Eu Bernice
79 S. Spring Ave.,
La Grange, Ill

MEN OF ART

Rembrandt: PORTRAIT OF HIMSELF.

National Gallery, London

MEN OF ART

by

THOMAS CRAVEN

NEW YORK
SIMON AND SCHUSTER
1931

PUBLISHED BY SIMON AND SCHUSTER, INC.
386 FOURTH AVENUE, NEW YORK, N. Y.
MANUFACTURED IN U. S. A.

TO MY FATHER

Contents

Illustrations

INTRODUCTION

MY SUBJECT is as old as the human race. Since the dawn of time, men have carved and painted—have moulded material substances into living forms which we call art. And art, being immemorial, is rich beyond measure, so rich indeed that the sum of its achievements is no longer within the grasp of any one mind. My aim then has been to organize and simplify, to reduce speculative and technical problems to the narrowest dimensions, to concentrate on significant movements and outstanding individuals. I have limited myself to painting in the Western World, beginning with Giotto and the occidental tradition, and driving a straight course through successive developments down to and including the latest French Modernism and the new mural art of North America.

Why some men should draw and paint, while others prefer to buy and sell, I do not know. I have accepted the fact that they do, and have tried to make the most of it. To account for the art impulse and to explain its origins would be to explain life itself—and that enigma I leave to the astrophysicists. But this does not mean that I have conceived of art as having no purpose in the world. On the contrary, my whole book is a tribute to the power and the glory of artists whose work is impregnated with human meanings and interwoven with the fabric of the social structure, as opposed to the futile practitioners of art for art's sake. Accordingly, I have been at pains to reconstruct backgrounds, to present the artist in relation to contemporary events, and events in relation to the special civilizations producing them. It has been a pleasant task to emphasize once more the humanity of the artist; to show that in the character and quality of his experiences, in his strength and his weakness, he is not a curious solitary with a unique emotional apparatus, but a sane, healthy, and industrious workman, differing from his fellows only in the intensity of his endowments. An exceptional relish for life involves him in wider experiences; having sharper susceptibilities, he is more deeply moved by his conflicts; aided by a stronger imagination, he is able to give vitality to lines and colors, and to create forms in which the dramatic forces of life are so composed as to play profoundly upon the feelings of the beholder.

Throughout the book, in every chapter and on every page, I have stressed with all the temper at my command, the fact that the only artist of any consequence is the one who has educated himself in the subjects he engages to paint; that strong preferences and special interests excite him to habits of observation and reflection; and that his knowledge of certain aspects of humanity is as extensive as the scientist's knowledge of abstractions. In this I have been supported by a galaxy of extraordinary personalities —Rubens, Rembrandt, Hogarth, Goya, Turner, and Daumier, to name but a few—whose art, by its scope and its depth, illuminates experiences common to all mankind. If I have dwelt at length on the lives of such men as Rubens and Hogarth, it has been, in part, to show that the great artist may be shrewd and formidable in practical affairs, adapting himself to the conditions of his time, and making a good living into the bargain. I have had no room for mere talent, manual cleverness, virtuosity, exhibitionism, opportunism, and tender souls who can only paint in the leisure of dead civilizations or romantic settings. I have considered character and conviction, knowledge and purpose. Talent implies limitations; it is a substitute for vitality, a disguise for emotional emptiness.

The growth of traditions is, in itself, a fascinating study. In the prehistoric beginnings of art, the first pictorial efforts of man consisted of images of animals carved in stone or bone, or painted on the walls of caves. The first images—probably made with some idea of facilitating the success of the hunter—were crude in the extreme; but the second artists, guided not only by their memory of animals actually observed but by the trials of their predecessors, did a little better; and as time went on, a tradition of animal painting of an astonishingly high order was consolidated among the cave men. This is the way all art grows into schools and movements. The artist takes the tools of his predecessors, uses them for his own purposes, and adds his increment of originality to the deposits of the past. Without pushing the metaphor too far, we may say that art is a great tree, a biological plant rooted in the same soil as other organic developments, putting forth new branches as new civilizations appear, and expanding with the fresh enrichments of individual genius. But, as I have told in detail, in certain periods when the soil is impoverished, art shrivels and dies. It becomes academic. It is tended by men whom contemporary life excites to no new activities and responses, who slavishly imitate the styles and forms of the past. With this kind of official pattern-making as exemplified in one department of French painting from Poussin to Puvis de Chavannes, I have had no sympathy.

I have no patent system of aesthetics to expound. The manifold expressions—the moods, habits and passions—of the human race cannot be reduced to a code or formula. It is only in times barren of creative energy that little systems of absolute aesthetics are brought forward to explain the whole of art. Plastic relationships are determined by human relationships. If art is to be stripped of all human and social values; if it is to be reduced to congestions of cubes and cones the sole meaning of which lies in mechanical ingenuity; if it has no higher function than is claimed for it by certain Modernist sects; then it is not worthy of consideration.

The vastness of the field has complicated the problem of selection. Naturally I could not include all the great men of art, but the omissions have been made with the greatest reluctance. In the end my choice has fallen upon painters who seemed to me to be typical of certain tendencies in the growth of civilization. Hence the exclusion of Raphael for the sake of more important Italians, and the sacrifice of Tintoretto. I do not believe for a moment that Titian is as great a painter as Tintoretto, but he is more characteristic of the Venetians—and there was space for only one. I am sorry about the Germans, but it could not be helped. Their influence on the art of painting has been relatively slight, but no one can deny the eminence of Dürer and Holbein.

I should have liked to include Holbein, if only to pay homage to his portrait of Erasmus. And a chapter on Audubon, who has never received his just deserts as a painter, had to be thrown out to make way for the Modernists. The French have been fully treated because of their predominant position in nineteenth century painting; and the Modernists as well, because they are our contemporaries. For, after all, our chief concern is in the art of our own time—whether we like it or not.

CHAPTER

I

THE WORLD BEFORE GIOTTO

IN OCTOBER 1927, the Italian Fascists celebrated the fifth anniversary of their march into the city of Rome. Informers, buried or in exile, have told us that the leader of the famous march travelled to the gates of the capital in a Pullman car, but such details do not rob the event of its historical significance. Mussolini is the new Caesar, the symbol of tyranny and the atrocious grandeur of imperial Rome. True, he is but a petty villain, a poor excuse for a man when compared to the rulers of old Rome or the magnificent bandits of the Renaissance, but he has irritated and inspired his people into something which resembles a national consciousness, and revived the gorgeous dreams of antiquity. For the Italians have always loved tyranny and bloodshed, and the great art with which we have to deal seems to have been the appanage of unbridled egoism, cupidity, violence and incessant political experiment.

To signalize his five years of despotism, *Il Duce* commanded his partisans to give the populace a good show, and every town from Verona to Naples was the scene of noisy and somewhat puerile demonstrations. In Florence the commotion was enough to wake the dead—to bring forth the imprecations of the enormously sensitive and irascible past. We can easily imagine what the old Florentines, renowned and feared for their sharp tongues and fierce wits, might have said on seeing their beloved city besmirched with a mob of insolent Black Shirts, and how the masters of art, accustomed to designing banners, uniforms and all sorts of processional devices, would have sneered at so stupid and colorless an emblem as that worn by the followers of

Mussolini. On almost the precise spot where Savonarola was hanged and burnt, one of the Premier's retainers addressed the people on the blessings of the new régime. The Italians have not lost their love for oratory. "Florence," he shouted, "Florence, the cradle of painting, the mother of Giotto, Michael Angelo and Leonardo da Vinci, will soon behold a second Renaissance, a new epoch of splendor, culture and riches inaugurated by the modern Lorenzo de' Medici—by the heroic leader of the people, Benito Mussolini!"

Behind the gusty sycophant rose the sombre Palazzo Vecchio, 600 years old, a majestic dungeon surmounted by the Tower of the Vacca—or the cow—so-called because of the bell it housed—the tocsin which was forever bellowing to the burghers to arm themselves against traitors, nobles, Popes and Germans. The tower was silent—the ferocious spirit of Florence is a thing of the past; today nothing remains but traditional pride. *"Viva Il Duce! Viva Il Fascismo!"* sang out the Black Shirts. The cry was repeated dutifully but much less vociferously by the populace; the band played the Fascist anthem; heads were uncovered; and the militia followed by children in uniforms marched off, fevered with wanton excitement and ready to perform noble and valorous deeds such as murdering helpless professors or throwing incendiary bombs into the offices of newspapers. There were, however, in the mixed audience of peasants and tradesmen, a number of scornful figures, their black eyes flashing indignation, and one serious young man with a copy of Dante under his arm—obviously a student—whispered to his companion, "*Il Duce* will be killed!" Tyrannicide, once the universal remedy for all ills, has not been forgotten; but as Machiavelli sarcastically remarked after observing the habitual intestine strife of his native city, "How perilous it is to free a people who prefer slavery!"

Let us not then suppose that it is environment alone that produces art. Florence is still one of the fairest cities on earth; and more, she has among the peasants and merchants, the classes from which her artists and leaders were almost invariably drawn, plenty of health and strength; but she is, as we say, a dead town, without spirit, imagination or courage. Lawless demonstrations and factional uprisings similar to the antics of the Fascists were at one time of daily occurrence within her walls, but they were opposed with the utmost energy and vindictiveness, and so high and exciting was the competition among political schemers that a mountebank like Mussolini would not have qualified as a hired assassin. It was in an atmosphere of peril and of despotic disregard for all established authority, combined with courage, intellectual curiosity and strong religious feeling, that art flourished. If environmental influence were the determining factor, the modern Florentine would be the most fortunate of men. His city has altered but slightly since the fifteenth century, and his natural surroundings not at all. He looks out upon the clearcut outlines of the Apennines, upon the sharp ridges traversed by Dante when, with tenderness and scorn he gazed down, a homesick exile, into the heartless city that had banished him from her gates; he sees the same hillsides striated with farms and villas, the same dry slopes silvered with olive groves and divided by solemn rows of cypresses; he lives and works amid the creations of his ancestors; he crosses the Ponte Vecchio, the old bridge where Cellini had his shop and where the goldsmiths still ply their trade; his business takes him by Giotto's Campanile, the Duomo, and those curious structures in which the strength of the fortress and the dignity of the palace are so perfectly united; and the very air he breathes, the thin, clear air of Tuscany, according to the authorities, is peculiarly favorable to the birth of men of genius. Yet he does nothing. In contemporary Florence there is not a single native artist worthy of the name, nor an architect capable of designing a building that is not a disgrace to the community—nor yet a tailor who can contrive a decent uniform for the Black Shirts. The old spirit has been dead for ages—the will to search and discover, to glorify the body and liberate the soul at any cost; to work fiercely, to fight, to test all things and to live fully, and above all to believe that art leads to the kingdom of heaven.

To understand that spirit we must review the trend of events during the Middle Ages, a dark and complicated epoch rendered all the more difficult by ceaseless movement and uninterrupted warfare. When the seat of the Roman Empire was transferred to the East, Italy became the battleground and the objective of wandering tribes from the North lured over the Alps by the magic name of the Eternal City. First came the Huns and Vandals, vicious nomads who left a trail of blood and spoliation and moved on; then the Goths, a much more formidable foe, who showed a disposition not only to conquer but to settle down in the more clement regions fronting the Mediterranean. The Goths were driven out by the Lombards, another barbarian nation called in by special invitation from the Eastern Emperor, a move leading to disastrous results. The Lombards established a kingdom in the mountains of northern Italy and proceeded at once to extend their sovereignty in many directions, thereby breaking up the peninsula into ill-balanced groups of hostile principalities. But they were outwitted by the Church. For some unknown reason these unorthodox warriors joined the Catholic communion; the Pope played upon their weaknesses, both spiritual and military, and at their expense enriched his bishoprics and enlarged his temporal dominions. When the Lombards retaliated and menaced his greatly increased possessions, Leo III appealed to the powerful leader of the Franks, Charles the Great, a measure which plunged Italy into centuries of iniquity and corruption.

Charlemagne, as every reader knows, subdued the Lombards and entered Rome where, in the year 800, by papal trickery he was crowned Emperor and invested with a half-interest in the Holy Roman Empire. The operations of that sublime and impracticable institution, as Bryce calls it—"the one perfect and self-consistent scheme of the union of Church and State"—concern us only so far as they relate to the dissolution of the mediaeval spirit, the creation of the modern state and the moulding of the modern man. The scheme did not work, and for five hundred years Italy was torn to pieces by the conflict between the two powers. On the one hand were the successors of Charles, for the most part, second-rate kings who aspired to become Caesars and who wasted their lives and impoverished their kingdoms trying to annex their hypothetical provinces in the South; on the other, the Papacy, strong enough to hinder unity but not to achieve it, inciting the people against the Emperors, fortifying its organization by placing its bishops on an equality with the German counts, steadily augmenting its institutions and its temporal authority, cultivating depravity and shrinking at no crime to remove its adversaries—in the end forfeiting the respect of the common man, and bringing down upon its head the consolidated heresy known as the Reformation.

But this prolonged combat was the making of Italy. Out of the shambles emerged the commune, or civic commonwealth, standing between the Church and the Empire. Early in the twelfth century the city-state comes into prominence and from this time forward assumes the commanding position in the development of Italian politics and culture. Feudalism, introduced by the German and Frankish nobles, took but feeble root in the South—in their impulses towards independence, the Italians were far in advance of their age, and were never noted for chivalry. Rallying round their bishops in common cause against the barbarians, the city states, in their first efforts at freedom, expelled the foreign nobility and set up a local government of their own, but once firmly established, with characteristic disloyalty and inordinate lust for individual power, they veered from one party to the other, according to their immediate selfish interests. As a consequence, the feud between the Guelphs and the Ghibellines, or the partisans of the Papacy and the Empire, eventually evolved into a maze of internecine squabbles between the jealous communes. The rivalry was incredibly bitter. "Penned up," as Symonds expresses it, "within narrow limits, throbbing with fresh life, overflowing with a populace inured to warfare, demanding channels for their energies in commerce, competing with each other on the paths of industry, they clashed in deadliest duels for breathing space and means of wealth."

We see in Italy today the remains of those wonderful centers of art, industry and murder, in towns like Urbino and Perugia, towns pitched upon hilltops and encircled by walls, with vast empty palaces and domestic architecture of the most varied and exquisite design. Such towns are in themselves works of art: they are, one might say, composed like pictures—the general effect is one of completeness and unity, while the individual parts, the tortuous streets binding together in curious circulating lines the public buildings and private houses, and the squares and churches, are of the most distinguished excellence. But they are lifeless and depopulated, and the laggard activity of the saturnine modern inhabitants serves only to enhance the disintegrated splendor of former times. Architecture is born of specific human needs; when a structure loses its function, that is to say, when it no longer fulfills its original purpose, it becomes a tomb.

The activity of the communes we can only imagine. It is the tendency of contemporary writers to exaggerate the artistic inclinations of the belligerent cities, but no one, I think, can overestimate their vitality. The practice of exiling offenders widened the scope of the unending animosities. The nobles, for example, ousted from one city, hurried forthwith to another, fomented smouldering jealousies, recruited an army and returned to wreak the most dreadful vengeance on their accusers. Thus were the isolated communities of Italy joined together by protracted hatreds and vacillating sympathies; thus were ideas and discoveries disseminated and utilized to the fullest advantage. Ultimately we find the social structure shaken down to a democratic level, and nobles, burghers and laborers dwelling together, not happily, but in abounding prosperity within the same walls. The nobles were never completely beaten. Though shorn of their power and compelled, at least nominally to descend to the ranks of the burghers, they retained their old prestige and the bulk of their wealth in the shape of outlying castles and lands. They built fighting towers and palatial fortresses to repel private enemies, and their hot-blooded bickerings and feuds among themselves were carried into the open, throwing the whole city into a tumult. But by all odds the most important issue of the conflicts which we have just outlined was the enfranchisement of the lower classes and the formation of the Guilds, or Arts, as they were officially designated. At the opening of the fourteenth century, the cities were practically controlled by admirably organized groups of merchants and artisans, and from these trade-unions or guilds appeared the greatest painters, sculptors and architects of modern times.

Under such circumstances Italy developed into a nation, or more precisely, into a collection of powerful and antagonistic city-states, sharing in common sharply defined ambitions and appetites. These states are sometimes called republics, sometimes despotisms; as a matter of fact, they were democracies founded upon wealth and individual audacity. While the machinery of the government was kept in motion by the people, the genius of the community was centralized in the tyrants who used the state as an instrument to realize their dreams of unrestrained energy and self-expression. But the tyrants were not necessarily of noble origin—as often as not they were mercenaries or illegitimates. Hereditary succession, though generally preferred, was not possible in a state composed of scoundrels and mongrels tempered by war and stimulated by the success of their rivals to extract from life the very marrow of sensual and intellectual excitement. The sons of popes effected alliances with the prominent families of merchants and bankers, and played politics on a grand scale. The common man needed only brains: opportunities awaited him on all sides, and everything conspired to spur him on to the highest and hardest undertakings. But without supreme intelligence and cunning he was nothing.

Gianpaolo Baglioni, for example, of that unmentionable Perugian family all the members of which are said to have died an evil death—twenty-seven on a single occasion—murdered his kinsmen and committed incest with his sister. But he was just a commonplace villain enticed to Rome and mercifully beheaded by Leo X. For a specimen of real ability we must turn to Ezzelino da Romano, the first and perhaps the worst of all modern despots. This cadaverous, ratty little monster had a passion for torture. Though his executioners worked day and night, his airless dungeons were always filled with fresh captives. His especial delight was to lay hold of a town and to cut off the noses and legs and pluck out the eyes of his victims irrespective of age, sex or occupation; his most infamous piece of scheming was to entrap in a body 11,000 soldiers and to allow all of them to perish in slow misery in his prisons. But, as Symonds points out, "by his absolute contempt of law, his inordinate cruelty, his interminable massacres, and his infliction of plagues upon whole peoples, Ezzelino established the ideal in Italy of a tyrant marching to his end by any means whatever. His fury captured the Italian imagination, and by the glamour of loathing that has strength to fascinate, proved in the end contagious."

This is not the place, however, to enumerate the abominations of tyrants—we must bear in mind the conditions that bred them. The morality of the Renaissance was of a very low order and to be conspicuous for his crimes, a man had to rise to the seventh heaven of iniquity. With the exception of Frederick of Urbino, a beneficent ruler, a great soldier, a scholar and patron of the arts, and a man of unblemished character, none of the usurpers was above baseness and treachery, not to mention more devilish habits. At the same time they were men of remarkable strength with nerves of steel and sensibilities embracing the entire gamut of emotions from exalted depravity to exalted aesthetic joy; in short, wolfish antinomians with transcendent gusto for life. There was not a hypocrite among them, nor a hypocrite in the society that supported them. What they did was theoretically within the reach of the humblest citizen, and it was only natural that the pattern of their careers should have provoked the hottest rivalry and emulation. The social forces which produced the tyrants also produced the popes, the artists, the historians, humanists and builders; great blessings and great evils went hand in hand, and that inscrutable thing known as imagination, or the creative will, found an outlet in the most diverse forms of activity. On the brighter side we must not forget that perpetual danger and competition sharpened the wits and desires of the people. Culture was diffused without reference to rank or wealth; the tyrants devoted their revenues and illicit gains to vast municipal benefactions, fostering the arts, restoring old churches and erecting new ones, protecting painters and providing them with honorable and lucrative commissions, financing palaces and halls of unsurpassed grandeur, gathering to their courts illustrious scholars and artists, maintaining police forces, insuring a supply of wine and grain, supervising trade routes, and looking after the sick and helpless. At certain moments when peace reigned and the burghers had time to breathe, art and commerce spurted forth with savage vigor. When the tyrants were antagonized or offended, hell broke loose, and the people, always the goats, flocked to the standards of their chieftains. How, we may well ask, did art manage to thrive in such a bedlam? There is no absolute answer, but an examination of the affairs of Florence will, I think, bring us to a closer understanding of the phenomenon.

Florence is one of the oldest of Italian cities, tracing her descent from a garrison-town founded by Julius Caesar. Materially her early history is much the same as that of her sister commonwealths, but in the malignancy and permanency of her quarrels she is without a peer. She could neither preserve liberty nor endure slavery, and Dante, disgusted by her instinctive restlessness, likened his city to a sick man continually changing his posture to escape pain. Throughout the twelfth and thirteenth centuries she was embroiled in deadly hostilities, domestic and foreign—no sooner had she asserted her independence than she set out with unconscionable cruelty to exterminate her rivals, Pisa, Siena, and Arezzo. Normally a Guelph town in her opposition to the Empire, she professed to love the Pope, but was quite ready to defy his decrees, repulse his armies, and tax his property, whenever it was to her best interests. When the democratic Guelphs, together with the titled families who had, as a last resort, enrolled in the lists of merchants, grew rich and overbearing, the people passed drastic sumptuary laws, confiscated wealth, and finally, with no regard for justice, completely excluded the nobles from any voice in the government. She would fight at the slightest provocation, as is witnessed by the duel between the Whites and Blacks, an event which had its origin in a silly family row in a neighboring city. Florentine sympathy, as usual, was divided; a civil war ensued, and after years of senseless killings, a French king was finally called in as mediator.

Despite the sanguinary outrages and the added disasters of fires, floods and plagues, Florence at the beginning of the fourteenth century was well on her way to her ascendency among Italian cities. It is at this point that our interest first centers upon her as a living organism occupied largely with commerce, but fertile in ideas and soon to produce an art which is not only the crowning achievement of Italian genius, but an active influence today in all civilized countries. Let us dismiss from our minds, once for all, the popular notion that Florence was a gay and romantic place. A compact little community of merchants and money-grubbers, she was too deeply concerned with ducats and florins to tolerate bohemian loafers, and her laws denied inheritances to sons without remunerative occupations. The idea that art is a refined pastime, the product of a carefully prepared romantic background, is a modern invention. Strange as it may seem to the American who looks upon art as an expensive plaything for millionaires or the obsession of freaks and incompetents, Florence actually needed artists and used them in exactly the same fashion as she used her bankers and dyers.

The pride of Florence exceeded that of modern Paris. Humiliated by the example of Pisa and Siena, she was resolved to build a cathedral of her own and issued a proclamation which Giovanni Villani, the first of her great historians, has preserved for us.

"The Florentine republic, soaring ever above the conception of the most capable judges, desires that an edifice should be constructed so magnificent in its height and beauty that it shall surpass everything of the kind produced in the time of the greatest power by the Greeks and Romans."

The cathedral, the work of Arnolfo and Brunelleschi was paid for, I may add, by taxing exports, and by the sale of indulgences from the Pope; and this same Villani, after recounting the glories of his city, was lodged in a debtor's prison when his bankers had ruined him, and died of the plague. Lamenting his fate, he wrote from his dungeon:

"It has been seen and experienced truly in Florence, in ancient and modern times, that whosoever has become leader of the people and the masses has been cast down, forasmuch as the ungrateful people never give men their reward."

The proud city had no room for the detached Leonardo da Vinci; Michael Angelo's statue of David was hated and stoned by the rabble, and at night had to be protected by an armed guard; a large reward was offered by public decree for the assassination of Alberti, whose only offense was that he happened to belong to a detested family. Because Dante opposed the subsidy granted to a French freebooter, he was sent into exile with the promise of death at the stake if he should ever set foot in Florence again. But the noble poet was also a politician, and we find him some years later a champion of the German invaders, praying that his city be forced to bite the dust in order that he might return in triumph. Vasari was so proud of Florentine artists that he endowed them with the characters of saints; Machiavelli was so captivated by the political crimes of the city that he ignored artists altogether in his long chronicle; and the artists themselves took it for granted that they were the best in the world in all departments of their profession.

Imagine then a small square city, rich, arrogant and envious, with fighting towers, palaces as solid as rocks, and houses tinted in warm earth colors, a city of 100,000 people dwelling together on as democratic a basis as is possible where wealth and fame are the dominant ambitions. Mediaeval simplicity was rapidly passing, and already we detect signs of that vehement assertion of personal rights which was to culminate in the elaborate self-indulgence of the Medici. Florence was not afraid of singularity; on the contrary she cultivated it assiduously, in dress, politics and art, and the old sumptuary statutes were so successfully evaded that in the end no attempt was made to interfere with private expenditures. Her temperament demanded the extremes of good and evil, and no other city was able to bring together in perfect harmony such seemingly irreconcilable passions as the love for the loftiest forms of art and the love for unmentionable carnalities. The masses, the bulwark of religious faith, were fond of gambling and horseracing; had a taste for practical jokes and buffoonery of the lowest sort; were not disturbed by the presence of pigs and goats at the threshold of their comely houses, nor by the filth and vermin accompanying defective sanitation. But they were not illiterate: the schools were open to boys and girls alike, and everyone could read and write—even the garbage carriers and the blacksmiths sang the feverish love songs of Dante. And they were capable of a certain amount of aesthetic enthusiasm. To insist, as many writers do, that every Florentine was an artist and a connoisseur is manifestly absurd, but the level of appreciation was probably higher than at any subsequent period. Of one thing we may be positive: the activity of Florence and her rivals was truly staggering, for Italy, after feeding the museums and galleries of the world for centuries, is still the richest of nations in art deposits.

Florence owed her commercial supremacy to her favorable situation, her skill in handling wool and in dying silks, and above all to her banking establishments. She was the clearing house of Europe, inventing the letter of credit, modern methods of finance, and in her confounded pride, the passport. At the crest of her prosperity she boasted of 120 banking houses, whole streets of them, the Bardi, the Strozzi and the Medici—the Morgans and Rothschilds of the old days. She had branch offices in the leading foreign cities and floated loans for popes and kings. Her industries were admirably organized and controlled by Guilds—the seven major arts including the money changers, judges and notaries, physicians and apothecaries, furriers and the separate merchant units, and the fourteen minor arts representing such trades as the butchers, tanners, blacksmiths, and carpenters. The Guilds were responsible for the distinguished appearance of the city; not only did they frame the building laws, but their own executive halls and coats of arms were designed by famous artists. The butchers were a lordly group, great showmen and notable patrons of the fine arts. It would require considerable stretching of the imagination to conceive of the American butchers as patrons of anything—still, they have been known, as in the case of the Swifts, to hand over a fraction of their blood-money to radical magazines. We might dwell at length on these fascinating trade-unions: how, through their councillors and priors, they constituted the governing body of the city; how they formed the standing army; how they quarreled with one another and shut their doors against outsiders; how they imposed religious observances upon their members; and how, for the sake of their pride and their markets, they maintained the highest standards of workmanship. But we must content ourselves with the important fact that the painters, while a distinct corporation, were under the jurisdiction of the doctors and apothecaries and were amenable to the same laws as the merchants and artisans.

There were no art schools in Florence. A boy of talent was apprenticed to some recognized master under whose guidance he was thoroughly trained in the business of picture-making. At first he is a menial, a janitor and valet; he must needs be an expert carpenter in order to prepare altar pieces and to construct scaffoldings used in mural decoration; he must understand gilding, the grinding of colors, the sizing of canvases and the behavior of the different mediums. Along with his routine duties, he learns to draw, and when sufficiently advanced, subordinate parts of pictures are assigned to him. If he is exceptionally gifted, as was Michael Angelo, the star pupil of Ghirlandaio, he is paid a small salary for his services. His apprenticeship over, he is matriculated into the guild of painters, but before setting up his own shop, he usually remains a while in the employ of his master, the association bringing him publicity and future commissions. His shop, or *bottega*, is the opposite of the modern studio. Today the artist prefers to live in Paris, in the enervating atmosphere of make-believe; at home, if he can afford the initial expense, he plays the social game and equips his studio into a seductive den to ensnare the uncritical rich. Or, being poverty-stricken and useless, he becomes a calamity-howler, painting to no purpose and trusting to his dealer to palm off his works on a gullible collector.

In Florence, exhibitions in the professional sense, that is, the display of pictures to attract buyers, were unheard of; on St. Luke's day, paintings not *in situ* were assembled in one of the big churches, but only for festive reasons and to impress strangers. The artist's shop was simply his place of business, and painting, at least officially, was a trade or a craft. Many of the most celebrated painters began their careers as goldsmiths, and in both occupations conducted their shops to serve the public. An artist did not spend years amassing a batch of pictures, hoping by good luck, or the cunning of an intermediary, to get rid of them; he executed commissions. The patrons of the arts were clients who came to the shops and ordered what they wanted, and the terms were carefully stipulated in writing, a happy and sensible arrangement when we think of the mystery, crookedness and aesthetic palaver of the modern gallery. As the market for fresco painting increased, the artists left their shops to their assistants and went on the road. They travelled up and down Italy filling churches and halls with sacred myths and stories—with the popular subject-matter of their time—exposing themselves to thieves and cut-throats and performing jobs which demanded not only sternly disciplined imaginations but exceptional strength and endurance. It was a man's work. But it had its compensations: artists were handsomely paid, and the best of them, being constantly employed, earned big incomes. Furthermore, they were praised and honored, enjoying the society of the most brilliant men and the most beautiful women.

Art, you see, was an excellent business; and more—it was a

useful, civilizing agency. Doubtless, as I have indicated, it was also a symbol of Florentine vanity, a means of showing-off before the world, but in essence it was a product of the powerfully stimulated activities of the human spirit. As art-forms multiplied, public taste correspondingly improved; ugliness became intolerable; the desire for new and finer things mounted incalculably, and the artist was taxed to the limit of his capacities. The fourteenth century in Italy was an epoch of building on a heroic scale; 110 churches and 25 nunneries appeared in Florence alone; every city had its town hall, and every town hall was a masterpiece; literally thousands of buildings were erected to replace the fighting towers of the dispossessed nobility, to say nothing of the palaces, monasteries, fountains, monuments, bell towers and private houses. In all these, architect, painter and sculptor worked in closest collaboration—indeed every artist of note combined the three offices to ensure a consistency of scheme in which the frescoes, bas-reliefs, statues and smaller decorations were part of the organic structure. It is with regret that we enter most of these buildings today, particularly the churches, where the original simplicity and purity of design have been ruined by the indiscriminate addition of gaudy altars and gimcrack tombs, the obliteration of the frescoes, the profusion of old bones ensconced in showcases, and the bastard carvings of the baroque period. In contrast we turn to twentieth century America, the home of the skyscraper and of industrial enterprises without parallel in history, the land of architectural engineers who have discovered no use for the abilities of painters and sculptors.

From the foregoing account we must not infer that art is merely a matter of business, and that another Renaissance would sweep over the world if wealthy experts like Mussolini, Kahn and Ford would only organize a chain of guilds and put a picture in every home. We have in America a class of hard-headed practical fellows known as "commercial artists" who are not artists at all, but skilled mechanics engaged in advertising popular merchandise. The genuine painter is not a machine to reflect commonplace events or to exploit physical appetites, and finds no more inspiration in soups and cigarettes than the poet or musician finds in popular merchandise. What the average man feels in his heart—his faith in his better self, his love for humanity, his vague consciousness of a more orderly world—what he experiences dimly in a mass of contradictory emotions, is presented by the artist with greater clarity, with completeness, assurance and power. In a word, art deals with problems of the spirit, with faiths and convictions. Whether it is limited to religious experiences is a debated question—the difficulty could be removed by separating the spiritual from the theological—but on one point there is no room for quibbling: the arts in their origin have always depended on religion, and the art of the Renaissance was indissolubly connected with the established Church. The struggles of art to give concrete form to Christian ideas were long and tangled, and we must tell them as summarily as possible.

The first manifestations of the struggles are to be found in the Catacombs of Rome. Into these cemeteries the persecuted Christians descended to bury their dead and to celebrate the forbidden Mass. Here, in their gloomy conclaves, they decorated tombs and walls with frescoes and carvings in low-relief. As art it is pretty poor stuff—even Lord Lindsay, one of those fine gentlemen of the old school who believe in the moral value of art, admitted that it is "inferior to the worst specimens of the contemporary heathen tradition." Indeed it is identical with the Graeco-Roman school in style and execution, and is Christian only in its crude substitution of biblical for pagan characters. Sometimes the substitution is purely nominal: the myth of Cupid and Psyche represents the union of the soul with God; and Christ, a beardless youth, is plainly Pan, the shepherd, or Orpheus taming the wild beasts. Catacomb art deserves mention because it shows how heavily art leans upon tradition, and because it delineates for the first time the Virgin, the nativity and many of the religious symbols which were to become the stock-in-trade of painters and sculptors for upwards of thousands of years.

Christian art came to the surface when Constantine officially adopted the new faith and moved the capitol of the Empire to Byzantium, or the East. For several centuries it groped along, in Italy adhering to Graeco-Roman models, in the more vigorous East speedily succumbing to Oriental influences. After 800, the year, you will remember, marking the advent of Charlemagne in Rome, the term Christian art was discarded, yielding to two well-defined tendencies, the Byzantine and the Romanesque. These two forms, fostered by the Church, followed the spreading Christianity into all parts of Europe and were radically modified by the builders of the various races. The history of their fusions and alterations is a study in itself, and it is enough to note that the natural process of evolution was from the old Roman and Byzantine to the Romanesque, and thence through the Gothic to the Renaissance. Byzantine art is characterized by the sumptuous ornamentation of the East; as a type we may cite the Church of St. Mark's, Venice, with its domes and vaults, its acres of mosaics, and its enamels and carvings in ivory and metal. The term Romanesque is more generally applied to architecture, to the ponderous northern churches with their round arches and heavy towers, and, on the other hand to the marvellous Cathedral of Pisa and the little Church of San Miniato at Florence, structures embodying the basic design of the Roman basilicas and the decorative embellishments derived from Byzantium. *Gothic* art, an expression coined by Raphael in a contemptuous reference to the barbaric work of the North, is exemplified by the great cathedrals of France, the incomparable town halls of the Flemish cities, and the painting of the early Flemish painters beginning with the Van Eycks. Italy, holding fast to her monuments of classical antiquity, was never strongly affected by the Pointed architecture of France and Germany, but Gothic sculpture, as we shall see, with its healthy naturalism, was destined to become one of the principal factors in the shaping of the new style of painting. Thus it is apparent that the Renaissance was not a sudden outburst of the imagination, but the result of tendencies in operation for a millennium.

We must again emphasize that art in the Middle Ages was not dead. It is commonly believed that after the disintegration of Rome the world was a dark and filthy chaos in which civilization, drained to the dregs by universal carnage, would have perished utterly but for the inexorable campaign of redemption waged by the Church. That the world was sad and bleeding, no one will deny, but it was neither sick nor decayed, and amid the most horrible adversities, art came to light here and there with splendid vitality. In the blackest of centuries the Byzantines swung the torch of enlightenment in the remotest corners of the West. Byzantine art is held far too cheaply by historians; it is stigmatized as a priest-ridden, sin-conscious formalism—hard, grandiose and sterile—in a word, devoid of soul. A glance at the city of Ravenna is enough to demolish this notion. Ravenna, where Byron carried on a beneficial intrigue with his girl-countess, is a pestilent town lying in a malarial sleep at the mouth of the Po. In the sixth and seventh centuries, as capital of the Empire, it was the home of a colony of Byzantine artists working under imperial authority, and among its extant treasures are four churches, externally unimposing, but within, of unparalleled grandeur. One of these, S. Apollinare in Classe, puts all other churches of Italy to shame; it is not over-ornamented like St. Mark's, nor is it a colossal bazaar like St. Peter's; it is sternly simple, as perfectly proportioned as a Greek temple, and brightened by exactly the right amount of mosaic color. Another, S. Apollinare Nuovo, is scarcely inferior, containing two processional friezes in mosaic which, as monumental decoration—figurative design conceived in relation to an architectural scheme—are unapproached by the frescoes of the Renaissance.

Byzantine art was almost scourged out oi existence in the eighth and ninth centuries by the Iconoclasts, or Eastern Puritans, who hated sacred images and destroyed vast quantities of them in Constantinople, but upon that heresy followed three centuries of great prosperity and wealth, and embroideries, enamels and ivories spread throughout Europe. The Eastern workmen, or Greeks, as they were called, migrated to Venice, Florence and Rome, and instructed the Italians in the secrets of design. They were the recognized masters of mosaic, but were equally adept in the illumination of religious manuscripts. In both departments, their work, dictated by the ascetic ideals of the Middle Ages, is totally devoid of sensuous qualities. It is essentially religious iconography, an art of silhouettes, patterns and symbols. The Byzantines supplied the traditional figure of Christ; standardized costumes, types and scenes; and their conceptions of the Nativity, the Holy Trinity, the Annunciation, Crucifixion, Resurrection and Ascension were common property from Giotto to Michael Angelo. Ultimately Byzantine art became academic, which means that it was made to order by hard and fast rules. Such is the fate of all art that feeds upon itself and ceases to refer to nature. No matter how deep the religious devotion, art cannot subsist without fresh experiences and new inspirations founded upon contacts with the real world of men and women. For more than four centuries the Greek mosaicists had been doing the same thing over and over again, copying stereotyped attitudes and reproducing the designs of their predecessors with about as much originality and creative fire as one finds in a gang of bricklayers. As a consequence the Virgin, once the majestic symbol of the Great Mother, became a sulky effigy, a lifeless, stiff-necked, empty symbol, and the Holy Child, a petrified little monster with square cheeks and the vacant glare of a witless old man. Byzantine art in the West had run its course.

While Byzantine art was dwindling into a barren method, the *imagiers* of France, proceeding in exactly the opposite fashion, were decorating the Gothic cathedrals with thousands of bas-reliefs and statues. The cathedral, though controlled alike in form and spirit by the Church, was a social achievement, the work of free men close to the soil; and the image-makers, let me add, were not contaminated by the chlorotic mysticism of the Middle Ages. They do not deal in agonies and tortures; their faith is healthy, and their carved allegories are based upon episodes in the lives of their people. In their facetious moments they create gargoyles, but normally their statues are remarkably realistic. The Gothic sculptors are slaves to no precepts or worn-out symbols; they are happy, earthy builders, and their love of life shows in their work. They draw upon nature for their forms, carving sheaves and vines, emblems of the seasons, reapers, wood-cutters and ploughmen. Gradually, since the cathedrals were centuries in building, their Saints and Virgins, passing from one generation to another, are evolved into types, but the types are always suggestive of the living model, and the Virgin is clearly a smiling peasant woman, slightly idealized by artists of profound conviction.

French critics say that Gothic and Greek art are sisters, a far-fetched relationship and difficult to sustain unless we fall back on the generalization that both are branches of the same old human tree. With much more reason they attempt to prove that the Gothic sculptors were the precursors of the early Renaissance in Italy. The argument runs as follows. In the latter part of the thirteenth century there lived at Pisa two extraordinary sculptors, Niccola Pisano and Giovanni, his son. Now this Niccola happened to observe certain Greek sarcophagi brought to his native town by traders, and with an artistic insight far in advance of his day, carved at Pisa and Siena pulpit decorations which can only be described as astounding combinations of nature and the antique. Niccola was scarcely touched by Gothic influences, but his deep interest in nature led his pupils, foremost of whom was his son, to an impassioned study of the French image-makers. Giovanni Pisano and his co-workers went from town to town spreading the seeds of the new gospel, and before long the ablest sculptors of Italy gathered their energies together to form a native tradition based on the Gothic. Nor was the French influence confined to sculpture. There was yet another Pisano, not a kinsman but a distinguished pupil called Andrea, who carried

Gothic naturalism to Florence, and carved for the campanile—probably from Giotto's designs—those reliefs which Ruskin worshipped so eloquently. How Giotto, an old man of seventy, profited by Gothic art is a riddle I do not pretend to solve. The French, however, have a ready explanation. When Giotto was a young man he went to Padua to decorate the Arena Chapel, and there, in the same church, encountered Giovanni Pisano working on the statue of a madonna. The madonna is still in existence, and the frescoes are the glory of Padua, hence it is not unlikely that the two artists were friends, and that Giotto was initiated into the mysteries of the Gothic style at this time. But Giotto was even then in command of his own mature style, and was named for the Arena Chapel because he was the most accomplished fresco painter in Italy! The business is a hopeless muddle.

Let us leave these speculations to the detectives of art who will expound and dispute and discover until Giotto's paintings shall have crumbled into colored dust. The important thing to remember is that art epochs are continually shifting and overlapping, that tendencies cannot be arbitrarily limited, and that no man, however original or independent, is big enough to abolish tradition and to create an art that is free from antecedent influences. To deny this would be to deny the permanent value of art. It is within the bounds of good sense to conclude that Giotto and his progenitors, whoever they may have been, travelling from city to city, must have associated with artists of all schools and classes—Byzantine, Gothic, Sienese, and Roman—that ideas were exchanged and stolen, methods compared and new tendencies slowly consolidated. Giotto, a shrewd peasant as well as the most intelligent artist of his time, had the wit to perceive that painting needed, more than anything else, a thorough humanization—more blood and less theology—and his experiments in this direction were undoubtedly facilitated by intercourse with Gothic sculptors. There were other influences of course—the fighting rivalry of Florence, and atmosphere charged with ideas, money, opportunity, and not least, the spirit of individual religious liberty promulgated by St. Francis.

The material side of Florence we have already discussed, and it now remains to inquire a little more specifically into the religious state of the city at the beginning of the first Renaissance. The term Renaissance, in its popular connotation, refers to the vast intellectual curiosity of the fifteenth century Italians and their general enthusiasm for classical antiquity; but there was an earlier spiritual awakening, which, though independent of the far distant past, was fully as significant in its artistic manifestations. The initial movement was inspired by the reaction against the corruption of official Christianity, and by the belief in the doctrine of the equality of all men before God, as preached by St. Francis. When we think of the immorality of the Roman Church, our vision is immediately dazzled by the resplendent rascals who precipitated the Reformation—Sixtus IV, Innocent VIII, who married the daughter of Lorenzo de' Medici and established a bank for the sale of pardons, and Alexander VI, the father of Lucrezia and Cesare Borgia; but the outline of iniquity goes back into the Middle Ages. "In fact," as Lecky has recorded, "it appears, from the uniform testimony of ecclesiastical writers, that immorality in the eighth and three following centuries, was little, if at all less outrageous, than at any other period. Simony was nearly universal. Barbarian chieftains married at an early age, and totally incapable of restraint, occupied the leading positions in the Church, and gross irregularities speedily became general. An Italian bishop epigrammatically described the morals of his time, when he declared, that if he were to enforce the canons against unchaste people administering ecclesiastical rites, no one would be left in the Church except the boys; and if he were to enforce the canons against bastards, these also must be excluded."

The Italian is not and never was a squeamish Puritan. He takes his religion more subjectively than other races and has always been able to separate the office from the incumbent; he is quite capable of genuine religious emotions and at the same time of charity toward human weaknesses and the natural appetites of his spiritual fathers. When it was the custom for priests to keep concubines, he did not hold it against them, nor deny the validity of their teachings; but when nunneries were turned into brothels, and the clergy sank far below the level of the laity, and worst of all, when he discovered the organized rottenness of Rome, the wholesale malversation and vice, he was sickened unto his very soul, and he joined the brotherhood of St. Francis to reclaim his shaken faith.

It is hard to magnify the importance of St. Francis. Roger Fry says that he brought about the great outburst of Italian art, proclaimed the idea of the immediate relationship of the individual soul to the Deity, and enabled every man to be his own priest. "To the fervor with which these ideas were grasped by his countrymen we may ascribe to some extent the extreme individualism of the Italian Renaissance, the absence of the barriers of social caste to the aspiration of the individual and the passionate assertions on his part of the right to the free use of his activities." St. Francis arrived on the scene at the close of the Middle Ages. For centuries man had been taught by his priests to despise that loathsome thing, the body, to mortify the flesh, and to purify the spirit by frenzied penance and excruciating tortures, and he had seen the hideous and unnatural vices that inevitably accompany excessive preoccupation with sin. St. Francis—he was half French—introduced a spirit closely akin to the naturalism of the Gothic communes. Not merely a poet, he was also a thoroughgoing modern with an essentially realistic grasp of human affairs, and with Giotto, one of the first to liberate the mediaeval mind from harrowing mysticism and ascetic superstition. He loved the corporeal world, shapes, colors and natural forms, his brother, the body, and his naïve acts, such as preaching to the birds, must not blind us to the rugged intelligence underlying his philosophy. To him the incompatibility of flesh and spirit did not exist. He advocated a religion in which the sensuous and the spiritual were at one, harmoniously interactive, mutually beneficial. A gospel of this sort was precisely what the Florentines needed most. Public faith was dying; the Papacy, debauched and humiliated, had eloped with the French to Avignon; and whereas the people had formerly blamed the nobles for everything, now they blamed the priests. St. Francis had already grown into a mighty legend: men, weary of corruption and killing, sought refuge by thousands in the brotherhood; and the monks of Assisi sent to Florence for the finest artists to decorate the church of the beloved founder of their order. St. Francis, restoring the human spirit to nature, opposing with marvellous gentleness both the violence and greed of tyrants and the abuses of the flesh as practiced by the masses, preaching not gruesome moralities, but poems filled with ecstatic joy in all outward forms and the divine union of the inward and outward man, and at his death, repenting his asceticism, revived the waning faith and provided the people with a religion which allowed for the expansion of their noblest faculties. The Florentine spirit, inflamed by wars and material supremacy, was cleansed by the artistic influence of St. Francis, artistic because it made for the exercise of the imagination and exhorted man to cultivate the sensuous elements of life without consciousness of sin. Later, in the second or High Renaissance, we shall see how the sensuous elements were conditioned by pagan ideals, and how the return to classicism affected religious forms.

St. Francis introduced an attitude toward life which made it possible for artists to co-ordinate a religion overlaid with scholastic subtleties and mystical abstractions with a race of egoists becoming more and more engrossed in objective realities. He enabled painters and sculptors to enter Christianity without sacrificing their intellectual interests, their freedom of mind and their sympathies with the world of the senses. Byzantine art, enslaved by hieratic rules, and vitiated by the repetition of prescribed motives, lingered on, hopelessly struggling with its mediaeval symbols. The sentiment of the people demanded a more human and exciting pictorial language. The artist was equal to the demand. The Florentine artist was a many-sided man, painter, sculptor, goldsmith and architect, all in one; he was not only dissatisfied with the vapid ceremonial spirit of the Byzantine, but with the rigidity of the mosaic as a vehicle of expression. To give full scope to his powers, he developed a more flexible medium, the fresco. The intangible metaphysical legacy of the Middle Ages, the mysteries and abstractions incapable of pictorial treatment, he was forced to abandon, but in the legends of the Church, the dramatic stories, martyrdoms, madonnas, nuns and saints, he had material into which he could infuse his own experiences and his observations on his own people. Profane subject-matter was practically unknown, and the artists vied with one another for the highest honors in the treatment of sacred themes. It has often been objected that Italian art with its multiplicity of madonnas and saints was of narrow compass. This objection will be fully answered as we pursue the lives of individual artists. At present we need only state, after admitting that in the course of time, minor painters fancied they had created something spiritual when they had affixed the madonna label to the portrait of a young and pretty matron, that artists, while keeping one eye on the Church, neither surrendered their personality nor denied themselves the right to use ecclesiastical subject-matter as a pretext for the expression of their own moods and experiences. Anyone familiar with the insufferable monotony of the modern gallery—the annual repetition of nudes, still-life and landscape—will not complain of the want of variety in the old Italians. But we must not lose sight of the fact that Florentine art was neither voluptuous nor physically seductive, that notwithstanding its richness and variety, it was from first to last an intellectual art, devoid alike of consciousness of sin and of sexual enticements and that the character and form of its imagery was undoubtedly colored by the noblest convictions of the Church to which it was the appointed servant.

Let us keep in mind the Florence of the first years of the fourteenth century: a little community avid of ideas and experiments; rich in the things of the spirit and of the senses; hardened by warfare and commerce; humanized by the teachings of St. Francis; proud, aggressive, revengeful, and capable of the extremes of good and evil; absorbed, for the most part, in trading and making money, but enormously imaginative and demanding—as compensation for her violent materialistic energies—the profound composure, the tranquilizing grandeur, the stern intellectual joy, afforded by the arts. Florence was a city of singularities. She made the artist a useful citizen, put him to work, respected him, paid him well for his services and appreciated his performances, but she would not tolerate him if he were cowardly, anti-social, precious or incomplete. The artists, as a class, were sensible fellows no different from other distinguished men, except in one particular—they would not go to war. They were famous for their singularities, but they were not more singular than the great men of other professions. Let us not forget that fact. Today we are in the habit of thinking of the artist as a freak endowed by the Lord Almighty with unique talents, a fragile touchy soul unfitted for the shocks and battles of the mundane world. The Florentine artist was not a freak, but he certainly was not just an ordinary man, and nothing can make him one. The current attempt to reduce great men to the level of clodhoppers or hide-cutters by recounting their weaknesses and ignoble deeds, is something to which no Florentine biographer would ever have stooped. The great Florentine artist was an infinitely exceptional man—to credit the Sistine Chapel and the *Last Supper* at Milan to ordinary talent is inconceivable; when he was human, as we say, he had the humanity of a hundred men; when strong he was a giant, when unhappy he created an eternal epic of scorn. He was not abnormal, he was superior. Florence understood this distinction and gloried in it, and bred a race of exceptional characters whose brains went into art. There are all sorts of artists, and their ways and habits are various and unclassifiable. Occasionally one is born who seems to be more or less like an ordinary human being. Such a man is Giotto.

Giotto: DESCENT FROM THE CROSS.

Arena Chapel, Padua

CHAPTER

II

GIOTTO

AS USUAL, Florence was at war. The old hatred between the burghers and the nobles broke out again with uncontrollable fury, and every man flaunted the emblem of his party and went to work with one hand on his sword. It was a civil inflammation utterly without sense, the hot-tempered avarice of men ready to kill and be killed in order to gratify an insane desire for temporary power. At length in the year 1260, the wealthy Ghibellines, the party of the minority, were banished from the city, but gathering reinforcements from surrounding communes, the nobility completely routed their opponents and returned as masters of Florence. Hereupon occurred an event which shows more clearly than anything we might name the vindictive cruelty and sadism of the old Florentines. These conquering braggarts, not outsiders, mind you, but sons of the great city they loved and sought to glorify beyond all rivals, voted in general council to raze Florence to the ground and to drive her people to the furthermost corners of Italy. And they would have done so but for the resistance of the infamous Farinata, the one man with enough public spirit to resist the flagitious designs of his comrades. Farinata, of detested lineage, was chained by Dante to a smouldering sepulchre in one of the hottest corners of hell, and his cries echo through the whole *Inferno*! "I was not alone in the deeds which moved the wrath of Florence against my race; but alone I stood when all around me would have destroyed Florence, and I defended her with open face."

After this there was no peace. The nobles had the upper hand, and nothing would do but for the people to put them down. Party lines were drawn with a knife, and the pretexts employed by both factions so that they might kill in good faith strike us today as springing from the minds of monstrous children to whom life was a murderous sport. The Ghibellines wore white roses and white hats, drank their wine from smooth goblets and cut their garlic and salami slantwise; the Guelphs wore red, drank out of chased cups and cut their food straight down. By such tokens a man was known wherever he went and his allegiance published by his most trivial actions. Everything he did was calculated to start a fight—he lived with a chip on his shoulder. No one was safe, not even in the churches, and at night the shrieks of assassinated victims had a familiar and, to many, a pleasing ring. And when men died, whether guilty or innocent, whether from foul or natural causes, they died with faith in their hearts, and the conviction that life had been worth while. These insurrections went on for forty years until the leaders of both parties were ostracized, and the Pope dispatched a Frenchman as visiting judge to sit upon all offences.

Into such a world was Giotto born. His full name was Ambrogiotto di Bondone, but he is known today, as he was in his own time, by the contraction, Giotto, a word which has come to stand for almost all the great things that art has accomplished. According to Leonardo da Vinci, he was born a few miles north of Florence, "in a wilderness of hills inhabited by goats." His father was a peasant, but a man of some means, and the boy was never to experience poverty, hardships or any struggle except that which every artist, big or little, must go through to attain mastery over his materials. The records of his life are meagre and disconnected, but we know that Giotto, from boyhood, was associated with the great minds of his time, and that he was counted by all who knew him as the most fortunate of men. Though undersized, he was endowed with strength and endurance and a finely balanced mind, a combination that enabled him to finish one monumental job after another without draining his energies or falling a prey to fits of temperament such as the modern painter is so fond of affecting; he had a large fund of good sense, practical wit, vast human sympathies, an amiable twinkle in his eye, and extraordinary powers of observation. These last, as his contemporaries attested, "made it possible for him to see everything with just measure, and to introduce the custom of drawing from nature," a simple custom, it would seem, but responsible for the greatest advance ever made by painting in a given period of time.

Giotto's climb to fame began with a stroke of good luck. His father gave him a few sheep to watch, and watch them the boy certainly did. He not only shepherded his lambs, he studied them and scratched his impressions on a piece of slate, using a pointed stone for a pencil. Throughout his life he retained his love of animals, and brought them into many of his greatest frescoes, painting them with tenderness and touching humor. He observed his father's sheep with the natural curiosity of a peasant in the habits of animals, their breeding, feeding and growth, but also he observed them with the eye of an artist, noting the twists and turns of their bodies when leaping and running, and their various postures when at rest. If a particular attitude pleased him, he would make a sketch of it, working as children do, with no purpose except to set down a simple combination of lines which, though only a crude symbol, would suffice to bring into his vision the perception of forms more or less precisely remembered.

Giotto was born with a sense of form. Now this word *form* is the incubus of art criticism. It has passed through so many hands and has been applied by writers and painters alike to so many obvious lunacies and abortions, that it no longer has any meaning to the layman. How often have we heard artists and critics praising or condemning this picture or that! "What marvellous form!" "A master of form!" "Utterly lacking in form!" And so on. Generally speaking, the term relates to fulness, solidity, and structure—something that is palpable, substantial and permanent, invested with life and reality. But a dynamo has structure and solidity, and so have these vacuous archaic nudes of Picasso, and rocks and elephants and sandbags! On the other hand we cannot question the life and reality of the comparatively flat art of the Chinese, or of Persian miniatures, the Byzantine mosaics of Ravenna, and the random sketches of Leonardo. One of the greatest intellects in the history of art, Leo Battista Alberti, writing from the middle of the fifteenth century, struck at the heart of the problem: "Nature produces the material, but genius brings forth the form." If there is any one point on which critics of all creeds and cults are agreed, it is that art is not imitation of nature. Art, like religion, draws its inner nourishment from the spiritual world and cannot be explained by the mechanical process of copying surfaces, textures and colors. This fact cannot be stressed too strongly. Nature is indispensable to the artist, but she is his servant not his master. In the epoch preceding Giotto, as we have already observed, art, for want of freshening contacts with nature, withered into a repetition of bloodless abstractions; at the other extreme, we have the period of too much nature which came directly before the Modernist upheaval of the closing years of the nineteenth century, a period in which painters forgot the example of Giotto, the mysteries of religion, and the grave philosophies of the old masters who had to live and labor and speculate for their interpretation of the world. As a result art was reduced to a formula of technical skill, a sensuous pastime based on duplicating the play of light and shade on flesh and flower and silk—and form dwindled into superficial ornamentation.

Form, then, is nature moulded by the artist, nature simplified, relieved of waste and profusion, organized and converted into an instrument for the transmission of human experiences. If this were not true, painting would be only a cumbersome substitute for photography. Training, talent, study and taste are not enough—to produce form, the painter must have genius, as Alberti said long ago; he must have something to say; passion, spiritual steam, pronounced desires, and the intellectual power to select and coordinate and reconstruct the external world into a new and individual creation. This artistic vitality, or form, cannot be induced by handmade rules. We have in our galleries, museums, and homes countless thousands of pictures which have been foisted upon us as works of art, but which are in reality only the pathetic performances of misguided painters who have taken the living material of nature and literally killed it by unimaginative copying; we have studies of the nude—cold, sterile things done according to rules laid down by the undertakers of the academies; portraits executed with meticulous skill, anatomically perfect, detailed to the last hair and highlight, but signifying nothing; landscapes in which the painter, contemplating a picturesque scene, is moved to tears, and fancies he can reduce others to the same condition by faithfully presenting the woods and hills before him; works of every description, scientific, sentimental, Cubist, and what not, that make no impression upon us for the reason that the painter brings nothing to them, or at least nothing worth communicating. The artist, like every other man with blood in his veins, can respond only to that part of his model which is also himself. An illustration from the field of literature will help to drive this home. Most of the great historical figures, when we read their biographies, are only puppets stuffed with facts; when presented to us by writers of genius, they become living individuals. There is Bernard Shaw's Saint Joan—a new creation, not the Saint Joan of the reader, perhaps, but a thoroughly modern conception. Mr. Shaw himself in doublet and hose, confounding the doctors with his wit.

Set a number of artists to work upon the same model and the results are radically different—each is colored by a distinctive personality. Renoir and Cézanne happened to choose the same model for portrait studies; in one canvas the man in question is a personable human being fashioned out of delicate colors kneaded together into a rich and sensuous mixture characteristic of Renoir; in the other he is a piece of still-life, a spherical unit of planes and angles. Raphael's madonnas are creatures of sweetness and light—portraits of himself; but Michael Angelo, who held portraiture in severest disesteem, converted the Italian woman into sexless sculpture burdened with his own tragic reflections. What, in the organic kingdom of nature, is so much dead matter, may be transmuted by the artist into living form. In Giotto's

Deposition, the crucified Christ, dead in obedience to physical laws, lives through the creative spirit of the painter, and in a picture of a flayed ox hanging in the Louvre, the spirit of Rembrandt shines out gloriously. With a few strokes of his pen, Goya depicted forms which fairly stretch and burst with vitality; his fellow artists, laboring under the example of a stupid court painter imported from Flanders learned the figure by rote, copied it like so many lazy sheep, and painted pictures that no one ever looks at.

But to return to the boy who was watching his sheep. Giotto continued to make drawings of his flock, and his efforts must have indicated more than ordinary ability. At any rate they were considered promising by Cimabue, and his days as a shepherd were over. Cimabue was the first Florentine artist of any stature. Latterly, the high priests of attributions have conspired to reduce him to a myth, but the man will not die. He was a mosaicist and fresco painter in the Byzantine tradition, his madonnas being patterned after the unbending scarecrows of the East, but he was a decorator of undeniable dignity and grandeur. Dante speaks of him as, "holding the field until Giotto came along," and Dante made no mistakes in estimating personalities. It was Cimabue's picture of the Virgin that "was carried in solemn procession, with the sound of trumpets and other festal demonstrations, from his house to the Church of Santa Maria Novella, and all the men and women of Florence hastened in crowds to admire it, and the inhabitants of the neighborhood, rejoicing in the occurrence, ever afterward called that place *Borgo Allegri*," which is to say, the Glad Quarter. How Cimabue met the boy Giotto is told by Vasari:

"It chanced that one day the affairs of Cimabue took him from Florence to Vespignano, where he perceived by the roadside the young Giotto who, while his sheep fed around him, was occupied in drawing one of them from the life upon a smooth clean piece of rock—and that without any teaching whatsoever, but such as nature had imparted. Halting in astonishment, Cimabue inquired of the boy if he would accompany him to his home, and the child replied he would go willingly, if his father were content to permit it. Cimabue therefore requesting the consent of Bondone, the latter granted it readily, and suffered the artist to conduct his son to Florence."

In the workshop of Cimabue the boy received sound and exhaustive training in all branches of his chosen profession. Every day he must draw—no exception was made for Sundays and holidays—and he must master the intricacies of the different mediums. Giotto was not greatly tempted by mosaic design; the medium had the advantages of permanence and magnificent color, but the setting of thousands of little glass cubes in a prearranged order was far too mechanical a process for a youth born with a plastic mind and an original zest for expressive freedom. Fresco painting was his ambition. "This form of art," to borrow from the *Treatise* of Cennino Cennini, a painting monk of the year 1400, "is the most delightful and charming work that can be." Before painting, the artist covered the rough plaster of the wall with a coat of lime, very fine and smooth and mixed with ground marble, and upon this the outlines of the drawing were stencilled in charcoal. While the plaster was still wet, the colors—powdered pigments mixed with water—were applied, and as the lime dried, it crystallized, and the paint was incorporated with the surface of the wall. The art called for precision, rapidity of execution and supreme confidence. Corrections were impossible after the plaster had dried—if an artist made a mistake, he had to scrape off the old lime, lay on a new coat and begin all over again. Alteration, of course, could be made in tempera—a medium compounded of glue and yolk of eggs—but this was an unsatisfactory expedient, and every precaution was taken to avoid it. The medium does not sink into the plaster; it is less permanent than true fresco and noticeably different in color effects. The pure unaltered fresco seems to have been an ideal infrequently attained, and in nearly all decorations retouchings in tempera are discernible. But the old painters knew their business, and when we fix our attention on the frescoes of Giotto, Masaccio and Michael Angelo, overpowered by their magnitude, we may be pardoned for repeating Michael Angelo's remark that "fresco is a man's art—oil painting is for women or idle and incapable men."

Oil painting was unknown, or undeveloped in Giotto's time. Besides the fresco, there was the tempera panel, the description of which is given at some length in Cennini with a few side-lights on other matters pertaining to art.

"The artist should eat and drink temperately twice a day, take care of his hands, and be careful of women, inasmuch as over-indulgence makes the hand so unsteady that it will tremble and flutter more than leaves shaken in the wind. In beginning a picture, the first step is to invoke God Omnipotent and the beloved Virgin, St. Luke, the first Christian painter, and all the saints in Paradise; the second is to put on the cloak of charity, fear, patience and obedience; the last to temper his colors with the yolks of eggs, and the juice of young fig branches mixed with wine, and to prepare his panels of old beechwood by rubbing them with the ashes of bones—if possible the wing-bones of capons."

To what extent the young Giotto observed these admonitions we do not know—he was both droll and devout, and his industry was incessant. Cimabue had the reputation of being very sedate, and his pupil annoyed him with rustic jokes which he bore magnanimously for the sake of the boy's unusual powers. Giotto's development was swift and astonishing, and he was soon regarded with envious glances by the Greek artists residing in Florence. This scrawny boy from the goat pastures was doing something in painting that had never been done before. When a mere youth he received his first commission, a fresco and altar-piece for the Church of the Badia, works which have long since disappeared. It was an age of precocity. Outside his master's workshop the world moved to a tempestuous measure: life was fevered with the high passion of accomplishment; men hungered for blood, loveliness and glory; every joy was dimmed by the shadow of tragedy; the spring festival, celebrated on May Day "with dance and delight" ended in a brawl between the jealous parties, and the streets were strewn with the dead and wounded. Giotto drank in this life, merged himself in the tumult, wondered what it was all about. He saw men stabbed and maimed; he remembered the faces and attitudes of women as they bent over the prostrate bodies of fallen warriors; he saw impudent children throwing stones at family enemies, solemn monks carrying the injured to the hospitals, and foolish workmen rushing to the support of demagogues who were willing to sacrifice the city to appease their spleen. But he did not lose his head and roam the piazzas with a red or white rose pinned to his smock. He had his own work to do; he must paint and learn and outstrip his rivals; as an artist he must preserve his serenity and his powers of reflection, and find order and meaning in the violence around him. But you will notice that his saints and angels, for the first time in art, come down to earth as living men and women, and you will notice, too, that all his work, though it speaks to us with the voice of youth and health and fresh discovery, throbs with the inescapable surge of human sorrow.

Giotto drew from the life, bringing into his shop any available monk or errant woman, so eager was he to chart his own course, and so swiftly did he exhaust the comparatively narrow art education of Florence. Why then, I have heard people ask, did he draw in such primitive style, and why was he unable to render more closely the facts of nature, the visual appearances of objects as they are presented with ease and accuracy by art students of today? There are several explanations. In the first place, it is a simple matter for a student to set down on paper what he sees before him, provided he has a definite notion of how an object should look when realistically copied; but without precedents to guide him, without examples accruing from a long tradition of science and experiment, he is at the mercy of his own instincts and foredoomed to remain in the primitive stage. Children, savages, half-wits and hermits, uninfluenced by artistic conventions, adapt nature to their own purposes, and are not in the least bothered by such arbitrary things as correct perspective and anatomical propriety. Roger Fry relates that he once asked a little girl about her method of drawing and got this answer: "First I have a think, and then I put a line around it." Sound aesthetics, this answer, and much more intelligent than the practice of the majority of professional artists who transcribe nature after the technical fashion of the moment and then try to persuade the public that they have put a "think" in their scrupulous imitations. Second, while it is unanimously admitted that the value of music does not lie in the reproduction of natural sounds, or in the evocation of associative ideas, and that architectural forms are independent creations not to be confused with trees, caves, or erosions, popular appreciation of painting is determined by the fidelity with which that art portrays the literal facts of the visible world. Giotto drew from models, and we have no means of ascertaining how closely his portraits resembled his sitters, but assuredly they were far from literal, for it was not until the invention of the camera that the public realized how deadly accurate a likeness could be, and began to demand that the painter turn himself into a soulless, unreflective machine. Giotto's audience was not only satisfied and delighted with the pictorial truth of his conceptions but actually amazed at his realism. "He was," to quote Boccaccio, "so great a genius that there was nothing in nature he had not so reproduced that it was not only like the thing, but seemed to be the thing itself."

Examining Giotto's drawing in the light of contemporary standards, we may perhaps smile at Boccaccio's criticism, but it is well to remember that the most hopeful signs of the regeneration of modern painting, as exemplified by the successors of Cézanne, point to a return to the principles established by the men of the early Renaissance in Italy. It may indeed be questioned whether painting, considered as a balance between deductions from nature and man's experiences, has ever again attained the expressive power of Giotto's best work. Take for example, the arms of his figures. Apart from their context, they are only elongated triangles encased in stiff folds of cloth; the hands are too small, the fingers thin and inflexible. Conjoined with his figures, outstretched in a gesture of supplication, as in the case of the kneeling Mary in the drama of the Resurrection, they become universal symbols conveying not only the overwhelming sentiment of a particular situation, but emotions that have troubled the human spirit since the beginning of time. Giotto's figures in the last analysis, stand for universal states of the soul, and we need not, in our modern sophistication and conceit, bemoan his technical limitations. Any inarticulate draughtsman can make an arm that is "in drawing," and dazzle us for a moment with clever foreshortenings and slippery tricks of brushing and modelling, but technical dexterity is valid in art only so far as it serves to enhance form; pursued for its own sake it is irrelevant finery.

There is no irrelevant finery in Giotto. Though he drew from nature, he looked at objects through the vision of his master Cimabue, an inevitable proceeding for reasons already noted. Accordingly, his early pictures were markedly Byzantine—the figures long and flat, the faces and attitudes stereotyped, the draperies woven into nets of hooks and hatchings—but the carvings of the Gothic sculptors showed him how the proper study of nature enables the artist to animate his forms and to give them convincing reality. Henceforth he is buoyant and secure: his figures become massive and sculpturesque; his draperies more simply folded; his faces no longer types and staring masks but the countenances of individuals. He surpasses his teacher, and in his early twenties is recognized as the most independent, original and far-seeing artist in Italy. All that he needed now was a big commission, an expanse of plaster upon which to unfold the panorama of his experiences—to reorganize the life around him in a cycle of dramatic pictures. The great church of St. Francis, at Assisi, awaited his genius, Assisi, the sanctuary of the oldest mendicant order and final resting place of the saint "whose life and miracles were audaciously compared with those of the Redeemer." On his deathbed Francis had prayed that he be laid away in humble ground, and that no monuments be erected to his name, but so intense was the enthusiasm of his followers, and so munificent the contributions from the whole of Italy, that he was canonized two years after his death, and against his wishes, his bones were deposited in the crypt of a costly Gothic shrine. The basilica is really two churches, one piled over the other, and when Cimabue, who had painted in the vaults of the lower church, was summoned again to work in the upper, he took with him his assistant, Giotto.

To a young man eager to demonstrate his ability and to challenge all comers, the church on the Umbrian hillside was an impressive sight. In nave, choir, and transepts, artists of various schools, Sienese, Roman and Florentine, were working together. It was a scene of inspiring activity, of rivalry that provoked boasting and argument, of tendencies that were to merge in the formation of a new style of painting. Giotto had no patience with the Sienese: they were delirious Byzantines who cluttered the market with devotional pictures; small-minded, delicate, sickly—makers of altar-pieces—but the Romans opened his eyes to the most advanced mural workmanship he had ever encountered. But after all, their frescoes were superior only in technical refinements, the work of men aloof from life who seemed to see, feel and realize little in the world of actualities. They were very possibly adapters of the old Graeco-Roman style of painting where figures were modelled after the manner of sculpture but rarely set up with any idea of deep spatial intervals. He would show them up. To decide on Giotto's first work at Assisi is to conjecture to no good purpose; it is probable that he had his hand in the series of frescoes devoted to scenes from the Old and New Testaments. At all events, with true Florentine push, he took care that his talents were recognized, and to the great discomfiture of the effeminate Sienese and the stately Romans, was named by the general of the order to decorate the lower walls of the nave with the history of St. Francis. His partnership with Cimabue was ended. He hired his own assistants and went to work.

At last Giotto had a subject after his own heart. Today, painters will tell you, and critics, too, who run after painters hunting for ideas, that subject-matter is of no consequence—it is all in the treatment, the handling, the composition. This is nonsense, the defence of sensitive creatures too timorous to face the world —or too stupid to understand it—and therefore constrained to secrete themselves in their dingy studios and to paint bowls of fruit, or arrangements of cubes and cones like children playing at life with piles of blocks. The artist must of course seek material that is congruous with his temperament, and his temperament, if he is to do anything worth preserving, must be receptive to human issues and a wide range of stimuli. Giotto was an anthropologist, the first in Italian painting and one of the greatest in all art. He did not subscribe to the more ecstatic ideas of St. Francis; he was thrifty, prudent, and a property holder, and he even went so far as to write a poem declaring that "poverty is not commendable; it leads the world to evil, judges to corruption, damsels to dishonor, and men in general to violence and lying; it requires no discretion or knowledge or qualities of any kind." But with the character of the man, his wonderful conviction, his provisions for the rights of the body as well as the soul, and his crusade against ecclesiastical corruption and materialism in general, Giotto, as an artist, had the profoundest sympathy. The life of St. Francis was an epic in itself. Furthermore it was a contemporary theme—to the popular imagination, an heroic legend; to the artist, a subject in which religious beliefs might be personified by living men and women.

The story of St. Francis as told by Giotto in the frescoes of the upper church at Assisi may be seen today. Many of the episodes have been partly obliterated by time; all of them have been restored and abominably repainted; the architectural backgrounds resemble stage settings and the scale of proportions is by no means consistent from one compartment to another; but in their present condition there is nothing in early Italian painting to compare with them, and they disclose not only the essential greatness of Giotto's mind, but the true beginnings of the monumental style which was to reach its summit in the decorations of Michael Angelo. In this cycle, Giotto proves himself, in his initial trial, the master story-teller in paint of all time. He translates the thoughts and feelings of his characters into action, penetrating at once to the heart of the situation with unerring psychological insight. He drags in no dummies to fill unmanageable spaces, no supernumeraries who bend and twist and stare in ridiculous studio poses for "the sake of the composition." Every actor belongs to the scene, and every attitude, gesture and facial expression contributes to the total dramatic effect. Like his friend Dante, he helps himself to the vulgar incidents of everyday life, a habit that grew upon him, and in his pictures at Assisi, Padua, and Florence, we find such familiar touches as maids spinning, a fat cooper tasting the wine in the representation of the Marriage at Cana, the infant Christ sucking his thumb, the new-born Mary making a face as her eyes are washed. One of the finest of the frescoes depicts the miracle play which St. Francis staged on a Christmas Eve for the benefit of the poor people of Assisi. The subject of the drama is the Nativity, but the performers, one of whom is St. Francis himself, are dressed in the costumes of Giotto's own time, an innovation as startling to his contemporaries as the versions of Shakespeare in twentieth century trappings are to modern audiences. The scene is indescribably convincing. Giotto, as we might expect, seizes the miraculous moment in which St. Francis takes hold of the wooden image of the infant Christ, and the Child comes to life in his arms with the most knowing, wondering and composed expression of self-recognition that was ever painted in a human face. Behind the saints is a Florentine pulpit, a trio of monks, brows wrinkled and mouths wide open, singing like trained mummers, a priest and groups of spectators transfixed with astonishment. The characters, as anyone can see, are ordinary Italians to whom Giotto has added his knowledge of all men, and who thus become emotional messengers of universal significance.

Here we enter into a most perplexing question: the abyss that lies between Giotto and artists who are more correctly described as illustrators. Both are story tellers; both translate literary material into pictures which are supposed to add clarity and dramatic emphasis to situations contrived in a verbal medium. The one creates visual forms that last forever; the work of the others hardly survives the day of its publication. The illustrator produces fashion plates, reflecting the whims of the moment in costumes, manners and sentiment, and when the tide of popular imagination has turned, his picture becomes as old-fashioned as the photographs in the family album. The true artist is never old-fashioned. Of recent painters, Cézanne alone rises above temporary styles. He takes a French peasant, strips him of all that is merely local or ephemeral, reconstructs him, moulds his clothing into a rigid integument scarcely separable from the flesh it covers, and the result is a new form that will never be obsolete—a unique creation, a French peasant with a soul. Giotto relates the legend of St. Francis with realistic truth—the actors are all doing something and doing it in a convincing manner—but going beyond historical events, he transmutes, by sheer imaginative force, the vulgar into the heroic, the most commonplace characters into immortal symbols. The modern man to whom the story of St. Francis is only a charming myth, may be deeply moved by these frescoes without understanding their historical import, a fact that has led artists to explain Giotto's pre-eminence by his command over composition, his ability to dispose his figures in harmonious groups in which line, mass and volume are so related as to fuse the scene into a powerful and compact unit. This is true as far as it goes. To unify his conceptions necessitated intellectual labor denied to all but the greatest, but design with Giotto was not an end but a means, and without his convictions he would have been only an illustrator concerned with external actions, and not an artist using his figures to embody the inner experiences of the race.

Giotto was now the most famous painter alive, and "all Italy," as Lord Lindsay says, "was on tiptoe waiting to see what he would do next." Abruptly and without warning, he entrusted the execution of the last three frescoes of the St. Francis series to his assistants, and hurried back to Florence where he married a damsel called Ciuta di Lapo. After this event we cannot follow him with any certainty, and his life in the main is a record of the cities in which he worked. We know that he opened a shop in Florence, that commissions poured in upon him, that he painted the altar-piece hanging in the Uffizi, that his Ciuta as speedily as possible bore him eight children described by Dante as "lumps of deformity as ugly as their sire," that he owned several houses in the city, and the estate inherited from his father, and that his wife and family remained in the country during his numerous wanderings. He accomplished an immense amount of work and is credited with a great deal more than any man could conceivably have done; and to the day of his death advanced steadily in his knowledge of art and the ways of the world. The anecdotes collected by Italian chroniclers are not worth retelling. They may be true, but if so, they represent Giotto in his most trivial moods, and reveal nothing except that he was not above the buffoonery of his time. From the following, which has been formidably authenticated, historians have deduced all sorts of esoteric meanings.

The Pope, Vasari tells us, proposing to have certain paintings executed in St. Peter's, sent a messenger to Florence to negotiate with Giotto and to procure specimens of his art. "Giotto, who was very courteous, took a sheet of vellum and fastened it upon the wall, and dipped his brush in a red color; then, resting his elbow against his side to form a sort of compass, with one turn of the hand he drew a circle so perfect and exact that it was a marvel to behold. This done, he turned, smiling to the courtier, saying, 'Here is your drawing.' 'And am I to have nothing more than this?' inquired the latter, conceiving himself to be jested with. 'That is enough and to spare,' returned Giotto. 'Take it along and you will see that it will be recognized.' The messenger, unable to obtain anything more, went away very ill-satisfied, and fearing he had been fooled." It seems that his holiness and "such of his courtiers as were well versed in the subject," were amazed at the red circle, and that they "perceived in it how far Giotto surpassed all the other painters of his time." The incident, needless to say, has no aesthetic significance. Any well-trained fresco painter could have done the same, and no artist, not even Giotto,

Giotto: DESCENT FROM THE CROSS. (Detail.)

Arena Chapel, Padua

could have imparted a personal touch to a perfect circle. Giotto was fooling, that is to say, he was, in his own jovial manner, asserting his independence. The man who had designed the enormous frescoes at Assisi needed no recommendation. If the Pope desired his services, let him say so.

In due time Giotto was called to Rome by the Pope's favorite cardinal. For the old Church of St. Peter he constructed a large mosaic of Christ walking on the water, receiving in payment 2200 florins—a sum equivalent to $22,000, if it is possible to translate the florin into modern values. The mosaic has been moved a number of times and each time mercilessly restored, and as it stands today in the porch of the mother church, it contains nothing of the original save the design. Giotto also painted the panels for the high altar, a gift to St. Peter's from the wealthy cardinal. He charged 800 florins for his services and immortalized the cardinal into the bargain, introducing him into the picture of the Enthronement. The generous Red Hat, kneeling at the feet of Christ, with angels hovering round him, is filled with appropriate ecstasy, and if he is conscious of the honor conferred upon him, he does not show it. Here Giotto paints one of the first portraits in Italian art, and sets the precedent of bringing into sacred themes recognizable personages from the artist's own time. Rome, the center of Christendom, was the logical destination of painters, but shortly after the great jubilee in 1300, Boniface VIII, Giotto's patron, suddenly died, and the new Pope fled to France. Giotto returned to Florence but conditions at home were worse than at Rome. A family quarrel had divided the people into two camps, the Whites and the Blacks, and the city was a battlefield. But it happened that a rich noble living in the town of Padua had just completed a chapel dedicated to the Annunciate Virgin, and erected ostensibly to "defend the dignity of the Virgin against various heretics," but actually to efface the memory of his father, a notorious usurer, stationed by Dante in the seventh circle of hell and compared to an ox licking his nose. Giotto, acknowledged master of painting in Italy, was summoned to decorate the walls, and happy at the turn of events, he took his family to Padua to begin the largest and most important job of his career.

Externally the church, built on the remains of a Roman arena, is drab and insignificant, but the interior is a new world in which heaven and earth are brought together in perfect harmony. Giotto was now about forty years old, in complete command over his powers, rich in experiences, and retaining, in spite of his triumphs and his maturity, the extraordinary freshness of his poetic vision. All of us, reading or hearing as children the stories of Christ and the Virgin, are filled with strange and contradictory feelings: joy, and terror shift and mingle; the miracles brighten our hearts and we can believe them, but over the tragedy of the crucifixion and the doctrine of redemption we grope and wonder—we try to visualize the stories and to connect them with our own lives and experiences. These feelings Giotto, with amazing directness and simplicity, has put into a language that is comprehensible to every one possessed of sight. He makes the stories incontrovertibly real and true. Legends consecrated by time, shaped by faith into supernatural dreams, he unrolls before us purged of everything that is vague and doubtful. He creates a world of robust men and women whom we can understand, whose actions speak to us, take hold of the spirit, communicating with matchless dignity and eloquence the agonies, the sublime gentleness, the subdued terrors of human passion. There is not a strained or artificial attitude in the whole church, and while some of the frescoes are more powerful than others, some deliberately reduced in potency to accentuate adjoining scenes, there is not one that cannot be ranked among the noblest masterpieces of art. The Arena chapel is a long rectangular box pierced on one side by six Gothic windows and ceiled with a barrel vault. Every square inch of the room is covered. The vaulting is a deep blue studded with gold stars and adorned with medallions of prophets; the space above the entrance contains *The Last Judgment*; the opposite end *Christ in Glory*, and the side walls are ruled into 36 compartments devoted to the life of the Virgin, as recorded in the apocryphal gospels, and the deeds of Christ. Below the tiers is a series of narrow panels filled with figures of the Virtues and Vices. The whole is a vast, illuminated book, a picture gallery displaying the consecutive workings of the creative mind as it explores the experiences of man, discovers their meanings, and embodies them in appropriate and unalterable forms. Giotto had few architectural difficulties to contend with; he grouped his stories in the simplest possible scheme, dividing the walls into squares, and breaking the monotony of the arrangement by intervening bands of geometrical ornament. The architecture of the chapel, in fact, never occurs to us; we see only pictures—wall decorations conceived as friezes and held together by uniform backgrounds of ultramarine.

The spirit of the frescoes is one of unadulterated solemnity, of deeply fathoming pathos, and cleansing tragedy. All sentimentality, all that is banal, grandiose and mawkish has been excluded from this world. Even in *The Last Judgment*, an enormous picture reminiscent of the old Byzantine model, the distribution of the component parts—the central figure of Christ framed by a rainbow, the grovelling damned, the flocks of angels in serried rows like spectators in the balcony of a theatre—is so adroitly managed that the monstrous Satan "munching sinners" is neither grotesque nor discordant. The tragic spirit is not immediately apparent to the spectator. On entering the chapel he seems suddenly to behold a world of happy splendor and youthful gaiety—the effect of the color. Giotto uses no local colors, that is, the natural colors of objects, selecting his pigments solely to ensure an harmonious ensemble. The Arena chapel, though somewhat effaced by moisture, has lost little of its original brightness. Golden yellows blend into pale greens; the whitish draperies are tinged with rose and violet, soft greys fade into the ultramarine background—and all glowing with the lightness and purity of water-color. But once accustomed to the splendor of the frescoes, you are sensible of the carefully measured flow of human sorrow, and of the tragic passions informing the groups of plain characters who enact the sacred stories. You see old St. Joachim returning to the sheepfold after his sacrifice has been refused—the most pathetic figure in art; you see the flight into Egypt, the betrayal, the Last Supper, the grief-stricken women holding the body of the crucified Christ, and the Magdalene imploring to touch his garments, and in all of them, depicted as simply and dramatically as in the Gospels, you feel the tenderness and compassion of a man who loved all suffering, blundering, human creatures.

The fundamental brainwork expended by Giotto on the Paduan frescoes is something few people take into account. The artist dwells in the same world as the rest of us; he sees and feels, enjoys and suffers but he does not, after an exceptionally poignant experience, burst forthwith into paint. As the word implies, the artist is a kind of carpenter or joiner, but one who imparts a living meaning to material within itself lifeless. The intellectual labor involved in one of Giotto's frescoes would have killed the average virtuoso—the man who paints lilies and fish and pretty faces and calls himself an artist. From the perfection of the Arena Chapel, its infallible rightness and precision, its marvellous bending of bodily action to abstract rhythm, and the clarity of its message, we might infer that the artist had a rather easy time of it. But Giotto sweated and struggled over the job for four years, designing, brushing and directing a corps of trained assistants. His friend Dante, living in exile at Padua, dropped in frequently to watch the progress of the work, and to offer suggestions, but I doubt if his council was of much help to the painter. Literary men, as a rule, do not understand pictorial problems. They seem to think that the painter gathers from one model or from many, a lot of fine facts which he whips together into an exciting aesthetic concoction. For instance, if he wishes to portray grief, he has only to observe a woman weeping and to photograph her on plaster or canvas. Nobody will confuse Giotto's frescoes with photography. He is as truly a poet as the man of whom the old women of Verona remarked, seeing how scorched and dark was Dante's complexion, "that he went to hell and came back when he pleased, bringing news of them below;" he pictures grief, despair, the dignity of motherhood and sacrifice, the vices and virtues, but he puts into these conceptions his inexhaustible store of assimilated knowledge, generalizing his figures into symbols that are above temporary circumstances. His poetry is expressed in visual forms, in terms of design, an intellectual labor as complex and exacting as the composition of a symphony. It is not a matter of rules or precepts, and though governed by the artist's individual preferences, resolves itself into an intricate scheme of relationships wherein line is arrayed against line, contour opposed to contour, mass balanced by mass, the whole welded together into a single unit. Sometimes the design does not come off: in each creation the artist embarks upon a voyage of discovery; nothing is absolutely predetermined—one movement calls up another, a rhythm demands its foil, new ideas intrude, the stubborn materials of life refuse to accommodate themselves to the formal plan, and must either force a change of structure or be cast aside; and the end is always a compromise between the human document and the abstraction. A design may be perfectly ordered, flawless in its adjustments and in the relationship of the integral parts, and still be without meaning. It is then, as we say, academic, for the reason that the artist, having nothing to say, has either revamped the examples of other men, or concentrated on a mechanical problem. For the variety of his compositions, which is only another way of saying the variety of his experiences, and for the ability to create forms in which emotions are carried to the highest pitch of dramatic intensity Giotto remains secure among the greatest artists of all time.

Technically, Giotto's problem was to relieve painting from the flatness of the wall, to liberate objects from a single plane and to force them into deep space, and to enhance the emotional appeal of forms by making them massive and solid. To a degree he succeeded; his figures have monumental bulk, and the solidity of sculpture, but they are in the nature of bas-reliefs; recession is limited, and a full century was to elapse before artists were able to move freely in a three-dimensional world. He had so many difficulties to surmount that he left anatomical details, the minute study of faces and muscular actions, and the intricacies of perspective and light and shade to men who were to begin where his work ended.

After finishing his commission at Padua, Giotto lived and worked in many cities. The records of his travels during the next twenty years are vague and untrustworthy. In all probability he painted in the lower church at Assisi; he may have gone with the popes to Avignon; his name is associated with Ravenna, Rimini, Pisa, Urbino, and Lucca. From time to time we hear of him at Florence, and in his later years, he decorated the chapels of Santa Croce with a series of frescoes which were without doubt, his masterpieces. I say *were*, for the walls were whitewashed in the eighteenth century, half-ruined when subsequently uncovered, and barbarously restored, but even in their present state, they are living witnesses of Giotto's faculties developed to their fullest capacity. These pictures exhibit the same psychological penetration that enthralls us at Padua, with a more advanced technical knowledge of color, light and shade, anatomy, and design in three dimensions. In his old age—he was a pretty tired man at 64—he was called to Naples by King Robert, and was attached to the southern court for three years. In 1334 the city council of Florence passed the following resolution.

"In order that works undertaken by the city may be carried out for the benefit of the commune and may proceed in the most perfect manner, which is not possible unless an eminent and experienced man is chosen leader of the whole works—and in the whole world none is to be found better qualified for that and much besides than Giotto di Bondone—it is resolved that Master Giotto shall be named *Magnus Magister*, and publicly regarded as such that he may have occasion to abide here, and the city shall gain no small honor because of him. Therefore the Lords Priors, twelve good men and true, select and designate Giotto as leader and master of building operations at the Cathedral, and for the construction and completion of city walls and fortifications, and for all the works of the said commune."

Giotto must have been a recognized architect, but how and

when he learned the principles of building nobody knows. The imagination of the old master was good for one more great work, the famous bell tower, which blossoms by the side of the Cathedral. He designed the tower, ornamenting the base with some of the noblest sculptures ever carved, but lived to complete only the first story of the Campanile. He was seventy years old when he died, and the Italians who have always loved a good funeral as well as a good picture, gave him a magnificent burial in the Cathedral of which he had been appointed master-builder—Our Lady of the Flower.

CHAPTER

III

FLORENCE

WE HAVE compared art to a great tree nourished in the soil of human experience. But for a clear understanding of this metaphor, we must bear in mind that art, while it may be truthfully considered as an organic development, does not and cannot have an independent life of its own, and that it is not, strictly speaking, an evolutional process governed by fixed genetic laws. In its growth from simple and primitive to larger and more complex forms, certain well defined characteristics appear which, in the course of time, are accepted by artists as structural principles. We have, for instance, the devices for maintaining equilibrium in design by the proper adjustment of weights around a centre; we know that lines and colors affect each other with almost mathematical exactitude, and that depth, movement and rhythm function according to special laws. Such matters however belong to the field of technology and have very little relation to art as the fulfilment of human needs.

As a medium for the transference of experiences, art becomes important in so far as it participates in the general evolution and development of thought. In this capacity it is far more than a mere reflection of the external world. Though ineradicably rooted in its environment, it is, in its genuine manifestations, creative; it moulds assimilated materials into forms, and in this respect rises above temporary circumstances. It becomes not only expressive of individual dreams, visions and dramatic moods but indicative of certain tendencies in the world of ideas, and takes a distinct place in the formation of the mental attitudes of its own and subsequent generations. In short, it becomes a civilizing influence, a protest against cheapness and vulgarity, rendering us intolerant of baseness and shams, sharpening our susceptibilities, and making for the realization of what Bertrand Russell has called "the good life." We cannot therefore endorse any view of art which confines itself to that vague and imponderable quality known as *beauty*, or to the representative values of objects considered apart from their sources—from the background of tendency and action in which they had their inception. Nor can we look upon art as a recreation for dilettantes, a voluptuous feast for connoisseurs, a cultural decoration for millionaires, or the exclusive property of aesthetes who profess to derive strange metaphysical joys from the analyses of technical exercises.

As to the evolution of art, we may say that within given periods ideas expand, multiply, culminate, lose their significance and in the end are absorbed in newer and more vital tendencies. Thus an historical survey may be resolved into a succession of movements, or more precisely, growths, such as the growth of realism, the revival of the antique, the epoch of the Baroque, the pseudo-classic age in France, the Romantic upheaval, and latterly the widespread interest in non-representational forms emanating from the experiments of Cézanne. But these growths, in the general scheme of things, are of limited duration, and do not describe a consistent outline of progress—they simply carry specific tendencies to a conclusion. With social changes, new discoveries, and the perpetual onrush of human activity, the artist feels the insufficiency of the old forms, and proceeds to create new ones to satisfy the needs of contemporary experiences. This does not mean that a movement perishes with the conditions that produced it. The various kinds of artists will always be with us—the classic precisionist, the headstrong romantic, the poetic painter, the intellectual abstractionist, the man who specializes in procedures—and these artists, both by the example of their work and by their direct affiliation with kindred temperaments of the past, will serve to keep the various traditions living and influential. Hence it is futile to seek in art an evolution of forms and types such as exist in biology and mechanics, and it is equally futile to expect the exact recurrences which our academicians are forever trying to bring about. Just now what we need more than anything else is an artist of the stature of Giotto, one who is bigger than formulas and studio obsessions, whose vision extends beyond inconsequential details into the main currents of modern life, who is capable of reorganizing the world on a vast and impressive scale, thus taking painting out of the hands of triflers and establishing it once more on an equality with the other arts. Doubtless such an artist will eventually arrive, but he will not be an imitator of Giotto, nor will he, for all his knowledge of optics and color, be superior to the first great Florentine; he will deal, of course, with the profound humanities of religious and social interests, but in his own way, and his pictures will be creations in harmony with the civilization of his own time.

We have told how this art tree, during the Middle Ages, was tended exclusively by the Church, and how, after bearing much good fruit, it severed its connection with human experiences and fell into decay, and how it was restored to life by Giotto, the first painter to make pictures conforming to the realistic demands of everyday themes. Giotto's accomplishments were tremendous, and we might well say, immortal, but after his death, the world changed rapidly, the last vestiges of mediaevalism disappeared, and the Italians, stimulated beyond belief by a systematic intellectual curiosity in all things—spiritual and phenomenal—in science, geographical exploration, invention, classical antiquity, infamy and power, produced such a multitude of great artists that it is scarcely possible even to enumerate them. We now approach the chain of events leading to the fullest bloom of art in the early decades of the 16th century, a period known historically as the High Renaissance. It was a time of continual agitation and alarm, of inexpressible iniquity, of contrasts and corruption, experiment and prosperity, and most important of all for our story, of perhaps the most complete emancipation of the mind of man from the fetters of authority and convention that the world has ever seen. In this brilliant chapter of events, Florence rises to the height of her development, dominates all Italy by virtue of her art, her wealth and her consummate political chicanery, and finally submits in shame to the hereditary sovereignty of a family of parvenus.

In the year 1348 a terrible plague raged in the city destroying three fifths of the population, and instead of chastening civic arrogance and curtailing private indulgences engendered a wave of relaxed morality and disorganized the entire social structure. In the anarchy that followed, capital and labor came together in a clash that swept away all class distinctions, and henceforth the source of power was vested solely in personal ability. What, we might reasonably ask, could be fairer or more conducive to the welfare of a progressive democracy? But it was not so in Florence where egoism was irresponsible, and personal ability unsatisfied with anything but the annihilation of all restraints. The city, as we have already shown, was a community of tradesmen and manufacturers, and once business was flourishing again, wealth was swiftly concentrated in the families of a few plutocrats who scrupled at nothing to gain control of the state for their own selfish purposes. Legally, these plutocrats received no special privileges; their weapons were crime, craft, and ducats. Springing from the humblest origins—generally illegitimate—they affected the airs of princes, and became so obnoxious to each other that constant feuds involving the resources of the whole city were waged, resulting in the extinction or exile of the least powerful offenders. The year 1427 marked the appearance of the Medici who guided the fortunes of Florence for four generations, slowly and with rigorously concealed cunning, transforming a loose-jointed democracy into a cringing despotism. Throughout this era of unparalleled energy and disorder, the state enjoyed at intervals remarkable prosperity: colossal sums accruing from fines levied against rich houses temporarily out of favor, and from the peace offerings of victorious oligarchs, poured into the treasury—the Medici alone in less than thirty years paid in taxes, charities and public works the equivalent of $7,000,000 in modern money. Rival cities were reduced to servitude or silence; leagues for good or ill were effected with France or with the Pope; every conceivable form of government was debated and tried, as if the state were something to be moulded at will to fit a constitution made over night, and in all these experiments were brought into play the conspiracies of exiles, the learning of scholars, the brains of artists, the machinations of demagogues, the greed of office holders, and the talents of intriguing financiers.

And throughout the era tragedy awaited the republic at every turn. Florence was doomed. The last struggle for freedom came in 1527 when it was too late for a constitution, when the burghers were whipped into ignominious subjection. "Unable to maintain liberty or submit to control," Symonds has written, "Florence over-reached herself; she was ruined by the petulant and variable temper of a democracy wherein an over-developed intelligence passed into cleverness. In the hour of need her Tuscan rivals threw off her yoke and aided her enemies. She suffered a memorable siege in a final effort for freedom that shed undying lustre on the noblest of Italian cities. At the end, menaced alike by the Pope and Emperor who shook hands over her prostrate corpse, betrayed by her own generals, sold by her own selfish citizens, the center of European civilization succumbed to the monarchy erected by the Medicis."

The spirit of St. Francis passed away with the great plague, and the old mendicant order, at first so inspiring and salutary, degenerated into a swarm of beggars despised by the masses and the cultured Popes. Morality, judged by modern standards, ceased to exist, and its disappearance, together with increasing wealth and the decline of public faith, undermined the courage of the people and vitiated the qualities of hardness and inflexibility which had placed Florence at the head of the Italian republics. Mercenaries were now hired to do the fighting, a dangerous policy so Machiavelli declared; processions, pageants, and plays, splendidly presented, furthered the growing taste for adornment; the Decameron was the favorite reading of the masses, even of the cloistered nuns; the extravagant use of ornaments prevailed, and we meet with false hair made of white or yellow silk, perfumes sprinkled upon everything with which human beings come into contact, cosmetics without limit, and an endless list of beautifying waters, plasters, and paints for every part of the face including the teeth and eyelids. Florence was trying to be carefree and gay, but she was never gay in the easy voluptuous style of Venice. Her rulers and artists were too sternly occupied with their own designs, too zealously burdened with intellectual pursuits to cultivate folly for its own sake, and the temper of the common people fluctuated between absurd pieties and fanatic excesses of an opposite cast. Whether public faith, as many writers assert, was completely wiped out, is a difficult question to decide. Certainly the common people, despite their fits of licentiousness, remained good Catholics to the bitter end—they are good Catholics today; certainly the artists, with one or two exceptions, the sons of tradesmen and mechanics, were religious to the core; and the leaders, however cruel and treacherous and self-seeking, were capable of genuine devotion to the doctrines of the Church. It is true that the scholars and humanists in their enthusiasm for the newly discovered treasures of pagan Greece and Rome ridiculed the monks and the ascetic life and controverted orthodox beliefs, but so long as their ideas were not openly hostile to the Church, they were unmolested. They were indeed as welcome in Rome as in the literary society of Florence, and added conspicuous brilliancy to Papal circles. We cannot estimate this age after our own modern notions of propriety, nor can we, least of all, condemn it because of its crimes and seeming inconsistencies. Modern America, notwithstanding her vicious disregard for personal liberty and her insensibility to the fine arts, has, in her commercial tendencies, her use of wealth, her submissions to plutocrats and her pride, many things in common with the Renaissance in Italy. These I shall discuss in a future chapter. It was an age when man was at liberty to make the most of himself, and individual contradictions, when viewed in relation to fully developed instincts, vanish in the vast abundance of individual attainments. There is Machiavelli whose life was filled with amours of the lowest order yet who was profoundly shocked when several dignitaries of the Church, at a public festival, violated the canon against eating meat during Lent. "What is our illustrious Florence coming to?" he moaned. Lorenzo de' Medici, on his deathbed, summoned the monk Savonarola for absolution. The monk came but recommended to the magnificent one that he first restore to the people the old liberties of Florence. The greatest of the Medici, so the story goes, literally scared to death at the prospect of facing God unshriven, turned his face to the wall and breathed no more. And there are the despots and *condottieri* who, as foemen, cursed the Pope and smote his armies hip and thigh, but who, as Churchmen, reverentially kissed his toe and received his blessing.

Occasionally, in her enslavement, Florence roused herself with a show of oldtime courage. When Charles VIII approached the city, the people were terrified, but after he had marched within the walls, and they saw the French king as he actually was, an ugly, misshapen, short-necked dwarf with a parrot nose, a fiery birthmark round his left eye, and splay feet, they were no longer afraid. His terms refused, Charles cried: "I will sound my trumpets!" The people answered, "We will ring our bells." And the cowardly king, hemmed in by palaces and houses that could be turned, while the tocsin was ringing, into fortresses, accepted a chest of florins and withdrew. When Cesare Borgia would bind Florence into an alliance, the people strongly opposed him, saying, "We did not fear the King of France with 30,000 soldiers; shall we fear a few ragamuffins led by the Pope's unfrocked bastard?" Again, inflamed by the eloquence of Savonarola, they raided the Medicean palace, expelled the family, and proclaimed Christ King of Florence. A theocracy was established with the mad monk in full control. He thundered his decrees from the pulpit and the people executed them with hysterical decision. The city of art, scourged by a Puritanical bigot, was changed into a revivalist camp-meeting. Children were dispatched from door to door to collect cards, dice, cosmetics, false hair, ear-rings, Decamerons, books of indecent poetry which circulated freely among the young, and nude pictures; and one night in the Piazza of the Signoria, a pyre seventy feet high was piled up and the famous "Bonfire of Vanities" lighted the heavens. It is doubtful if any valuable works of art were consumed, although Fra Bartolommeo and other converted painters are said to have tossed masterpieces into the holy flames. But like all attempts to regulate morality by arbitrary laws, Savonarola's reforms did not last. The Florentines, attracted for the moment by the picturesque side of the monk's crusade, had no confidence in his political abilities; the reaction came swiftly and the defiant preacher was hanged and burnt on the very spot where the excited rabble had danced round his bonfire; the Medici were recalled, and the city reverted to her old ways.

The corruption of Renaissance Italy has fascinated historians for centuries. Unfortunately the sensational aspects of the period have been so meretriciously exploited that the Medici, the Borgias and the popes are remembered, in popular imagination, as the prototypes of the gaudy villains of a motion picture melodrama. The great families do not concern us except as examples of the contrasts, capabilities, and excesses of an unprecedently productive age. The Medici were scoundrels, enlightened, ingratiating and generous, but scoundrels none the less. From simple tradesmen they advanced themselves to bankers and international financiers; two members of the house were elevated to the Papacy; one became Queen of France, and the three golden balls taken from their coat of arms hang today above the doors of the shops of pawnbrokers the world over. Gradually they absorbed the government of Florence, and suspended the machinery of the state in favor of their own retainers; they diverted public moneys to their own uses and so artfully entangled the general revenues with their private ventures that the state, under peril of bankruptcy, dared not repudiate them; they intimidated the burghers and enslaved the people; "in effect, they bought and sold the honor of the public officials, jobbed posts for profit, worked at crime and created a court of corrupt men willing to govern by permitting iniquity." On the credit side, they were, in their most distinguished representatives, Cosimo and his grandson, Lorenzo, men of solid intellectual attainments and sympathies, and patrons of the arts in the true sense of the word. They contributed enormous sums to public utilities, founded monasteries, libraries and academies for encouraging the study of Greek and Latin; they were great collectors, sensitive alike to classic and contemporary art, and summoned to their palaces the finest artists, the most brilliant wits and the most learned scholars—and their aesthetic activities were free from snobbery and condescension.

The real centre of iniquity was Rome, with its 7,000 public prostitutes (in 1490), its army of degraded monks, and its scum of visiting sensualists from all parts of the world. Those who care for the wickedness of the popes can find plenty of authenticated material to gratify their curiosity. The best source that I know of is Burchard's Diary. Burchard was master of ceremonies to Alexander VI, and he relates in a cold, routine fashion, without the slightest feelings of indignation or censure, but with incontestable veracity, the daily happenings in the lives of the Spanish Pope and his two illegitimates. Life in the Vatican was revolting enough, and the Spanish Vicar seems to have been guilty of most of the crimes that have made him the favorite target for the assaults of the enemies of the Church, but he was infinitely less "the unspeakable monster" than Sixtus IV, who lent his support to a conspiracy formed to assassinate two of the Medici in the Cathedral of Florence, *the signal for the deed being the moment of the elevation of the Host*, and who authorized the Inquisition in Spain for the extermination of the Jews, one of the most horrible crimes on the pages of history. Nor was the private life of Alexander VI offensive or even startling to his own generation. From Burchard's account of the nature of the sins for which the Pope granted unlimited indulgence, we may readily understand why his besetting weakness for women—even his own daughter—may have been looked upon so lightly. It was Alexander's frank acceptance of the Papacy as a secular institution and his superb skill in enlarging and protecting the dominions of the Church that made him so odious to his ambitious adversaries. In many ways he was an excellent Pope, handsome and amiable, punctilious in matters of business, unceasingly energetic, humanely considerate of the wants of the poor, abstemious in food and drink and averse to luxury and laziness. In common with the other powerful figures of the Renaissance he knew what he wanted and proceeded to get it with the means at his disposal. His ability as a poisoner has been ridiculously overrated. If we were to believe the stories handed down to us, the Pope and his family were more adept at compounding drugs than the most eminent of modern chemists—magicians, in fact, whose dainty boluses worked slowly and imperceptibly, bringing death after an interval of thirty days! We have ample evidence that the famous white powder, now known to have been arsenic, was employed with marked success by the Borgias, but it was the boldness and frequency with which it was administered that made the family name so mysterious and terrifying.

Alexander's children, Cesare and Lucrezia Borgia, interest us as examples of the Renaissance tendency to extract from life all that it had to give. Cesare was endowed with immense physical strength, a forceful intelligence, and more than ordinary qualities of military leadership. He remains one of the most devilish characters on record, friendless, heartless, carnivorous, an educated animal who threw off his cardinal's hat and put on the sword, hoping the more quickly to make himself master of Italy. He was a son after his father's own heart, and the Pope was exorbitantly devoted to him, assisting him in all his dastardly enterprises. But Cesare despised affection of any sort. During his father's last illness he never once set foot in the Vatican, and at the end sent his men to steal the silver and the papal cash. There have been greater criminals than Cesare Borgia, and more memorable and gifted exemplars of depravity, but he is the world's prize specimen of a being in whom the loathsome instincts of man reigned to the utter exclusion of everything worthy of respect. Only one blemish mars the perfection of his vile career: he appreciated the genius of Leonardo da Vinci, and made the versatile artist his chief military engineer.

Lucrezia Borgia typifies the capricious spirit of the age. We could hardly expect a girl reared as she was to grow up into decent womanhood, but that is exactly what she did. Her early life was godless and lively, and she could enjoy with bursts of laughter the famous banquet given by her brother—a supper party for which fifty prostitutes were employed to test the concupiscence of the male guests. "She seems," says Creighton, "to have inherited her father's frank and joyous nature, but she was in no way remarkable. Her fine figure, her long golden hair, her sweet childish face, her pleasant expression and graceful ways struck all who saw her." At the age of twenty-two she married her third husband and settled down at Ferrara where her life was not only blameless but full of good works.

The intellectual life of Rome developed through external influences, Florence supplying the main stimulus. The popes, on the whole, were munificent patrons, whimsical and autocratic, but providing great artists with great commissions, and attaching to their court the most accomplished writers and orators to whom were entrusted bulls, diplomatic letters, state papers, and such like. Alexander VI had no time for painting and sculpture, but Julius II, a man of heroic mould, one of the master spirits of the Renaissance and one of the noblest of all the popes, imprisoned Michael Angelo in the Sistine Chapel—to the Eternal glory of the art of painting, called forth the best in Raphael and conceived the idea of St. Peter's—"the materialized idea symbolizing the transition from the Church of the Middle Ages to the modern semi-secular supremacy of Papal Rome." His successor Leo X, the son of Lorenzo de' Medici, was a man of entirely different stamp. Leo, whose name is associated with the "golden age of art," remarked on his coronation, "Let us all enjoy the Papacy, since God has given it to us." The remark was characteristic. He was a smiling sybarite infected with the germs of the popular neo-pagan culture. His Pontificate was a gorgeous carnival that left the Church bankrupt. But to his flair for bacchanalian diversions, he added a reckless patronage of the arts, worked Raphael to death and adorned his court with all the entertainers, scholars, and poets that money could buy.

From our picture of the Renaissance, its rapacity and crime, its bewildering profusion of baseness, bloodshed and unsettling violence, the reader may well wonder why it was that art flourished so magnificently. There is no absolute explanation. No one knows precisely why art is produced, why Michael Angelo, at such a terrific cost of mental agony, forfeiting all the pleasures of companionship and good living, sold himself to endless creative toil, why Donatello and Brunelleschi, penniless and starving, went off to Rome in their youth to spend their days and nights digging among the bones of antiquity. But this we do know: art inheres in the human soul and under certain conditions manifests itself with extraordinary fertility. Impulses, which, for want of a more definite name, are called spiritual, demand fulfilment, and the artist, viewing the gross activities of life with reason and contemplation finds order in lawless violence, significance in all experiences and permanence in transitory events. What circumstances are favorable to art is a question we will not attempt to decide. It is, I think, beyond dispute that when man is most free, when no artificial restraints are imposed upon him and it is possible for him to develop his individuality to its fullest capacities, that art is most likely to thrive. Does anyone suppose for a moment, considering the incomparable wealth and variety of Italian art, that such monumental records of imaginative power could have been produced by a civilization that ran along with the humdrum regularity of a Swiss village? The grandeur of Michael Angelo has its analogue in the grandeur of Julius II; we remember Cesare Borgia for his appalling brutality, but the frescoes of Andrea del Castagno contain similar qualities of terrible energy and vengeance; the fanaticism of

Savonarola is matched by Uccello's obsession with the scientific problems of perspective; the sexual proclivities of Alexander VI are not more notorious than those of Cellini; the spirit of mysticism and simple faith, before it was extinguished in the hearts of the ineffectual minority, found its perfect spokesman in Fra Angelico; at the other end of the scale, the elegant and sophisticated tastes of Leo X created a congenial atmosphere for the classical decorum of Raphael. Today we demand more stability and less art, and we may rest assured that whenever life is secure and uneventful, art in the aggregate is bound to be a reflex of commonplace experiences.

There are no ideal conditions for the growth of art. Or perhaps it would be better to say that conditions popularly believed to be favorable to art give rise to the lighter and more agreeable forms of expression. We may dispense with the idea that nations struggle and fight, accumulate wealth, and then in a period of cultured leisure, direct their refined energies to the production of art. This fallacy is perfectly illustrated by the aggressive cultural pretensions of our own millionaires. The American plutocrat, having won his fortune and bought himself an enviable social position, sets out, in the same parvenu spirit, to buy culture. Generally he invests his superfluous millions in the carefully authenticated treasures of the past and hoards masterpieces to symbolize his vanity. His life, however, remains unchanged save for those moments when, surrounded by his costly plunder, he fancies that he, too, has something of the artist in his soul, thus exalting himself above his kind. A similar delusion is shared by our "commercial artist." These money-grubbers, to a man, look forward to the day when they can retire from business and go in for painting "in a serious way." They will go to Paris where, in an ideal background, breathing the joyous Bohemian air, they will saturate their starved souls with culture and become real artists. But art, unfortunately, does not proceed from culture—it is the child of new evaluations and fresh enthusiasms for old and native things. It appears most abundantly when the life of a nation is strong, healthy and unrefined. Eventually, of course, art exhausts its virility, acquires graceful manners, and degenerates into sweetness and imitation. Culture is only the organization of stereotyped attitudes, and though originally based on actual objects soon loses its direct connection with art and becomes a matter of etiquette. During the last, or cultural stage of art, painters and sculptors lean heavily upon tradition and talk wistfully of the ideal conditions of the past. In the palmy days of the Renaissance, after the great constructive minds had done their work, the little men of culture, engulfed in the humanistic tide of paganism, looked at the world through the golden haze of Greece and Rome. They believed that the Greeks had created, for all time, the ideal figure, and sought by measurement and imitation to duplicate that ideal. Such is the academic point of view, the attempt to make art out of other art, the belief in the perfection of the past. The best Greek sculptures are perhaps the most subtle reconstructions of the human body that have ever been made, but even so they are only one form of art, and are no more to be worshipped as ideal creations than the figures of Giotto and Rembrandt which are respectively idealizations of Italian and Dutch types.

The Renaissance in Italy affords striking proof of the fact that great art is not a literal reflection of the external world. An examination of Florentine painting from Giotto to Michael Angelo discloses no signs of corruption or sensuality. The reason is not far to seek. Art, whenever it is worthy of the name, deals with the meanings behind man's activities and with experiences as they affect the spirit; and it cannot therefore, be used as an agent for vice, or an instrument to glorify corruption. Those who look upon art as a stimulus to erotic desires and carnal recreations will find small comfort in Italian painting—or for that matter in any genuine painting. They will even find that the obscene photographs peddled surreptitiously in Paris—such things are now sold in America as well—are pretty poor substitutes for flesh and blood. It is also worth noting that the Italians esteemed themselves as the inventors of painting and practiced the art with peculiar reverence. Their secular plays, their novels and their poems were unblushingly salacious, at least by modern standards, but they allowed nothing even remotely suggestive to tarnish the nobility of the plastic arts. We might think that the Venetians were less censorious, but when Aretino persuaded his friend, Giulio Romano, to engrave a series of dirty designs to accompany some lewd sonnets he had written, the patrons of art were profoundly shocked, and the plates were immediately confiscated by the Pope. No one objected to the sonnets, but the profanation of the sacred name of art by a distinguished painter like Romano was nothing less than treason.

We must regard the art of Italy as a record of spiritual achievements, a depository of documents representing the inquiries, speculations and organized experiences of men who rose above the fierce materialism of their age, discarded all that was irrelevant and inconsequential, and gathered together in permanent form ideas and emotions common to the human race at all times. Art is great in proportion to its power to attract the largest audiences throughout the longest period of time and the greatest art, because of its humanity and philosophy, is inexhaustible. The creative genius of Italy was primarily pictorial and her painters aiming at what Leonardo defined as the goal of all art—universality—conferred upon the world more pictures which may without reservation be called inexhaustible than the artists of any other nation. Thus, after 400 years Michael Angelo is a living influence and Leonardo more discussed than ever before, to say nothing of lesser painters like Uccello whose purely scientific studies in planes and angles are so fresh and modern that they seem to have inspired the Cubists of yesterday. The extraordinary variety of intellectual interests bred men of protean talents, and the great figures of the Renaissance, for the most part, were eminent in every department of the fine arts. Follow the career of almost any artist, and you will discover that he began as a craftsman—more often than not a goldsmith—studied with a recognized master, practiced with distinction painting, sculpture and architecture, and still unsatisfied, cultivated as side-lines poetry, music and mathematics. Not all the artists, of course, were giants. The rank and file were far more numerous but we do not hear so much about them. For the sake of convenience, in charting the stream of development, we may divide the artists into two classes: the first includes the followers of Giotto, the men interested in universals; the second, the specialists absorbed in more particular problems, in landscape, portraiture, pageantry, and the reconciliation of Christianity with pagan culture.

Giotto's immediate successors were a set of submissive, agreeable and second-rate story-tellers. Like the crowd of small souls who tag along after every great man, they capitalized the externals of their master's art without understanding his constructive principles. These little Giottos deserve no mention; let them lie unexhumed in that prolific interlude of the Renaissance when painters, blinded by the light of prophetic genius and incapable of grasping new ideas, filled the churches of Italy with commonplace dreams and nice symmetrical inventions. But perhaps it is better to dismiss this school than to flout it. What we now take for granted—that painting should give the impression of reality—was not always an axiom. "There was a time," Wölfflin explains, "when this requirement was quite unknown, and for the sufficient reason that it was believed to be impossible to suggest the tactile quality of natural objects on a flat surface. This was the opinion of the whole mediaeval period. Men were content with a representation that merely suggested objects and their relations to one another in space. It was undoubtedly one of the greatest advances ever made by humanity when this limitation was recognized as prejudicial and men began to believe that it might be possible to achieve something closer to the actual impression made by nature."

In short, mediaeval painting was restricted to two dimensions; it was a symbolical art of flat surfaces. From Giotto to Masaccio, the trend was toward a greater and more intense relief of objects in space—toward realism. Now the word realism has received so many different interpretations that we must define it carefully. The term, as we shall use it, bears no relation to photography; it refers to an abstraction of substantial qualities from actual experience and not to literal representation; it is based upon an imaginative conception of life, creating a new order of things by means of new combinations and strengthening the emotional appeal of two-dimensional art by the addition of solidity and depth, both universal characteristics of our experience of things. The photographic painter trains his eye and hand to register what he sees before him; the creative artist looks upon his materials with a synthetic vision; he fortifies his immediate visual impression with knowledge gained from all his experiences; he reinforces the appeal of the human body by enlargements and alterations rendering the figure, not after its appearance from a given point of view, but according to searching studies of hundreds of attitudes and movements. This new order—this reality—is far more stimulating than a camera record for the obvious reason that it is more than a mere impression of nature. It is nature disciplined and humanized. Art, then, considered as reality, enters the realm of the spirit, and becomes, in the words of Havelock Ellis, "the remaking of the world after the heart's desire"—that is, after conceptions of order and meaning.

With the inception of depth, painting simulated sculpture in its use of detail, that is to say, forms were modelled. Instead of the tangible reality of sculpture, which, of course, could never be approached, painting extended solid form far beyond the limits of true sculpture and opened up a new and voluminous world of deep space. The loss of surface, the liberation of objects from a background, first became a positive fact in Masaccio. This austere genius, a direct descendent of Giotto, was the progenitor of a movement destined to include veritable giants of art, some of the greatest men of all time.

The new style by releasing objects from a single plane, brought an extraordinary impetus to art, and at the same time imposed upon painters the most difficult problems. To make a flat design was relatively simple; to control insurgent forces operating in three dimensions called for the superior intelligence of the masters of composition. For a long and magnificent period the genius of the artist was concentrated on the study of form, and on the sequences of line and mass necessary to hold together groups of objects presented in actual space. Form, as delineated from Masaccio to Michael Angelo, was an *artistic* reality. It was not imitation. It imparted to the substance of the fleeting world of the Renaissance a permanent beauty infinitely surpassing anything merely phenomenal; it embodied the higher reality born of mind.

I must apologize for this technical digression, but it is unavoidable if we are to have a clear perception of the transition from mediaeval to modern painting. For it was at this time that the occidental tradition of art came into existence, and the men who formed the tradition were technical pioneers and indefatigable students of new methods. It is difficult to believe that perspective, anatomy, and light and shade should have aroused in the old painters such unbounded enthusiasm and admiration, but we must remember that technical implements now regarded as part of every student's equipment were once fresh discoveries by means of which the artist might conceivably make himself lord of all creation. Imagine the furore that would attend the discovery of a sane and convincing method of depicting the fourth dimension! Think of what would happen if a contemporary artist should evolve an entirely new color gamut! Something of this sort did happen a few years ago when Cézanne abolished light and shade and modelled his forms in planes of pure color. The result was a new school of painting, a school so radical in its departure that it is still popularly referred to as the new movement in art. But the early painters, let it be observed, were not mechanics intoxicated with technical experiments; they were many-sided men concerned with perspective, anatomy, and light and shade only as properties to facilitate their artistic conceptions.

The change from the mediaeval to the modern style was not effected by one man, nor by a single generation of men. The change came slowly working always toward the establishment of substantial, massive forms in deep space. The primitive masters could portray figures only at rest or in slow motion; the complex ideals of the Florentines required a more varied and realistic art. Giotto started the movement, but Giotto's pictures are comparatively flat. His figures stand on their toes—they are substantial but incapable of free muscular action. His architectural backgrounds are flimsy stage settings and all out of proportion. His faces, despite individual characterizations, are cast in the hard Byzantine mould, and his knowledge of anatomy is limited. This is not to deny his greatness; as I have already pointed out, his name stands for most of the highest things in art, and his work prefigures all the outstanding excellencies of the Florentine school. He fixed the direction of modern painting; his large simple forms, clearly defined in pure line, showed his successors how the deepest feelings might be made dramatic and heroic; his frescoes testify to the power of the will and to a firmly controlled imagination, qualities which lent to Florentine art monumental vigor and nobility and sharpness of expression seldom to be found outside of Italy, and which have attracted all subsequent artists who believe that painting is more than soft, seductive color and the surrender to momentary physical excitement. After Giotto we are overwhelmed by scientific inquiry. Space was geometrically explored; light and shade analysed; the anatomy of the human body and all the intricacies of rhythmical action, weight and volume systematically investigated. Each discovery had its band of devotees, and painters competed with one another to prove the value of new technical means. As a result, an abundance of detail was laid upon art, but in due course, after new methods were accepted and mastered, simplification set in, and the Renaissance culminated in frescoes as clearly defined as those of Giotto but infinitely more subtle in rhythmical construction.

Giotto, you will recall, was greatly aided by the Gothic carvers; his followers, in turn, were instructed in realism by the first sculptors in Florence. About 1400 the city decided to complete the bronze doors of the Baptistry and invited sculptors from all parts of Italy to submit designs. The commission was awarded to

Lorenzo Ghiberti, a young goldsmith who devoted fifty years, or the rest of his life, to the job. But what a marvellous job he did! "These designs," said Michael Angelo, "are worthy to adorn the gates of paradise." Ghiberti's bas-reliefs are really pictures in bronze. Modelled after a perspective plan with the figures in the receding planes gradually diminishing in size and relief, graceful in outline and wrought with the delicacy of the goldsmith's craft, the doors stand outside the Florentine tradition of heroic art, but in surmounting, with consummate skill, pictorial difficulties of the most baffling nature, they were of inestimable benefit to painters. Another competitor, Brunelleschi, on seeing the designs, graciously retired to his more special province of architecture, and composed a treatise on perspective which was used as a handbook by painters in their efforts to achieve verisimilitude in backgrounds and scenic accessories. Brunelleschi was also a mathematician and engineer and "left formulae for the resolution of all problems." The great Donatello, though only a boy of seventeen, is said to have been consulted by the judge before the verdict was finally awarded. We may well believe it. Donatello's genius does not lie within the scope of our story—nothing short of a volume could do justice to his "terrible fury"—but his invincible realism—he carved a statue of Christ which provoked the comment from Brunelleschi that "he had crucified a rustic," his ability to study the antique and at the same time to combine his studies with a voracious and untiring observation of nature, to produce therefrom sculptures of incomparable vitality and free from classic staleness; his judgment, his sanity, his versatility, his technical daring—in sum, all that makes Donatello's carvings of children, serene youths, warriors and men so old and wizened that they appear to be skinned alive, perpetually modern, all that makes him one of the monarchs of art, was as profound a source of inspiration to Florentine painters as to sculptors.

To Masaccio belongs the honor of planting the new style squarely on its own feet. The life of this young Titan is shrouded in obscurity. He was the son of a notary and he must have been a slouchy fellow for his contemporaries gave him the nickname Masaccio which is to say, "dirty Tom." From evidence adduced by his pictures, it is probable that he studied antique sculpture; certain it is that his precocious powers were directed by Brunelleschi and Donatello and that he knew Giotto like a book. He was favorably noticed by one of the Medici, seems to have had trouble keeping out of debt, and died in Rome in 1428 at the age of twenty-six, possibly by foul means.

Anatole France called this unkempt prodigy the master of masters. The phrase is a happy one. There was, and is today, in Florence a Church of the Carmine, and in this church a little chapel decorated with frescoes by Masaccio. During the middle years of the fifteenth century, every celebrated painter, in his student days, came to the chapel to learn how to draw—Andrea del Castagno, Filippino Lippi, Verrocchio, Ghirlandaio, Botticelli, Perugino, Leonardo da Vinci, and Michael Angelo. At first the frescoes are disappointing; the light is poor; the colors have darkened under layers of soot and dust, and the backgrounds, once dramatic landscapes, are clouded with a smoky grey atmosphere through which we may discern straight, dead trees and slaty hills. But stay awhile, and the qualities that elicited the homage of the above-named masters will be slowly revealed. Masaccio, as if by instinct, anticipated the maturity of the Renaissance, and the painters who studied him confirmed and elaborated his amazing technical discoveries by scientific experiment. It is easy to see that he is the direct heir of Giotto, but at one stride, the constricted world of his forerunner is extended far back into space. For the first time in painting, at least to any appreciable extent, he uses aerial perspective. This is a studio phrase. It means that his figures are bathed in light and air; they are not glued to a background, but move freely in space with plenty of elbow room between them. He models his forms with strong oppositions of light and shade; in his hands architecture becomes stable, convincing and inhabitable; he lays hold of the secrets of foreshortening and of giving objects the appearance of solidity by superimposing one upon the other; his landscapes have a massive grandeur and scenic appropriateness.

At the present time Masaccio is one of the gods of the Modernist school of painting. This recent apotheosis may be ascribed, in part, to a venomous reaction against evils with which Masaccio, fortunately, did not have to contend—salon art with its offensively clever array of imitated textures, and its flashing meaningless nudes; flattering portraiture done with the machine-like finish of photography; and soulless virtuosity controlled by ignorant and unscrupulous dealers—and in part to a laudable and salutary interest in the constructive aspects of art. The intelligent Modernist will tell you that Masaccio is a master of three-dimensional space, that every figure and every object has its geometrically determined position in a perfectly ordered scheme of relationships, and that he is one of the world's greatest draughtsmen, realizing with a few swift strokes forms of terrifying bulk and solidity. He will also tell you that Masaccio is a master of *plastic form*. Another studio phrase and a good one. Form becomes plastic when it conveys the substance and thickness of sculpture, when it is so firm and palpable and real that it stimulates through impressions received by the eye, our sense of touch and feeling. Also when it has resilience—when we are not conscious of a painted surface but of living shapes that bend and move and unite with one another.

All of which is true and praiseworthy. Most of us, I think, take delight in beholding the triumph over difficulties. We do not need to be artists to derive a keen sense of pleasure from fine forms and attitudes, from human figures in rhythmical movement, and the balanced distribution of weights and masses and colors. But this is not, I hope, the end and aim of art. The Modernist painter has had to fight his way through a wilderness of trash, and has been so closely preoccupied with questions of plastic form and structure that he imagines he has produced a work of art when he has only solved a technical problem. He forgets that great painting, over and beyond technical necessaries, is animated by a profound human purpose. In the Florentine chapel, Masaccio painted a picture of the *Expulsion of Adam and Eve*. Now it is quite possible that in conceiving this fresco he was prompted by the desire to show his rivals how the nude should be painted, how the inert figures of Giotto might be put in motion, and how, in the form of Eve, suggested, it is said, by a statue of the pudic Venus—whose attitude I am reliably informed, is that assumed by every modest woman when surprised in her nudity, he could, in fresco, surpass the carvings of the antique. But look at the pair of sinners! The lines, muscles, and features, the postures and facial expression, are deliberately calculated to make the two figures eternal effigies of shame and suffering. If it were not so, they would be only a couple of studio nudes, doing nothing, expressing nothing. Masaccio selected for models a pair of miserable Italians—his faces are individualized into portraits—and by means of plastic modelling and the other expedients noted above, transmuted the local into the universal. The legend of the Expulsion was peculiarly suited to his tragic genius, for it is the spirit of tragedy that unites him with the greatest Florentine artists, and with Rembrandt, Daumier, and all contemplative mortals.

The tragic art of Masaccio is not a weak and whimpering wail, not a sweet plea for mercy, nor the plaintive moan of defeat. It is, first of all, the sharp and magnificent tragedy of his native city, a city in which men, despising the softer virtues of Christian charity, meekness and humility, and armed with pride and power, played a desperate game with life—and lost, a city famed for its hard anguish and austere suffering, and personified in a papal festival at Rome by a strong lady plunged in woe. Second, it is the tragedy of the whole human race. In the dark chapel of the Carmine there is a fresco which represents St. Peter baptising a group of men, two of whom are naked. Here again the artist may have wished to demonstrate his knowledge of the nude—for purely illustrative purposes the rugged young men might better have been clothed—but I doubt it. The novelist and poet have other means of showing what a small and painful specimen man is in the face of the universe, but if the artist wishes to portray this idea let him follow Masaccio's example—let him strip man to the skin and expose him to the world in a sublime shiver. So it is with the rest of his pictures, which I regret to say, are not many. Whether the scene contains few figures or a crowd, the action is dominated by one idea, and that idea is tragic. It is the tragedy that cleanses the soul. We feel it in the commanding figure of Christ in *The Tribute Money*, in the *Crucifixion* of Santa Maria Novella, and in his madonnas, the last being, not languorous maidens beaming with vapid ecstasies, but stern women acquainted with grief.

Masaccio, as we have learned, was a remarkable man, and how far he might have gone, had he lived longer, is a conjecture that must be reserved for idle theorists. Luckily, those who came immediately after him were hardly less remarkable, and their discoveries so far reaching and fertile, that modern painting, save for the momentary flurry of Impressionism, has added practically nothing to their science. What a mighty lot of painters they were! Not merely scientists illuminating abstruse technical processes, but artists filled with the religious melancholy and tragic power of the Renaissance! And how grandly they give the lie to the notion that painting should be a *pure* art, that it should contain nothing literary—whatever that may mean—that it should be the spontaneous gushing of unbridled feelings and not the workings of a rigorously controlled intellect, that it should be independent of subject-matter, and to the hundred and one theories binding art to this or that ingenious postulate. They saw life as a whole, seeking always to present man, not as a visual bulk of bones and clothing, but as a unit in a universal scheme; they delved into anatomy and perspective, not for the sake of verisimilitude but to give their ideas coherence: though serving the Church, they treated all subjects with absolute freedom, investing their materials with spiritual qualities which transcend all institutions and creeds. The love which the earlier painters had for their art and the energy with which they pursued it move the modern mind to wonder. I know that it is easy to sing the praises of the past, but let any one who doubts visit those hot hill towns of Tuscany and Umbria, the miasmatic districts of the North, and Rome in August, and let him, sweltering in some unclean tavern, project his fancy back into the Renaissance, when it was equally hot and much less sanitary, and when one's peace and safety were constantly imperilled by wars and civic brawls, and then, pondering the physical impediments of the past, let him wander through the churches, museums and palaces and take stock of the incalculable treasures remaining in Italy after the depredations of centuries. Painting, of course, was a profitable business—but that is only the beginning of the matter. For reasons that I will leave to the psychologists—when their science becomes more trustworthy—the Italians had a genius for the plastic arts. All that was fine and noble and generous and civilizing, went into painting and sculpture. The rest is literature, and the literature, excepting the work of the historians, is mannered frivolity and sensual declamation touched up with hot conceits and theatrical gestures and pretty tangles of incestuous copulation. Today it is unreadable, whereas the old painting, besides being an active influence on all who care seriously for art, is the redeeming glory of a hapless nation overrun by political brigands.

The main current of Florentine painting moved swiftly onward fed by the intellectual resources of six great men. These artists had no time for the minor graces of painting—for smooth, melting color, innocuous piety, charming landscape and tender sentiment—they conquered the stubborn forces of life by the strength of the individual will; their purpose was definite and concrete and they remade the world into an architectural edifice from which was excluded everything soft and vague and uncertain. Paolo Uccello, a barber's son, was a mathematician and an expert in perspective—not the atmospheric perspective of Masaccio, but the science which deals with converging lines, foreshortening and receding planes—and would stay up all night with his studies, drawing polygons with 80 facets and other such oddities, and exclaiming to his wife when she besought him to go to bed, "O what a delightful thing is this perspective!" He

Masaccio: THE TRIBUTE MONEY. (Detail.)

Carmelite Church, Florence

had little interest in sacred themes, and introduced into painting, for the first time, since the Pompeian freizes, battle scenes and historical motives. The battle pictures, alive with clashing planes and radiating lines are, as I have said, strangely modern. Uccello was a curious soul, a scholar and a precisionist, and yet fascinated with all the wonder and faith of youth by the expanding brilliancy of the Renaissance. His battles are not dramatic by reason of any truth to nature or war—his knights are tin soldiers, his steeds hobby horses—but commanding the most advanced technique of his time, he contrived by means of clear-cut design, to give exciting movement and rhythmical form to his somewhat fantastic visions.

We have commented on Donatello's search for realistic truth, that is to say, how he studied the human body in order to make his sculptures living organisms. The same spirit of deep tireless inquiry characterizes the two painters Andrea del Castagno and Antonio Pollaiuolo. Both were masters of muscular action, both exponents of the trenchant Florentine style. For savage strength that makes no concessions to delicacy or refinement, for hard power and massive vigor, Andrea del Castagno, the son of a laborer, has no equal in Renaissance or any other art. He is not, however, a giant exulting in feats of strength; his sardonic mind reaches out into the realm of tragedy; his domineering military heroes are types of august and merciless energy; his *Last Supper*, an assemblage of ennobled peasants, is one of the greatest of pictures, and the only one inviting comparison with Leonardo's treatment of the subject, and his conception of Christ the most robust and masculine in Italian painting. Pollaiuolo, son of a poulterer, was painter, sculptor, engraver and anatomist. His knowledge of the nude was enormous, but it was the artist's knowledge gained to exhibit tension, flexibility and movement. His passion for the figure led him, naturally, to choose subjects, mainly mythological, allowing him to revel, to his heart's content, in naked forms. The wildest attitudes bringing into prominence complex muscular articulations were as child's play to him, and it is not to be doubted that in some of his pictures he was carried away by his frenetic thirst for experimentation. Pollaiuolo was a pathfinder, the first painter to give close attention to anatomy and to test its aesthetic potenialities. He was a great teacher, but a great artist as well, and his work is a perfect expression of the mobility, the athletic paganism and the exaggerated violence of the Renaissance.

The fame of Piero della Francesca, never seriously contested during the passing of the ages, has lately risen to Olympian heights. The Modernists claim him for their own; connoisseurs read cabalistic meanings into his perspicuous designs; it is fashionable to praise him at the expense of Michael Angelo; Mr. Aldous Huxley has written an essay extolling his *Resurrection*, as "the greatest picture in the world." But the master will survive this hero-worshipping—he has lived down worse things in the past. Piero, you must understand, is now celebrated as one who is all head and no heart, great because of his "cool, intellectual detachment." Must artists always be *cool* and *detached*, or are these stigmata only the rationalizations of modern painters who are social outcasts? It happens that Piero was not cool. He was a more rabid student of mathematics and perspective than his master Uccello, and almost as much of an anatomist as Pollaiuolo. Nor was he detached. A man cannot remain aloof from life and paint pictures of any considerable appeal. True he spent most of his days in Umbria, but Umbria was then at war, and the town of Arezzo was not the sunburnt graveyard that it is today. Piero was fond of war and his battle pictures could hardly have been painted from second-hand information. There is something lordly and militant in all his work. Moreover he was a traveller, he was patronized by Dukes and Popes, painted at Rome, and in all probability was in Florence during the patriarchal festival of 1439. He loved festivals and parades, strange costumes and head-dresses and archaic faces, but he had a philosophical mind, and that, I think, accounts for the belief that he set himself apart from his age. He was an heroic soul who suggests, in the modern world, Joseph Conrad, an artist who has also been accused of detachment. For all his color, his curious costumes, and his processions, it was the sombre side of life that acted upon Piero's imagination. His mind is orderly, exact and severe, he has no room in his world for dainty sentiment, frailties, and homely affections; with the utmost clarity, with never a sign of insecurity, he refines his characters into types of poised and unapproachable nobility. His sense of placement is infallible, and he composes his frescoes with a diagrammatic perfection that tempts one to conclude that he was in possession of some magic formula. Technically, he contributed as much or more than any of his great contemporaries to the science of space and depth: it was his practice to paint directly from clay models so that his forms might have the rounded solidity of sculpture; his serene, carefully observed landscapes, with their astonishing effects in light and shadow, run back into vast distances; as a mural decorator combining colors, lights and forms on a large architectural scale, he is one of the few supreme masters in painting.

The serenity of Piero della Francesca is changed into furious turmoil in the art of his pupil, Luca Signorelli, another heroic soul, but one charged with terrible agonies and fiery compassions. Signorelli was a lowly Umbrian who moved to Florence, studied Pollaiuolo, worked for the Medici and the Pope, but meeting with little success in the centers of culture, wandered from town to town painting altarpieces and small devotional pictures. His industry was enormous, and his delight in the nude inexhaustible. Vasari relates of Luca Signorelli "that he had a son killed in Cortona, a youth of singular beauty in face and person, whom he tenderly loved. In his deep grief, the father caused the child to be despoiled of his clothing and with extraordinary constancy of soul, uttering no complaint and shedding no tear, he painted the portrait of the dead child, to the end that he might still have the power of contemplating, by means of the work of his own hands, that which nature had given him, but which an adverse fortune had taken away." His life-long ambition was to use the naked figure as a motive in monumental decoration, and in his 60th year he was called to Orvieto to paint *The Last Judgment* for the Cathedral. Here, in one of the foulest, most God-forsaken towns on earth we may behold one of the wonders of art. We may see the *Souls of the Damned* and the *Resurrection* symbolized by nude forms in the most audacious positions, swirling through space, contorted to reveal violent tension and muscular energy, skeletons, demons and angels—the whole range of tormented human life expressed with the same tragic pity and controlled sorrow that marked the artist when he painted the portrait of his murdered son.

The sixth great man was the son of a Paduan farmer. Andrea Mantegna is the noblest Roman of them all. Though he belongs more or less to the Venetian school, he is allied with the Florentines in his scientific tendencies, and in his perfection of design in fresco. The grandeur of antiquity which cast such a fervent spell upon Renaissance humanism and which in the end was debased into an ignoble fad and a blighting disease, was Mantegna's birthright. He did not play the ape to the conventional worship of Roman culture, he was indeed, a Roman reborn, or more precisely, an original artist whose temperament responded naturally and with profound reverence to the grimness, the nobility and power of his ancestors. As a boy he was initiated into antique scholarship by a famous teacher of the North; when he grew wealthy he collected Greek and Roman statues and bas-reliefs, but his scholarship was enriched and saved from pedantry by travel and by unceasing intercourse with men and women of all classes. He painted his frescoes from casts and clay models, but the finished works, instead of impressing the spectator as copies of sculpture, contain in pigment qualities of living fierceness and grandeur similar to those which animate the antique marbles. His drawings have been admired and studied by artists from Dürer to Burne-Jones and Beardsley; his engravings are among the most distinguished things bequeathed by the Renaissance; a French critic ventured the opinion that "Mantegna is the prince of draughtsmen of all time."

Having considered the great constructive minds that developed the tradition of art founded by Giotto and Masaccio, we may note briefly the secondary figures. First comes Sandro Botticelli, the son of a tanner, the pet of swooning connoisseurs and neurotic aesthetes, an artist of indisputable charm, and in the narrow sense of the word, of excessive originality. He was esteemed in his own time as a superior draughtsman, and we may still honor him for his sensitive tremulous line which he weaves into eccentric rhythms. But he was entirely too sensitive, and his influence upon painting has been, on the whole, baleful. A sick soul, half-pagan and half-Presbyterian, he brings into art the atmosphere of the unhealthy studio and becomes the father of precious dabblers and quack mystics who try to convince us that the world owes them a living because they are expressing themselves. In Botticelli's pictures we see, for the first time, figures set in vacant studio poses. His art is popular for what it suggests rather than expresses—he was incapable of defining emotions with decision and clarity—and his wistful elusiveness has received far-fetched and incredible interpretations by moping literary rhapsodists.

Fra Filippo Lippi, son of a barber, turned monk, eloped with a nun, and executed religious pictures with faint conviction, but being a jovial family man, employed his madonnas and saints as characters in little domestic dramas painted affectionately and with a touch of poetry. His most important contribution to art is his color which is modern not only in its richness, but in its subtle blending of broken tones. His gifted son Filippino, adopted Botticelli's mannerisms, and after completing, amid great applause, several of Masaccio's unfinished frescoes, went to Rome where he forgot all he had learned and wound up in baroque sensationalism.

Everybody loves Fra Angelico, the holy monk who prayed before taking up his brushes and who covered the walls of San Marco with his celestial visions. Technically, he is a highly sophisticated painter, spiritually, he is a thousand years behind the times—or many thousand ahead, if we are to believe the modern monks and their lay brother, Mr. Gilbert K. Chesterton. However that may be, no one has ever expressed primitive faith and the mediaeval conception of heavenly bliss, and the joys of suffering with such exquisite clarity and truth. There is an echo of this faith in the mad designs of Vincent Van Gogh. Fra Angelico was not mad—he lived within himself in an unbroken dream of holiness. He is a painter of one mood and an anomaly in Renaissance art. His pupil, Benozzo Gozzoli, was also a dreamer, but a superficial one. Gozzoli possessed a staggering inventiveness and a Gothic eye for engaging details—nothing save death and space could limit his narrative skill. He covered wall after wall with huge pictures of lords and ladies, landscapes, animals, architecture and pageantry—frescoes which are not particularly interesting as works of art, but delightful illustrations of the careless and picturesque court life of the Renaissance.

The enormously capable, sane and admirable painter, Domenico Ghirlandaio, son of a garland maker, sums up the whole Florentine tradition—but in a prosaic fashion. Fresco painting was as easy to him as oil painting to Rubens, and he regretted that he had not the walls of Florence to decorate. I must confess that Ghirlandaio leaves me cold. He could handle the largest spaces without the slightest difficulty or embarrassment; his figures are arranged with judgment and skill; he is as accomplished as the best of them in portraiture, and his costumes and ornaments are beautifully subordinated to his general decorative scheme. But he lacked genius. He is respectable, not dignified; inventive, not creative; agreeable, not inspiring; and forceful rather than dramatic.

Two other artists epitomize the fulness of the Renaissance tradition. In Leonardo da Vinci and Michael Angelo, the qualities of intellectual discovery, science, power and deep human feeling are gathered together, organized and individualized into works which seem to be destined to remain forever as examples of the greatest things that art can accomplish.

Leonardo da Vinci: SELF-PORTRAIT.

Turin Gallery

CHAPTER

IV

LEONARDO DA VINCI

O wretched mortals, open your eyes!
LEONARDO'S NOTEBOOKS

LEONARDO DA VINCI is perhaps the most resplendent figure in the history of the human race. In person, distinguished and strong; in bearing, generous and gentle; in intellect, a giant; in art, the most perfect painter who ever held a brush, he stands so far above the ordinary mortal that his name, for centuries, has signified less a man than a legend, less an artist than a magician. During his lifetime his presence stirred people to wonder and admiration, and to uncomfortable conjectures on his marvellous powers. When he walked through the streets of Milan, his long fair hair crowned with a black cap, and his blond beard flowing down over his favorite rose-colored tunic, passers-by drew aside, and whispered to one another, "There he goes to paint *The Last Supper!*" He would travel from his house across the whole length of the city to work on the picture, mount the scaffold, add two or three touches of color, and then go away; at other times he would paint in the deepest concentration from morning till night, without food or drink. Kings and cities bid for him, as if he were, himself, a work of art; commissions were thrust upon him by public opinion; and when one of his cartoons was exhibited at Florence "a vast crowd of men and women, old and young—a concourse such as one sees flocking to the most solemn festivals—hastened to behold the wonders produced by Leonardo." The loveliest woman in Italy, a duchess whose habit it was to dictate to artists the pictures she fancied, implored him again and again to paint for her a little twelve-year-old Christ, or "at least a little picture of the Madonna, devout and sweet." The picture was never painted. Leonardo was also an artist in warfare, and pressed by all sorts of demands, entered the service of Cesare Borgia as chief military engineer. It is no wonder that such a figure should have passed so swiftly into legend.

The legend was not of Leonardo's making. No man ever labored so steadfastly and scientifically to destroy mysteries and to enlighten the world by discoveries proceeding from observation and experiment. Profoundly religious, he was the enemy of superstition and magic; disillusioned and skeptical, ceaselessly inquiring into the operations of all phenomena, he was at the same time, a poet who loved all outward shapes and forms—children, stern old men, enchanting women, horses, flowers, mountains and moving waters—and who tracked every outward manifestation of life down to the secret source of its energy. "O marvellous necessity," he declared, "thou with supreme reason constrainest all effects to issue from their causes in the briefest possible way!" This law burned in his mind, colored his ambitions, provided him with a scientific basis for his investigations, determined the nature of all his performances. He saw no essential difference between art and science; his mind was serene, strikingly deliberate, realistic, and endlessly experimental, and yet filled with the artist's delight in the making of new things. Whatever he applied himself to—and we shall see that he attempted everything under the sun—he considered as a problem in construction. He put no trust in inspiration or momentary impulses; he was a master of calculations, a thoroughly modern man, superbly conscious in his methods and perfectly balanced in his procedures. He believed with Blake that "if the doors of perception were cleansed, everything would appear to man, as it is, infinite"; and to the end that he might understand the connection of all things, he trained his faculties consciously and with the utmost rigor, and with immense toil and no small amount of pain. He believed that all the laws of structure are within the scope of the human mind, and that once these laws have been grasped, then all things become of equal importance, and man can create spontaneously, like God himself. It scarcely needs to be said that his passion for omniscience was not realized. After all, he was mortal, a Florentine susceptible to human influences and predisposed to certain forms, gestures and scenes. And he was never able to create spontaneously. He painted but few pictures, and those after infinite reflections and readjustments. He struggled for sixteen years with an equestrian statue that was never finished. But in the completeness of his knowledge and in his conception of the world and the whole celestial system as one vast design, he came closer to universality than any other man.

When Leonardo was fifty-two years old, he entered the following item in his note-book:

"On July 6, 1504, Wednesday, at seven in the morning, died Ser Piero da Vinci, notary to the Palazzo del Podestá, my father. He was eighty years of age and left ten sons and two daughters." There is no further comment. His relations with his father had been pleasant and honorable, but he had freed himself from fears and lamentations and had learned to accept events with excellent composure. His mind contained the whole of the past and the beginning of everything that was to come. "In rivers," he said, "the water that you touch is the last of what has passed and the first of that which comes: so with time present." His father's family rose from the soil, produced four generations of notaries, and by accident, an artist, and then reverted to the land again. It was a virile stock: Ser Piero's youngest child appeared fifty years after his first born, Leonardo; recently a genealogist, exploring the ancestral properties of the family, discovered a direct descendant of one of the artist's brothers. The man was a peasant, crushed and silent and overworked, but not without memorable dignity as he drove his oxen over the steep hillsides—and his name was Leonardo da Vinci!

Leonardo was born in the village of Vinci, a few miles west of Florence. He was an illegitimate, his mother being a peasant girl of sixteen who, for a consideration, surrendered her child and became the wife of a craftsman. His first years were spent among the mountains of his grandfather's country estate; at the age of thirteen he was received in his father's house at Florence. As a youth he saw the shining Tuscan city rise to the height of her physical power and artistic grandeur. The Prince of the Medici, Lorenzo the Magnificent, the most civilized scoundrel of the Renaissance, was engaged in strangling the commonwealth with despotic bonds forged by an unexampled mastery of statecraft, and to cajole the favor of the populace kept the city riotous with festivals and tournaments worthy of his splendid title. Always the politician, Lorenzo was as well a lavish patron of the arts, a poet and classical scholar, and his villa was the meeting-place of the most brilliant minds in Italy. But the old austerity of Florence was gone forever. The masses, incapable of genuine gaiety and relaxation, yielded to organized frivolity and subtle tyranny, and at length, ashamed of their silly levity and softness, hearkened to the ravings of the Puritan spellbinder, Savonarola. The artists, debilitated by culture, substituted taste for strength, and affected the ideals and unseemly refinements of the old Greeks and Romans. The glory of the city lingered on in the genius of Leonardo and Michael Angelo.

Leonardo was never at ease in Florence. Though it has, with reason, been urged and echoed that he is the matchless composite of all that the Renaissance contributed to civilization, he was a lonely figure in the center of culture. He was above the coarse mercantile spirit of his age; he was lacking in the push and harsh aggressiveness necessary to material success; he would not be hurried or commanded; he did not venerate the past—he studied it only to be delivered from it; he had a wise contempt for book-learning and declared that "whoever in discussion adduces authority uses not intellect but rather memory"; he was suspicious of the wholesale worship of Greek and Latin—a fetish the world has not yet shaken off; his decency and self-respect made it impossible for him to solicit favors from corrupt prelates—"friars," he wrote down, "that is to say, Pharisees"—and to find a convenient outlet for his comprehensive energies. Thus he was, for all his delight in life, and his social graces, a man of few friendships. Very early he learned to keep his own counsel, and depend on his own resources. His solitary habits were enhanced by his position in the Vinci family. There was no particular dishonor attached to illegitimacy, but his half-brothers and sisters—his father married four times—a swinish lot, jealous of his superior gifts, seized upon his irregular birth as an excuse to get rid of him. But it did not matter. The world was bigger than a quarrelsome family circle. He avoided and forgave them, and in his will left them some money.

The young Leonardo was extraordinarily precocious. When a boy he displayed his ability in many directions, in mathematics, music and every branch of design. He played the lute, "singing to that instrument most divinely," as Vasari fondly relates, and improvising both words and music; he modelled figures in bas-relief and made drawings of faces, animals and flowers. His father, a fashionable lawyer but a man of sense, showed some of the drawings to his friend, Verrocchio, and so astonished was that master at the quality of the work that he accepted the boy immediately as his pupil. No better teacher could have been found in Florence. Verrocchio was a bachelor whose life was devoted entirely to intellectual pursuits. He was not the greatest painter in the world, but in sculpture he was unsurpassed, and he was also renowned for his skill in goldsmithing, geometry, music and wood-inlaying. Leonardo's loyalty to his master was the only personal tie formed in his youth. He remained in Verrocchio's workshop from his thirteenth to his twenty-fifth year, probably the most purely enjoyable period of his career. It was the time of learning rather than accomplishment. Here he found support in his scientific researches; here he met Botticelli, Perugino, and Lorenzo di Credi; close by were the brothers Pollaiuolo whose studies of the nude were among the latest marvels of art. He lived soberly in his master's house; his fame was rising and he was by common consent the most richly gifted and enviable young man in Italy. Reluctantly, five or six years after he had become a licensed painter, he set up his own shop, for he had little interest in art as a physical exercise or a means to a livelihood, and disliked having to finish a work within a specified time. Nor was he, like Michael Angelo, possessed of a mad competitive fury which drove him to impossible commissions and bound him to the service of thankless popes.

During Leonardo's first residence at Florence his mind was enormously active. He was continually experimenting—striving to perfect new methods of expression. Art absorbed only a part of his attention, or, as he would have said, he encompassed the union of art and science, analyzing natural forces and phenomena empirically and co-ordinating them with creative vision. It was not, of course, a new thing for an artist to concern himself with scientific problems: his master was a mathematician and an engineer, and most of his distinguished predecessors had studied anatomy, perspective and light and shade—but only so far as such matters had a practical bearing upon art. Leonardo was the first modern man of science. He observed life minutely and patiently, testing his theories by laboratory methods; he was the founder of the science of geology; he was a botanist with a classified herbarium; he formulated the law of the parallelogram of forces and invented deadly engines of warfare; he dissected corpses to ascertain the relation between function and structure and ascribed the deaths of persons of advanced age to hardening of the arteries. And he went further. He believed that all substances are inherently connected, mutually dependent, and in the final analysis, as modern chemistry insists, interchangeable. Hence he regarded every fact as sacred and every form as a symbol of universal significance. He conceived the world as a living organism warmed by the sun and nourished by the circulation of rivers just as the human body is maintained by the movement of the blood. But his view did not lead him into quack metaphysics or astrology. He conceded the supernatural but did not invoke it, confining himself to observable issues. His universe, as Paul Valéry has aptly pointed out, was entered by a well-devised perspective.

Applying his ideas to art, he scorned the specialists, avowing that no man is so big a fool that he cannot succeed in one thing, if he persists in it, and calling attention to the infinite diversity of nature, "the various kinds of animals there are, the different trees, herbs, and flowers, mountains and plains, springs, rivers and towns." Occasionally, when he felt he was ripe for the task, he painted a picture, and his pictures are, structurally, so perfectly put together that every part takes its position in space with scientific inevitability. And all the components—the rocks, trees, fingers and faces—are painted with equal tenderness and care, with the devotion of one who said, "we have no right to love or hate anything unless we have full knowledge of it."

Naturally, with this unlimited range of interests, Leonardo painted less than the average artist, but it is certain that he painted, at least in his early years, a great deal more than has been preserved. His reputation among his contemporaries, though fabulous and somewhat sinister because of his inventive powers, was primarily that of an artist. It was the general opinion that whenever Leonardo undertook a commission, he would produce something wonderful to behold—and he generally did. But from 1478 to 1483, his first years as an independent artist, we have only three authenticated pictures, the *St. Jerome* in the Vatican, the *Adoration* in the Uffizi, and the *Virgin of the Rocks* in the Louvre. None of these brought him any money, and the first and second are unfinished. Yet he contrived to live, not sumptuously, but well, keeping servants and horses. The conclusion is that he supported himself by painting, and that a number of canvases from this period are still in existence.

In his apprenticeship Leonardo seems to have been a faithful assistant to his master. Precocious as he was, he was obliged to learn the essentials of art. It is a fact not sufficiently recognized that the painter leans heavily on tradition and that his originality asserts itself slowly, after laborious study of past developments. The reason is clear enough. The writer has the advantage of a medium which is shaped and cultivated and enriched by conversation, and it is not necessary for him to read anything—many authors apparently have not—to produce a sophisticated and moving work. But the language of painting is limited to a few practitioners, and the artist, without instruction and without examples to guide his initial efforts, would be as helpless as a child. Leonardo's first work was in sculpture: Vasari mentions certain heads of "smiling women and children, done in his first youth, which might be supposed to have come from the hand of a master." He likewise "formed models of different figures in clay on which he would arrange fragments of soft drapery dipped in plaster, and from these he would then set himself patiently to draw on very fine cambric or linen with the point of a pencil in the most admirable manner." He must have seen specimens of Greek sculpture; he studied the men who had founded the great tradition of Florentine art, especially Masaccio; he journeyed to Arezzo to examine the frescoes of Piero della Francesca, another painter who worked from clay models, and incidentally to make drawings of stratified rocks.

From the scanty records dealing with his early years we might infer that Leonardo was shadowy and mysterious and something of a dilettante. Nothing could be more false. His personality was vivid and ingenuous, his intentions definite and consistent. But his contemporaries could not fathom his complex mind—and he did not turn out pictures with the regularity expected of one so magnificently endowed. Stories went round of his exceptional strength: how he could mount unbroken stallions and how he could bend a horseshoe as if it were a coil of lead; he was left-handed or ambidextrous, as has been fairly well proved, drawing with his left hand and painting with his right; he was fond of animals, "treating them with infinite kindness and consideration," a singular thing in an Italian, and when he passed shops where birds were sold, so Vasari tells us, "he would frequently take them from their cages, pay the price demanded, and let them fly away." It has been suggested that Leonardo's kindness to birds arose from another motive—his interest in flying-machines and aerial problems. He made models and drawings of mechanical appliances of every description, demonstrating by diagrams to the city magistrates, who could not refute him and could not believe, how the church of San Giovanni might be raised and steps placed beneath it without injury. He consorted with mutes to observe the expression of feelings by gesticulations; extraordinarily receptive to visual impressions, he adorned his note-books with sketches, done from memory, of unusual types he had encountered, handsome or hideous—heads as delicately proportioned as the finest Greek sculptures, faces as repulsive as Savonarola and "The Ugly Duchess"; he invited peasants to his house, entertained them with stories, marked their peculiarities, and threw them into fits of laughter by caricaturing their queer faces.

At the age of seventeen, if we are to judge by the angel and the landscape which he painted in Verrocchio's *Baptism*, Leonardo was a remarkably mature artist commanding a style of his own. With such a beginning, most painters would have rushed into a fervent career of profitable commissions and popular acclaim. Not so Leonardo. The modelling of forms by the subtle flow of light into dark; the scientific analysis of atmospheric effects; the psychology of emotions and the relation of gestures and facial expressions to the deepest feelings:—such things possessed him, and hundreds of others. He was indifferent to the hero-worshipping of a populace which boasted so loudly and understood so little. And, as I have said, he would not be hurried. We need not vex ourselves over the pictures done in collaboration with his master: the quarreling micrologists will never agree upon these joint products. Of more importance are his innumerable drawings. In his *Treatise on Painting*, he places the graphic arts at the top of all forms of expression, arguing, among other things, that the visual image is much more explicit and convincing than any image evoked by words. Accordingly, when he describes a machine, engages to prove a theory, or record an observation, he supplements his text with drawings. There are literally thousands of these sketches, some purely expository, others elaborate studies for paintings or memories of scenes and figures. It would be difficult to exaggerate the radiant animation of Leonardo's work in black-and-white, but let us not fall into the error frequently committed by cranks and connoisseurs and set his drawings above his finished pictures. All drawings, in a certain small sense, are more satisfactory than paintings for the reason that they fulfil more perfectly a specific purpose. But how much more limited the purpose! Artists know this, if the critics do not. A drawing is essentially a framework, a study in structure. In most cases it is simply a preliminary sketch. Even the etching, a work complete in itself, is a pale thing of slight, suggestive charm when compared to a painting with its full-bodied splendor of color and mass.

Corot called Leonardo "the father of modern landscape." In a drawing dating from his twenty-first year, the first work entirely by his own hand to come down to us, we have the earliest independent landscape in western art. It was, however, probably intended for a background. Despite his universal interests, his major concern, as a painter, was with the figure. The sketch is remarkable for its dramatic distribution of lights and darks, the beginnings of *chiaroscuro*, a technical method practically invented by Leonardo and destined to exert a tremendous influence on painting, for good and ill. He employed this method to accentuate modelling, that is, to give his forms greater bulk and relief. The richest effects in chiaroscuro are, of course, to be had in paint, but he obtains in black-and-white, by the simplest means imaginable, results almost equally astonishing. He has a series of madonna studies—a fine Florentine mother holding in her lap a child who is playing with a cat—which fairly glow with life. It is impossible to analyze the incomparable vitality of these diminutive sketches. We may say that his elastic outlines swell and recede with a wavy motion, that his knowledge of anatomy and muscular action enabled him to twist the figure into positions of exquisite movement, that, with his subtle power over light and shade, "he had only to stroke the surface with parallel hatchings in order to bring out relief, and to give an inestimable homogeneity of effect to his sheets." Such comments are true but largely technical, and they do not explain—nor can it be explained—how his figures reflect his own ideas, and how he caught and clarified within the mesh of a few lines, certain

Leonardo da Vinci: MADONNA WITH ST. ANN.

Louvre, Paris

smiles and movements and attitudes which reveal the workings of the spirit.

In Florence, when important malefactors had been apprehended and hanged, the magistrates appointed a prominent artist to paint the portraits of the rascals, head downward, on the walls of the town-hall, an excellent custom, and one which, I think, might be advantageously revived in modern America. It would probably have no deterrent effect upon crime, but it would be a great boon to art. Every city would have an annual exhibition of genuine social significance, and Washington would be the center of American art! After the infamous Pazzi conspiracy to extinguish the Medici, eighty criminals were lynched and thrown down to a rejoicing mob, and Botticelli was honored with the job of painting the leaders. The chief man of blood, Bandino, escaped to the East, was extradited by the Turks, and five days after he arrived at Florence was swinging from a rope. On a cold day in December, Leonardo, aged twenty-seven, notebook in hand, viewed the spectacle at close range and calmly sketched the victim, emphasizing the peculiar spinal stiffness and gaping terror of one whose neck had been suddenly broken, and jotting down for reasons known only to himself the various details and colors of Bandino's last costume. Another opportunity to observe the behavior of man under unusual circumstances. But he did not share the common hunger of the Florentines for slaughter; he believed that fighting and killing were senseless and uncivilized. Towards the end of his life he became a vegetarian.

About a year later he began his first great painting. The work was ordered by the monks of San Donato; the subject was the *Adoration of the Magi,* and he agreed to finish it in thirty months for a sum equivalent to $3000. The picture was never finished. It never, in fact, got beyond the greenish-red monochrome of the under-painting, and it remains a colossal sketch of the greatest complexity. Apart from its position in the development of Renaissance art, the chief claim of the *Adoration* on modern interest lies in its constructive transformations. It shows us that a work of art is never preconceived, that it begins simply, grows resolutely, and suffers endless alterations. The subject was dear to Leonardo's heart. Long before he accepted the commission he had experimented with it. He made drawings for the principal characters—dozens of them, nude and draped; he plotted out a marvellous perspective graph; three times he elaborated the idea into a tentative composition and as many times was dissatisfied; finally, he found, by trial and error, what he wanted and the actual painting was begun. But his newly discovered chiaroscuro defeated him. Determined to achieve the maximum of relief—the very perfection of modelling—by the use of strong lights and shadows gradually deepening into the densest blacks, he worked the picture into so low a key that he could no longer control it. Whereupon the monks lost patience and appealed to that handy manufacturer, Filippino Lippi, who, in short order, gave them exactly what their tastes required, a pretty thing of small artistic merit.

Leonardo abandoned the project with few regrets. The fundamental brainwork was done, the problem solved. Design, he said, was for the master, execution for servants. He had completely severed painting from ecclesiastical authority; to his own satisfaction he had proved that a multiplicity of forms could be put together with geometrical clarity. From the studies, Michael Angelo derived his idea for his slaves; Raphael imitated the central figures, the Madonna and Child; before the design modern artists stare and gasp. There is nothing to be gained by considering the work as a philosophical criticism of Christianity. I do not believe Leonardo intended anything of the kind: the painting must be regarded as an experiment. Notwithstanding the sweeping movement, the intense characterizations and significant gestures, and the flowing unity, it is, as a subject picture, unconvincing: the entire background—the galloping horsemen, the architectural ruins, and the broken landscape—though structurally related to, is emotionally isolated from the rest of the drama. More convincing is the *Virgin of the Rocks*, the Louvre version, painted a year or so afterward. Here again he departed from the conventional treatment and stationed an enchanting and youthful Florentine woman, an angel, and two naked children in a grotto reminiscent of the caves of the Arno which fascinated him in his geological studies. But the idea is devoid of all incongruity. Science and observation and sentiment are perfectly fused; the design is flawless; the faces are refined to the last degree—carried further by Raphael, the type becomes, not more spiritual but vacuous, and with Luini, sickening; and the flesh painting has never been equalled—the children seem to have been fashioned in heaven by a creator who is a plastic artist.

Leonardo did not thrive at Florence and in his thirtieth year entered the service of the Duke of Milan. The occasion of his departure for the North is unknown. It seems that he made a certain musical instrument, a lute of silver in the shape of a horse's skull, and that Lorenzo de' Medici, greatly pleased with the invention, despatched him to Milan to play before the Duke for whom music had especial charms. At all events, he was only too glad to leave Florence, and aware of the wealth of Milan and the prodigality of the unlawful Duke, wrote a letter to his Excellency enumerating the various capacities in which he might be useful—if attached to the court. The letter is one of the most amazing documents on record. Coming from any one else, we might dismiss it as egregious bounce; in reality it is an application for employment from a man whose vast powers had never received more than passing consideration. In part Leonardo wrote:

"I have a method of constructing very light and portable bridges, to be used in pursuit of, or in retreat from, the enemy, with others of a stronger sort, proof against fire, and easy to fix or remove.

"For the service of sieges, I am prepared to remove the water from the ditches, and to make an infinite variety of scaling-ladders and other engines proper to such purposes.

"I have also most convenient and portable bombs, proper for throwing showers of small missiles, and with the smoke thereof causing great terror to the enemy.

"By means of excavations made without noise, and forming

tortuous and narrow ways, I have means of reaching any given point, even though it be necessary to pass beneath rivers.

"I can also construct covered wagons, secure and indestructible, which, entering among the enemy, will break the strongest bodies of men; and behind these the infantry can follow in safety and without impediment.

"I can make mortars and field-pieces of beautiful and useful shape, entirely different from those in common use.

"For naval conflicts, I have methods for making numerous instruments, offensive and defensive . . . and I can also make powders or vapors for the offense of the enemy.

"In time of peace, I believe that I could equal any other as regards works in architecture. I can prepare designs for buildings, whether public or private, and also conduct water from one place to another.

"Furthermore, I can execute works in sculpture, marble, bronze, or terra-cotta. In painting also I can do what may be done, as well as any other, whosoever he may be.

"I can likewise undertake the execution of the bronze horse which is a monument that will be to the perpetual glory of my lord your father of happy memory, and of the illustrious house of Sforza.

"And if any of the above-named things shall seem to any man impossible or impracticable, I am perfectly ready to make trial of them in whatever place you shall be pleased to command, commending myself to you with all possible humility."

The Duke did not hesitate, and Leonardo was engaged forthwith as general constructionist and court utilitarian; and remembering that he remained with his Excellency for sixteen years, we may conclude that he made good his claims. The records of his life at Milan are confused and sparse, and in our ignorance we must be content with a few details. Besides a substantial salary, his position carried with it a house and vineyard and numerous perquisites. He lived unostentatiously with his pupils and apprentices, avoiding the princely splendor of Raphael and the squalid loneliness of Michael Angelo, kept strict accounts and saved a little money. "It is only those who have too much who cannot bear vicissitudes and losses," he said. He painted the Duke's mistresses, designed costumes, organized festivals and supervised weddings—in a word, supplied the court with an artistic background. Whether these minor exactions bored Leonardo we do not know. Probably not. He had what most Florentine artists lacked—the ability to play and to enjoy life. Also, he looked upon his ceremonial duties as the price paid for his freedom. He had an assured living; was free to come and go as he pleased; and his obligations to the Duke did not interrupt his scientific studies. In a more serious vein, he assisted in the completion of the Cathedral, acted as hydraulic engineer, built canals with wonderfully improved locks, drained marshes, and invented the machine gun and breech-loading cannon. His intellectual activities at Milan fall into three divisions: the equestrian statue; the notebooks; and *The Last Supper.*

The Duke, Ludovico Sforza, known as Il Moro because of his swarthy skin, desired to honor the memory of his father with a bronze monument and gave out that "there was only one man capable of the task, Leonardo, the Florentine; he alone was equal to it—and even he might not be able to finish it, inasmuch as it was the work of a lifetime." Leonardo entered into the plan with characteristic thoroughness, having in mind a horse that would throw the monuments of Donatello and Verrocchio into the shade and indeed surpass the efforts of the Greeks. He knew more about the subject than any man of his time—had he not outlined a book on the anatomy of the horse? For six years he fought with the idea of a horse in violent action—something unheard of in sculpture—making countless designs and studies of animal movement, then abandoning the scheme as too pictorial. At length he fixed upon a more restrained attitude, and at the end of ten more years of intermittent labor, constructed a clay model twenty-six feet high, devising a new kind of armature to support the beast. It must have been a stupendous sight—but alas, it was never cast! He needed eighty tons of bronze for the horse alone—and the ducal exchequer was empty. Shortly afterward the French invaded Milan, Il Moro was captured, and the model was used as a target by Gascon bowmen. Soon it crumbled into the earth again—one of the greatest tragedies in art. Some years later, in Florence, Leonardo was arguing a passage from Dante with a friend when Michael Angelo, an authority on the Inferno, happened to pass by. On being asked civilly to expound the quotation, Michael Angelo, who envied the composure and freedom of Leonardo, turned upon his rival savagely. "You're the one who made an equestrian model that was never finished—to your eternal shame! You couldn't cast it!" As a parting shot: "And those castrated Milanese believed in your ability to do it!" Leonardo, in his fifties, smiled at the impudence of youth and said nothing.

The notebooks of Leonardo constitute a repository of incalculable scientific research and speculative inquiry. From boyhood it was his habit to record his theories and observations; the habit grew with years, and at the age of thirty-seven, in Milan, he began to revise and collate his papers, and to keep his notes on a more extended scale with a view to complete formulation. But other duties continually interfered; his experiments multiplied; his writings piled up, and he was never able to give them anything like systematic arrangement. As a consequence, we have today, dispersed in European libraries, 5000 manuscript pages of unclassified reflections set down in reversed, or mirror writing, and embellished with drawings of the highest value. Let us make no mistake about the notebooks. They are not the maunderings of a metaphysician nor the pompous effusions of the professional hemlock-drinker. In method and in terminology, in magnitude and limpidity, they reveal one of the finest brains ever put in a human head, the brain of the artist-scientist, or shall we say, the universal artist? Havelock Ellis, examining these documents from a scientific point of view, credits Leonardo with being the founder of engineering and the study of anatomy and geology, a biologist in every field of mechanism, an hydrographer, geometrician, master of optics, and inventor of innumerable varieties of ballistic machines and ordnance. And these were only a fraction of the man! But unfortunately he did not give many of his discoveries to the world. Possibly he feared the Church and "the timid friends of God," as he called them, his ideas being so greatly at variance from orthodox Christianity, and including the belief that the soul, though divine, does not exist apart from the body. For whatever cause, the manuscripts lay concealed for centuries, and science in the meantime had produced Bacon, Newton and Watt. In geology he established the laws of petrifaction; he was aware of the circulation of the blood; he invented the military tank, hydrophonic devices for communication among ships, roller bearings, and the wheel barrow; he described the flight of birds and made drawings of a "bird-man" and of aeroplanes driven by a propellor attached to a spring motor; he worked out every possible type of domed architecture and designed a cupola for St. Peter's sixty years before Michael Angelo; he planned hygienic cities with underground avenues flushed by canals and houses limited in height to the width of the streets, complaining that "people should not be packed together like goats and pollute the air for one another"; he had a cure for sea-sickness—the list is endless.

In all the 5000 pages there is but one reference to women, a certain "Catarina who worked in a hospital—and had a fantastic face"; in the whole life of Leonardo there is no record of a single love affair, or indeed of a distant Platonic friendship. He who dissected the human body, studied its proportions and movements, and made cross sections of embryos, who penetrated the soul of woman and painted madonnas of divine serenity and charm, declared that "intellectual passion drives out sensuality," and that "the act of procreation and everything connected with it is so disgusting that the human race would soon die out if there were no pretty faces and sensual dispositions."

In the section devoted to painting, Leonardo deals with the fundamental values of art, presenting the subject both scientifically and in the universal terms of God and man. He defines painting technically as modelling, "the task of giving corporeal shape to the three dimensions on a flat surface," spiritually as the rendering of emotions, or states of the soul, by means of appropriate postures and movements. He advises the artist to acquaint himself with all phases of life and to subject its details to the severest criticism—to go directly to nature and experience for his materials and not to make pictures out of other pictures. On the other hand, he counsels against imitation, emphasizing repeatedly the necessity for synthesis and organization. "The painter," he points out, "who draws merely by practice and by eye, without any vision, is like a mirror which copies all the objects placed before it, without being conscious of their existence." The treatise contains, besides directions for depicting everything imaginable from draperies to deluges, an intricate and exhaustive analysis of optical phenomena accompanied by illustrations of the most searching and portentous character. It is not too much to say that Leonardo's knowledge of light and atmospheric effects is equal to that of the modern Impressionists, or even superior. He describes at length the division of tones, the color of shadows—particularly the variable blues and violets—and the vivid illumination obtained by the use of complementaries, but he rejects the methods of the Impressionists on the ground that they dissolve form and wreck design. Though he said that "the eye is the window of the soul," he could not think of art as a chromatic formula or the mechanical imitation of visual appearances.

The illustrations to the notebooks afford us beautiful proof of the difference between artistic drawing and photography. Here we have sketches of scientific apparatus, interiors of gun foundries, cannon, hydraulic engines, median sections of the skull, muscles, bones, fossils, leaves, trees, and cloud formations, all of which are a joy to behold. None but Leonardo could have made these drawings. They are separated from the photograph by a gulf as wide as that which separates the poetry of Shelley from the tabulated reports of the New York Stock Exchange. Did he, as a scientist, merely attempt to represent and describe with cold-blooded accuracy the object before him? Obviously not. The artistic impulse, co-existent and predominant, incited him to reconstruct his materials, to add himself to them, to make infinitesimal alterations of contour, to introduce light and shade and subtle variations of natural appearances for the sake of harmony. Thus a dead skull or a cogwheel becomes a living organism—a creature of Leonardo's brain, a dynamic part of the world remade.

With such a brain a man should be capable of anything. But there is, let me explain, an idea that will not down, a superstition widespread, mischievous and nonsensical, that a painter should not have any brains, that he is, when really artistic, a sensitive instrument through which God's will automatically functions, a gilded harp upon which the winds of life play tremulously, plucking out divine melodies. And if, perchance, a painter does possess a brain, the sensitive numskulls who faint before a shapely bosom or a bowl of fruit, snuffle with fear and sigh contemptuously, "He thinks too much!" They cry "He has no feeling, no inspiration! He works by formula!" Now if ever a man were able to paint by formula, surely Leonardo would be the man. But the more he studied, the deeper his wisdom, the sharper his experiences, the more troublesome did the making of pictures become. Each new undertaking implied a new and unique design. Inspiration meant nothing to him except the choice of subject-matter which he could mould to his own ends. In the popular sense, he was not sensitive at all: he was calculating, penetrative, and rational. It took him three years to paint *The Last Supper*.

This masterpiece was finished in the year 1497. It was painted in the damp refectory of Saint Mary of the Graces, at the command of the Duke of Milan who wished to erect a memorial to his deceased wife in the church that had been her favorite place of worship. The theme was common property and had been conventionalized by many treatments. It had been in Leonardo's mind for years, and long before he received the commission he had made provisional studies for the work. It was a challenge to his highest powers, a stimulus to perfection. The painting immediately lifted him above his contemporaries, and throughout the ages has remained not only the most famous picture in the world but the supreme exemplification of monumental design. Of the grandeur of the undamaged original we can only guess. Leonardo, impatient of fresco, painted in tempera on a ground prepared to resist the clamminess of the wall. The medium was a disastrous choice. The ground began to contract and flake, and within fifty years the picture was covered with spots; deterioration went ahead slowly; dreadful restorations were made by heavy-handed meddlers; some imbecile Dominican monks cut a door through the lower central part; Napoleon's dragoons stabled their horses in the refectory and threw their boots at Judas Iscariot; more restorations and more disfigurements. About twenty years ago an Italian of genius completely removed the unsightly smears laid on by alien retouchers and found a way to prevent further decay. Today *The Last Supper* is in fair condition. What we see is genuine Leonardo, and it is enough to warrant an appraisal based on the fact itself and not on historical panegyrics or misleading copies. The popularity of the picture may be attributed, in a large measure, to the engraving made by Raphael Morghen in 1800, an engraving that resembles a Sunday School chromo. Morghen copied, not the original, but a drawing executed by a nondescript Florentine, diluted Leonardo's stern conception into pervasive sentimentality, and substituted for the noble figure of Christ, a nice lymphatic gentleman, sleepy and a little sad.

The greatness of a work is not an indeterminate quality. Without reciting the theories propounded in behalf of a pure aesthetic, or talking the language of abstractions, it is possible, I think, to specify one or two things which those who have trained themselves to look at pictures acknowledge to be implicit in a great painting. In the first place, the conception must not be mawkish, sentimental or eccentric. It must be apparent that what the artist has to say is worthy of his best efforts. He must show us that he has good reason for the selection of his theme, that he knows vastly more about it than we do, and he must illuminate it with the sympathy born of closest intimacy and the gusto that comes from exceptional wisdom. If the idea is old—and what idea is not?—he must bring to it new evaluations and fresh considerations. Second, the purpose must be transcendently certain and definite. The artist must express his meaning with clarity and power, throwing aside all needless accessories, disturbing flourishes, and exhibitions of virtuosity. What we experience vaguely and with mixed emotions he must present with singleness and undivided emphasis. Third, the picture must give us something to think about; it must have many avenues of interest, many sources of appeal. Avoiding merely physical seductiveness, it must ask for the cooperation of our noblest faculties, emancipating our emotions and stimulating us to feel and live deeply and liberally. In short, it must act upon the spirit and lift us out of our daily round of mean preoccupations into a realm of purging tragedy, exhilarating joy, profound human pity, dramatic power.

Does *The Last Supper* fulfil these requirements? We may say that it does, without question and without reserve. The picture is too well known to call for description. The subject was consummately suited to test his theory that in painting the "facial expressions must vary according to the emotional state of the person, and that the attitudes of the figures must correspond to the emotions reflected in the faces." He prepared his studies with extraordinary care, giving minute attention to detailed characterizations—to hands, beards, and costumes—roving the Ghetto for a model to serve as Judas, and experimenting with the design. He has left us, in his notebooks, an eloquent account of the psychological action which he regarded as the mainspring of the drama. At first he adhered to the conventionl arrangement, with St. John asleep by the side of Christ, and Judas by himself in the foreground, but the actual work of construction changed his plans. At last, with a stroke of genius, he found the one and only way to tell the story. Christ sits in the middle of the table with the apostles in groups of three on either side: He has said, "One among you shall betray me." The utterance is a proclamation of tragedy, and to reveal the tragedy, Leonardo portrays the effects of the word as it pierces the souls of the twelve men. Everything in the picture conspires to this end: the lighting; the architecture; the bare walls stripped of distracting ornament and converging to carry us directly into the scene; the perspective plan; the heads, gestures and faces. Never was a painting so perfectly put together. Structurally, all the lines focus in the right eye of Christ, the movement beginning slowly in the distant figures and increasing in agitation as it approaches the center; emotionally, the prophetic word of the Lord reverberates among the two groups of His followers, provoking horror, consternation and curiosity, and binding the groups together by the force of spiritual tension.

It is an undeniable fact that every one comes to a picture of *The Last Supper* in a peculiarly receptive mood, with a mind preattuned to the tragic situation and eager to participate in the religious sentiment. Hence the subject, if only tolerably presented, is more moving and impressive to the average person than the magnificent mythological compositions of Rubens, which as illustrations have lost their significance. Theoretically one art should not be dependent upon another; it should express itself fully in its own language. Painting should be self-revealing and not rely upon literature to complete its meaning. Acting on this premise, certain critics advocate a "pure approach" to art, that is to say, they tell us, in all seriousness, that when they look at a picture they judge it as the only thing of its kind in existence, suppressing all associatory elements, and responding like infants with eyes and souls but no experiences, to the emotional appeal of lines, colors and volumes. Perhaps they are able to behave in this fashion when looking at the utterly negative and empty nudes and still-lifes—pictures done by artists who seem to have no connection with life whatever—comprising most exhibitions, but when confronted with Leonardo's *The Last Supper* they cannot overlook the subject-matter. Despite their anaesthetic theories, something irritatingly human and eternally sad gets under their skins. So they say, "It is not art. It is exaggerated illustration."

I mention these unpleasant matters only to remind the reader that all art partakes of illustration. The moment an artist contrives a unit of form, a figure, let us say, he makes a representation clothed with habitual associations and memories from which the beholder cannot remove himself by an act of will. Leonardo did not consider it vulgar to tell a story in paint. Nor did he imagine that to create a spiritual type one had merely to represent an effeminate figure with the traditional blond beard and label it Christ. *The Last Supper* is illustration in that it brings before us with convincing reality a situation first described in the medium of words. But we cannot say that it is the counterpart of the Biblical story. It is Leonardo's *The Last Supper*, a part of his mind, containing his science, his understanding, and his preferences. It is more than illustration: on one side of a table large enough to accommodate only six or seven guests he has placed thirteen figures, but we are not conscious of any crowding; the disciples are Italians, and no one seems to notice that they have no legs; his Christ is beardless; there is, in truth, nothing oriental in the conception. The psychological import is conveyed with such absolute precision and dramatic force that the meaning of the picture would not, I think, be lost on any one ignorant of the Christian legend. Into these excited and gesticulating apostles Leonardo has infused his immense fund of human experiences; he has indeed so thoroughly filled his characters with their appropriate emotions that they become, not Italians posing as vehement Jews, but living symbols of grief, terror, bewilderment, and woe. And the Christ has the grandeur, the imperturbable grace and tranquillity characteristic of Leonardo himself in his noblest moods.

I have watched painters go into ecstasies over this picture—over the plastic form, the marvellous composition, the distribution of the figures, apparently so simply ordered yet, on analysis, so complexly balanced and inextricably united; the rushing, involute rhythms, the expressive hands, et cet.—and I have wondered what Leonardo would have done, had he wished to represent, not a group of men bound together by a community of tragic purpose, but merely an assemblage of plastic forms. He would, I fancy, have produced something analogous to those compositions of Picasso, so astonishing and yet so meaningless; for Picasso is a man who has tried to learn the secrets of art from other art and not from life. It was the subject that released Leonardo's creative activity and inspired him to incorporate a great idea into a great design. And I have also fancied, in moments when I permit myself a little indulgence in the more esoteric meanings of art, that Leonardo, having finished *The Last Supper*, must have surveyed the work with a smile of satisfaction seeing that he had represented once and for all time how men of ordinary clay are appalled by the presence of supreme intelligence.

The following year the French crossed the Alps and captured the swarthy tyrant of Milan. Leonardo noted the event succinctly. "This day the Duke lost his state, his possessions and his liberty—and none of his works is completed." By unfinished works he probably meant "the horse" and certain enterprises in engineering, and with the hope of carrying them out under the new régime, he tarried a while in the North. It is told that on being entreated to make something extraordinary for the reception of the foreign monarch, he constructed a mechanical toy in the shape of a golden lion which, after advancing a few steps, opened its huge jaws, and disgorged a bundle of lilies. We next hear of him in Venice where he invented a diving-bell and swimming-belt, and at the opening of the new century he is in Florence again, deep in geometry and anatomy, and painting little. As field engineer for Cesare Borgia, he explored central Italy from coast to coast and proved himself a cartographer of immense skill. These maps are still useful, showing mountains, roads, rivers and towns that have changed but slightly since the sixteenth century—all accurate in configuration and drawn in relief with as much care as he bestowed upon his madonnas. The political manoeuvres of the Borgias did not concern him, and after Cesare's collapse, he returned to Florence and prepared for one of the monasteries a cartoon of the *Virgin and St. Anne*, a study which caused great commotion in the greedy city, reviving for a moment the ancient custom of celebrating the appearance of a new masterpiece with processions and ecclesiastical extravagance. At the same date he made his only venture in mythology, a drawing of *Leda and the Swan*. More than likely he painted the subject as well, for there are half a dozen Ledas in the European galleries, all springing from a common ancestor and imitative of Leonardo's style.

Finally it occurred to one of the burghers to remind his fellow citizens that Leonardo was beginning to look like an old man, that he was much given to wandering, and that if the people desired to wring from him something to the eternal lustre of the commonwealth, they had best lay hands on him while he was residing among them. It was therefore decreed that the Grand Council chamber, speedily completed after the expulsion of the Medici, should be decorated with martial scenes witnessing the power of Florentine arms, one wall being entrusted to Leonardo da Vinci, and the other to Michael Angelo, a young man of unlimited promise. With her usual malice and to humiliate an errant son, the city imposed on Leonardo the *Battle of Anghiari*, an encounter in which the Milanese were conquered by the warriors of Florence. But war to him was an exhibition of energy and he had no faith in patriotic motives. He chose a cavalry episode, a number of horsemen fighting for a lost standard, intending to paint the personification of bestial frenzy—the diametrical opposite of *The Last Supper*. The cartoon raised a tumult of applause. Such cyclonic fury, such concentrated energy and rhythm had never before been even suggested in art. But the painting itself came to grief. Leonardo, always trying new things, used an encaustic medium, and the colors, instead of fusing with the plaster under the action of heat, ran down the wall. The picture was ruined. Nothing that relates to it has survived except some wonderful drawings and two or three copies of part of the design, one by Rubens. Leonardo abandoned the work without more ado, and the Florentine council, naturally, was plunged in gloom. The artist, however, does not appear to have been troubled by the catastrophe: he was interested in Mona Lisa.

The *Mona Lisa* shines out among the portraits of the world like a star. Though time has appreciably impaired the color of the picture, the glory of it increases with the passing years. The canvas hangs in the Louvre, a veritable shrine attracting pilgrims from every land, all of whom gaze upon it with a liquid reverence not accorded to any of the more essentially sacred pieces in that gigantic morgue. Fable and gossip have made the famous lady a strange and uncanny charmer, a sphinx whose smile entrapped the soul of a great artist and impelled him, bit by bit, to build up an image of unfathomable mystery. The image lives on, but the legend also endures—and the soul of the artist is buried in the mystery of a woman's smile!

The story is that in the year 1502, Leonardo looked upon Mona Lisa, the third wife of Francesco del Giocondo, and found her fascinating, for she was, according to contemporary opinion, "exceedingly beautiful," and he was by no means insensitive to feminine charms. She was young and her husband was old and impotent and unkind. He had pawned her jewels and forced her to put on mourning so that the absence of personal ornaments might not be suspected. When Leonardo desired to paint her portrait, she assented eagerly, cast a spell upon him, and became his mistress. She had lost her only daughter and was chronically sad, and it is told that he hired an orchestra to lighten her melancholy and jesters to make her smile. And it was the smile that held him in her toils and called up the secrets of his soul.

The legend is damaged by several inconsistencies. Leonardo was not a youth at this time: he was in his fifties and fearfully venerable, appearing indeed in a portrait sketch made three years later, an octogenarian. He worked on the picture for four years, but not merely to preserve the features of a striking woman—likenesses came easy to him and he had no use for them as such. Nor was much of the period devoted to Mona Lisa. Florentine artists did not paint directly from models but from black-and-white studies. Furthermore, we know that Mona Lisa posed for the head alone—the torso and hands were drawn from other

Leonardo da Vinci: HEAD OF A YOUNG WOMAN.

Uffizi Gallery, Florence

sitters, a fact which may account for the rather stiff joining of the neck and shoulders—and that Leonardo, the most painstaking of painters, in solitude, undisturbed by music and a beautiful woman, slowly created a figure of imperishable vitality. Whatever he may have thought of the sitter, he prized the picture more, as an artist should, keeping it in his possession to the end of his days. All things considered, it would seem that his interest in the model was neither protracted nor sentimental, and that he found in nature a face which helped him to realize in paint an ideal type towards which he had constantly moved from his earliest efforts. His concessions to portraiture only served to enhance this ideal: Mona Lisa was a lady and he gave her the sensitive hands of an aristocrat; he observed the mourner's costume but turned it into living drapery; the high forehead and the plucked eyebrows, current marks of distinction, facilitated the modelling of the features. But Mona Lisa, the woman, the mistress, the Neapolitan, has vanished from the picture forever. It may fairly be questioned whether the work is a portrait at all, that is, as we understand the term today. Certainly the head resembles all the other heads that he painted, male or female, and might be substituted for any one of his madonnas. Mona Lisa is the sister to his other forms, only more exquisitely embodied.

She is purely a devotional creation, devotional in the largest sense; the incarnation of Leonardo's love for life, and women, and all perfect forms, the nexus between the world of memories, experiments and disappointments, and the flawlessly appointed world of his imagination. Into this picture he has projected all of himself and all his arts—his subtlety, his elaborate and dazzling refinement, his scientific perfection, his psychological penetration, his puzzling serenity, his infallible knowledge of structure. In comparison most of the paintings of the world seem flat and lifeless. Like it you may not, but you cannot escape its reality. It stops you and holds you with confounding directness. Many other canvases are perhaps corporeally as substantial and convincing; other figures are even more truthful representations of flesh and blood, but this, you feel, is more than flesh and blood. The face is that of a more sentient being, a more highly organized intelligence. You are not conscious of paint, of color, or of canvas. Lifeless material has been shaped into a human face, and the face, as Leonardo said and intended, becomes "the mirror of the soul." Your spirit is somehow touched by another spirit, and for a moment you may be repelled—repelled by a figure that is made in the form of a human being and yet made without weaknesses or imperfections. To apprehend the *Mona Lisa*, you must remain with the picture, see it again and again, for it contains, like all works of art, the history of its creator, and you cannot, at a single glance, enter into the mind of Leonardo da Vinci.

The figure is as solid and as permanently established as the rocks behind it, yet plastic, and free to bend and breathe and move, and brought into fullest relief by the purposely strange background of dwindling rivers and shadowy peaks; the landscape, wrought out with as much affection as the face of the woman, is a living thing; the smile is achieved by imperceptible variations in the lines of the eyes and mouth—so delicately modelled, in fact, that it is lost in coarsely screened reproductions. The smile is not peculiar to Mona Lisa; it was not original with Leonardo. It is written in the faces of the archaic goddesses of Greece; we find it in the sculptures of his master, Verrocchio, and in other paintings of the time. If Leonardo was prepossessed with it, then so is every artist with certain expressions and attitudes. Why he so loved the smile we cannot say, but we do know that by means of it he made his faces conclusively real and emblematic of the deepest emotional states. The mystery of the *Mona Lisa* arises from the romantic gossip attaching to the model and to repeated misconceptions of the artist's purpose. The emotional life of art is, in the final analysis, like all life, insoluble. We can no more explain it than we can explain a tree or a woman or any organic thing, and when we attempt to do so, we are driven into dreams and mysteries. Leonardo's aim was to dispel mysteries, not to create them. His purpose was to create a form which should be neither vague nor enigmatical—not a stimulus to reveries, but actually and in all its parts, an articulate and convincing expression of the spirit. He succeeded, and that, I think, is enough.

His business with the city of Florence having ended in monumental disaster, Leonardo departed for Milan again, taking the *Mona Lisa* along with him. The Republic granted him a leave of absence, but with an ill grace, strongly bent on forcing him to attend to the unfortunate battle picture. He never returned. From time to time he received angry protests and sarcastic communications from the Florentine magistrates reminding him that he had made "only a little beginning on a great work," but these he calmly disregarded. In the employ of the French viceroy, he superintended the building of canals and other public utilities, and prepared designs for an equestrian statue. His second venture in heroic sculpture, like his first, was never to be cast. His painting was limited to two pictures, both religious, both of the highest importance. One, the London version of the *Madonna of the Rocks*, was executed with the help of a colleague to appease an unforgetting group of Franciscans who compelled him by legal action to live up to a contract made twenty years before; the other, *St. Anne with the Virgin and the Infant Christ*, now in the Louvre, though faded and unfinished, is a marvellous reconstruction of an old subject. Disregarding the inflexible arrangements of his predecessors, he poured into a recalcitrant theme all his wisdom and all his skill, and developed a group of human forms which, for expressive power, plastic richness, and intricacy of design, cannot be too lavishly extolled. It was his last great picture. The French were expelled from Milan, and he travelled to Rome to work for the Pope.

His visit to Rome was a mistake. Leo X, sleek and superficial, was busy exploiting Raphael's fresco factory, and could not understand a man of Leonardo's leisurely habits and interminable ponderings. At the end of two unprofitable years he journeyed to France, invited thither by Francis I, one of his warmest admirers. Comfortably lodged in a chateau in Touraine, exempt from creative toil, he was eminently at peace with the world.

His hands were paralyzed and he could not paint, but nothing could interrupt his speculations, his desire to discover the connection between all things so that he might create spontaneously, like God himself. One day he wrote in his notebook, "When I thought I had been learning how to live, I had only been learning how to die." In his will he commended his soul "to our Lord Almighty God and to the glorious Virgin Mary, to all the blessed Angels and Saints, male and female, in Paradise." He died on the first of May, 1519, in his sixty-seventh year.

CHAPTER

V

MICHAEL ANGELO

HE WAS born in an old castle on the summit of a rock. Round him were mountain ridges; close by, the village of Caprese where his father, a citizen of Florence, was serving as chief magistrate. His mother, a girl of nineteen, returning to a family property a few miles above Florence, put the boy out to nurse with the wife of a stone-carver in a hilly district rich in marble quarries. The music of mallets and chisels rang in his ears from infancy; the world, as he first saw it, was a place where every man's work was to hew the unyielding earth and to struggle with stone. In after years he said, "It is only well with me when I have a chisel in my hand," and the world which he made with his own hands is a sculptor's creation inhabited by heroic men and women imprisoning his own convulsive struggles and the struggles of the human race, and carved into forms as solid and indestructible as the crust of the earth.

His father, an ignorant man claiming descent from imperial blood, reading propitious signs in the aspect of the heavens, believed that his second-born was blest with celestial powers, and gave him the name Michael Angelo. The family was ancient and honorable, but at the time of Michael Angelo's birth, phlegmatic and shiftless. There were three more sons, grumbling, ungrateful wretches not worth mentioning except for the great sculptor's singular generosity toward them and his persistence in trying to scold them into decent employment. From a decaying stock, from a family marked by a peasant composure, he came with unaccountable qualities of extreme nervousness, enormous vitality, and sensitivity to all the arts and all superior human forms. He lived to be ninety years old, productive to the last; he saw Popes come and go, nine of them, and he slaved for them all; he saw the Renaissance fade into hypocritical culture, and Italy ruined forever by Lutheran butchers and Spaniards excelling in deliberate cruelty; and he saw Florence whom he loved and hated as he loved and hated his own family, betrayed and sold by her own sons. In his tough old age, when he was too feeble to carve or paint, he made many drawings for a great picture of the Crucifixion—wonderful drawings but pathetic witnesses to the fact that at last he had come upon a theme which, with his slackened energies, he could not conquer. In his face are sadness and death and the agony of creative toil, but it is the face of one who had experienced the highest joy of life: the consciousness that he had used himself for a mighty purpose. He was born with the will to subdue and command the intractable elements of life, and he refashioned those elements into an overwhelming humanity commensurate with his own vision. No other mortal, in art, science, warfare or any field whatever, has left upon the world the impress of a personality so powerful, concentrated and irresistible.

Michael Angelo, passing through a sickly childhood, soon developed into a boy of deceptive vigor and endurance. Rather small than large of frame, he was capable of such protracted labors of mind and body as to defy belief, were they not attested by living evidence. His father, remembering the omens attending the birth of his son, sent him to a school in Florence kept by a scholar of some repute, hoping that he might devote himself to letters and thus revive the glory of the Buonarroti family. It was not to be. Art captured him from the first: he filled his copy-books with sketches and sought the society of youths apprenticed to the leading painters and sculptors. He visited the workshop of Domenico Ghirlandaio and after that there was no stopping him. Day and night he sketched and painted, opposing the wishes of the family and suffering bitterly for his disobedience. His father and uncles regarded painting as a low business, a trade for peasants and craftsmen, and such indeed it had always been in Italy until Leonardo da Vinci practiced it with the graces of a gentleman. They took turns beating the boy, trusting to break his spirit, but this stupid cruelty only strengthened his determination, and in 1488, he was formally articled to Ghirlandaio, the most popular master in Florence. He was then in his thirteenth year.

For one so young he was extraordinarily advanced in art: though nominally an apprentice, he went to Ghirlandaio as a qualified assistant, his contract calling for a small salary to be paid annually. He was not precocious in the sense that his work was merely of brilliant promise and exceptionally dextrous in execution; his earliest studies were definite in intention and of such commanding maturity as to fill his fellow pupils with active jealousy. Harsh and irritable, he dominated his master's shop; he was hot-tempered, insultingly frank, unrestrained in his criticisms and scornful of everyone whose ideal of art fell short of absolute perfection. These traits increased in vehemence as he grew older, and there is scarcely an artist of his own or former times upon whom he failed to pass merciless judgment. But his judgments, let us take note, were honest and almost invariably correct; and he was as generous in praise as he was in condemnation. He was neither jealous nor selfish; concerning his own performances he said little, maintaining a formidable modesty and allowing his art to proclaim its own virtues. He was aware that great art presupposes unending labor and infinite self-denials and it never occurred to him that the long hard journey was not worth the trouble. Disappointments piled upon him and ingenious malcontents plotted his ruin; he fought back fiercely and silenced his accusers with works which no man, before or since, has ever approached. He was disgusted with the iniquity of his age, but he was no reformer, and he did not expect the world to cease its foolish crimes and devote itself to soothing his exasperated soul.

It is not probable that he learned anything from Ghirlandaio except the technique of fresco-painting. This master, as I have already said, was an artist of surpassing competence, but much too conventional to assist a boy of Michael Angelo's impetuous originality. Moreover, he seems to have been of an envious nature and to have claimed partnership in his pupil's first painting, a prodigious piece of draughtsmanship done, as an old biographer relates, "with that perfection of his which never failed to excite the wonder of the world." Fortunately, the relationship was terminated at the end of a year. The Magnificent Lorenzo, deploring the scarcity of sculptors in Florence, begged Ghirlandaio to send to him his two most promising pupils in order that they might have the advantages of the collection of Graeco-Roman statues which he had assembled in the Medicean gardens, and Michael Angelo was named immediately as one of the candidates. His master was not only glad to be rid of him, but glad to see such audacious talent withdrawn from painting.

Three happy years followed, the most tranquil years of Michael Angelo's life. In the gardens of the Medici he breathed for the first time the atmosphere of antiquity. Here he caught something of the spirit of classic Greece—little, perhaps, for Lorenzo's collection contained few, if any, Hellenic masterpieces; and here his natural inclination toward large and powerful forms was stimulated by the carvings of the old Romans. In one part of the gardens, sculptors and stone-cutters were preparing marble for a library which was to house Lorenzo's books and manuscripts. Again the sound of mallets and chisels rang in the boy's ears, reminding him of his sculptor's birthright. He began as a practical workman, assisting the masons in dressing blocks of stone, and rapidly acquiring facility with tools. In the course of his studies he came upon the grinning mask of a faun, an antique greatly damaged by time. The thing amused him and he proceeded to copy it, restoring from imagination the injured features. As he was polishing the head, the Magnificent happened to pass by on a tour of inspection, and, as Condivi tells us, "noticing in the first place the beauty of the work, and having regard to the lad's youth, he marvelled exceedingly, and although he praised the workmanship he none the less joked with him as with a child saying: 'Oh! you have made this Faun very old, and yet you have left him all his teeth. Do you not know that old men of that age always lack a few teeth?' When alone Michael Angelo corrected the error, cutting away a tooth from the upper jaw, and drilling a hole in the gums as though it had come out by the roots. Some days later Lorenzo returned, and seeing the single-mindedness of the child, and appreciating the beauty of the head, resolved, as father of all talent, to take the boy into his house. Learning from Michael Angelo whose son he was he said, 'Let your father know I would like to speak with him.'"

The sequel is a slight corrective to the glorious notion that all Florentines loved and appreciated art. On hearing the news, old Buonarroti was sick at heart, and burst into tears at the thought of his son entering the lowly walks of the stone-masons. In vain did Michael Angelo explain the difference between a sculptor and a mason—the obtuse remnant of petty nobility would not be convinced. But Lorenzo's will was not to be denied, and accordingly Michael Angelo left his father's house for lodgings in a palace. Henceforth the young sculptor was to be the main support of the family, and though his father lived to see him the foremost artist in the world, the old man never gained the faintest appreciation of the works upon which that fame rested, and never ceased to regard his son as a sort of obstinate stone-mason who had managed, at the sacrifice of everything worth having, to hack his way into a profitable, if ignominious, profession.

Lorenzo treated his protégé as one of his own sons, bestowing upon him a violet mantle and a liberal allowance, furnishing him a room to work in with the right to hold as his own property whatever he might choose to make, seating him at the famous table where men of the noblest birth and highest rank were daily assembled, favoring him with the keys to his museum of sculpture, painting, antique gems and manuscripts, and exacting nothing in return except that he keep his interests centralized on sculpture and employ his diligence toward pre-eminence in the hardest field of art. The importance of this space in Michael

Angelo's life—he remained with Lorenzo from his sixteenth to his eighteenth year—cannot be emphasized too strongly. The finest intellects of Italy—the luminaries of Renaissance learning—were his counsellors: from the mystic Ficino he learned to love Plato, and Platonic ideas, as we shall see, entered into his art and into his variously interpreted passion for ideal beauty; through Pico della Mirandola, the seraph of oriental culture, he was attracted to the prophetic books of the Old Testament; he read Dante with Poliziano, and was a companion of Luigi Pulci, the best of the improvisatori, who, as Cellini describes, "met together during the summer nights on the open streets to match their skill in singing and reciting."

But the growing genius of the young artist was not enfeebled by culture—despite the violet mantle and the princely environment. Ceremonies, polished manners, and the somewhat affected refinement of Lorenzo's guests made little impression upon him. On rare occasions he comported himself with diplomatic gentility, but just as he opposed in art all that was soft and conventional and asserted, even in his first carvings, a defiant individuality, so he was, in his dealings with his fellows, harsh and rude, and disdainful of polite breeding. But the value of his association with the distinguished brains of his time cannot be questioned. It enabled him to develop all his faculties and to frame a conception of art which should represent the complete dominion of the spirit and not a technical triumph in a particular field, and it enabled him to approach his special creative problems in a philosophical mind, with the constantly enlarging vision of an heroic world. Thus, through mental habits formed in the first years of adolescence he saved himself from the ranks of the mechanics, panders and virtuosi, and from the malady all too common among modern artists—the preoccupation with eccentric details. It is probable too that the material nature of the sculptor's medium balanced his high-strung energies. Steel and marble were needed to strike fire from his soul, and he loved the sculptor's art. There were no pointing and scaling machines to help him; it was hard and healthy work; and he learned to carve with great rapidity, using his left hand as easily as his right.

During this period he continued his studies in anatomy, "occupying himself," in Vasari's account, "by night and on all holidays with drawing in his own room, by which means he produced better works in the garden than any other student and accordingly was much favored by Lorenzo." Having pleased the Prior of one of the churches with a Crucifix carved in wood, he was given in return a room into which he secretly brought dead bodies and dissected them. He has left us a curious record of those ghoulish experiments in a pen sketch showing two men dissecting a body by the light of a candle that has been stuck into the corpse's belly. In his later years he confessed that the fetid sessions turned his stomach permanently and that never again was he able to eat or drink with any relish. Ruskin, with snarling eloquence, complains that Michael Angelo learned his anatomy from corpses instead of from the living figure. So he did—but only in part. He learned it from many sources—from models living and dead and from all the strong men of the past. A native Tuscan, he was deeply influenced by Florentine painting, especially the frescoes of Masaccio which indeed formed a part of the education of every serious artist. Among the many students who frequented the Chapel of the Carmine, where he worked daily, there was a sculptor named Torrigiano, a pugnacious youth who hated Michael Angelo with a vengeance. The hostility ended in bloodshed. Torrigiano reported the quarrel to Cellini in the following manner.

"This Buonarroti and I used, when we were boys, to go into the Church of the Carmine to learn drawing from the Chapel of Masaccio. It was Buonarroti's habit to banter all who were drawing there; and one day when he was annoying me, I got more angry than usual, and, clenching my fist, I gave him such a blow on the nose that I felt bone and cartilage go down like biscuit beneath my knuckles; and this mark of mine he will carry with him to the grave."

For this act of violence Torrigiano was shunned by all his

comrades, and fearing punishment from Lorenzo de' Medici, left Florence in a hurry. From all that we know of the circumstance, Michael Angelo accepted the injury without resistance. He possessed any amount of moral courage, but physically was timorous and shrinking, subject to fits of terror and forebodings, and inclined to withdraw from impending dangers. These faults were the weaknesses of his virtues. While Florence was putting forth her final efforts at gaiety and Lorenzo was concealing his corruption behind a carnival of wanton amusements, Michael Angelo was listening to the voice of the prophet who was groaning his sermons from the pulpit of the Duomo, warning the people of the woes that were about to descend upon them. Leonardo, you will remember, was indifferent to the philippics of Savonarola and caricatured the monk's grotesque features; Michael Angelo was made of sterner, if less coldly penetrating, stuff. He was now on the verge of manhood, and had, in two trials, proved himself not merely the greatest sculptor alive but ready to challenge the whole of antiquity; he was haunted by the consciousness of mysterious and untempered strength, burdened by maturing dreams of a positive and colossal humanity; and confronting him was the doom of Florence—"the nest where he was born," as he expressed it in a moment of tenderness—the death of his patron, and the downfall of the House that had honored and protected him.

At the age of eighteen, Michael Angelo stood alone in the realm of art. In two works he had demonstrated his powers and indicated the decisive nature of the world which he was to erect, block by block, into the most comprehensive materialization of the struggles of the human spirit that man has been privileged to create. If, as we reconstruct this world, the labors of its maker seem to be superhuman, and the organizing energy behind it to transcend belief, let us bear in mind that it would have been impossible at any other time and in any other circumstances, and that Michael Angelo stood at the apex of a long and mighty tradition. And let us not forget the pressure exerted upon the artist: the popular recognition of his genius, the social curiosity in, if not understanding of, his performances—when the Sistine decorations were first exposed to the public, the crowds flocked in before the floor of the chapel had been swept, like the rabble at a Roman circus, and kicked up an immense cloud of dust some of which still darkens the glorious ceiling—the demands, papal and civic, for work, more work and greater work; all of which inflamed his imagination and emboldened him to undertake and carry out commissions involving what would have been, in any other age, insuperable difficulties of execution. Similarly today, the capitalist, the engineer, or the moving picture director, controlling armies of men, exulting in his power over money and raw materials, seems to possess an inexhaustible vitality as he performs those herculean labors which make the multitude stare and applaud; while the painter or sculptor, out of joint with life and untouched by any social pressure, wastes his energies contriving little samples of his talent, a feverish starveling who breaks his health and his strength over jobs that should cost him no effort whatever. When we consider Michael Angelo in relation to his antecedents and to Renaissance ideals, he becomes more than a churlish demi-god shielded by impenetrable sublimity, he becomes a creative artist; and his world is no longer an isolated and disparate phenomenon but a completely possible humanity.

Michael Angelo did less apprentice work than any other artist of the first rank. He had, as we have shown, profound and audible contempt for mediocrity; his trenchant originality prompted him, from the outset, to regard his contemporaries with suspicion; and it was inevitable that such a man should quarry his materials alone, abjuring and cursing assistants, and that his world should be a unique and indivisible structure entirely of his own making. But again we must remember that he was not an independent phenomenon. For two centuries the old art tree had been flourishing, and Florentine painters and sculptors had been occupied with the problems of mass and movement. That is to say, they had, first, to learn how to present objects as convincing materials with the force and realistic truth of nature—an elementary task to the modern artist; next to endow the inert masses with potential energy and action, to make the painted or sculptural image a living, breathing form; and last, to individualize these plastic forms and use them as symbols expressing the artist's specific philosophy of life. The preponderant concern of the art of this epoch was the figure, and the landmarks in the liberation of the human form from the conventional flatness of the Middle Ages were Giotto, Masaccio, Signorelli, and Leonardo, four anthropologists whose special sensibilities were guided by scientific methods. These men, and many others, including Donatello and the Tuscan sculptors, forged the tools with which Michael Angelo was to work. Without them he would have been absolutely impotent. To imagine him without his predecessors would be as fantastical as to imagine Einstein without his immense heritage of scientific discovery reconstructing the universe on the point of a pin.

Upon the past then, as a foundation, Michael Angelo erected his world. Let us not think of this world as a poet's dream, a confusion of disembodied fragments and a litter of dislocated images strewn through unbounded space; let us think of it as an existent fact, a solid objective reality planned and put together by a master of design. It was the custom of the Florentines to speak of the *art of design*, meaning that creative or tectonic faculty by means of which the artist shapes old things into new combinations or new forms. Michael Angelo possessed this faculty in the highest degree and explained it most eloquently. "The artist," he says, "will be instructed not only in painting, sculpture and architecture, which are his own province, but in all other manual crafts practiced throughout the world. I find amongst men but one single art or science, and that is drawing or design, all others being members proceeding therefrom; for if you carefully consider all that is being done in life you will find that each person is, whether he knows it or not, a designer, creating and producing new forms and figures, in dress and various garbs, in building and occupying spaces with houses, in cultivating the fields and ploughing the land into pictures and sketches, in navigating the seas with sails, in fighting and dividing the spoil, in burials and all other movements and actions."

It is a scientific world. The space in which his huge forms are established is charted and resolved with geometrical precision; he uses the principles of perspective, foreshortening and light and shade as handed down to him by a race of scientific draughtsmen; he obtains movement and rhythm by his knowledge of thrusts and balances and the opposition of forces; he goes to life and death for his anatomy, adding the joy of the artist to the curiosity of the surgeon.

It is an architectural world. His universe, like Einstein's is finite and bounded. Before he creates his men and women he provides a dwelling place for them. For him an isolated picture or statue is a still-born thing, since it belongs to nothing; it is not even a severed member but a freakish orphan—a head that never had a body.

It is a sculptor's world, projected in three dimensions, composed of crests and hollows, free from charming makeshifts and pasty uncertainties, foursquare and impregnable. "Painting," said Michael Angelo, "should be considered excellent in proportion as it approaches the effect of relief, and relief should be considered bad as it approaches the effect of painting. Leonardo da Vinci wrote saying that painting was more noble than sculpture, as though he knew as much about it as he did of the other subjects on which he has written. Why, my serving-maid would have written better!"

Finally, it is a human world. "The highest object of art for thinking men," he declared, "is man." And we must take this statement to mean not only man in the generic but in the individual and masculine sense. Women, of course, he carved and painted, but he formed them after the pattern of his men, large, and sinewy and heroic, with no regard to physical loveliness or the charms of sex. There are no sexual enticements, in fact, almost no sexual differentiations, in his world. One might as well expect to find sex in an earthquake or a hurricane as in Michael Angelo. It is true that Rabelais also created giants and made them capable of marvellous copulations—but he was working with satire and low comedy. Shift the vein to tragedy and the idea becomes monstrous and revolting. Sex appeal in Michael Angelo's figures would be nothing less than a cosmic mistake. A naked woman eighteen feet in height cannot exhibit sexual attractions. There is another reason for the absence of seductive qualities: during the Renaissance the sexual impulses found a satisfactory requital in organic life, and it never occurred to the artist to sublimate conventional sex-experiences into a curious symbolism. That was reserved for a more modern age when art had lost its architectural significance and had become submerged in introspective psychology.

The subject-matter of his world is primarily religious—in externals, ecclesiastical. In his first efforts he emulates the old paganism of the Greeks and Romans, but once he is sure of himself, he adopts the time-honored themes of his countrymen, themes close to the hearts of the people and a traditional challenge to all artists. But his treatment of the old subjects is essentially personal; and he departs radically from canonical observances. The wonders of nature which had so fascinated Leonardo leave him unmoved; landscapes, trees, flowers, and stuffs he casts out as cheap makeshifts for Flemings and sentimentalists, things "deceiving the external eye," he said, and impossible to anthropomorphize. For he wished, as Berenson puts it, "to endow the universe with human attributes"; to reduce the world to a single factor into which he could translate all his thoughts and feelings. His one instrument is the human body, preferably the nude, and he uses it to express his moods, his mental habits, and every shade and depth of emotion.

Two sculptures adorn the entrance of Michael Angelo's world. They were done in his first youth and are by no means perfect—they are only the beginning. But what a beginning! They reveal the tenor of his mature mind, and the fabric of the entire structure is woven into them. One, his single work in low-relief, is a Madonna and Child. It is only a small plaque, showing clearly, in its sharp edges and flat surfaces, that the artist had

PORTRAIT OF MICHAEL ANGELO.

Uffizi Gallery, Florence

not quite mastered the problem of uniting his planes to give the effect of rounded forms, but it has the largeness and stature of monumental carving. The Madonna is a little ponderous, the Child a potential weight-thrower, but the whole is austere and dignified, and the face of the mother is generalized into a type of grave brooding and heavy tenderness characteristic of all his women. At the age of seventeen, he would do nothing as it had been done before, and this Madonna is figuratively the mother of a new genus of massive progeny.

The other piece is the *Battle of the Centaurs*, suggested to him by one of Lorenzo's scholars. As if to put behind him, once for all, the influence of Donatello discernible in his Madonna, he compresses in a small block of marble some twenty nude figures thrown into mortal combat by an explosion of energy. This relief is overcrowded and inharmonious, a *tour de force* representing, with extraordinary creative gusto, his preference for dramatic movements, violent contrasts of action and resistance, involved compositions—in sum, everything that pertains to his use of the nude as an expressive instrument.

He had scarcely finished his *Centaurs* when Lorenzo died leaving the control of Florence to his eldest son, Piero, an insolent fool. Michael Angelo, overcome by grief, returned to his father's house, and spent the winter in an unheated room carving a statue of Hercules. During a great storm he was recalled to the palace of the Medici and ordered to model a snow image for Piero's courtyard—the only employment Piero seems to have found for the young master who stayed on as guest for several months. One of the inmates of the palace, a musician and very friendly to the sculptor, had a talent for hallucinations. Twice the ghost of Lorenzo appeared to this man, bearing sinister tidings of the collapse of the Medicean tyranny. Michael Angelo, believing the whispered tale of woe, was according to Condivi, "so convinced of the truth of the vision that he left Florence with a couple of comrades two days afterward, dreading that if what the musician had predicted should come true, he would no longer be safe in the city."

He travelled to Bologna and thence to Venice where his comrades squandered all his money. Returning to Bologna, he neglected a certain formality required of foreigners and would have been lodged in jail but for the intercession of a nobleman who, hearing that Buonarroti was a sculptor, paid his fine and gave him rooms in his own house. Michael Angelo remained with his new patron for more than a year, delighting him with his genius and "reading aloud to him every night out of Dante until the old gentleman went to sleep." While in Bologna he studied the reliefs of Della Quercia, and for the shrine of San Domenico carved a highly finished statuette of a kneeling angel holding a candlestick, his first professional work. But the local sculptors accused him of taking the bread out of their mouths, and fearing personal injury, he returned to Florence.

Savonarola was now the ruling spirit and the city was strangely sober and well-behaved. A distant branch of the Medici, however, had, under an assumed name, managed to escape the wrath of the people, and for the third time, Michael Angelo, a republican at heart, was affiliated with a house of despots. For a prominent member of this division of the family, he designed a *Sleeping Cupid* which compared so favorably with the work of the ancients that his patron advised him to doctor it, saying, "If you can make it look as if it had been buried under the earth, I will forward it to Rome; it will be taken for an antique, and you will sell it much better." The sculptor fell in with the fraud, for what motives we cannot be sure. Possibly he wished to show that he was familiar with all the secrets of his craft; or perhaps he needed money, his father and brothers being in poor condition. The Cupid was placed in the hands of a dealer who carried it to Rome and sold it as a genuine antique to a cardinal for 200 ducats. Out of this sum Michael Angelo was paid thirty ducats, which goes to prove that the ways of dealers have always been the same. But in time it was rumored that the putto was a modern invention, and the cardinal despatched an agent to Florence to investigate the chicanery. When Michael Angelo learned how small was his share of the spoils, he flew into a passion, confessed his guilt, and accompanied the agent to Rome, hoping to get a larger percentage of the money. His claims were unrewarded. The cardinal recovered his 200 ducats; the dealer took back the Cupid; and the sculptor still protested that he had been cheated.

He was twenty-one years old when he first arrived in Rome. It was at this time that he formed, partly through necessity, but largely because of some inexplicable weakness, those miserly and squalid habits which he never cared to relinquish. But he was miserly only with himself. When, after a year or two of hardships, he began to make money, he sent most of it home; he established his brothers in business; bought a villa for his father, and town properties as well, and wrote that he would "advance the honor of the family if he had to sell himself into slavery." He took no pleasure in eating or drinking, or in carnal recreations. A little bread rubbed with garlic, a bit of cheese, wine—very dry and light, a bed and a workshop—he wanted nothing more. A creator of immortal forms, he dwelt with the gods. He slept in his clothes to save time, and worked so hard that his sides were swollen, his face seamed with wrinkles, his back misshapen. His brother found him living like a dog and reported the unseemly matter to his father who wrote a word of admonition, alarmed lest the fruitful branch might be cut off. "Above all, do not be penurious; live moderately but do not stint yourself; above all things avoid hardships, because in your art, if you fall ill, which God forbid, you are a lost man; above all things have a care of your head, keep it moderately warm, and never wash; have yourself rubbed down, *but never wash*."

He made for a Roman banker a statue of Bacchus, larger than life, and wrought out with a manual perfection that is almost repugnant. This is one of the few works by Michael Angelo which I cannot write of with sympathy. It is not because it fails to embody the Greek spirit as some critics have objected—the spirit which produced the masterpieces of Greek art was dead a thousand years before Michael Angelo was born, and a man cannot by an act of will live in the past; it is simply that the Bacchus is a squint-eyed, tipsy nude and little more. It is neither flesh nor spirit; it is polished marble so faintly impregnated with the mind of the artist that we cannot forget the material substance, a work modelled in all seriousness, but plainly one in which Michael Angelo had no special interest. It occupies a subordinate niche in his world and is to be remembered chiefly for its astounding craftsmanship and the impeccable finish and completion that he bestowed upon his works when not harassed by more commissions than he could handle.

About this time he produced his first indisputable masterpiece, the *Pietà* which stands at present in a chapel of St. Peter's where, as Wölfflin points out, "it is most barbarously placed—raised so high that it is impossible to get the chief point of view—lost in vast space." The commission came from a French cardinal, the contract stipulating that "Michael Angelo shall make a Pietà of marble at his own cost; that is, a Virgin Mary clothed, with the dead Christ in her arms, of the size of a proper man, for the price of 450 golden ducats, within the term of one year from the beginning of the work"—certain sums payable in advance. The Roman banker, acting as intermediary, pledged his faith that the artist "will finish the said statue within the given time, and that no master of our days shall be able to produce a better."

There are greater statues by Michael Angelo, and more tremendous Madonnas, but none that springs more fully from the heart. When we look at this group, we immediately ascribe to it movement, feelings, crushing tenderness, and terrible pity; the cold tissue of stone solicits our emotions and calls into action the muscular play attending those emotions; the dead body of Christ becomes, as we say, living form—more living indeed than the youthful Mother; it actually bends into the lap that contains it; the muscles contract; the head droops down in agony, and we are not conscious of inorganic materials, of stationary marble, but of forms which express in every line and limb the voice of suffering humanity.

The *Pietà* plunges us into the torrent of pity that flows through Michael Angelo's world—pity that is positive and controlled;

pity that is an active force; pity affirmed by creative joy and made heroic. To realize this emotion in marble was a task for the one man who accomplished it—it has never been done again. The Virgin does not weep—for weeping women are not heroic, at least not in sculpture—and her half-opened hand is more expressive than tears. She has the face of one who never grows old, and the body of one whom God and Michael Angelo have endowed with more than human strength. Both in conception and treatment the group is modern; it makes all previous representations of the subject curiously archaic. The two figures are combined into an harmonious unit, a single block-form in which the constituent parts are related without the use of distortions or enlargements. One would think that the Catholic Church, the justly proud possessor of this monument, would provide replicas of the *Pietà* to replace the hideous wax-work effigies which disfigure its shrines throughout the world.

To those who, in his own day, objected to the youthfulness of the mother, Michael Angelo replied: "Do you not know that chaste women retain their freshness far longer than the unchaste? How much more would this be the case with a virgin, into whose breast there never crept the least lascivious desire which could affect the body! Nay, I will go further, and hazard the belief that this unsullied bloom of youth, besides being maintained in her by natural causes, may have been miraculously wrought to convince the world of the virginity and perpetual purity of the mother."

This is his only signed work. It is said that a party of Lombards, passing through St. Peter's, praised the *Pietà* and attributed it to one of their own sculptors, and Michael Angelo, overhearing their remarks, was indignant that his art should be mistaken for another's. So one night he stole into the chapel and carved his name in the belt of the Madonna's robe.

He was now the foremost sculptor of his time. He returned to Florence, preceded by a great reputation, to relieve the troubles of a family that was always clamoring for ducats. Commissions awaited him and he accepted them all. He promised a cardinal, the future Pius III, to complete, within three years, fifteen saints for the Cathedral of Siena, a large order which he proceeded to fill with his customary confidence and energy. He had no sooner begun work than a far more tempting offer presented itself. The Board of Public Works owned a large marble slab, popularly known as the *Giant,* which had lain in the Cathedral yard for a hundred years, having baffled the ingenuity not only of the sculptor who had originally abandoned it, but of all subsequent artists. Michael Angelo was sent for.

"Is the marble good for anything?" asked the warden.

The slab was eighteen feet long, disproportionately thin and narrow, with an ugly cleft in one end.

"It was ruined at the quarries! The man who caused it to be blocked out was not a sculptor, he was a bungling knave and a wood-chopper ——"

"Andrea del Monte San Savino has applied for it. He says that by adding certain pieces ——"

"Let me have it! I will use it just as it is."

Whereupon a contract was signed and the *Giant* removed to a shed not far away.

Two years later the holy quiet of the city was changed into wild excitement. Word went abroad that the *Giant* had come to life in the form of *David* and that it was a miracle of art. An assembly of the most important artists, including Leonardo da Vinci and Botticelli, was convoked to determine where the miracle should reside. After many long and eloquent arguments, the committee agreed to leave the site to the judgment of Michael Angelo—a decision it should have reached in the beginning—who chose the steps of the Palazzo Vecchio. When the statue was first placed upon its pedestal, the populace, in an aberrant state of prudery, was shocked, or rather offended, by its extensive nudity, and an armed guard was posted by night to protect the young king from mutilation; but after Savonarola had been disposed of and the moralists had recovered their normal candor, the *David* became the most popular statue in the city and the symbol of the power and glory of Florence.

Much has been written about the naturalistic aspects of the *David*. The Germans criticize the enormous hands and feet, the wrestler's neck, and the angularity of the figure, asserting that the sculptor committed an aesthetic error in treating an adolescent body on such large scale, and that he created a colossal hobbledehoy instead of an ideal of youthful beauty; and Symonds interprets the motive as a "moment caught from palpitating life," and explains at length the relation of the attitude to the movement described by a warrior in wielding his sling. These matters are interesting but beside the point. It is plain that Michael Angelo had no intention of depicting the legendary *David*. His conception was conditioned by the limitations of the marble. He had promised to deliver the *Giant* from a flat matrix, and there was but one solution: an heroic youth whose incomplete development would allow him to carve to the limits of the block, that is, to combine great height with a flatness that would have been impossible in a mature figure. As a marvel of execution the statue is without an equal: Michael Angelo—in this instance only—made no life-size model in clay; he depended upon a small wax model eighteen inches high and a few drawings; and so exact were his calculations that he preserved, on the top of the *David's* head, a vestige of the old carving in order to show his employers that he had nothing left over.

The white *Giant* would be as great under another name. It might be called *Youth* or *Victory*, and if any one wishes to think of it as the quintessence of Florentine ideals, there is ample ground for the association. Certainly Michael Angelo was filled with thoughts of the grandeur of his native city, and it would be foolish to deny that he was the product and culmination of that grandeur. More specifically, I should say that, taking into account the difficulties of the marble, he was absorbed by a single purpose: to disencumber from the block, a figure synonymous with power—power in the abstract, gigantic strength from which the dross of brutality has been eliminated, intellectual as well as physical energy, the inestimable force generated by spiritual wrath. Those who seek in sculpture the voluptuous charms of the later and more androgynous Greeks, or the soft contours of female nakedness, had best avoid the *Giant*; as an anthropomorphic realization of godlike power identified with a plausible human engine, it is the most majestic statue since the Olympian Zeus. Michael Angelo was twenty-six years old when he finished the work and was paid 400 ducats for his trouble.

In his first extant sculpture, the *Madonna and Child* in low relief, he puts forth tentatively but unmistakably, that quality which the Italians call *terribilità*—the dreadful force that shakes the soul, the clap of doom that beats through a Greek tragedy; with his *David* this note crashes into his world with an awful power. It will be sounded again and again, finally to die out in a prophetic echo. We find it in the abundant works immediately following the *David*; three more Madonnas, two in high relief, one in the round; *St. Matthew*, an unfinished statue, one of the twelve apostles he agreed to make for the Cathedral but for which he found no time; a painting in tempera of the Holy Family, his only finished easel-picture. Perhaps this last should be excepted. It is a powerful picture, both in design and draughtsmanship, but hard and glittering and spiritually barren. We cannot pronounce it a failure, nor even a mistake; save for the color which is hot and unpleasant, it seems to possess all the attributes of Michael Angelo's genius—the incomparable drawing, the elaborate finish, the twistings of the bodies to ensure dramatic movement, the nude youths placed in the background as decorative properties. It is the product of titanic determination. No other man could have painted it, and yet somehow we wish that it had never been painted.

Together with Leonardo da Vinci, he was appointed to decorate the Grand Council Chamber of Florence. The unhappy lot of Leonardo's mural we have already noticed. Michael Angelo's design suffered a similar fate—the fresco was never painted and the cartoon was either lost or cut into pieces and stolen by envious rivals. Cellini tells us that "Michael Angelo portrayed a number of foot soldiers, who, the season being summer had gone to bathe in the Arno. He drew them at the moment the alarm is sounded, and the men, all naked, rush to arms. So splendid is their action, that nothing survives of ancient or of modern art which touches the same lofty point of excellence. Though the divine Michael Angelo in later life finished that great Chapel of Pope Julius, he never rose half-way to the same pitch of power; his genius never afterwards attained to the force of those first studies." This opinion is open to dispute but of one thing we may be assured: "the great drawing," as it was everywhere known, became the training school of all artists, a sort of anatomy lesson, revealing for the first time, and by some fresh and stupendous insight, the infinite potentialities of the human body and the connection between dramatic action and organic structure. While engaged in the cartoon and the twelve apostles, Michael Angelo was called to Rome by the Pope, receiving 100 ducats for travelling expenses.

His return to Rome marks the beginning of a long series of struggles and disappointments—appalling cheats of fortune that would have killed an artist of less resolution. Julius II was a Caesarian type, a man of the sword rather than a man of God. The last of those truculent individualists whose implacable ambitions fill the pages of Renaissance history with such spectacular careers of art and crime, he had acceded to the Papacy by means which could hardly be called honorable, but after he had seized the tiara, his course was fearless and straightforward. His desire was to be absolute ruler of the papal states, and to effect this, he was willing to cripple the rest of Italy. His head teemed with political schemes: he was rough and irascible, and a hard taskmaster, in short a bold imperialist, but almost unique in his frankness and his aversion to pompous nonsense and courtly splendor. His knowledge of art was meagre—he was essentially a man of action—but his general ideas were sound and practicable. He wished to restore the dignity of ancient Rome and to fill the city with vast and imposing monuments. He was accustomed to treat his artists like prisoners of war, but in Michael Angelo he encountered a spirit as haughty and unbending as his own.

They quarrelled and insulted each other, but in the end the Pope was the victor: he held most of the cards, and if the game went against him, jangled the sword.

Giving thought as to how he might employ his sculptor, Julius suggested a sepulchre, and in less than two months Michael Angelo came forward with the design. His Holiness chuckled in gruff approval—he had found his man. The conception was colossal; the tomb would be a monument worthy of a great pontiff.

"But," explained Michael Angelo, "it is too large for St. Peter's."

"I will have a church big enough to hold it."

With a peremptoriness that shocked the whole of Christendom, Julius ordered the destruction of the mother-church, the old Basilica erected in the reign of Constantine. In vain did the cardinals and bishops cry "Sacrilege," and urge him to reconsider his decree. The walls were pulled down with such indecent rapidity by Bramante, the architect chosen to plan the new Cathedral, that Michael Angelo personally complained to the Pope that "the marvellous antique columns were broken into fragments when they might have been lowered gently and preserved intact." The Pope was engrossed in military affairs and sent the sculptor off to Carrara to quarry marbles for the tomb.

Now follows what Condivi has called "The Tragedy of the Tomb," a heart-breaking business lasting for more than forty years. Michael Angelo in his original designs intended to build a tomb surpassing all existing monuments, an enormous edifice three stories in height, with forty major statues and numerous subsidiary carvings in marble and bronze relief. But the world of the imagination crumbled before the world of fact, and the mighty sepulchre slowly shrank into a mural shadow. The Pope's enthusiasm chilled; the Pope died; his executors demanded that the work continue but on a reduced scale; the Medicean Popes drafted the sculptor into their own enterprises; the heirs of Julius accused him of malversation and the triple quarrel went on; five times the plans were altered, and the six *Slaves* two of them among Michael Angelo's supreme masterpieces, were shuffled out of the design; at last the dreary project was concluded in a single statue, the horned *Moses* presumably conceived as a symbol of Julius, the leader of men, but more truthfully, I think, the compacted fury of the two score years in which the artist's vision clashed and compromised with the world of fact.

He spent eight months in the mountains of Carrara, with two assistants and his horse, at the close of each day going down to the sea to study a piece of headland which, because of its convenient shape, he hoped one day to carve into a Colossus for the guidance of sailors. The marble was shipped to Rome and carted to the Piazza of St. Peter's where its immense bulk astonished the people and filled the stern old Pope with joy. Julius treated Michael Angelo like a brother and had a drawbridge thrown from the Vatican to his workshop in order to visit him privately. So far all was well.

But Bramante was an enemy of the sculptor. A great architect, he was also a spendthrift and had been guilty of cheap building to save money for high living. This knavery Michael Angelo had exposed as well as the wanton destruction of the old church, and Bramante secretly plotted revenge. There was another reason for his intrigues: he was Raphael's uncle, and wished a clear field for the talents of the young god from Urbino. Referring to the dirty business years afterwards, Michael Angelo said, "All the dissensions between Pope Julius and me arose from the envy of Bramante and Raffaello da Urbino, and this was the cause of my not finishing the tomb in his lifetime. They wanted to ruin me, Raffaello indeed had good reason; for all he had of art he owed to me."

It seems that the architect worked insidiously upon the temperamental Pope, warning him that "men who built their own tombs soon occupied them," and Julius was the more receptive to such prattle since he was about to make war on Bologna and needed all his revenues for that purpose. One day Michael

Angelo heard the Pope say that "he would not spend another cent for stones, either big ones or little ones." The remark naturally perturbed him, and when he applied for funds to pay his workmen and the freightage of the marbles, he was chased out of the Vatican by an insolent groom. He ran back to his shop and served the following notice on His Holiness.

"Most blessed Father, I have been turned out of the Palace today by your orders; wherefore I give you notice that from this time forward, if you want me, you must look for me elsewhere than at Rome."

Then he called out to his servant, "Find a Jew, and sell everything in the house, and come to Florence."

The city of Florence, having surrendered Michael Angelo reluctantly in the first place, welcomed him home with open arms and bade him finish the cartoon for the Grand Council Chamber. The Pope was enraged and hurled a bull at the city, "full of menace, demanding that he should be sent back by fair means or force." Michael Angelo replied briefly, "that he would never return, that he had given good and faithful service and had been treated like a rogue, that he was free and did not wish to bind himself again."

The Pope sent a second bull and a third, and the Gonfaloniere of Florence, trembling for the safety of the Republic summoned the sculptor and said, "You have braved the Pope as the King of France would not have done. Therefore there is no longer any occasion to make yourself sought after. We do not wish to go to war with him on your account and risk the State, so prepare yourself to return."

It is pleasant to record this incident if only as a reminder that there was a time when states were prepared to fight for the services of an artist. Today conditions are a little different; the Pope has no use for artists; nor has any state, nor any city, nor any individual unless it be the brigand called the dealer and the snobbish collector.

Meantime the warrior Pope had captured Bologna, and we find him, a few days later, renewing his demands for Michael

Angelo. "I was forced," the artist wrote to a friend, "to go to Bologna with a rope around my neck to beg his pardon. He ordered me to make his portrait in bronze, sitting, about fourteen feet in height. When he asked the cost, I answered that I thought I could cast it for 1000 ducats, but that bronze was not my trade and I did not wish to undertake it. He answered, 'Go to work: you shall cast it over and over again till it succeeds; and I will give you enough to satisfy your wishes.' To put it briefly, I cast the thing twice; and at the end of two years at Bologna, I found that I had four and a half ducats left. I never received anything more for this job; and all the moneys I paid out during the said two years were the 1000 ducats with which I promised to cast it."

Julius was always poor pay. The statue was hoisted to a pedestal above the central door of the cathedral where it remained for less than three years. When the enemies of the Pope regained the city, they razed the great bronze to the ground and cast a huge cannon out of it which, in mockery, they named Julia. The head, weighing 600 pounds, was saved but what became of it nobody knows. Michael Angelo lived like a vagabond in Bologna. He hated the place. "The wine," he said, "like everything else, is dear and bad"; the plague was spreading; his craftsmen were thieves and incompetents; and when his brother wished to pay him a visit he replied, "Don't come. I pass my life here in the greatest discomfort and with the hardest labor, doing nothing but work day and night. I am lodged in one wretched room, and have bought one single bed in which myself and my three assistants all sleep. I shall not be able to receive you suitably."

At liberty now, so he fancied, to resume work on the tomb, he returned to Rome to look after his pile of marbles which, in his absence had been considerably reduced by the inroads of marauding sculptors. The Pope, however, was ill-disposed toward the tomb and commanded him to decorate the vault of the Sistine Chapel. The old biographers inform us that Michael Angelo was again the victim of Bramante's intrigues, the architect desiring to have him withdrawn from the province of sculpture, where his attainments were above all rivalry, into painting where it appeared certain that he would be eclipsed by Raphael. The story is not without plausibility inasmuch as the Chapel offered technical difficulties beyond the abilities of any but the most experienced master of fresco and Michael Angelo had not touched this medium since he was a boy of thirteen. On the other hand, Bramante could not possibly have been ignorant of the successful issue of the cartoon for the *Battle of Pisa* which, though never carried into color, was an unsurpassed example of mural design and draughtsmanship. There can be no doubt that Michael Angelo vigorously resisted the new commission, unwilling to forsake a project which had cost him so much time and money rather than through any fear of being disgraced as a painter.

"It is not my trade!" he exclaimed. "Raphael is the proper man for the job."

"I am the one to estimate your abilities," replied the Pope. "Go to work."

The Sistine Chapel is long and narrow, 132 feet by 44; the ceiling is a plain barrel-vault 68 feet from the floor; the lateral walls are cut by twelve high windows, six on either side, running up to the spring of the vault. These walls were already decorated in fresco by such celebrities as Signorelli, Botticelli, Ghirlandaio, Perugino and Rosselli, and Michael Angelo's task was to finish the chamber, that is, to proceed from the space bordering on the rounded arches of the windows, upward through the bend of the vault and thence across the large flat expanse of ceiling. Morosely he surveyed the uncovered area, and eager to discharge the commission as expeditiously as possible, "made," as he said, "a design for twelve apostles in the lunettes, and for the rest of the ceiling certain compartments filled with ornaments of the usual sort." But when he unfolded his plan to the Pope, his spirits revolted at the meagerness of the conception.

"It is a poor thing," he said, "I will make another."

"Do whatever you like," replied Julius, "and you shall have 3000 ducats for your pains."

He began anew and as he examined the vast territory to be conquered, his imagination was unleashed and he let himself go, filled with a terrible audacity. He had hated painting, calling it a woman's work, but his antipathies disappeared when he discovered that his world might be extended into illimitable space, retaining the strength and certainty of sculpture and enriched by color. Fortunately he was in the flower of his physical and mental development, and in virtue of his past triumphs, ready to acknowledge no limit to his capacities. The magnitude of his labors cannot be conveyed by words: one must see the chapel, and to see it is an ordeal. There were 10,000 square feet of plaster to be painted—not merely covered but organized into a structural unit, and the expanded design necessitated 343 figures, some 225 of which ranged from ten to eighteen feet in height. Any other artist, Raphael, for instance, who was working in the chamber next door, would have hired a band of assistants whom he had trained to do his bidding to the letter, and have done a tidy acceptable job in a short time. But not Michael Angelo. He did nothing except from the depths of his soul, and none but himself was capable of objectifying the complex harmonies flowing from his impassioned spirit.

All that Bramante got from the Pope was an order to build the scaffolding and the renowned architect could devise nothing better than a clumsy platform suspended by ropes from the vault. Michael Angelo inquired how the holes would be stopped up, and receiving no answer, had the thing taken down, and erected a new scaffold in the form of a huge deck supported by trestles and pierced by apertures through which he could view the ceiling in perspective from the pavement. Vasari adds that the "wasted ropes which the new construction had rendered needless, were given by Michael Angelo to a poor carpenter who sold them for a sum which enabled him to make up a dower for his daughter."

His next step was to prepare the cartoons, or working stencils. Vasari is authority for the statement that he finished all the cartoons before beginning to paint, a manifest impossibility, even for an artist of Michael Angelo's genius. A work of art cannot be so comprehensively visualized or so mathematically predetermined; it is protracted agony and a growth, reborn many times, and altered not only by exigencies of the medium which no man can foresee but by practical circumstances which cannot be anticipated. First he made a tentative design for the entire ceiling and then gave his attention to the several compartments. Each subdivision was carefully composed throughout—evolved from small drawings made directly from models into cartoons of the same dimensions as the figures to be painted on the vault. After the first three compartments or Histories were finished in fresco, the scale of the figures was radically enlarged, which shows conclusively that Michael Angelo, like all artists, obeyed the fundamental creative law of trial and error. This in no wise detracts from the truly marvellous character of his performance. In fresco, the artist paints on the wet plaster, and a recent inspection of the seams dividing each day's work reveals that he painted with incredible speed—the great Adam was finished in three days!—and that some of the genre scenes were executed without the help of stencilled outlines. And in the handling of the medium, experts are agreed that his technical skill has never been equalled. The wonder grows when we recall that the Sistine Chapel was his first mural commission!

At the beginning Michael Angelo intended to use assistants and did indeed engage five painters from Florence, men of recognized excellence in fresco, but their timid efforts infuriated him. He destroyed the plaster they had decorated, locked the doors of the Chapel against them, and refused to confer with them at his house. One of the unfortunates was his oldest friend, Francesco Granacci, who as a boy had roamed the streets of Florence with him, gazing at the treasures of art, had studied with him in the shop of Ghirlandaio, and had been promoted with him to the gardens of Lorenzo—and now he was disgraced by the artist whom he loved and admired above all men!

In the first stage of the painting, the creative zeal which rose

Michael Angelo: THE CUMEAN SIBYL.

Sistine Chapel, Rome

within him as the great cartoons took shape, lapsed into despair, and for a moment he believed that he had labored in vain. "He had hardly finished the picture of the Deluge," writes Condivi, "when the work began to throw out mould to such an extent that the figures could not be distinguished through it. Michael Angelo thought that this excuse would be enough to get himself relieved of the whole job. So he went to the Pope and said: 'I told your Holiness that painting is not my trade; what I have done is spoiled; if you don't believe it, send and see.' The Pope sent San Gallo, who, after inspecting the fresco, pronounced 'that the lime basis had been put on too wet, and that water oozing out produced this mouldy surface.' He told Michael Angelo what the cause was, and bade him proceed with the work. So the excuse helped him nothing."

For four years he was the Pope's prisoner. He did not, of course, work uninterruptedly. There were times when the weather was too cold for plastering, times when he had to relax and revise his designs. To rest his weary soul, he read Dante and the Old Testament, or brought his models into the chapel for further studies. Twice he journeyed all the way to Bologna to beg money from the Pope and obtained nothing. A second depression seized him and he complained to his father: "I am still in great distress of mind, because it is now a year since I had a penny from the Pope, and I do not ask, because my work is not going forward in a way that seems to me to deserve it. That comes from its difficulty and also from *this not being my art*. And so I waste my time without results. God help me!" His family kept up its perpetual whine for aid and he retorted: "I live here in the utmost bodily fatigue, without money and with no one to look after me. I have no friends and seek none. I have not even time to eat what I require. Therefore let no additional burdens be put upon me." He had no one to look after him because he could not stand women meddling in his affairs. "The serving-maids of Rome are all whores and swine," he said.

Yet his purpose never flagged; in truth, as the work progressed, his confidence and his imagination rose higher and higher end-ing in a tumult of exalted humanity, which, instead of exposing his sublime contempt for life, as critics are wont to declare, renders the ordinary mortal infirm and insignificant. Day after day, month after month, he lay on his back, his head swathed in a towel, and painted, with an astounding delicacy of finish, the creation and fall of man, the collective effects of which were to be seen at a distance of sixty feet! He painted this world alone. I do not mean that he was without mechanical assistance—he employed workmen to lay the plaster, to pounce the designs through the large and unwieldy cartoons, to fill in the architectural framework and minor decorative accessories—but it is no exaggeration to say that the whole of the artistic work proceeded from the hand of this one man. When but half of the vault was done, the impatient Pope insisted on uncovering it to the public; the mob rushed in and many necks were broken; the gentle Raphael came and saw, and sought by the aid of Bramante, to get the rest of the Chapel to paint. Michael Angelo went to the Pope and swore by all that was holy, that he would not tolerate such effrontery; Julius upheld him, and the Umbrian retreated, borrowing from the heroic style all that his facile talents could assimilate.

What happens to a man when he lies on his back for four years is described by Michael Angelo in the following sonnet addressed to his friend Giovanni da Pistoia. The translation is by Symonds.

I've grown a goitre by dwelling in this den—
As cats from stagnant streams in Lombardy,
Or in what other land they hap to be—
Which drives the belly close beneath the chin:
My beard turns up to heaven; my nape falls in,
Fixed on my spine: my breast-bone visibly
Grows like a harp: a rich embroidery
Bedews my face from brush-drops thick and thin.
My loins into my paunch like levers grind:
My buttock like a crupper bears my weight;
My feet unguided wander to and fro;
In front my skin grows loose and long; behind,

By bending it becomes more taut and strait;
Crosswise I strain me like a Syrian bow:
Whence false and quaint, I know
Must be the fruit of squinting brain and eye;
For ill can aim the gun that bends awry.
Come then, Giovanni, try
To succour my dead pictures and my fame,
Since foul I fare and painting is my shame.

Before the second portion was finished, the Pope, whose habit it was to inspect the work in person, climbed up to the deck and shouted to the artist:

"When are you going to finish my chapel?"

"When I can," Michael Angelo replied.

"When you can!" cried the choleric Pope, "when you can! Do you want me to throw you down from this scaffold?"

"You won't do that to me," muttered the painter under his breath.

Michael Angelo had planned to retouch certain places with ultramarine and gold, but as soon as the Pope had gone, ordered the scaffolding removed. Julius hearing what had been done, rushed back to the chapel.

"It needs gilding and more color!" he insisted.

"I'm through. What is missing is of no importance."

"You should touch it up with gold," replied the Pope.

"I have not observed that men wear gold," Michael Angelo said casually.

"It will look poor," Julius repeated.

"Those who are painted here were poor men."

The Pope smiled and gave the artist his blessing. The great job was done. Michael Angelo, knowing what poor and impertinent things words are, either big ones or little ones, wrote home to his father: "Today I finished the Chapel I was painting. The Pope is very well satisfied."

The physical difficulties which he successfully surmounted in the colossal undertaking are, after all, of secondary interest: our main concern is with the pictures. As a parallel we may remember that Beethoven composed symphonies when he was stone deaf, an extraordinary fact and possibly of profound aesthetic significance, but irrelevant until aesthetics and behaviorism shall have been scientifically correlated. Let us consider then the general nature of the decorations. If you should enter the Sistine Chapel with your head bowed, and then should suddenly look up, you would behold an intricate architectonic system supporting and combining single figures and groups of figures whose various actions symbolize the creation of the world, man's first disobedience and the prophecies of redemption; you would see Jeremiah and David and the sibyls seated on deep-set thrones and other forms apparently much closer; and lunettes, spandrels, caryatids, pilasters, and compartments opening into the vault of heaven and God Almighty Himself sailing through chaos. All this appears real and convincing, but the architecture is painted. Michael Angelo annihilated the existing shape of the ceiling and remodelled it to suit his own purposes.

You would see, in the central portion, the nine Histories representing the origin of the sun and moon and of man and woman, the temptation, the expulsion from Paradise, the Flood and the sacrifice and drunkenness of Noah. You would see on either side of the subject-pictures rows of alternate prophets and sibyls and above each of these powerful forms two seated slaves, nude and bursting with vitality. In the lunettes and recesses above the windows are scenes depicting the genealogy of Christ, and in the corners of the vault episodes symbolical of the redemption. Continuing to gaze into the firmament, you would discover, by degrees, that the decoration is not a heterogeneous mixture of nude and draped figures, but a world in which heaven's—and art's—first law has been wonderfully observed, that the effect of order and unity has been obtained by the basic architectural lines, the perfect consistency of the scenes and actors, and the binding harmony of the color, and that the danger of overpowering monotony has been avoided by the infinite diversity of the postures and the changes in the scale of the compartments and the size and number of figures grouped together.

The decorations in the Sistine Chapel constitute the greatest single-handed work of art that man has ever produced. So transcending indeed is this achievement that it reduces most of the paintings of the world to miniatures or granulated fragments. "Such," to quote Melville on Moby Dick, "is the virtue of a large and liberal theme. We expand to its bulk. To produce a mighty volume you must choose a mighty theme. No great and enduring work can ever be written upon the flea, though many there be who have tried it." And many there be who have tried to produce great and enduring work by painting pieces of still-life, or geometrical foetuses, or disembodied particles of pure form. Michael Angelo's theme had possessed the minds of artists since the Middle Ages, and though he treated it in his own way, he respected the story. It was appropriate; it allowed unfettered play of his favorite motif, the human figure, and he believed in it, believed in it with such absorbing passion that he created from it a world which Darwin and all the modern scientists have not been able to destroy.

I have seen the Sistine Chapel in the most auspicious circumstances—when the Pope was celebrating a special mass with all the cardinals in attendance—and the decorations in the vault struck me as being extraordinarily apposite. But they would, I think, be fully as congenial to any civilized religious ceremony, Catholic or Pagan. The reason is that Michael Angelo, as he developed his story, rose above representation and created a race of men and women whose very existence proves its humanity and its indestructible truth. He depicted God, for instance, an omnipotent conception possible only in paint, a majestic foreshortened personage who, in spite of his tremendous bulk, flies lightly through space as if impelled by some celestial means of locomotion. But who can think of this figure as the Supreme Being?

Look at Jeremiah! If this patriarch should spread his arms, the momentum generated would atomize a dozen Hebrew prophets. And the superb giant called Adam—a more delicately articulated and immeasurably richer and more vital figure than anything the Greeks ever did—should this dormant giant rise to his feet, and he seems perfectly capable of it, he would be more than a match for all the agents above and below the earth. The compressed energies of Eve are not less puissant, and the little children—they are only six-footers—are positively frolicsome as they hold up their heavy architectural burdens. Michael Angelo respected the biblical legend but he was not content with realistic presentment, with a pretty Italian garden for Eden's bower, an amorous nude couple for the first parents and Pope Julius, perhaps, for God the Father. The creation of the world was a mighty theme, but the Mosaic account could only be visualized in terms of his own experiences. Accordingly he made his own creation and placed within it a breed of men constructed with all his science and animated by the noblest outpourings of his soul.

His world is a universal tribute to a superior human race. Landscape is abolished or stripped to its barest essentials; the vegetable kingdom is symbolized by a bunch of herbs; Paradise is a waste land with a few rocks and a single tree. It is the story of heroic man in every phase of his development—his infancy, his fall and his redemption. But painting cannot tell a story as a continous narrative, it can only portray certain instants of action, and contemplation; certain moods which reflect the character of the artist. These great figures, let us understand, have no duplicates in nature: Michael Angelo made them from his fund of accumulated knowledge, inventing new proportions and new attitudes. If they seem to us perfectly possible, it is because they are so perfectly put together. Nothing in art is so difficult or so rare as a completely convincing human figure. Study any work by any master and you will discover without much trouble one or more organic weaknesses: a leg, while exquisitely drawn, seems detached from the trunk; the concealed fingers, you feel, do not actually exist; a foreshortening destroys the form; a head has too little depth, and so on. There are few weaknesses in Michael Angelo, and that is why many modern critics find him intolerable: they cannot expand to his bulk, and talk wistfully of Giotto and the primitives. He is the lord almighty of the naked form. One would think, on examining the vault of the Sistine Chapel, that he had used up every imaginable human attitude; but no, he returned thirty years later, a tired old man, and painted 200 more figures in *The Last Judgment* without a single repetition of posture! And these figures, let me add, are not exhibitions of anatomical skill but inter-related forms struggling under extreme emotional tension.

The much talked of despair of Michael Angelo is largely mythical. Personally, I find in the Sistine decorations the most glorious draughts of creative joy that an artist ever breathed into his creatures. Apart from their historical context, the validity of which has for most of us evaporated, these figures move us today because of their living reality. Is it not enough that they still exist and are unhampered by the disturbances of actual life? Is it not enough that the twenty nude slaves should be eternally and exhilaratingly young? That the old prophets should unburden their souls to us? What more can one ask than to dwell among the gods?

One word more. It has been said many times that Michael Angelo employed methods illegitimate to painting, that is to say, the methods of sculpture, and that his ruthless example contributed to the ruin of that art. This academic absurdity we may pass over in silent contempt. If he ruined painting that is the fault of those who came after him. When an artist selects from the field of his experiences those elements necessary to the building of his own world, and when he has successfully created his world and given it coherent vitality, then we need not quarrel about his methods, nor deplore the fact that he did not paint like a Venetian or a modern Frenchman.

With the Sistine Chapel the main fabric of his world was finished, his universe bounded, we might say. In the fifty years of life that remained to him he was to labor in many fields—in sculpture, painting, poetry, architecture, and engineering—and was destined, as the fates presiding over his birth had augured, to conceive stupendous things, but in most of his undertakings to accomplish only a fraction of what he had intended. He was continually at war with the world of fact; like every artist, he must needs adjust himself to an economic background or perish, and the background of the Renaissance, as Gibbon has characterized it, was "a society in which the loftiest cultural ideals and the most magnificent art were interfused with the bloodthirsty habits and degrading political morality of barbarians." It would be a waste of time to speculate on what Michael Angelo might have done had conditions been otherwise. Who shall say that his fights and misfortunes were not good for him? He never weakened and unceasing struggle toughened his spirit; his art never grew soft or sentimental or conciliatory. Nor did success enfeeble his purpose and lead him into cheap performances to please the mob.

In 1513, a year after the completion of the Chapel, Julius died, and his heirs promptly ordered Michael Angelo to go ahead with the interrupted tomb. This, as we know, was his cherished ambition, and in the next three years he produced the foundation and most of the extant sculptures—the two *Slaves* of the Louvre, a rough draft of the *Moses*, and the four troglodytes now in the Academy of Florence. In 1516 he scented trouble and wrote to his father: "I shall have to hurry, for soon, I fear, the new Pope will be after me." Leo X, son of Lorenzo the Magnificent, and a sensual aesthete, has been severely criticized for wasting Michael Angelo's powers at the height of their development, but a share of the blame must be charged against the artist's temperament. In view of his extraordinary attainments, it was believed that he could do anything and he was perfectly willing to try; in common with the other great artists of Italy he was not satisfied with anything less than universality, but the following instance, and in fact his whole life, is an illustration of how dearly universality was sometimes purchased.

Leo took a notion to complete the façade of San Lorenzo, the family church at Florence, and called for designs. Michael Angelo, understand, was not obliged to submit designs, but when he heard that Raphael and Bramante had entered the contest he could not resist the temptation to beat them. As ill-luck would have it, his plans were approved, and then, warming up to the job with intemperate enthusiasm, he informed the Pope: "I feel it in me to make a façade that shall be the mirror of architecture and sculpture to all Italy." Nothing came of the project except a wooden model and that has been lost. Somehow he had persuaded himself that he could finish the tomb and the church at the same time and in consequence squandered his years in futile negotiations, quarreling and cutting stone. Three of those years were spent in the mountains: he was forced by the Pope to work a new quarry belonging to dealers at Florence, and to transport his marbles to the sea. "A new road had to be constructed for several miles over the mountains with pickaxes and across the plains, which were very marshy, on piles. During this interval he entrusted his property to a faithful servant, writing him 'to tie up the vines in the garden, and not to use rotten sticks, to take care of the house and to go to confession.' "

Pneumonia claimed the corpulent Pope, and Michael Angelo did not weep. "Leo ruined me!" he declared. "Not wishing me to work on the tomb of Julius, he *pretended that he wanted to complete the façade of San Lorenzo*." The accusation must be taken as the cry of an artist who, in combating the objective realities of life, had finished but one work in ten years. But it is a mistake to regard those years as wasted. The immense physical and mental energies which he concentrated on his art could not have been continuously sustained, and it was a human necessity that he recover from one epic of toil in order to engage in another. Hard indeed was his life in the marble quarries, but still it must have been a holiday after his recumbent years in the Chapel. And besides, he was compelled to master mechanical engineering and to gain a practical knowledge of building, an experience which prepared him for future architectural triumphs. Up to this time he had considered architecture less as a logical construction than as a framework for sculpture; now he was better equipped to understand the reciprocal dependence of the two forms and to combine them harmoniously.

Leo was succeeded by a Fleming, a glum and frugal pontiff who died after a brief reign of twenty months. The next Pope chose the title of Clement VII, and Michael Angelo expressed the general satisfaction of the Italians in a letter to a friend: "You will have heard that Medici is made Pope; all the world seems to be delighted, and I think that here at Florence great things will soon be set on foot in our art." Great things in art and great woe for Italy! Clement was devoted to Michael Angelo and would gladly have made him a bosom companion had such a relationship been possible. "But Buonarroti frightens everybody," explained His Holiness, "even the Popes. When he comes to see me I always sit down and bid him be seated at once, feeling sure that he will do so without leave or licence." Buonarroti resented this charge of eccentricity. "The Pope," he said, "thinks I'm terrible because I mind my own business. An artist has no time for idle trivialities and flattery. Sometimes when I am talking to the Pope, I put this old felt hat on my head without thinking and talk to him very frankly—but even for that he does not kill me. On the contrary, he has given me a house and a pension. He knows that I serve him better by doing my work, than by standing before him all day, as the others do."

The Pope, wishing to secure a firmer hold on Michael Angelo, tried to make him promise that he would never marry and offered him an ecclesiastical sinecure as compensation. "I am wedded to my art," replied the sculptor, "and she has given me trouble enough. And if I became a monk, I should lose what little freedom you popes are now willing to grant me." Clement admired the man, and setting aside the lawful claims of the heirs of Julius, immediately commissioned him to furnish plans for the Laurentian Library and for a memorial chapel in the church of San Lorenzo. The two projects occupied him intermittently for thirteen years, brought forth his greatest sculpture, and disabled him permanently. "He eats little and poorly," said one of his friends in alarm, "sleeps badly and takes no rest. If he does not change his habits, he will die." But Michael Angelo had no intention of dying: at the age of sixty he could carve faster than three ordinary sculptors; his thin body shrivelled to a bag of bones but his energy was inexhaustible and his mind retained its lucid grandeur to the last.

During these dark years the Imperial army from the North marched into Italy and in the name of Charles V sacked the city of Rome. Clement, whose irritating policy had been partly responsible for the slaughter, hid himself away in Hadrian's Mausoleum for nine months, watching, in the words of Symonds, "the smoke ascend from desolated palaces and desecrated temples, hearing the wails of women and the groans of tortured men, the ribald jests of German drunkards and the curses of Castilian bandits." Gazing from the windows of the pagan tomb, the pusillanimous Pope borrowed the language of Job and cursed the day of his birth.

The sack of Rome roused the burghers of Florence to action: again the Medici were thrown out and the city fortified herself in her final stand for freedom. Michael Angelo's share in the tragedy was not an unmixed glory. His sympathies were with the men of Florence, and yet he was bound by contract to serve the tyrannous family whose name it was now death to mention. His brother died of the plague and at the risk of his own life, he held him in his arms while he expired; he took care of the widow and the children, placed his niece in a convent, and subsequently arranged her marriage, giving her many presents and a farm for a dowry. He was appointed governor and procurator-general over the construction and fortification of the city walls, and in this capacity erected the bastions which may still be seen on the hill of San Miniato. Experts have decided that while he protected the strategic position for the defence of the city, his constructive work was not exceptional and that he lacked the brilliant military genius of Leonardo da Vinci.

Thus employed he kept close watch on the other members of the Board of Control, suspecting treachery, and one night, in a sudden panic, secretly left the city, taking with him two companions and all his money—about 3000 ducats. In other words he used his official position to pass beyond the walls and deserted his post in time of war. In extenuation, it may be said that he was perfectly right in his suspicions of treason on the part of the leaders, and that he had good reason to believe that his own life was in danger because of his connections with the Medicean Pope, at this moment, Florence's bitterest enemy. He fled to Venice, realized his guilt, applied for and received safe-conduct, and in two months returned to Florence. Almost immediately he resumed his military duties and prevented the destruction of the bell-tower of San Miniato by shielding it with bales of wool against the cannonade of the enemy. In the midst of his military labors, so Vasari insists, he continued to work secretly on the Medicean tombs. When the city was delivered by local traitors into the hands of the Pope and the Prince of Orange, Michael Angelo went into hiding and but for Clement's intercession would probably have been put to death.

"You ought to be hanged," remarked the Pope. "You were one of the ringleaders against me. But I forgive you—for the glory of art. Finish the memorial chapel and come to Rome."

He toiled on for three more years and then, alarmed by the machinations of his enemies, suddenly left the stricken city for good. The Medicean Sacristy was only half-finished, but in these tombs the emotional sweep of his imaginative world reaches its climax, and the existing monuments, together with the two *Slaves* in the Louvre, comprise the greatest sculptures since Phidias designed his passive gods. And if it is the purpose of art—I mean the individual object—to stimulate the beholder into active response, to transport him into a state of mind which is not merely a moment of enjoyment but a deep-plumbing agitation that searches and purifies the soul, then we are justified in saying that the Chapel contains the greatest statues ever modelled by the hand of man. The vast and impressive monuments of the Egyptians and the Chinese, and the subtle and serene figures of the Greeks seem to be static and lacking in spiritual virility when compared to the best of Michael Angelo.

The Sacristy, as Wölfflin points out, "is one of those rare instances in the history of art in which building and figures were created not only contemporaneously but with a definite regard one for the other." Michael Angelo's first plan was to utilize the whole interior to commemorate the Medici family, but time and trouble compelled him to modify his plan into two mural tombs of similar configuration. Unfortunately, the Sacristy, like most of his art, is hard to see. Photographs give a false impression of spaciousness and height: actually there is scant distance from which to view the tombs. You see two squat sarcophagi, each of which supports on its convex lid two colossal nude forms, a male and female, whose reclining bodies carry the eye upward to the figure of a warrior seated within a niche. The sculptures seem to be oppressively amplified and to fill the entire room, perhaps a calculated measure. If so, the inclusion of eight additional figures, as the artist originally had in mind, would have produced an effect beyond human endurance.

Sculpture, perhaps the most difficult of all the arts, was Michael Angelo's *métier*, and when he was forced into other fields he was miserable. He was master of the architecture of the human body. He knew how to get his ideas and feelings into marble—to think, one might say in three dimensions; to endow stone with meaning and vitality; to create a form that thrills us with the accent of a new personality and invades our whole being like a fresh and powerful experience. A miraculous ability! "A statue," he said, "should be so compactly put together that it would suffer no injury if rolled down hill—" his own way of stating the inviolability of the block-form, the necessity of solidly fencing-in the imagination instead of disbursing it into flying fragments of arms and legs. His work, technically speaking, is a perfect expression of our tactile and motor experiences. His figures are synthetic structures—flexible bodies in attitudes of grave and terrible restraint, and the mind that conceived them felt their massive forms through and through; bound them together with muscles that weave in and out and up and down and around their giant frames; and filled them with the burden of tragic thought.

The sombre cast of his thought at this time is indicated by

the quatrain which he composed to correct the misleading rhapsodies written by a nameless poetaster in praise of *Night*, one of the four nudes in the Sacristy.

"Dear is my sleep, but more to be mere stone,
So long as ruin and dishonor reign:
To hear naught, to feel naught, is my great gain;
Then wake me not; speak in an undertone."

I do not cite these verses as criticism but to remind the reader of the symbolical implications of the statues. It is self-evident that the art of the man who defended the honor of Florence, and who saw his native city sold by traitors, should have been colored by his bitter experiences; and it is one of the grimmest pieces of irony on record that he should have used his art to perpetuate the name of the pernicious family that enslaved and ruined Florence and made it intolerable as a dwelling place of an honest man! As an artist, old loyalties running back to Lorenzo the Magnificent bound him to the Medici; as a republican, he could not choose but aid in the extermination of tyrants. Thus, in carving the figures of the two warriors—obscure dukes whom he could not respect—he idealized them into contemplative types. When asked why he did not make portrait studies, he answered, "In a thousand—nay in a hundred years, no one will know or care who they were." The helmeted warrior was called *Il Penseroso* by the patriots of Florence and was regarded as the symbol of one "condemned to contemplate forever the woes of Italy he helped to cause."

The four nudes have been traditionally named *Day* and *Night*, *Morning* and *Evening*. The names, with reservations, are as fitting as any that might be chosen. The figures do seem to personify certain abstract states, but just what, it is impossible to define. Reactions vary according to temperament. Perhaps *Evening* typifies the evening of life? It may be that *Night*, a woman of many pregnancies, nurses in the depths of her slumbering despair eternal shame for the sons of men? Perhaps the awakening of the soul and the closing sadness of life are expressed here? But only in a general way, in the pervading tone of tragedy, can the figures now be related to a given historical event. No matter how profoundly afflicted Michael Angelo may have been by the woes of Italy, his despair, or a good part of it, was submerged in a store of creative energy when he encountered the marble block. In modelling the figures he was guided by his cumulative knowledge of forms and of art and by the infinite variety of experiences bound up in those forms; and the finished product is too complex an organism to be translated into a single mood or emotion.

When the modern man looks at the tombs of the Medici, he is not carried back to the woes of Florence: he is moved by something much closer, something that enters immediately and directly into the spirit. He has never found such forms in real life and he never will. He has seen many nude figures but he cannot recall one of them. These figures, once seen, will never be forgotten. Their marble forms stand for the complex personality—the soul, if you please, of Michael Angelo—and the qualities which that great personality possessed. We cannot respond to all those qualities but only to such as exist within ourselves. Our latent feelings and ideas are here magnified and presented powerfully in concrete form. Our spirits expand to acknowledge kinship with forms far richer in humanity than those of our mundane intercourse. We identify ourselves with a stronger and finer race, and our souls are emptied of all that is mean and weak and trivial and submissive. The experience is ennobling. We have penetrated to the heart of Michael Angelo's world; we emerge the better for it.

The peculiar property of sculpture—within intelligent limits, of course—to excite our emotions with a rising scale of distinctness and intensity as it approaches the abstract, may be illustrated by contrasting an early work of Michael Angelo's, the *Pietà* of St. Peter's, with the *Madonna and Child* of the Medici Chapel. In the former the drapery is wrought carefully and elaborately, and great emphasis placed upon facial characterizations; in the latter the block of marble seems to have been altered but little—as if the sculptor, with enormous manual strength, had simply pressed his material into human shape. The effect of the Medici statues is immeasurably more direct and powerful. This must not be taken as a plea for a purely abstract art, that is, an art where representation is completely abolished; for every rhythm and movement contributes to a human attitude and the total effect is what it should be—a mother holding a child. But by removing every disturbing detail and by uniting the two figures into a single compact unit, Michael Angelo created a sculptural form which assails the spirit with the utmost simplicity and concentration.

He was now in his sixtieth year, and having satisfactorily discharged his debt to the Medici, went to Rome with the expectation of finishing that old and agonizing business, the tomb of Julius. But the new Pope, Paul III, soon put an end to his hopes. "For thirty years," exclaimed Paul, "I have cherished a desire for your services, and now that I am Pope, may I not indulge it? Where is the contract? I mean to tear it up." Truthfully indeed did Michael Angelo complain "that he served the Popes, but under compulsion." So acute was his distress of mind at the abrogation of the contract that he wrote to the Pope's representative: "For the loyalty of thirty-six years, do I deserve no better fate? Painting and sculpture, labor and good faith, have been my ruin. Better would it have been for me if I had set myself to making sulphur matches in my youth! Your lordship tells me that I must begin to paint. I answer that one paints with the brain and not with the hands, and he who has not his brains at his command produces work that shames him. I am daily stoned [by the heirs of Julius] as though I had crucified Christ."

He spoke bluntly and bitterly, but he always spoke like a man. Unlike Goethe, he did not parade through life with the grand condescension of a demi-god; unlike Cellini, he never bragged nor lied; nor was he, like Balzac, filled with monstrous conceit and gross desires for fame. And in his whole life he produced not one cheap or unworthy piece of art.

Paul appointed him chief architect, sculptor and painter at

Michael Angelo: SKETCH FOR HEAD OF A SIBYL.

British Museum, London

the Vatican and ordered him to decorate the end wall of the Sistine Chapel. The wall had already been painted by Perugino, for whom Michael Angelo had nothing but contempt, calling him a dolt and a blockhead. Unhesitatingly he destroyed the old frescoes and substituted his own. For seven years he painted on a theme which had occupied the minds of artists from the Ninth Century, and when the doors of the Chapel were again opened *The Last Judgment* was revealed to the world with a finality of expression that no painter has dared to challenge. *The Last Judgment*, in spite of all that has been said against it—the tendency of an old man to rely upon his scientific knowledge of anatomy instead of refreshing his mind with new experiences, and the devitalizing consequences; the confusing masses of figures; the Herculean Christ—remains one of the great paintings of the world.

When the fresco was uncovered, the hypocrites of Italy who appeared for the first time in an age of moral laxity and refined indecency, raised a chorus of defamation. The loudest voice in the chorus issued from the foul mouth of Aretino whose attempts to flatter a drawing out of Michael Angelo had been unrewarded. Here is an extract from one of his letters to the artist.

"The pagans, when they modelled a Diana, gave her clothes; when they made a naked Venus, they hid the parts which are not shown by the hand of modesty. And here there comes a Christian, who, because he rates art higher than the faith, deems it a royal spectacle to portray martyrs and virgins in improper attitudes, to show men dragged down by their shame, before which things houses of ill-fame would shut their eyes. Your art would be at home in some bagnio, certainly not in the highest chapel of the world."

Aretino, a blackmailer by profession, kept a harem in his house at Venice, displayed a picture of the Virgin as a portrait of his mother, a courtesan, and boasted that he was, himself, the original Antichrist. To these infamous slanders the artist replied, "They created a Michael Angelo out of the stuff of which their own vile hearts were made." With the Pope's master of ceremonies, however, he dealt more severely. On hearing that this functionary had publicly denounced the nakedness of the fresco, Michael Angelo painted a recognizable portrait of him, with a pair of horns on his head and a serpent coiled around his waist, and thrust him into a corner of Hell—the right hand corner of *The Last Judgment.* The poor hypocrite, now the laughing-stock of Rome, appealed to the Vatican, but the Pope, who was not without humor, gave him no comfort. "If the painter had sent you to Purgatory, I would have used all my efforts to get you out—but I have no jurisdiction in Hell." Some years later Paul IV decided to expurgate the picture, but first sent a messenger to confer with Michael Angelo. "Tell His Holiness," the artist answered, "that to reform a picture is a small matter. Let him look to setting the world in order." The Pope entrusted the job to the painter, Daniele da Volterra, whose judiciously placed draperies brought him undying fame as *Il Braghettone*, or the breeches-maker. More clothing was prescribed by Pius V; and so, with one breech-clout and another, *The Last Judgment* has been sadly damaged in color and composition.

In his declining years, in Rome, Michael Angelo turned frequently to poetry as an outlet for his creative powers. Verse was no stranger to him—he had practiced writing it since his youth—but in old age, drawing upon two strong sources of inspiration, he used it to express sentiments and passions foreign to the plastic arts. When he was sixty-three, he met Vittoria Colonna, a widow of noble birth, forty-six, childless and famous in literary circles for her religious verses. She wrote him chaste and gentle letters and brought a little joy to his weary, overworked mind. On Sunday mornings, in a convent in Rome, Vittoria Colonna and her friends gathered together to discuss in a very lofty strain the kingdom of the spirit. These conversations were preserved by one of the group, a Portuguese painter, who gives us a charming picture of Michael Angelo holding forth to his enraptured audience. The old master for once forgot his brusqueness and his enemies, and uttered more truths about art, in a given space, than any man before or since. And a woman inspired him? Possibly.

She was not a fascinating widow: she was, in fact, angular and ugly, with a sharp hard face, high brow, long nose, and prominent chin. Her charms were spiritual and her friendship with Michael Angelo purely Platonic. She discovered his hidden vein of tenderness and "her love," he said, "kept his old heart, so near the point of death, alive." He gave her several magnificent drawings of the Crucifixion, and addressed a series of sonnets to her, dry, knotty poems, crackling with passionate abstractions but totally devoid of physical warmth. When Vittoria Colonna died, he regretted that "when he went to visit her upon the moment of her passage from this life, he did not kiss her forehead, as he did kiss her hand."

The other source of inspiration was Tomasso Cavalieri, described by a contemporary poet, as "a young Roman of very noble origin, incomparable physical beauty, excellent intelligence and graceful behavior." To this young man Michael Angelo wrote several epistles of labored and extravagant affection and a number of sonnets which have been compared to those of Shakespeare and which his grand-nephew altered so as to persuade posterity that the sentiments had been inspired by Vittoria Colonna. Both sets of documents have provided a feast for the Freudians. To the modern mind, or perhaps I should say, to the Victorian mind, the tone of the communications may appear singular and absurd, but in Michael Angelo's friends neither his conduct nor his written words aroused the slightest anxiety or suspicions of an irregular attachment. The poems bear less resemblance to the sonnets of Shakespeare than do the figures in the Sistine Chapel to the nudes of Rubens. Michael Angelo, like many other artists, notably Plato, esteemed beauty as an absolute quality dissociated from sex, and when he beheld any superior manifestation of it, either mental or physical, male or female, he was powerfully affected, and became, as he said himself, a worshiper. In the sonnets and letters he has expressed—and rather badly for him—his appreciation of abstract, or "divine beauty," a phrase common enough in his day; but the fact that the object of his addresses was a man has filled the introspective psychologists with unholy horror. Anyone who deduces from these writings evidence of a sexual relationship would find incest in the conjunction of the planets.

The infirmities of age—gout, gall-stones and fever—slowly weakened the old artist and he grew more and more careless in his habits. "He wore stockings of dog-skin," so Vasari tells us, "for months together, and when these were removed, the skin of the leg sometimes came with them. Over his stockings he had boots of Cordovan leather, as a protection against swellings, to which he had become liable." He lived by himself in Rome, with one servant to take care of him, to saddle his horse, and feed his cats and his fowls. "I live alone," he said with his grotesque humor, "confined like the pith in a tree. My teeth rattle like the keys of a musical instrument; my face is a scarecrow; in one ear a spider spins its web, in the other a cricket chirps all night; my catarrh rattles in my throat and will not let me sleep. This is the end to which art, which proves my glory, has brought me."

He was too old for sculpture but he could not resist the joy of it—his greatest joy in life. His last work in marble is the unfinished *Deposition from the Cross* which stands in the dark behind the high altar of the Duomo in Florence. He began this Pietà purely for the love of it, but as the work developed, he designed it for his own monument, carving the figure of Nicodemus, who holds the body of the dead Christ, after his own likeness. But his hand was unequal to the task, and in an old man's rage, he seized a hammer and began to demolish the group. His strength failed him; and angrier than ever, he gave the broken marble to his servant. He used to work on the Pietà at night, with a candle stuck in a cap made of heavy paper. One night Vasari called upon him, and while they were talking, began to examine the leg of Christ "on which Michael Angelo was working. To prevent Vasari from seeing this, he suffered the lamp to fall from his hand and they remained in darkness. Then he remarked, 'I am so old that death often pulls me by the cape, and bids me go with him; some day I shall fall myself, like this lamp, and the light of life will be extinguished.' "

When Renoir, in extreme age, was stricken with paralysis, he took up sculpture, modelling his beloved nudes in clay for his own amusement. Rodin, in a resentful spirit, asked him why he did not stick to painting. "You see," answered Renoir with a smile, "I am too old to paint. I must do something easier." With Michael Angelo it was the other way round. Sculpture meant cutting marble and not fumbling with clay, and when the exercise became too strenuous, he returned to his brushes with an ease and vigor that astonished the jealous painters who had whispered to the Pope that the old man was getting senile. "If I am in my second childhood," remarked Michael Angelo, "I might as well act up to the part and begin to paint." In his seventy-second year he completed the frescoes in the Pauline Chapel—the *Conversion of St. Paul* and the *Crucifixion of St. Peter*. There is nothing senile in these pictures. The wonderful freshness, the living, leaping vitality of his first decorations in the Sistine Chapel, are missing, but in powerful construction and command of the figure, his last work in paint is fully as distinguished as his early frescoes.

Henceforth he devoted himself to architecture and engineering, and the abstract elements of his world come to the front. Life, which had never tempted him into luxuries, now afforded his haggard body little solace, and his only comfort was in the use of his brain. He journeyed to a famous mineral spring to drink the medicinal waters and returned to Rome with his bladder much improved. He still carried on a voluminous correspondence with the remaining members of the Buonarroti family, at Florence, advising them in the management of his properties, warning his niece not to send him such fancy shirts; and instructing his nephew to choose a plain woman for a wife. The people of Florence begged him to spend his last years among them, offering to make him Senator, but the younger Medici were a treacherous lot, and he deemed it safer to remain away from them. Besides, he had work to do. As chief architect to the

Pope, he was crowded with commissions, and with his usual creative avarice, he undertook more than he could fulfil. The architect whom he had displaced organized forces against him and made the rest of his life a continual row. He gave them better than he received, lashing them with a tongue that had lost none of its sharpness. A deputation of cardinals came to consult with him on the lighting of St. Peter's. "You never told us about your plans," said one. "I am not," retorted Michael Angelo, "nor do I mean to be obliged to tell your lordship or anybody else what I ought or wish to do. It is your business to provide money, and to see that it is not stolen. As regards the plans of the building, you leave those to me."

After his death, his plans were either lost or set aside, and he cannot be held responsible for the present clumsiness of St. Peter's. The dome alone is his, and all the architects, past and present, who have discounted his capacities as a builder, have looked up to this vast cupola with unqualified veneration. It is one of the masterpieces of architecture. With the great dome Michael Angelo's world is complete. It is the crowning triumph of his imagination. Through the force of its mighty lines, it carries us upward, higher and higher, into the pure realm of the spirit.

In his eighty-ninth year he was bothered by spells of sleepiness, but he was strong enough to ride out every afternoon to inspect his building. He discovered that his men were cheating him in their purchases of lime and his blood warmed again. Winter came, and he could no longer venture from his house. He crept close to the fire and with a piece of red chalk made designs for a great picture of the Crucifixion. A slow fever began to consume him and he made his will, "leaving his soul to God, his body to the earth, and his goods to his nearest relations." His goods consisted of several unfinished statues, a few drawings, six houses and seven estates in Florence, and in a sealed cash box, 8000 crowns—the equivalent of $100,000 in modern money.

On the afternoon of February 18, 1564, the light of life was extinguished.

CHAPTER

VI

VENICE: THE COURTESAN CITY

VENICE was the courtesan of the Italian Renaissance. During her long youth she grew slowly and warily, developing her talents for adventure and luxury, mastering the arts of intercourse and espionage; when she was fully grown—for a courtesan to be at her best must be amply formed, practiced in cunning and competent to traffic with strangers—she devoted her strength and her stolen wealth to the leisured cultivation of sensual splendor. Secure, isolated and insolent, she avoided all entangling alliances, at the same time maintaining spies and agents in every leading city so that her commercial supremacy might not be imperilled. Like all courtesans her tastes were extravagant, her desires insatiable; she loved color and excessive ornamentation, music and parades, costly trinkets, fantastic houses, lavish display—everything that appealed to the eye and catered to a passion for pleasure. Her patrician keepers called her the bride of the Adriatic. Bride she never was: queen perhaps, but mistress always. Much as she loved ceremonies, she had no place in her glittering selfishness for the rites of marriage.

The merchants of Venice were gentlemen, those of Florence only titled parvenus. Not one of them was ever known to be of the party of Luther or Calvin. Through their mouthpiece, Aretino, they sang, "Eat, drink and be merry, like liberal men." And liberal men they were unquestionably, although they allowed no one a voice in the government save those nobles whose names were inscribed in the book of Gold. They made their city the safest and most humanely regulated in Italy; there were no foreign invasions, no internal rebellions, no class rivalries;

to safeguard their commerce they relied upon a large and powerful navy, and when they had troubles on land, employed mercenaries to fight their battles. That boundless individualism which was the glory and ruination of Florence did not flourish in Venice, and speedy and cruel remedies were prescribed for busy-bodies with political ambitions. The people were perfectly content to leave the business of ruling to the secret councils of the crop-headed nobles; pleasure was a state institution; wealth was equitably distributed; fathers provided their sons with mistresses; every young nun had her cavalier; the carnival lasted for six months; there were adequate foundling hospitals; life was exciting and delightful, and no one gave thought of the hereafter.

The patrician lovers of the courtesan of the Adriatic never wearied of her charms. She was avaricious and ingratiating, cruel and irresistibly voluptuous. She demanded the treasures of the East and the West, and her merchants, to gratify her rich desires, resorted to spoliation and piracy. They sold one of the Crusades to their own profit and bled their inland tributaries without conscience; to appease the whims of their mistress they stole the ashes of St. Mark and buried them in a church which remains the most engaging and gorgeous example of courtesan taste that has ever been put together; they welcomed foreign traders and money-changers—Jews, Germans, Arabs, Greeks and Armenians—offering them amorous excitement in return for gold; they bought and sold slaves, white Circassian girls for the Turks and for the education of young nobles, black Ethiopian monsters for the galleys; they rejected papal authority, but were kind to renegade priests and monks; from the East they learned silk-weaving, glass-blowing, and the more subtle Asiatic vices; to prepare young girls for the fullest enjoyment of life they recommended Aretino's handbook for the instruction of courtesans; and most remarkable of all, by a magical blending of the styles of the Goths and the Orientals, they created a city which intoxicated the senses, a perfect setting for their profane goddess of pleasure.

Towards the close of the fifteenth century Leonardo da Vinci came to Venice. The city was then at meridian glory, "the jewel-casket of the world," as one of her paramours expressed it. He did not stay long: something of an aristocrat himself and accustomed to the splendor of court life, he found the pageantry of Venice a little rank and tinged with frivolity. It was too obvious, this enthronement of sensuality, this persistent stimulation of physical desires. He saw the Doge marching with his costumed servitors into St. Mark's, a magnificent affair, but on learning that it was only one of his thirty-six annual processions to the various churches, he turned aside wearily. When told that the baptism of a noble's son was attended by 150 godfathers he could not conceal his impatience to travel. He saw boat races on the Grand Canal in which crews of girls bent to the oars like men, but he did not care for sunburnt Amazons with strained muscles. He saw chambermaids decorated with pearls and Eastern finery, but he did not care for gaudy servants; he watched haughty strumpets, as they embarked in their gondolas after mass to visit the palaces of lords; he saw them on balconies exchanging signals with members of the Grand Council; and on the roofs of houses playing with doves, dogs and parrots, or bleaching their hair in the sun. With the eye of an architect he examined the work of the Venetian builders; the palaces inlaid with marble and mosaics; the arched windows; the domes and minarets; the rows of houses shining like a spectrum; the façades emblazoned with frescoes; the flags, banners and pavilions. It was exquisite and exciting to the eye, but spectacular and indiscriminate. A confusion of color and ornament, an embroidered bagnio.

Venice was too much for Leonardo. The poverty of intellectual pursuits, the absence of deeper feelings and dramatic complications, the perpetual flaunting of one phase of life, disheartened him. Venice produced no poets, no sculptors, no chroniclers, no school of literature; even her architects were imported and most of her painters were provincials. In Florence an artist was a master of all the arts of design, an architect, sculptor, scientist, engineer and humanist; in Venice he was merely a painter. And the freedom of expression accorded to the Florentines in their public commissions, enabling them to depict, in their own way, themes of the profoundest human significance and intellectual content was denied to the Venetian decorators. The aristocrats demanded of painting that it advertise the republic, celebrate her charms, and flatter her rulers.

Leonardo was not an orthodox believer, but the spiritual emptiness of Venice, and the narrow outlook of her artists palled upon him. In this riotous atmosphere there was no stimulus to philosophical speculation, scientific inquiry and the solving of mysteries. An art that appealed almost entirely to feminine sensibilities could not long detain him; he did not work for years on a picture merely to amuse people, or to produce a shining object which men should praise as they praised their mistresses, or enjoy for its surface brilliancy as they enjoyed stuffs and precious stones. To him art was essentially an affair of the mind, a constructive problem to be solved by science and imagination. But the courtesan city had no use for thinking men. Once she had called in a Greek scholar to educate her, but discovering that education was not to be had lightly, withdrew her favors and allowed the poor humanist to die of starvation. Leonardo returned to Florence. Better the city of Savonarola with its villainies and disorders than the suffocating splendor of Venice.

It is hard to draw distinctions between the various historical manifestations of sensuality. The delirious vices of Babylon, the orgies of imperial Rome, the sottish bestiality of Restoration England and the pomaded lechery of eighteenth century France all seem to be identical occurrences of ungovernable energy. Venice, however, was a unique city: by raising pleasure to the rank of a state institution, by entrusting its administration to nobles who were at once economists and connoisseurs, and by making it easily accessible to all classes, she kept her sensuality free from obscenity and from degenerating into stupid debauchery. When a rich and flourishing city employs its highest inventive genius for the glorification of a common ideal, we may expect an art of immediate and widespread popularity. That is precisely what happened in Venice. Her painters invested pleasure with poetic dignity, a lustrous romantic grandeur and refinement consistent with the ideals of a city that existed for the exquisite enjoyment of life. For a courtesan she was singularly well-behaved and orderly, abiding under the same form of government for five centuries. Eventually, after Napoleon had ruined her, she fell into viciousness and decay; at the beginning of the nineteenth century she was known as the brothel of Europe and Lord Byron came to dwell with her.

Painting came late to Venice. While her merchants and traders were accumulating wealth and establishing commercial relations with the East, she had no time for art, and it was not until the completion of the Ducal Palace in 1365 that she gave official attention to the matter. Before that date painting was more or less an applied art regulated by the guilds and designed to meet the requirements of the local churches; it was tame and mediocre, adhering closely to the Byzantine style and exhibiting no signs of originality except in the use of color which was soon to become the distinguishing characteristic of the great Venetian masters. When it was discovered that no native painters were equal to the task of decorating the Ducal Palace, the city, constrained to look elsewhere for talent, summoned Gentile da Fabriano, Pisanello of Verona, and Antonello da Messina, a Sicilian. Those three men practically killed the cobwebbed Byzantine tradition, and by the example of an authentic style of narration and portraiture, directed the attention of the Venetians to the rich and picturesque materials of their own environment. Antonello, a marvellous craftsman who is supposed to have traveled in Flanders, introduced superior methods of painting in oil, a fact of the first importance in the technical development of the Venetian school. But it was not oil painting as practiced by artists from Velasquez down to the present time: Antonello and his pupils at Venice, executed the body of their canvases in tempera, adding transparent glazes in oil to enhance the intensity of the colors.

The real beginnings of Venetian art are centered in one family, the Bellini, father and sons. Jacopo, the father, was an eccentric and inquisitive old gentleman and a great traveller. He wandered through Italy, notebook in hand, visiting Florence and Rome and making sketches of all sorts of things, elaborate architectural settings, animals, antiquities, mountains, cities, and Madonnas. On his return to Venice, he stopped at Padua, at that moment the home of Francesco Squarcione, perhaps the most famous of all Renaissance teachers of art. Squarcione, an iron disciplinarian and humanist, is said to have attracted to his academy 140 pupils, foremost of whom was Mantegna, and to have given them the severest training in anatomy, perspective and the imitation of the antique. From the classic school of Padua, but particularly from Mantegna to whom he gave his daughter in marriage, Jacopo Bellini acquired a scientific knowledge of painting and this knowledge he imparted to his sons Gentile and Giovanni.

Gentile Bellini, less imaginative than his brother, gained renown for his church decorations and his portraits, but his position as one of the founders of Venetian art rests mainly upon his processional pictures. Turning from the religious tradition, which had never been very marked in Venice, he entered into the pageantry of the city, portraying the stately crowds, the marching priests, the background of light and air and color, with a scenic truth that far surpassed the realistic efforts of the Florentines. Giovanni, the great glory of the Bellini family and the first of the Venetian masters, lived long and passed through many stages of development, painting Madonnas, portraits, altarpieces, landscapes, allegories and pastorals and if his fame has been dimmed by his pupils Giorgione and Titian, and by Tintoretto and Veronese, it is because his followers profited by his discoveries and carried them forward to a higher degree of perfection. Giovanni was a man of remarkably good sense and reasonableness: nothing failed to excite him, but nothing excited him immoderately; he was incapable of tragic passions, but equally incapable of banality and violence; his Madonnas are too sweet and self-possessed to pass as the Mother of God; but they are thoroughly human and free from the witch-like agonies of the earlier Florentine school. Though painter to the State, he was never perfunctory and his flattery was always dressed in dignified raiment; in the use of color and of light and shade as a means to bind his forms together in a harmony of tones, he anticipated Rubens and Rembrandt.

Once the courtesan of the Adriatic had tasted the joys of self-glorification, she smiled upon painting and it flourished as no art had ever flourished before. It abandoned the guild for the dealer; it spread from the church to the Schools, or Mutual Aid Societies, from the palace to the private house; it ceased to be the servant of architecture and circulated in the form of the easel-picture; it appeared as portraiture, pageantry, legend and pastorals—anything that was happy and voluptuous and untouched by the sterner realities of life; it shone in the naked bosom of the city like a cluster of jewels. If ever painting was a popular art, a common language understood and relished by a whole community, it was in Venice in the first half of the sixteenth century. And this popular conception of painting has held to the present day, for the Venetians are generally credited with having brought the element of beauty into picture making. We must beware of that word beauty: if we restrict it to the radiant clarified sensuality of Giorgione and Titian, then what shall we say of the frescoes of Masaccio and Michael Angelo? What shall we say of El Greco and Rembrandt? Of Daumier and Cézanne? We shall say with Havelock Ellis that "beauty is not always soft and smooth, but more often than not filled with harshness and asperity."

The aim and end of Venice was the celebration of pleasure; and her painters with untroubled consciences reflected this singleness of purpose. The struggles and miseries of man; his abjectness and nobility; his weakness and his might; the qualities of courage and pity; the whole range of human passions—all these she arrogantly ruled out of her art, content to play upon a single mood. Whatever man or woman she painted she must decorate with aristocratic graces; Carpaccio presents St. Ursula exactly as if she were a charming Venetian girl; Veronese's *Marriage at Cana* is a local feast attended by living characters including the artist himself and his friends, Titian and Tintoretto.

The name of Giorgione rings with the sound of gold; his art charms us with the golden gleams of magic. His masterpiece, the *Concert Champêtre*, or *Pastoral Symphony* in the Louvre, is a landscape with figures: at the left, a large nude woman holds a crystal jug over the mouth of a well; at the right, a seated nude woman of the same generous proportions fingers a shepherd's pipe; in the centre a young courtier splendidly clad strums a lute while his companion, a youth in sylvan garb, looks on serenely. If this bald description means anything at all, it means that the scene, as an actuality, is frankly preposterous. Not in the environs of Venice nor anywhere else did young ladies roam the countryside without any clothes on; nothing happens in this picture and there is no apparent reason why these four people, two of them undressed, two of them overdressed, should be where they are and doing what they are doing; conceivably such a foregathering might have taken place in a bagnio, but in that case, the attitude of the youths would not have been one of indifference. I stress the illogical nature of the *Pastoral Symphony* only to point out more clearly the miracle Giorgione has brought to pass. The work does not offend our sense of fitness, nor is anyone, not even a Scotch aesthetician, conscious of any representational incongruity.

The picture is a young man's dream, the luxurious vision of a hedonist who has enjoyed the charms of his mistress, and by the poetic magic of his brush, has transformed his sensual experiences into a harmony of supreme loveliness. To say that Giorgione achieved the miracle by means of light and color is to repeat a half-truth. Manet, a technician of rare excellence, attempted a modern version of the theme—and failed: he could not imitate, much less experience, that unforced delight in the physical world which was the natural propensity of the Venetians. Giorgione was not a great draughtsman: the right leg of the seated nude is formless and flat as a board, and the head of the lute-player is a silhouette. Such carelessness in Michael Angelo, whose art depends upon the strength and construction of the figure, would be fatal; in Giorgione it is immaterial. When a painter arrives at such absolute perfection of purpose, we need not cavil at his draughtsmanship. He is one of the great colorists: his palette compared to that of the modern Impressionists is sombre rather than brilliant, but the balance of tones and values —the relation of tones in a scale of light and dark—is flawless. A glowing envelope of light and air drifts over the scene binding the figures to the landscape; the color seems to be embedded in the forms—in the golden nudes, the red costume of the lute player, the light that breaks among the trees, the faint blue hills, and the streak of clouds. In the *Pastoral Symphony*, so named because the harmony of light and color and form seems to affect us like a musical composition, Giorgione has perpetuated the spirit of youth so typical of the Venetian Renaissance. This spirit, of course, is not dead: it is present in varying degrees in all of us, but with Giorgione it was the whole of life, and he gave to it a perfection of expression that no modern painter, unless it be Renoir, has ever approached.

If Giorgione glorifies the sensual youth of Venice, Paolo Veronese celebrates her magnificent maturity. Changing the golden notes of the earlier artists into lighter, crisper tones of grey and silver, Veronese raises pageantry, ceremonials and local episodes, which with Carpaccio and Gentile Bellini are delightful genre pieces, to a high level of decorative splendor. He loved the free, healthy and unrestrained existence of Venice; her strapping, sportive nudity; her frank and full enjoyment of good things; her nobles who behaved like nobles; her gorgeous architecture; and all his pictures, whether biblical histories, mythologies, or contemporary festivals, are rejoicings in the untrammelled amplitude of the city of charm. Berenson has noted that Veronese's "chief employers were the monasteries," adding slyly that "the joyous worldliness and the qualities which we find in his huge pictures of feasts seem to have been particularly welcome to those who were expected to make their meat and drink of the very opposite qualities." On one occasion the Tribunal of the Holy Office objected to the presence of "fools, drunken Germans, dwarfs and other follies," in a sacred picture and demanded an explanation. Veronese answered that he had made the Scriptures not only delightful but seductive and that he should be commended for his good offices.

The Venetians called Tintoretto, "The Thunderbolt" because of his terrible energy and frightening impulsiveness. He is one of the world's most prolific painters, his enormous works in square feet amounting to ten times the product of Titian's industrious brush; his *Paradise* in the Ducal Palace, completed when he was seventy years old, measures seventy-five by thirty feet, and contains 500 figures! Many of his pictures, owing to the rapidity of execution, are marred by inferior parts and time has played havoc with much of his color, but judged by his best work of which a vast quantity survives in good condition, he remains one of the most original and amazing artists of all time. Tintoretto was an odd and surprising character in Venice: a domestic fellow with a happy family of legitimate children, he had an annoying habit of accepting commissions for the love of art and not for pay. He is the one great draughtsman of the Venetian school, the only painter rivalling the Florentines in monumental design. "The drawing of Michael Angelo and the coloring of Titian," he wrote on the walls of his studio; and it may fairly be said that what Michael Angelo accomplished with the single figure, he accomplished with groups of figures. In his portraits he does honor to the splendor of his native city, but with a deeper humanity than we find in Titian; in his nudes he lends dignity and grandeur to nakedness; like Veronese he fills his religious pictures with the people of his own time, not however to emphasize elegance and display, but as a pretext for dramatic action. There is, I think, more energy and agitation in his huge designs than drama, but no one can question the powerful effect of his groupings. Through his mastery of light and shadow and movement, and his ability to compose his figures in a convincing world of three dimensions, Tintoretto gave a greater impetus to the modernization of painting than any other man in Venice, and his influence has been transmitted by the Spanish, Flemish and French schools to artists of the present day.

It requires no very searching analysis of the habits, tastes and desires of man to explain the popularity of Venetian painting. The notion that the artists of Venice, as a school, caught and expressed the spirit of youth, the gladness of the morning of life, is not altogether tenable when we bring against it the cold fact that the city in the first centuries of her development produced no art worth mentioning, and not until she was adult and rich and calculating did she pretend to culture and seek in painting an adornment for her possessions. Just as the modern millionaire, choosing his mistress for her fleshly masteries, lavishes upon her all the garniture that money can buy, has her painted by fashionable artists, puts her on the stage and in the public prints, and in the end, deceived himself, tries to pass her off as a lady of quality, so did the Venetians enjoy and exploit their city and invent a resplendent style of painting as an ornament to her physical pre-occupations.

The Venetians are the great decorators of sensuality. They disguise the yahoo that dwells in all of us and adorn man, the animal, with the qualities of civility and splendor. They go further: experts in the use of light and color and atmosphere, in smooth surfaces, arcadian landscapes, romantic costumes and delicately rounded forms, they create pictures which assail the senses with an appeal so enchanting and inescapable that we forget the basic voluptuous facts and ascribe to them the higher attributes of spiritual ecstasy and contemplative imagination. It is no wonder that such an art continues to be popular. There is not one of us but loves to see himself as an aristocratic animal, dignified in actions which are without intrinsic dignity, romantic in vulgar rôles, poetic in an age of prose. The Venetians endow commonplace ideals with pompous distinction and grandeur; they paint the physical side of man with an heroic touch. If this is what painting is for—and there are many who seem to think so—then the Venetians stand alone in art. The French, their closest competitors, have done well, but there is too much artifice in their adornment of pleasure, and not a little sham in their elaborate tact and good taste. The men of Venice serve up sensuality as a feast for the gods.

Titian: PORTRAIT OF ARTIST.

Berlin Gallery

CHAPTER

VII

TITIAN

WHEN his exceptionally prolonged and fruitful career came to an end in 1576, Titian was acclaimed by his countrymen as "the father of modern painting." This epithet, I find, has caught the critical fancy, and if we first consider its true meaning, it will serve as well as another to indicate the changing social conditions which made the new, or modern art, possible. In the representation of universal passions, that is to say, of the pity, tenderness and tragedy that move the heart of man to anguish or joy, Titian is manifestly inferior to Giotto; in scientific knowledge and psychological penetration into the springs of human emotions, he is not to be mentioned in the same breath as that thoroughly modern man Leonardo da Vinci; nor is he, in the ability to visualize humanity in godlike forms—to create a race of supermen fitted to conquer the earth—to be compared to Michael Angelo. In what, then, does the modernity of Titian's art consist? The answer to this question, I am sorry to say, reflects little glory on the present status of painting and not too much on the foremost of the Venetian masters.

Titian was the first *professional* painter. I use the word professional in the sense that it is used today: a specialist without convictions; a virtuoso who, with great talent and greater industry, perfects a technical method of rendering the appearances and externals of life, and employs his method, with no special beliefs, for any subject that possesses a cash value; like Manet, a painter and nothing more. The difference between Titian and the modern painter is this: the Venetian was an educated man, a master of the predominant interests of the civilization that produced him; the modern painter, disavowing the value of subject-matter, is ignorant and ineffectual, ignorant because he refuses to accommodate himself to the intensely stimulating materials of an industrial age, ineffectual because his isolation binds him to a narrow aestheticism that scarcely touches reality.

With the Venetians as a school, but with Titian in particular, painting ceases to be an expression of collective religious interests and becomes a speculative profession. Henceforward, instead of a large number of artists working cooperatively under an admirably regulated system of guilds, insured of steady employment and a fair wage, we have a few talented schemers capturing all the rich prizes. When royal and wealthy patronage displaced the guilds, the great body of artists followed the only course open to them: deprived of an organic market, they gradually withdrew from society and delivered themselves into the hands of the dealer. Titian, of course, cannot be held responsible for this reversal of conditions: he merely brought to a focus the ideals of Venice, and his painting, though ostensibly religious in much of its subject-matter, illuminates only one aspect of life, and that certainly not the spiritual. But in his attitude toward his work, his greedy haggling over prices, his flattery, and his reliance upon the press agent, he introduced into painting methods of self-exploitation without which the modern artist would find it very difficult to get a hearing.

But Titian's chief claim to the title, "the father of modern painting" is to be found in his craftsmanship. Adopting the discoveries of Bellini and Giorgione, he perfected the craft of solid oil-painting and set a standard of tonality which remained unchallenged for more than three hundred years. And in his extreme old age, when his hand was shaky and his vision less acute, he began to paint in a bold and broken style which was soon to influence Rembrandt, to be enlarged upon by Turner and carried to scientific completion by the modern Impressionists.

Titian is the business man of painting. His life was singularly successful in every sense of the word, and he shaped its course with the foresight and practicality of a stock-jobber. Other artists, to be sure, have been men of the world, and have far outclassed Titian in the variety of their attainments, but none has ever approached his work so thoroughly in the spirit of the merchant. And, I might add, no merchant ever transacted his business with so much refinement and distinction. There is no reason why a painter should not be shrewd and sensible, and there is no reason why he should be indifferent to the material comforts of life, but dealing with spiritual values which cannot be assessed in terms of money, his first duty is to his art. Having discharged that obligation, he may then dispose of his work as he pleases and drive as hard a bargain as his wits permit. Titian, we feel, painted with one eye on the box-office; as one of his clients remarked on receipt of a portrait that did not quite conform to the master's standard, "Perhaps the silks and brocades would have been better if he had been paid a few more ducats for working them out."

Few artists have been so fortunate in natural endowments. Titian was industrious without being hasty or temperamental; he loved the good things of life but never descended to gluttony or excesses; though hard and avaricious in his business affairs, he was liberal in domestic expenditures, hospitable, an entertaining host, at home with kings, courtesans and prelates; he was never too old to learn; his life was disturbed by no struggles of hand or soul; he experienced no suffering; he was honored beyond any other painter of his time; and active to his ninety-ninth year, when the plague carried him off.

He was born in the Alps of Cadore, a commune seventy miles north of Venice. A pretty story tells us that when "quite a little boy he painted, entirely by himself, with the juice of flowers, the figure of the virgin; in consequence of this, he was sent by his father to Venice, and placed in the house of his uncle, and that he might make good use of his natural talent, he was put with Giovanni Bellini." He fell readily into the ways of Venice and seldom returned to his birthplace, except in later years to sell his hay and his timber. But he did not forget the picturesque landscapes of Cadore, and typical Venetian that he became, never once painted the city of canals, drawing upon his memories of Alpine scenes for all his backgrounds.

Titian was not precocious; he had a natural aptitude for painting, but lacking the strongly marked individuality so abundant among the Florentines, he was slow to find himself. His tardy development did not discourage him; on the contrary, it sharpened his perceptions, taught him self-discipline, and equipped him to take his place, at an opportune moment, as the leading artist of Venice. There is not a single existing document relating to the first thirty-five years of his life, and all descriptions of this period are purely fictional, or founded upon hearsay. We are not even certain that he was Bellini's pupil; the one incontestable fact is that he was intimately associated with Giorgione, and that the canvases of the two painters, in some cases, are so similar in theme, color and treatment as to be indistinguishable. When Giorgione died of the plague in 1510, at the age of thirty-three, he left the destinies of the new style of painting to the capable guardianship of his comrade Titian.

Technically the new style of painting originated with the Flemings, the greatest craftsmen in the history of art. As employed by Giorgione and more expertly by Titian, it consisted briefly in this: first the canvas was covered with a flat ground of tempera upon which successive layers of semi-transparent oil glazes were superimposed. With each thin coat of oil paint, the lights were intensified, the shadows warmed with color, harsh outlines softened and blurred, tones fused and blended. The general effect is one of extraordinary richness of color; the light seems to radiate from the interior of the forms, and not to be thrown upon them from an external source, the color to penetrate deeply into solid objects, and the whole to be bathed in an atmospheric lustre. Titian remarked that he painted the flesh in layers according to the course of nature when she wrapped the body in the several coverings of skin.

It is commonly said that the Venetians excelled in the use of color, the Florentines in the use of form, a meaningless distinction unless we make sure that we understand our terms.

There is no such thing as the "intrinsic value of color." To describe colors as noble, spiritual or profound is to talk in empty metaphors. One might, with a better show of reason, attribute such abstract qualities to wines and beers. In painting, unless color is related to a specific object, it is of no more significance than a rainbow, a fading sunset in a cloudless sky, or an old palette thick with the excrescences of dried pigments.

When a painter represents an object as a concrete form, he does so by means of lights and darks. Without using a single color, he may build up a figure as solid as a rock; if color is to function as an element of structure, it must, as the artist puts it, be "in value." This means that colors contain relative amounts of light and dark, and that to model with them, the painter must have precise knowledge of their black-and-white equivalents. Generally speaking, we may say that the Florentines, being primarily involved in problems of mass and structure, modelled their forms in monochrome and added color as a decorative accessory, as one would gild a statue or brighten a piece of architecture; whereas the Venetians, living in a showy, sensual world, steeped their nudes in color and drenched them with vaporous lights and tones which seemed to be exhaled from the forms themselves. Let us not be mistaken on this point. There is no more harmonious or effective color in western art than in the decorations on the ceiling of the Sistine Chapel; it is fresco color, an architectural embellishment, clean and transparent, but thin and dry in comparison to the dense and lucent richness of the Venetian glazes.

The structural test of a painting is the black-and-white reproduction. Titian, when subjected to this decolorizing ordeal, fares badly. If we were to judge his work solely by photographs, we should wonder how the grand old man of Venice ever got his reputation. His color covers a multitude of sins, conceals weaknesses in draughtsmanship, creates an illusion of magnificent life that is harshly dispelled by the negative. Michael

Angelo said that Titian would have been a great artist if he had only learned how to draw. The remark should not be misinterpreted. As the Florentines understood and practiced drawing, Titian deserved to be called second-rate, but his great fame does not rest upon his conformity to the standards of Florence. He did not attempt to mould the lives of men; he dealt with a less rigorous but much more pleasurable form of human behavior and to the accomplishment of his purpose, brought the happiest combination of pictorial gifts that have ever been centered in one painter. But without color, his hypnotic charm is lost. In the original, his famous *Flora*, for example, is the most gracious strumpet in art, an ivory-skinned beauty who wears the seal of her profession but with an immaculate delicacy that makes her a paragon among her kind and among all women; in black-and-white, alas, she is a vacuous, wooden-headed, pretty thing in a white nightgown! Her hand is swollen; her head formless and bulging; her mouth stamped; her nose an afterthought.

To conclude these technical questions, let me repeat that form in art is not the unique property of any one man or group of men. Certain tendencies of civilization, the religious, economic or social drift of mankind, give rise to similar mental and physical habits, and these the artist inevitably reflects, clarifying and organizing them, and presenting them in the different mediums of speech, sound and color. Thus the manifestations of art, at given periods, assume general characteristics, and we may rightly speak of Florentine and Venetian form. In a more limited sense, form becomes individual expression; general habits and ideals, passing through the artist's vision and impressed by his own special experiences, are moulded into fresh statements which have the appeal of living personalities. Estimated by the realization of its intentions—the transfiguration of the courtesan—Venetian painting is as rich in form as the art of Florence. Whether it is as profound or ennobling is another matter.

It was the genius of Giorgione that first discovered the domain of poetic sensuality in painting, and this fragrant domain

Titian cultivated for all he was worth. It was new; it was popular; it was profitable; and he exploited it with canny diligence for thirty years, painting portraits, religious pieces which have no value as such, and poesies—groups of draped and undraped figures assembled for no purpose that can be realistically described. Thus far, I have said little about portraiture, mainly because it has played an inconspicuous rôle in art; but from now on, with the separation of painting from architecture, the example of aristocratic patronage, and the rise of the easel-picture, its popularity increases by leaps and bounds, and after Titian has dipped the human form in a bath of gold, after Velasquez has preserved the degenerate Hapsburgs as monumental studies in still-life, and Rembrandt has illuminated the faces of nameless Jews and hags with the light and majesty of his own soul, it bows to English charm and French cleverness, and towards the close of the nineteenth century falls prostrate before the camera. At the present time it is the painter's most effectual instrument to lure the public into the exhibition room, and through its fashionable clientele, the most lucrative form of art.

We have no means of ascertaining how closely the portraits executed by the old painters resembled the sitters, but certainly they are far from literal, for it was not until the invention of the camera that the public realized how deadly accurate a portrait could be, and began to demand that the painter turn himself into a soulless, unreflective machine. The old portraits are not remarkable for physiognomical truth, but for such qualities of strength, dignity and individuality as the artists were able to bring to their models. Today it is the opposite; and the painter has but one course to follow—to compete with the camera. If he deviates at all from servile copying, it is not for artistic reasons but to clinch his commission by flattering the self-esteem of his subjects.

Titian, as I have hinted, was something of a politician and sycophant, but he is one of the kings of portraiture. In fact, it is in this field that his art is most distinguished. Look at his self-portraits. What a foxy old rogue he was! What piercing eyes!

What trenchant aquilinity! Here, you will say, was a man who knew what life was about, who knew how the Venetians esteemed themselves and depicted them with much more nobility of face and bearing than they actually possessed. Did he flatter them? Not exactly: he cast them all in the same mould, made them conform to his own ideal of aristocratic superiority. He never painted an old woman, and seldom an old man. He loved the ripeness and roundness of life at the maximum of its physical development.

One of his best portraits, called *The Man with the Glove* for want of a more descriptive title, hangs in the Louvre. This crop-headed young noble has exceptionally broad shoulders, a device used again and again by Titian to emphasize the masculinity of his characters and to give largeness and stability to the design. The picture is painted with the utmost simplicity and is free from every suggestion of trickery: a head, a dark body against a background almost as dark, a segment of shirt, one hand uncovered, one gloved—that is all. The design is nothing extraordinary—a graceful attitude slightly accentuated. Why then so much fuss over the canvas? The reason is that there is not a weak spot in the whole picture, not an infinitesimal trace of imperfection. With marvellous dexterity, planting light in low tones, Titian has pulled his figure out of the background, modelled a head of noble proportions, created a living presence. And this presence is the essence of princeliness. Everything that is tawdry, bourgeois and mean has been left out; the young man is a lord, or at least, he satisfies our romantic conception of a lord. He is Byron without the boorishness; he is the image of man as he would have himself created; he has dignity and strength, and at the same time, an inscrutable commanding wistfulness that women adore.

Sometime later Titian painted another great portrait, *The Young Englishman* of the Pitti, which in workmanship and design surpasses, if possible, *The Man with the Glove*. These two canvases represent the highest reaches of his genius. Who these gentlemen were and what they did are irrelevant questions. In them he created an ideal which epitomizes the aristocratic complacency of Venice and which appeals to the deep-seated pride and romantic aspirations lurking in all of us. I have said they are perfect, and so they are, in their own vein; but we cannot forget that they are lordly souls. In Rembrandt's portraits we are not conscious of birth, rank or breeding but of an overwhelming humanity that annuls all distinctions and embraces the entire range of our emotions. To this universality, Titian, with his narrower sympathies and circumscribed vision, could not pretend, but in his own province he is a master.

Like every portrait painter who is also an artist, Titian was intent on making a good picture rather than a faithful likeness. He finished his canvases without models, slowly and systematically altering color, form and features into a type of physical excellence that should be a credit to Venice and to art. It was his habit to keep a number of works in progress at the same time and his studio was filled with canvases in various stages of construction. Face to the wall, some stood untouched for months; when he resumed them, "it was," according to one of his servants, "as if he were attacking his worst enemy." He was more successful in his portraits of men; he preferred women in the nude. On occasion he was not above cold-blooded flattery, treating the Duchess of Urbino, wife of one of his wealthiest patrons and known to be a woman of morose ugliness, with the dexterity of a beauty specialist. Retaining a vestige of a likeness, he transformed the sour repulsiveness of this ill-favored lady into a formidable dignity that is not unpleasing. The Duchess, needless to say, was delighted. Going further, he renounced personal implications and painted her as the flower of Venetian sensuality, the imperious *La Bella* in the Pitti. The Duchess was overjoyed. Having idealized her face, Titian paid the final compliment to her figure, and in so doing, committed aesthetic forgery. The head of *La Bella* was annexed to an indefectible nude body painted from a courtesan, and the composite has come down to us under the title *The Venus of Urbino*. What the Duchess thought of the final compliment history does not say; no doubt her vanity became unbearable, and no doubt she boasted that she had posed for the *Venus.*

During his earlier period, when he was about thirty-five, Titian painted the most famous of his poesies, the *Sacred and Profane Love* in the Borghese Gallery at Rome. The title is not Titian's, and all suggestions for a more appropriate one are equally futile. Round this picture interminable and pointless controversy has raged, the idea being to translate it into some cogent fable or realistic circumstance. The picture needs no far-flung exegesis, and when so expounded conveys the impression that the artist set out to tell a story and told it so poorly that no one has ever discovered its purport.

The conception is plainly derived from Giorgione's *Pastoral Symphony*: here, in the foreground of a landscape, is a long ornate bathtub upon the edge of which two women are sitting, one gorgeously dressed, the other nude. The scene is the exemplification of a poetic mood, a mood in which figures, trees, skies, hills and textures are conjoined with color in praise of the loveliness of woman, clothed and nude, and of all natural forms. The difficulty, in works of this kind, is to prevent the representational element from overweighing the poetic intention, and the galleries of the world are cluttered with nude models posing against sylvan backgrounds in pictures which, through the collision of illustration and fancy, are manifestly absurd. There is a little of the studio atmosphere in *Sacred and Profane Love*: the figures seem to have been transferred to the spot in predetermined attitudes, to fit less perfectly in the scene than those in Giorgione's masterpiece, and the dressed lady is apparently sitting upon nothing at all. But these are trifles. The mood was sufficiently strong in the young Titian to claim authentic expression; the picture works; it has always been popular, for it embodies the sensuous aspects of life in forms of concentrated loveliness.

He had worked hard and had gained considerable fame but not much money, and to put himself beyond financial worries, petitioned the City Council of Venice in the following style:

High and Mighty Lords:

I, Titian of Cadore, have from childhood upwards studied the art of painting, desirous of a little fame rather than of profit. And although in the past as well as in the present I have been urgently invited by His Holiness the Pope and other lords to enter their service, I, as the faithful subject of Your Excellencies, have preferred to leave behind me in this famous town a memorial; and therefore, if it seems good to your Excellencies, I am eager to paint in the Hall of the Great Council, employing thereto all my powers, and to begin with the canvas of the battle on the side toward the piazza, which is so difficult that no one has yet had courage to attempt it. I should be willing to accept for my labor any reward that may be thought proper, or even less. Therefore, being as aforesaid studious only of honor and to please Your Excellencies, I beg to ask for the first broker's patent for life that shall be vacant, irrespective of all promised reversions of such patent. In return for which I promise to do the work above named with such speed and excellence as will satisfy the Signory.

The broker's patent was in effect the job of painter to the State and carried with it an annual salary, tax exemptions and the services of two assistants. Old John Bellini, who held the office and who seemed to be immortal, fearing that he should be ousted or poisoned, grumbled mightily and the other artists supported him. The petition was disallowed but fortunately, three years later, Bellini died, and the post went to Titian. Thereupon the painter "desirous of a little fame" returned calmly to his own business, satisfied old patrons, contracted to serve invading kings, drew his salary and defied the importunities of the State. The Council scolded and threatened him, but to no avail; his fame increased and they basked in its light; but for twenty-five years save for the painting of a Doge or two, he did nothing for the official glory of Venice. At last the Council bore down upon him without equivocation and gave him a week to begin the battlepiece or refund all unearned moneys. The prospect of losing money drove him into action, and he painted, so it is said, a battle of such boldness and magnificence that the town went mad with excitement. The picture was destroyed by fire the year of Titian's death.

While bargaining for this sinecure, he painted *The Assumption* for the Church of the Friars in Venice. "He was constantly annoyed," so an old chronicler relates, "by the visits and reproaches of the fathers who objected that he made the apostles too large, and it gave him no little trouble to clear up their misapprehensions and to make them understand that figures must be in proportion to the great space that was to be filled." They held their tongues but were not completely pacified until the Imperial ambassador tried with large offers to obtain the work for the Emperor. Upon this the fathers decided that it must be a great picture and would on no terms part with it.

There is no use pretending that Titian's religious works are great pictures. They are hack jobs, marvellously executed, brilliant in the manipulation of light and color, theatrically effective, but hack jobs none the less. The man at heart had few religious convictions. Let him paint the aristocracy and he was second to none; let him paint a sumptuously bodied nymph and the heat of his blood caught fire within his light and color and instilled vitality into his forms; but give him a religious theme and he produced stagey collections of fine people masquerading as saints. Furthermore, great technician that he was in his mastery of light and of the modelling of flesh by imperceptible changes of tone, he was not a great composer. Two or three figures he could manage well enough, but when it came to combining larger groups he was, in contrast with Tintoretto, El Greco and Rubens, confused and inept. The relation of line to line, and of mass to mass he could never learn to control, and he attempted, with some success, to hide his deficiencies beneath the splendor of his color and the enameled lustre of his surfaces. His *Bacchus and Ariadne*, for all its blues and scarlets, its greens and purples, is a scrambled affair. Twice—in the *Entombment* of the Louvre and the Munich version of *Christ Crowned With Thorns*—actuated by a curious spiritual impulsion, mastering, no one knows how, his weaknesses in design, he rose above pageantry and painted religious compositions of a high rank.

The Assumption is one of the most popular pot-boilers in painting. The design is broken in two by a Christmas garland of cherubs; God the Father in his flying robes resembles a hoary bat; but the superb figure of Our Lady, a ravishing Venetian type, soaring gently aloft, with inviting arms and an expression of pathetic dignity and sweetness, fetches the popular imagination. The little fame that Titian had so earnestly coveted had now grown into an international reputation; royal patrons came to his studio and he had more work than he could take care of; he was rich, renowned and contented. Venice escaped the fury of the Imperial armies and went on in her serene lasciviousness, the courtesan rejoicing in the destruction of her rivals. While Florence was dying, Titian was calmly painting bacchanals for Alphonso d'Este or a nude Magdalen "as beautiful and as tearful as possible" for the Gonzagas.

At the age of forty-eight he married Cecilia, a barber's daughter, who bore him three children, one, or possibly two, before he consented to make her his wife. His marriage was purely nominal, and when Cecilia died, five years afterward, he did not grieve. His handsome daughter Lavinia was very dear to him and he painted her many times, as a bride, as Salome and as Venus. One of his sons was a poor but honorable painter; the other an indolent rascal whom, as a last resort, he made a priest.

His wife out of the way, Titian bought a house in the suburbs of Venice and established himself on a scale worthy of his high position. Here he lived magnificently. His studio looked down upon terraced gardens into the open sea; a young mistress with curly red hair relieved the tedium of incessant painting; the choicest courtesans supplied him with nude models; kings and princes passing through the city counted it a signal honor to be his guests. He lived magnificently but with habitual prudence, squandering neither his vitality nor his money; he drove sharp bargains, wisely invested his savings, kept track of every penny; but if there were royal visitors to be entertained, he tossed his purse to his servants and bade them prepare a banquet. Summoned to Ferrara by the Duke, he traveled in style with five servants; again, journeying thither at his own expense, he went up the Po alone on the cheapest boat. He worked methodically, as other men spun silk or glass, without haste, inspiration or exuberance, but without fatigue or loss of interest in his art. Never was a painter more astute in procuring commissions; never were commissions executed more painstakingly. Titian was always in good health; he had nerves of steel; his productivity was enormous.

At this time Pietro Aretino arrived in Venice. Expelled from Rome for peddling filthy drawings, he became a friar at Ravenna, but even the Capuchins could not stomach him and he wandered about Italy, hurtled from pillar to post, picking up dastardly gossip and salable scandal. Only in the free air of Venice could his peculiar talents prosper and he lived like a prince on the Grand Canal, a parasite by profession and a spy of Italy's most dreaded enemies Charles V and Francis I. In his palace he kept as many as twenty-two women—some, the wives of men whose careers he had blasted, some with infants at the breast, some, lovely fledglings whom he groomed for the fancy Venetian trade.

"I am a free man," he boasted. "I live by the sweat of my pen. I do not need to copy Boccaccio or Petrarch. Let others worry about style and cease to be themselves. Without master, without a model, without a guide, without artifice, I go to work and earn my living, my well-being and my fame. With a goose quill and a few sheets of paper I mock the universe."

Well might Aretino boast that he needed only to be himself to earn a living. Corrupt as Italy had become, she had room for only one man of his kidney. He was not a covert defamer but an out-and-out publicist of infamy, loathed and feared in every part of the peninsula, a genius who grew fat upon evil, whose bravura was dazzling in an age of boldness. After a particularly successful coup, or after inexpressible debauchery and fornication in the carnival season, he closed the doors of his palace and curbed his energies in solemn penitence to square himself

Titian: VENUS OF URBINO.

Uffizi Gallery, Florence

with the Pope. Out of the profundities of his own baseness he developed a brilliant epistolary style with which he caught his victims, sometimes by consummate flattery, more frequently by blackmail or published insult. This man had hardly been in Venice three months when he captivated Titian, and they were boon companions for thirty years. The partnership was decidedly interesting.

Aretino had other qualities than those of villainy: he was generous and humane, and would ride all night to comfort a forlorn inmate of his harem who was dying of consumption in the uplands; he loved music and painting and had access to the most desirable patrons; and he was an incomparable talker. His loyalty to Titian was the only disinterested attachment in his shameless career, and although he enjoyed the prestige of the association, he made no attempt to extort money from his friend. It is possible that he had a decent respect for the painter's pugnacity—Titian was remorseless in his dealings with rivals and trouble-makers—it is possible too that while gratitude comprised the smallest part of his character, he was grateful for one friendship in a world of enmity. And Venice, a liberal city, thought none the worse of Titian for hobnobbing with a blackmailer.

We see him in his orange robes as Titian painted him, a Satyr with a well-furnished beard, as the old stylists put it, thickset and powerful, the golden chain of knighthood round his neck—he had been honored for his perfidy—and a sneering regality in his repulsive face. At the end of the day, having finished a glittering piece of invective calculated to make some unstable potentate quake with terror, he stood by his window exulting. A golden mist dragged over the Canal, and then suddenly, the veil lifted and an amazing sunset burst upon him. The burly animal sniffed and blinked, and with an artist's eye, noted the half-tints, the complementaries, the fabulous architecture dissolved in color.

"Nature," he exclaimed, "the mistress of all masters! How miraculous is her brush! How wonderful her pencil! I know that your brush, my Titian, is the rival of nature, and that you are her best beloved son." And three times he cried out, "O Titian, where art thou?"

Titian, a long day's work behind him, appeared with his plump blonde. A feast awaited them. Aretino, drinking heartily, extemporized a hymn in honor of hares, but when the pheasants were served, he shouted, "I will now sing the praises of the winged! And my good friend Titian, bestowing glances on these savory morsels, will have a duet with me." The blackguard, kissing the beautiful hands of his favorite Franceschina, murmured in his well-furnished beard, "Two charming robbers which steal not only men's purses but their hearts." And so the night began.

Aretino became Titian's publicity agent, and for a generation piloted the artist through diplomatic entanglements and the hazards of royal patronage. He sang the praises of Titian in bulletins of persuasive eloquence, instructed him in courtly palaver, advised him whom to flatter and when, dictated the tone of his correspondence, widened the scope of his commissions, and tripled his income. When we read the following bit of polite begging addressed to King Ferdinand, "The portraits of the serene daughters of your Majesty [there were seven noble little daughters, all in one picture] will be finished in two days, and I shall send them to you at once. As soon as your Majesty has seen them, I am convinced that I shall receive much greater favors than those with which your Majesty has previously honored me," we see behind it the grinning face and itching palms of Pietro Aretino.

Through the offices of his agent, Titian won the support of the Hapsburgs and painted the great Emperor Charles V and all his family; at the instigation of Aretino, he painted Paul III while his Holiness was visiting at Ferrara. Finishing the portrait, as was his custom, in his studio at Venice, he placed it outside on a terrace, to dry, and the passing crowds took off their hats and crossed themselves as if they were in the presence of the Pope himself. For the nuns of Murano he painted an

Annunciation, but failing to come to terms with the holy ladies, he sent the picture, on the advice of Aretino, to the Empress, receiving, as he had fully expected, a handsome check for the present.

During these years he was busy, for the most part, with royal portraits and nudes. Success, honors, fame, friends, money —these had not spoilt him, and his capacity for steady toil had not diminished. But the poetic vein of his earlier period was worked out, and he was now the professional picture-maker. To hold his aristocratic clientele, it was absolutely necessary that he endow his sitters with factitious dignity and grace, and this Titian did with remarkable uniformity and forbearance. He could not afford to incur the displeasure of his patrons and his position, at times, must have been painful; but fame and money were ample compensation for flattery. And besides, there were Aretino's parties; and the satisfaction that he had performed his tasks with a technical agility that no other painter could touch. He had carried craftsmanship to an enigmatical splendor. Perhaps the highest tribute to his skill was paid by Rubens when, on a diplomatic mission to Madrid, he spent all his spare time copying Titian's pictures.

The nudes painted during these years are voluptuous jobs. They were designed for the cabinets of dukes and cardinals and designed deliberately as aphrodisiacs for connoisseurs. Those who go to art for a glimpse of stunning nakedness doubtless experience a momentary quickening of the blood from Titian's indolent courtesans; to artists they mean little. The signs of manufacture are too obvious; the purpose too transparent. Exquisitely painted in textures and flesh tones they have, structurally, a certain puffiness that betrays an incomplete knowledge of artistic anatomy. Not that they are commonplace—they put most nudes to shame, and in the modelling of flesh by means of minute gradations of tone, they have never been excelled—but their appeal is wholly sexual.

At one of them, the *Venus of Urbino*, Mark Twain was profoundly incensed. The bare flesh he professed to tolerate, but the position of the left hand was the most brazen piece of impudicity he had ever looked upon—that is, in public! If literature were allowed such license the human race would soon go to the dogs! Today we smile at Mark Twain's moral indignation, but his criticism has the uncommon merit of honesty: he saw what every one sees in the *Venus*—the left hand—it is the center of attraction. He acknowledged it and recoiled in disgust. But no false sense of delicacy prevented him from publishing his reactions; and so far as I am aware, he is the only writer who has mentioned the inescapable fact. The defenders of the nude, enjoying what Mark Twain condemned, talk about the "slender body, the rosy shadows and creamy skin," but are discreetly silent on the subject of the hand; and the aesthetic writers, pretending to respond only to the formal relationships, have been so carried away by the suggestiveness of the Venus, that they have failed to perceive how feebly the hand is drawn. Incidentally, Mark Twain raised the perfectly valid question of the aesthetic properties of exhibitionism in art.

When Titian was about seventy, he went to Rome at the invitation of Cardinal Farnese. The Pope welcomed him cordially and gave him quarters in the Belvedere of the Vatican; Vasari showed him the city, and Michael Angelo, curiously enough, treated him with the greatest respect. He painted a number of things for the Cardinal, and the portrait of Paul III, one of the most powerful of all his works, but receiving nothing in return but promises and fine words, he returned to Venice. The next year he was summoned to Germany and there, at the Imperial court, painted Charles V, for the third time—"in bronze armor worked with gold as he was in his old age"—and a host of sovereigns and princes. During one of the ceremonials the Emperor made Titian ride at his side, remarking to his courtiers, "I can make as many lords as I wish, but God only can make a Titian." Besides the large sums which he commanded for his portraits, he was honored as no painter had ever been honored before. Charles conferred upon him the titles of Count Palatine, Count of the Aulic Council, of the Lateran Palace and of the Consistory; his children took the rank of nobles of the Empire; he became Knight of the Golden Spur, and was given certain special privileges in his native province, such as the appointment of judges and notaries and the legitimatizing of children.

But all these were not enough. We find him, in his eightieth year, complaining of his lot to the Emperor and begging for the concession of cutting timber in the Tyrol. "He was in ill-health," he wrote—an exaggeration, for he was painting as vigorously as ever; "the marriage of his daughter had set him back considerably"—the marriage had occurred a year before this; and "he was in straitened circumstances"—a distortion of facts, to say the least. With Aretino's help he falsified his income tax returns, omitting the sales of his pictures, his principal source of revenue. That same year Aretino died and the people rejoiced—tired, they said, of paying tribute to the brute. Roaring with laughter at an obscene joke, he burst a blood-vessel and fell to the floor. A priest was called in to administer extreme unction. The priest performed the rites and departed. He lay still, extinguished at last. But not quite. His eyes opened and his face broke into an enormous smile. "Now that I'm oiled," he cried, "keep me from the rats!" So saying he passed out.

At ninety, hale and hearty, Titian sent fifteen pictures to Philip II, and a characteristic letter.

"In these pieces, your Majesty, I have put all the knowledge which God has given me, and which has always been and ever will be dedicated to the services of your Majesty. That you will please accept this service as long as I can use my limbs, borne down by weight of age, I hope; and though the burden is heavy, it becomes lighter, as if by a miracle, whenever I remember that I am living to serve and do something grateful to your Majesty."

After wailing that he is obliged to sell his personal effects in order to live, he concludes in this strain:

"I beg your Majesty most humbly, and out of old friendship,

before I die to do me the grace and give me the consolation and utility of the privilege of importing corn from Naples."

In the last decade of his life a change came over the old painter. Technically, the change appeared in the final portrait of Charles V: the Emperor, a scarecrow Don Quixote, rides out from a wood on a deformed horse—a terrible conception, a symphony in blood and black. Titian's eyes failed him; his hand twitched, and he began to paint in a style that astonished the people. Outlines grow more and more indistinct; color gives way to luminous veils of tone; paint is applied in broad streaks which at close range reveal nothing, but when viewed at a distance blend into forms of startling animation. These works foreshadow Impressionism, a modern method of painting in which design and structure are subordinated to the vibrating effects of sunlight and atmospheric tones.

He outlived his family and all his friends. One by one he saw them go. The pleasures of the flesh were over; mistresses could do him no good; he was lonely and thoughts of approaching death revived in him the poetry that had lain so long in abeyance. But how different from the poetry of his early years! No more does he celebrate the glory and loveliness of the courtesan city; no more, with inimitable delicacy, does he create an ideal of composed and lordly manhood. The Renaissance has passed and Italy has been ruined by barbarian rulers whom he has flattered for money. The poetry returns but with a deeper humanity—his brush trembles with the shuddering touch of tragedy. He paints a bacchanal, but in name only: a nymph without a vestige of physical charm and a ferocious shepherd thrown together in an alarming landscape; he paints himself, an ancient goblin in a skull-cap, ready to join Aretino; he paints, for once in his life, a great dramatic composition, the *Crowning With Thorns*, a picture in which Christ is modelled in a burst of light worthy of Rembrandt, and the clubbing brutes around him are portrayed with wonderful realism and energy. With this picture, Titian, the invincible portrait painter, at the age of ninety-five, enters the company of the religious masters.

The old bargaining instinct never deserted him. He wished to be buried in the Church of the Frari, but rather than pay for the privilege, offered to paint a Pietà for one of the chapels. The offer was accepted and he went to work, but before the picture was finished he died of the plague.

CHAPTER

VIII

THE EARLY FLEMINGS

IN OUTWARD appearances, Belgium seems to have recovered from the War. The battle scars—the shell-holes, the filthy trenches, the desolate landscapes and ruined villages—these are gone now, and the little country blooms again. The lands are green and tidy and the poppies are growing in the wheat; women and children, like patient beasts of burden, work in the fields as they have always done, and the buildings demolished by German bombs have been replaced by new structures overlaid with an artificial quaintness to efface the memory of recent horrors, and to remind a poverty-stricken nation of her irrevocable glories in art and commerce. But spiritually and materially Belgium is bankrupt. The cities tell the story most painfully.

Brussels, before the War a smaller Paris, a city of wine and beer and uncensored abandon, of Flemish sensuality leavened with French taste, is today pathetically shabby and unclean. Disfigured and vicious, she is like a rich and charming woman reduced to beggary and striving raffishly to regain her charms and her revenues. The fashionable quarter on the heights, now bleak and overbearing in its elegance, contrasts oddly with the bedraggled commercial centre fringed with pot-houses and brothels. The wines are still superior but the restaurants are empty save for a few disobliging English clerks attracted by the low rate of exchange and a handful of American tourists on their way to Paris or London. There is no joy to be found anywhere. The solid worldliness and feasting gaiety are things of the past; sick and weary, the people are trying to forget their despair in the cheapest forms of American jazz. The movie palaces exhibit the flashy orgiastic splendors of Hollywood and the dingy cafés, haunted by underfed women eager to make a few honest francs, resound with Broadway melodies. The girls wear cotton stockings and no rouge; at night prostitutes, hungry, ill-clad and very young, prowl the streets in search of bespectacled Americans, and when they find one, fight among themselves for his gallant offices. They tempt him, in scraps of English with unmentionable offers, and if he refuses, curse his stingy soul to hell in shrieks of obscenity.

Ghent is solemn and kindly, with her weavers at work again, but hopelessly crushed and dull. Bruges is a scrubbed corpse, bright and clean in her renovated mediaeval dress, but dead these many years. The carillon in the old Belfry plays a dirge as a solitary barge, without visible means of propulsion, floats slowly down the canal to the sea. Living is cheaper here, perhaps, than in any other town in Europe, but the modern traveller demands excitement, and there is no excitement in Bruges—nothing but convents, canals, a collection of inimitable paintings and memories of Burgundian dukes and the luxurious days of the Hanseatic league. Antwerp alone promises to regain her former prosperity, and in this admirable city one sees again a return to the good old Flemish customs—a happy mixture of thriftiness, animal comforts, intelligent pleasures and a great delight in the material world.

There is no art being produced in Belgium today, a lamentable fact, and the only one, so far as I am aware, that has not been attributed to the German occupation. The great art of Flanders began with the Van Eycks in the fifteenth century and ended with Rubens in the seventeenth; since Rubens no man of any consequence has appeared and no spiritual movement has interrupted the narrow pursuit of commonplace satisfactions. The modern rooms of the museums at Brussels and Ghent are the dreariest I have ever encountered; an exhibition of the industrial arts at Antwerp revealed nothing beyond a rather pitiable imitation of the fraudulent designs of the French Modernists.

Travel from Liège to Bruges, from Antwerp to Mons; observe the habits of these Flemings; think of the sufferings they have endured, not only in the last twenty years, but continually since the Spanish terror; and you will marvel that they have the heart to produce anything: lace, linen, Brussels sprouts, cut diamonds for the American trade, much less works of art. The War did not kill the artistic aspirations of Belgium, but before the rape of 1914, it was easier to understand the spirit of a people, who, in times past, founded a tradition of painting which, in its origins, is the only European school independent of Italian influences.

Under present conditions it is hard to believe in the existence of that spirit, but turn from the squalor of Brussels to the Royal Museum of Old Masters; enter the Cathedral of St. Bavon at Ghent, or the Hospital of St. John at Bruges, and the creative industry of the early Flemings becomes a phenomenal reality. It was a long time ago that the wonderful art of the Low Countries flourished—five hundred years, to be exact, since the Van Eycks and their followers painted their portraits and altar-pieces, and yet these old pictures are as fresh and limpid as if done yesterday! In the fourteenth century the wealth of Flanders was the talk of Europe, and when Philip the Fair made his triumphal entry into Bruges, "the luxury displayed in the costumes of the burghers' wives excited the envy of his queen." At the end of the century there were 4000 master weavers at Louvain, each employing thirty to forty workmen; the weavers' guild of Ghent registered more than 40,000 members; Malines boasted of 3500 woolen factories with Ypres running a close second. Bruges, the chief emporium of the Hanseatic League, and famous all over the world for her commerce, tapestries, pictures, and her wealthy bourgeoisie, was a greater port than Venice, and received at her quays as many as 150 vessels in a single day.

"In those days", says Weale, "the squares of Bruges were adorned with fountains; its bridges with statues in bronze; the public buildings and many of the private houses with statuary and carved work, the beauty of which was heightened and brought out by gilding and polychrome; the windows were rich with storied glass, and the walls of the interiors adorned with paintings or hung with gorgeous tapestry. If but little of all this now remains, it must be borne in mind that, during the past centuries, Bruges has seen its works of art exported by Spaniards; destroyed, when not sold, by Calvinist iconoclasts and French Revolutionists; and carried off by picture dealers of all nations." The cities, in spite of feudal suzerains, were the most democratic communities in Europe; illiteracy was unknown; the spirit of the people was strong and hearty; and in conjunction with their material prosperity, in truth, as a part of it, developed the art of painting to a degree of excellence that is an endless source of despair to the modern artist.

"These Gothic people," wrote an old Italian historian, "are courageous and sociable; they eat and drink and carouse, but they work with marvellous and disgusting patience. They are very jealous of gain and vigilant of profit, but without anything feverish or irrational in their desire to provide for themselves. They are by nature cool and self-possessed. The women are extremely circumspect and are allowed much freedom, going out alone, and making visits and journeys without evil report. They love their homes and hold adultery in horror. All of them delight in wealth and other worldly things prudently, and are not easily disturbed, which is at once apparent both in their discourse and in their physiognomies. They are not too prone to anger or to pride, but live together on good terms and are especially of a gay and lively humor. They invented woolen fabrics, have a special and happy talent for the ready inventions of all sorts of machines, ingenious and suitable for facilitating shortening and dispatching everything they do, even in the matters of cooking."

By 1520 Bruges and Ghent had already declined, "because," as a Belgian professor explains, "of their hopeless spirit of routine, and their old-fashioned ideas of protectionism," while Antwerp, embracing free-trade principles, was transformed into a cosmopolitan and hospitable city. When Dürer visited Antwerp, the painters invited him to their guild-hall with his wife and maid-servant. "They had," he relates, "a great quantity of silver-plate, and costly furniture and most expensive food. All their wives were with them, and as I was led in to table, every one stood up in a row on either side, as if they had been bringing in some great lord. The syndic of the magistrates came in with two servants and gave me four cans of wine in their name; next came Master Peter, the town carpenter, and gave me two cans of wine with the offer of his services. When we had long been merry together, up to a late hour of the night, they accompanied us home in honor with lanterns, and prayed me to rely confidently on their good-will."

Dürer describes the famous procession held on Lady Day. "There were 400 triumphal arches, each two stories high and forty feet long, and decorated with allegorical paintings. The whole town was gathered together, and every rank and guild had its sign by which it could be known. I saw pass through the streets the Guilds of the Goldsmiths, Painters, Masons and Broderers, the Butchers, Joiners, Carpenters, Sculptors, Sailors, Weavers, Bakers, and workmen of all kinds. There were merchants and traders, men-at-arms, travellers and pedlars; and then a great company of very stately people, nobly and costly habited. Before them, I forgot to say, went all the religious orders, all in their various garbs, very piously; and also a great body of widows who support themselves with the work of their hands; all clothed from head to foot in white linen, very pitiful to look upon. At the end came the Canons of Our Lady's Church, with all the priests, scholars and treasures. Twenty persons bore the image of the Virgin Mary with the Child Jesus, adorned in the most gorgeous fashion, to the honor of the Lord God. In this procession were brought along many heart-gladdening things splendidly arranged: wagons with plays upon ships and other stages; the Annunciation; the Three Kings upon great camels and other strange beasts most cleverly done; also how our Lady fled into Egypt, most pious to behold; youths and maidens representing various saints, and last of all a great dragon, whom St. Margaret with her maidens led by a girdle. There was one young girl almost naked and very beautiful, and I gazed at her attentively, passionately and innocently, being a painter. This procession took more than two hours to pass by our house, and in it there were such a number of things that I could never write them all in a whole book, so I leave well alone."

In this atmosphere of healthy communism art prospered as a useful and respectable industry. When men get together freely, when they regard the occupations of one another without jealousy or conceit and are not too desirous of fame; when they are public-spirited and take pride in the comeliness of their city; when they welcome strangers with wine and feasting and dance a jig in the streets; you may depend upon it that they will put their artistic talents to a good purpose. And these Flemings, mark me, created an art within the reach of the humblest son of toil, and to make their works acceptable to the Lord God, first made them enjoyable to their fellow men. Art, as in Italy, was in the hands of the guilds, but more rigidly controlled, with longer apprenticeships and little incentive to competition or individual distinction. The Guild of St. Luke included painters, saddlers, glass makers and mirror-makers; only painters were allowed to work in oil, and the right to use water-color was restricted to the illuminators. Even after an artist became a master craftsman, unless he were in the direct employ of a Prince, his contracts, materials and tools were supervised by his guild. This system insured thoroughness, durability and fine craftsmanship, qualities in which Flemish painting has never been equalled. Dürer, a product of similar conditions in Germany, worked for seven years upon six pictures, and observed with just pride "that his canvases, 300 years later, would be as fresh as the day he painted them."

Partisans of Italian painting have always looked down upon the art of the Low Countries. When certain Flemish pictures were carried into Italy, in the fifteenth century, Michael Angelo rose up against them.

"The painting of Flanders," he said, "will generally satisfy any devout person more than the painting of Italy, which will never cause him to shed a single tear; this is not owing to the vigor and goodness of that painting, but to the goodness of such devout person.

"Women will like it, especially very old or very young ones. It will likewise please friars and nuns and also some noble persons who have no true eye for harmony. They paint in Flanders, only to deceive the external eye, things that gladden you and of which you cannot speak ill, and saints and prophets. Their painting is of stuffs—bricks and mortar, the grass of the fields, the shadows of trees, and bridges and rivers, which they call landscapes, and little figures here and there; and all this, though it may appear good to some eyes, is in truth done without reasonableness or art, without symmetry or proportion, without care in selecting and rejecting, and finally without any substance or energy. I do not speak so badly of Flemish painting because I think it all bad, but because it tries to do so many things at once—each of which alone would suffice for a great work—so that it does not do anything, really well."

The sharp disfavor with which Michael Angelo spoke of Flemish painting has been echoed again and again, and all subsequent objections are merely corollaries from his point of view. But let us not be deceived by his criticisms. Michael Angelo, you will remember, regarded all painting as a little womanish, especially oil-painting. Reared in a tradition of monumental frescoes, hating portraiture and landscape, and accustomed to express the tragedy of man in heroic nudes, "in a music which," he said, "intellect alone can appreciate, and that with great difficulty," he could not but feel that Flemish art was a trifling accumulation of details, a sop to the unduly pious, and that pictures of saints boiling in oil, sinners being skinned alive, and bishops having ther tongues pulled out were suitable for the gross appetites of savage ploughmen and stupid weavers.

Undeniably he fastened upon the weak spots in the Northern school, for the Flemings collectively were more literal-minded and sentimental than the Italians, and when they were bad they were horrible, but their simple humanity, their rich earthliness and warm delight in visible realities he was constitutionally incapable of appreciating. I have noticed too that for every writer who dresses up the opinions of Michael Angelo in modern aesthetic style and harps on the vulgarity of Flemish painting, there are a hundred honest laymen who enjoy that painting with unfeigned relish.

During the Middle Ages the general Gothic movement spreading over Europe was modified by local characteristics, and by the end of the thirteenth century had developed into two well-defined traditions of design. In Italy, as we have seen, the dry atmosphere and the structure of the churches favored the fresco, and mural painting predominated; in the North Countries, the damp climate was destructive to the fresco medium; the great cathedrals, built to admit every available ray of light, had no room for wall decorations, and oil painting came to the front in the form of miniatures, panels, portraits and easel pictures. Early Flemish painting is the direct offspring of the Gothic miniatures—sacred manuscripts, missals, and Books of Hours illuminated by the monks—and notwithstanding its rapid advancement in color and craftsmanship, retained the stamp of the miniature until Rubens returned from Italy in the seventeenth century. At first it was imitative and conventional, resembling closely the flat symbolical types of goggle-eyed saints who stare at us from the Italian decorations up to Giotto; but in 1384, Flanders was annexed by the Duke of Burgundy and her artists began to open their eyes to the world of nature. At the French court they saw illuminators working from life instead of rehashing worn-out abstractions, and Gothic carvers following the attitudes and faces of living persons; and this naturalistic influence was exactly what the Flemings needed most. They were plain people with no cultural pretentions and no classical tradition to draw upon, and they must make their art out of the homely materials of their own environment. While France was impoverished by wars and plagues, and wolves roamed the streets of Paris, Bruges and Ghent were booming with wealth, and the Flemish painters went back to their native clay to serve the church and the opulent burghers.

The time was ripe for something extraordinary. The blight of mediaevalism had been lifted; men and women struggling and starving for centuries like plodding beasts—but beasts subdued by superstitions and cherishing a grotesque reverence for torture—reclaiming swamps, fighting inundations, learning to spin and weave, and all the while looking for salvation in the next world, suddenly found themselves in possession of abundance. Not only enough but a feast; not rags but fine raiment; not merely a roof over their heads but houses that make sheds of our flimsy modern dwellings! There was a mighty fermentation of animal spirits, a robust conviviality, a clean breath of physical rapture, and now and then, for the novelty of it, a gorging of appetites. Their bellies were filled; their hearts glad; their hands not idle. The Flemings had awakened to the world of the senses.

But how different their sensuality from the refined fleshliness of the South! The Venetians made a cult of pleasure and dwelt upon the composed loveliness of nudes and idealized portraits; the Flemings, unspoilt by affectation and refinement, were grosser, but more candid and whole-hearted in their physical proclivities. They found the human body harsh of face, angular and long-limbed, lean for the most part, but sometimes awkwardly fat, and so they painted it. No seductive nudes to garnish the cabinets of lecherous dukes and cardinals; no princely heads to arouse the envy of the common man. Their attention reposed on the ordinary business of life; and in their childlike curiosity in everyday things we must look for the secrets of their enormously effective art. The Italians viewed the world from a greater distance, considered the abstract nature of objects and established universals—the relation of man to the sum of all things; the Flemings inquired passionately into the familiar

John Van Eyck: JOHN ARNOLFINI AND HIS WIFE.

National Gallery, London

facts of life—perhaps the heartiest and most sterling inquiry into homely realities that has ever been made. From time to time painters grow weary of the heroic principles inculcated by the Italians and return to the kitchen-minded simplicity of the Flemings, but they have never succeeded in recapturing the naïve vision of the early Northerners. The Flemings themselves could not long preserve the freshness of their first inspiration, and in less than ninety years their art had lost its local characteristics and had put on Italian mannerisms to please the wealthy patrons of Antwerp.

Flemish painting, a continuation of the mediaeval tradition, was naturally of a religious character, and remained so throughout its entire development. The Renaissance, striking at the roots of the mediaeval order, destroyed Christianity in Italy, but in the North Countries revived it. The Flemings found no incompatibility between their homely pieties and the teachings of Christ; they found indeed no irreconcilable differences between their matter-of-fact sensuality and the precepts of the Roman Church. Thus Rubens, a strictly orthodox Catholic and religious painter, was also the painter of the most fleshly but at the same time the most spontaneous, the most decent and genuine nakedness in modern art. About 1420 when the old school of manuscript illumination had reached its climax, the Van Eyck brothers appeared, two painters in oil, the greatest artists of the early Flemish awakening, marvellous technicians and remarkable men from any point of view.

The Van Eycks were not the first to use the oil medium, as was formerly believed; nor were they oil painters in the modern understanding of the term. "Oil and varnish," according to Sir Charles Holmes, "had long been employed as surface protectives for work in tempera (paintings in which the colors are tempered with yolk of egg) but the Van Eycks were the first to make them clear and tractable, so that they could be mixed with the colors and used for the painting itself." Before a century had elapsed, this new method was adopted by the other European schools; Leonardo da Vinci used it, and all the Venetians;

in Spain, Velasquez carried the process a step further, discarded the tempera base, and painted in oil pigments alone, establishing a precedent that has held, with practically no deviations, down to the present time. But no single artist or group of artists has ever matched the clean and brilliant color, the perfection of the finished surface and the durability of the efforts of the Flemish masters. The discovery of the Van Eycks was prized as a miracle by their countrymen, and in St. Bavon of Ghent, the bones of the right arm of Hubert, the elder brother, were enshrined in a casket and placed above the door as a sacred relic.

Technical methods mean little or nothing to the average person. Walking through the museums at home or abroad, trying his best to admire what he has been told to admire and to discover qualities which have long since disappeared, he believes that all pictures are painted in oil; and without reflecting on this fact, he believes, in the depths of his heart, that most of them are profoundly boring. And so they are. Dead mealy browns; gummy, resinous ochres; dirty smears of burnt umber. Every color seems to have been mixed with dung. What has happened is that inferior pigments ground in heavy oils have gone dead and brown, ruining the tonality upon which the life and form and meaning of a picture depend. All painting in oil, in the course of time, will deteriorate in color, and nothing can stop it; and yet pure oil painting is practiced today to the exclusion of all other mediums. But the Flemish masterpieces, after more than 500 years, have suffered no perceptible decline, and greet the eye with the glowing freshness of a spring morning. The Van Eycks and their followers, in the first instance, were craftsmen who kept the business of painting close to its original source—an honest business demanding the same intelligence and skill as the craft of the enamellers, engravers and goldsmiths from which it proceeded. But what amazingly patient and conscientious craftsmen they were! The body of their panels was painted in tempera to which were added successive coats of transparent oil glazes, a laborious and exacting method but the most permanent and satisfactory ever devised. The general nature of their processes conceals no mystery, but the formula for their oil glazes and the manipulation of their pigments remain a secret. Painting is the only art which, in technical equipment, has not improved with the advancement of science, and the modern painter has actually at his disposal a more limited set of working tools than the Flemish primitives. And the worst of it is that he does not care, and is perfectly content with the cheap and deceptive effects of commercial tube colors rather than experiment with the old oil and tempera medium. Even so scrupulous a craftsman as Whistler was careless of his materials and his *Portrait of His Mother*, executed with poor pigments and far too much oil, has already faded into a dingy monochrome. In a few more years the exceedingly delicate qualities of his oils, never very tangible, will have vanished in a fuliginous scum.

Besides perfecting a new means of painting, the Van Eyck brothers explored and conquered the mechanics of picture-making, mastered and taught linear and atmospheric perspective and revolutionized the mediaeval notions of landscape. You will recall how the Italians, beginning with Giotto, wrestled with space-construction for 150 years; how Brunelleschi, wrote a treatise on perspective; how Uccello became a maniac on the subject; and how most of the artists of Florence were scientists and mathematicians, forever theorizing and endeavoring, by abstract calculations, to construct the human figure and to formulate laws for the position of objects in space. While all this was going on; while Masaccio was astonishing the Florentines by his elementary discoveries in the division of the picture-planes and by so simple a thing as planting a figure squarely upon its feet, the Van Eycks, without aesthetic fuss and without any speculating whatever, by sheer accuracy of observation, solved most of the technical problems of painting. But skill of hand and an unerring eye for naturalistic truth and correct perspective will not, in themselves, produce art. There is in the National Gallery a sixteenth century Flemish picture by Mabuse called

Adoration of the Kings which in verisimilitude and the minute imitation of all sorts of material substances, has probably never been equalled. For a moment or two we are fascinated by the incredible craftsmanship of the picture, but after our interest in technical ingenuity has been exhausted, we see the work for what it is—a purposeless collection of details, broken tiles, dogs, angels, and figures painted to advertise the artist's skill with stuffs and surfaces. The merchants of Antwerp, admiring in art the things which they counted most desirable in real life, praised this gaudy profusion of rich materials as a work of the highest genius.

With the Van Eycks craftsmanship was not an end in itself, as is the case with so many painters, but a means for moulding the forms of the every day world into a poetic vision. They had that rare faculty which we name imagination, the power to take the old familiar concomitants of life which to the ordinary prosaic mind have no special significance and, recombining them, to charge them with their own intense feelings and experiences so that the ordinary man, beholding forms he had once taken for granted, is carried into a world that is new and strange and enchanting. We know little of these remarkable brothers and less of the painters preceding them. Certainly such a marvellous art as theirs did not spring full-blown from the illuminated pages of sacred manuscripts. In the opinion of the experts, their joint masterpiece, *The Adoration of the Lamb*, in the St. Bavon Cathedral at Ghent, is largely the work of the elder brother, and if the experts for once are right, Hubert Van Eyck is by all odds the greater artist. This altarpiece contains all the properties that Michael Angelo deprecated so splenetically in Flemish art—"saints and martyrs and little figures here and there; grass, the shadows of trees, and rivers and hills which they call landscapes," and a multitude of microscopic forms; it contains all that is memorable in early Flemish painting; and in its triumphant organization of little things, it surpasses anything that has ever come out of Italy.

Ghent, as I have said, is a solemn city, and a solemn stench fills the dark nave of the Cathedral. But grope your way down the aisle to the sixth chapel and a celestial light breaks suddenly upon you. I know of nothing in art so enchanting as the first peep at the apocalyptic vision unfolded on the twelve panels of this magnificent polyptych. The essential splendor of a new dawn; the translucent whiteness of the morning light; a pale sky tinted with ultramarine; vernal greens, deep blues, brilliant reds and shining gold; in the central panel of the upper tier, Christ the King of Heaven, neither proud nor powerful, nor soft and effeminate, as the Italians painted Him, but grave and ruddy; a hairy John the Baptist in a green gown; a piquant Virgin Mary; choirs of full-lipped Flemish angels earnestly singing; Adam and Eve in their scrawny nakedness. In the lower tier, a vast lawn dotted with spring flowers; in the front the Fountain of Life; the White Lamb on an altar surrounded by small white angels; prophets, philosophers, apostles, priests and the citizens of Ghent; behind the Lamb running far into the distance, a great expanse of turf blossoming with Easter daisies, orange trees and roses; a cortege of martyrs; Knights of Christ; the Just Judges and holy women; a ridge of darker hills; and then the new Jerusalem outlined against bluish mountains. Your heart leaps, and if you have been properly brought up, you will kneel before the altar and thank God for the pure soul and the joyous imagination of Hubert Van Eyck.

All this is direct and clear and exquisitely put together; the figures are solid, the lines firm and certain, and the colors, locked up against the damp air in transparent varnishes, as bright as the illuminations of the manuscript books. Not elsewhere in Flemish painting, or for that matter, in all painting, shall we find a picture in which so many small forms—pebbles, precious stones, leaves and flowers, banners, brocades, tiled patterns, and carved woods drawn with the minute observation of the miniaturists—have been included without prejudice to the general design. And the design is the vision of Hubert Van Eyck, who looked at the world and found it good, a strong and noble and devout character whose generous humanity informs every one of the hundreds of figures, irrespective of age or rank, whose gentleness and sympathy are traced in every folded robe and starry flower and rounded brow.

The altarpiece illustrates the vision of St. John as described in Revelation, but it is difficult, even in our most reverent moments, to associate these Flemish characters, most of them unquestionably portraits, with the actors in the biblical drama, to believe that the Gothic towers represent the celestial architecture of the new Jerusalem, and to construe the whole scene as symbolical of the redemption of mankind by the blood of the Immaculate Lamb. Not only is it difficult, it is unnecessary. The story worked vividly upon Van Eyck's imagination, but the wonders illustrating St. John's vision he discovered within himself; his love for mankind and for all things great and small, he projected into his characters and his landscapes, purging his men and women of the sacrificial agonies and tortures common to mediaeval art, and filling them with ecstatic kindliness. The picture is exalting; there is nothing quite like it in all painting; in its directness, its refreshing integrity and its clean poetic imagery, it may be compared to the tales of Chaucer.

John Van Eyck outlived his brother many years and was sent by the Duke of Burgundy on confidential missions into Spain and Portugal. He was a portrait painter, and in the literal meaning of the term, he remains without a peer. Acrid, unflattering and cold-blooded, he first examined the human face with an infallible eye for the plastic relations of lines and features; next he proceeded to rebuild the head in order to compel the face to yield the psychological secrets of the sitter. Because of his plebeian interest in the minutiae of objects, he has been called "a marvellous photographic machine" and a "preternatural reporter," reproaches which, I assure you, do him great injury. If he only copied visual appearances, and recorded everything that impressed its image on his retina, without selection or purpose, then, I ask why no other painter in the course of 500 years, has ever duplicated his performances and why the photographic method has never again produced an artistic picture?

John Van Eyck was a constructive artist and a great one. It happened that he deliberately avoided those "large generalized masses" which so many painters affect because they cannot draw and because they cannot manage detailed forms without falling into offensive distortions, and that he frowned upon glorified sensuality and "beautiful faces." Just as his brother excels in the organization of a multiplicity of figures and objects into a single unit, so does he excel all painters in the organization of the smallest components of the face into a synthetic countenance. The man had a biological passion for probing into homeliness. Instead of leaving out wrinkles, wens and blemishes, he seems actually to add to the natural allotments, blending innumerable items into a downright, speaking reality. Sometimes he signed his pictures with a great flourish, but the signatures are superfluous: the heads portray not only the subject but the maker, the coldest and most precise personality that ever got itself into paint.

The indigenous flavor of Flemish painting was maintained by Robert Campin, Roger van der Weyden, Peter Christus and Hans Memling, the last by reason of the appealing delicacy of his portraits and the quaint mediaeval sentimentality of his religious pieces, the most popular artist of the early school; but in the sixteenth century the Flemish painters went down into Italy and learned just enough about the heroic style to ruin the native tradition which the Van Eycks and their successors had so patiently erected. Unable to assimilate Renaissance culture and to fathom the principles of mural design, they loaded their own honest realism with theatrical decoration and Italian clap-trap—the mixture being the more ridiculous because of its mechanical competency and its glassy smoothness—and charmed the florid tastes of the Antwerp burgesses. In the thick of this false elegance and foolish Italian-worship, Pieter Bruegel, the Elder, appeared.

It is one of the enigmas of art that Bruegel should have remained in obscurity for nearly four centuries. Today, outside of Belgium and Germany, his name has little meaning to a public familiar with the Italian masters, and artists are only just beginning to overcome their curious prejudice against his irony and his humor. For a long time after his death he was remembered as "Pieter the Droll," a Rabelaisian fellow with an unsavory interest in diableries and the coarser aspects of peasant life. Were it not for the fact that painting has been regarded as a matter of feeling and sensitivity rather than brains and intelligence, he would long ago have received his full meed of appreciation.

Bruegel possesses most of the essentials of the great artist. His concern with life is vast and anthropological: no dabbling in still-life for him; no paltry studies of isolated bits of landscape; no stupid copying of models in Italian attitudes. He is interested in people, in the whole business of mankind from the intimate habits of peasants to the industrial and spiritual problems of his beloved Antwerp. His canvases are alive with figures, crowds, processions and cataracts of them, conveying not only a marvellously accurate sense of the given scene, but an allegorical significance as convincing as *The Pilgrim's Progress.* Like Giotto and Daumier, he delved into the homely human stuff around him and ennobled it into dramatic art. He had no need to plunder the Renaissance and the Primitives, and to make pictures out of the deposits of the past. When a very young man—he was only forty when he died—he journeyed to Italy, but if the southern painters impressed him at all, it was only to strengthen his conviction that he had nothing in common with their glorious Madonnas. He had other battles to fight; he was a Northerner to the marrow of his bones; and in more than one direction he surpassed the Italians.

As an ironist Bruegel is, perhaps, the most distinguished in the history of painting. He is without the fierceness of Goya, but his vision is larger and mellowed by philosophical tolerance. *The Carrying of the Cross* is one of the most amazing pictures in existence. Swarms of sightseers, on foot and horse, ramble merrily up a long hillside on a bright spring morning. "Other artists," observes Aldous Huxley, "have pretended to be angels, painting the scene with a knowledge of its significance. But Bruegel resolutely remains a human onlooker. Round the crosses of the two thieves on the bare cliff stands a ring of people who have come out with their picnic baskets to look at the free entertainment offered by the ministers of justice. Those who have already taken the stand are the prudent ones: in these days we should see them with camp stools and thermos flasks six hours ahead of time. The less provident or more adventurous are in the crowd coming up the hill with the third and greatest of the criminals whose cross is to take the place of honor between the other two."

Not less remarkable is *The Fall of Icarus*. In the foreground, on a piece of land by the sea, a Flemish laborer is serenely plowing; near by a shepherd gazes amusedly at the heavens; in the right-hand corner, visible by one flying leg, Icarus, a mere detail, disappears beneath the waves.

Those who are skeptical of allegories in paint will be comforted to know that Bruegel's work will pass the most rigid aesthetic tests. He is a first-rate composer; the countless figures in his canvases are not thrown together in the haphazard fashion of the modern illustrator, but are conceived as parts of an elaborate synthesis of black and white masses; his landscapes are beautifully constructed in a series of recessive planes; in his use of snow as a background for figures and natural forms revealed as silhouettes, he has no rivals in the western world; and he is a draughtsman of extraordinary ease and power.

But not even the stout imagination of Bruegel could redeem Flemish painting from the banality of the Italianates. A greater man was needed, one capable of going to school to the Mediterranean masters without sacrificing his own originality. That man was Peter Paul Rubens.

CHAPTER

IX

RUBENS

THE most magnificent of painters came from bourgeois stock. The stock was typically Flemish, solid, substantial and undistinguished, an Antwerp family which, for many generations, had dealt in hides, drugs and groceries. In 1531, John Rubens, the father of the artist, was born, and the line of petty tradesmen was ended. John Rubens was ambitious; he studied at Padua and Louvain, acquired, after the fashion of the times, a great deal of pedantic Latin, took his degree of Doctor of Laws at Rome and, but for his religious inconsistencies and his feebly sinful character, might have claimed the highest honors in the legal profession. After winning recognition as an advocate and serving as alderman of Antwerp for six years, he decided, at the worst possible moment, to become a Calvinist.

His decision was the act of a blunderer and a coward. When the Protestant iconoclasts began to destroy the sacred relics of the Romanist churches and to oppose the dominion of Spain, Philip II despatched the Duke of Alba to Antwerp to put down the heresy. What the terrible Duke did to the people of Flanders is well known, and Dr. John Rubens, the most learned Calvinist in the Low Countries, soon found himself on the lists of the famous Council of Blood. To save his skin he gathered together his money, his wife, the daughter of a tapestry weaver, his three children, and escaped to Cologne, where he obediently rejoined the Catholic Church.

At Cologne Dr. Rubens seems to have prospered, and all went well until he became the legal advisor to Princess Anne, the second wife of William of Orange. The Princess was an ugly

Rubens: SELF-PORTRAIT.

Hofmuseum, Vienna

woman and a notorious drinker and seducer, but being a Princess she captivated her advisor, made a fool of him and utterly ruined him. When she gave birth to a sickly child, that as one writer expresses it, "could have had nothing to do with her husband," William the Silent had the guilty doctor thrown into jail as an adulterer. The penalty for adultery was death, and John Rubens would have suffered it, but for the courage and patience of his wife, Maria Pypelinckx, the tapestry weaver. Maria Pypelinckx, with a magnanimity unknown to the modern woman, forgave her erring husband and sent letter after letter to the House of Nassau, petitioning his release. Her appeals were ignored until, after two years of continual solicitation, she threatened to expose the scandal to the world. At last, at a cost of the bulk of her savings, she obtained a pardon from the Prince of Orange and the united family retired to Siegen, a town west of Cologne, to live down their shame. Here, on June 28th, 1577, she bore her last child and named him Peter-Paul after the two great apostles on whose feast day he was baptized. Dr. Rubens resumed his practice in Cologne—without danger now since Princess Anne had died of drink in an asylum, and thoroughly chastened, gradually restored the family fortune which had been expended to get him out of his trouble. But he had not long to live, and after his death in 1587, Maria Pypelinckx returned with her children to Antwerp.

The great state of Flanders had been reduced to a great desert. The "Spanish Fury", opposing with the foulest tortures those who had dared "to criticize the best of kings," had accomplished its purpose with an abominable thoroughness compared to which the late Teutonic occupation was only a harmless holiday. Alba boasted that he had slain 18,000 people; half the population of Antwerp had emigrated and horses cropped grass in the streets; Bruges and Ghent were deserted villages, their factories destroyed, their weavers gone to England. The Church was the only flourishing industry, and convents sprang up everywhere to comfort the poor in heart.

Rubens, a boy of eleven, had been spared the horrors of the

Spanish tribunal. Nor was he ever to know the cause of his father's exile and his mother's sorrows. In Cologne his mother, with a shrewd and unfailing tenderness, had prepared him to love the city of his ancestors. Antwerp was depopulated but the spirit of the burgesses was not extinguished, and when the tyranny of Spain was lightened, the city began to thrive again, and through the mind and art of Peter-Paul Rubens to rise to unexampled splendor and renown. Maria Pypelinckx, a hard-headed woman as well as a noble mother, recovered the family possessions, and resolved that her son should have every advantage in the world.

The boy, already a good Latinist, thanks to his father's tutoring, was sent, with the sons of the best families, to a school kept by an old gentleman who had been reading the classics for fifty-two years. The old gentleman was an excellent master, but there was not much that he could teach his gifted pupil. Rubens learned everything with extraordinary rapidity, not without effort but with a clear head and remarkable powers of application. German he spoke from infancy along with his native tongue; he used Latin with facility and elegance; at the outset of his career as an artist he was a master of seven languages. Not in his whole lifetime was he idle; not in all history is there another such example of great natural endowments united to great industry and imperturbable common sense. As a boy he was reserved and amiable, always occupied—and occupied intelligently—free from moods and cheap distractions, without vanity, arrogance and meanness. He preserved these qualities throughout his brilliant life as painter, diplomatist and scholar: not one base or shabby trick has ever been charged against him. He kept his feet on the earth; he suffered no delusions, and with his candor, his wisdom, his kindliness, and his universal sympathies conquered the whole world, leaving heaven and hell to such harassed souls as Michael Angelo and a disreputable Dutchman, thirty years his junior, named Rembrandt.

At the age of thirteen he said goodbye to the aged Latinist and was attached by his ambitious mother to the court of a princess.

He served as page to the princess for a year, learned French, and improved his manners, but the frivolity of court life disgusted him and he returned home and announced his intention of becoming an artist. His mother was pained; she saw neither money nor glory in art, now that the Spaniards had pillaged the country, and she had, moreover, been secretly scheming to make a lawyer out of Peter-Paul, notwithstanding the example of her late husband. So she called the family together—a council of honest tradesmen who were deeply impressed by the unexpected eloquence and courtly address of the young man. Rubens gained his point. His intention was not based on a sudden desire but on his progress in drawing which he had worked at for a number of years, in fact, since his childhood in Cologne when he had first copied the illustrations in a famous Swiss bible.

Rubens studied with three masters, all servile worshipers of the grandiose style of dying Italy. He remained with the first, Verhaecht, a distant relative, only six months and learned nothing; the second, Van Noort, gave him the severest training in the fundamentals of painting. Van Noort was a coarse-tongued sot whose abusive behavior was a sorry trial to a sensitive youth with a decent regard for the feelings of others. The third, Van Veen, or Vaenius, as he preferred to call himself, was a man of wide learning in the arts and sciences, an inveterate traveller, a poet in several languages, and a handsome cavalier. He was a poor painter whose originality, if he had ever possessed any, had been lost in the overwhelming influence of the great designers of Florence and Venice, but of all the forgotten Flemings who were wrestling with the grand style, he was the only one with any real knowledge of Italian design, and this knowledge he imparted to his pupil. In 1599, when Phillip II married his daughter Isabella to Archduke Albert, and awarded them, as a wedding present, the sovereignty of Flanders, Van Veen and his young assistant made the decorations for the triumphal entry of the royal couple into the city of Antwerp. In 1560, Rubens, having taken all that his master could give him, twenty-three years old, a free-master of the Guild of St. Luke since his majority, departed for Italy, travelling on horseback from Antwerp to Venice.

The world of art and of material success lay before him. No painter, before or since, at the age of twenty-three was more certain in his aims or more excellently equipped, mentally and physically, to accomplish them. Born into an impoverished country, trained in a land that could not truthfully boast of a single artist of merit, a student of the Italians when contemporary Italy was dominated by eclectics like the Carracci and the sensational Caravaggio, he did not complain, as Michael Angelo had cried out, some years before him, that "the times were unfavorable for art", but swept away all obstructions and climbed steadily to the heights which he had envisaged as a boy in the studio of the brutal Van Noort. With a magnanimity not common to artists he employed his diplomatic talents to placate the tempers of kings and ministers, and despite his political interruptions, surpassed all other painters in fecundity, "relieving himself," as Taine says, "by creating new worlds." His development followed a straight ascending line, the variations in his style being purely technical and of small spiritual importance, but so vast was his program and so prodigious his imagination that twelve years of systematic labor were to elapse from his arrival in Italy to the completion of his first masterpiece. His ambition was not to imitate the Italians but to rival them, to extend the closed, or classical type of composition into a freer and more pliable instrument of expression, one congenial to his own rich and expansive nature, one by which Flemish earthiness and the strong savor of material abundance which he loved so ardently might be fused into a comprehensive organism of refreshing nakedness and blooming color, of undefiled splendor and healthy passion and dramatic energy.

He went to Italy as a student but no sooner had he set foot in Venice than he was snapped up by the Duke of Mantua. It has been said that his life was a golden chain of lucky accidents. Nothing could be more libelous. Rubens was a striking figure;

he was tall and fair, his forehead high and clear, his lips full, his complexion ruddy, and his brown eyes gay and gentle; his long auburn hair was carefully parted and brushed back; he wore a trim beard, a twirled moustache and the best of clothes. He had the manners of a prince and the discretion of a gentleman; aware that art was now in the hands of the aristocrats he took pains to make himself *persona grata* to his patrons. This, I think, was only good sense. But he was not addled by nobility. He truckled to no one, and we do not find him, like Titian, begging fulsomely for favors from royal alms-givers or allowing himself to be advertised by a bloodsucker. His tastes were luxurious; he loved baroque castles, blooded horses, and spacious studios lined with the original works of the greatest masters, but to obtain these things was willing to labor beyond the capacities of a dozen ordinary men, and to operate his business on the large-scale productive methods of the modern capitalist. As a young man of twenty-three on a modest allowance, he was not likely to overlook an opportunity to pursue his studies under the most enjoyable circumstances.

Vicenzo de Gonzaga, Duke of Mantua, connected by blood and marriage with many royal houses and a sovereign in his own right, was a reckless spendthrift and a collector of art treasures of every kind and category: Italian pictures, Chinese ceramics, Cremona fiddles, Dutch tulips, German engravers, actors, prostitutes and Flemish painters. Before he married his second wife, a Medici and a sister of the future Queen of France, he had been terribly humiliated by a bit of scandalous tattle circulated by one of his enemies. The tale ran that the Duke had lost his manhood and on account of such disability had been divorced by his first wife. Though a little mad, the Duke was far from impotent, but the Medici, rightly enough, would not consent to the completion of the marriage contract until he had satisfactorily proved that he was a functioning male. The Duke accepted the challenge and the ordeal was held in Venice, "a specially selected virgin" cooperating, before trustworthy witnesses and experts in such matters. The Church, it seems, authorized the experiment with the stipulation that it must not be performed on a Friday. In due course the anxious Duke was pronounced competent and two noble families were happily united.

As court painter Rubens had an easy time of it. He was obliged, now and then, to glorify the spiritual pretensions of his keeper—to paint the Gonzaga family adoring the Holy Trinity and other sublimities—but these ambitious decorations enabled him to compare his own conceptions with the great Italian pictures surrounding him. In the Duke's palaces were murals by Mantegna, Lorenzo Costa, Perugino and Giulio Romano which he might examine at his leisure; and he was at liberty to travel and to accept commissions from outsiders. Already he showed signs of that superhuman productivity which, at the fulness of his powers, gave credence to the legend that he created magically, with godlike spontaneity, and without trials or reflections. The truth is that he worked incessantly, with confidence perhaps, but in a more equable spirit than is characteristic of artists. His experiences broadened; he went frequently to Venice to study Titian and Tintoretto, visited Florence, and lived in Rome, dividing his time between the Sistine Chapel and the Church of Santa Croce for which he was painting an altarpiece. His interests embraced science, architecture, and antiquities; and he corresponded with numerous specialists in the arts, always writing in Latin.

Nor did he neglect his duties as a courtier. His charm, his tact and his intelligence completely won the Duke, and in 1603, Gonzaga, to maintain the political sympathies of Philip III, ordered Rubens to carry a quantity of presents to the Spanish court. The journey was long and the presents included many objects difficult to transport. The King was to have a coach and seven bay horses, a set of arquebuses and a rock-crystal vase filled with perfumes; for the Duke of Lerma there were many paintings, all copies, and a chest of silver; for the ladies of the court crucifixes, candlesticks and all sorts of fragile trumpery; and for the lesser functionaries money and clothes. After many delays by land and sea, and a month of rain, the embassy arrived at

Rubens: HEADS OF NEGROES.

Royal Museum, Brussels

Valladolid with the precious baggage in perfect condition except the paintings which had been seriously damaged by moisture. While waiting for the slothful court to arrange an audience, Rubens, politely refusing the services of the Spanish artists of whom he held a very poor opinion, restored the canvases and for two that were beyond redemption, substituted a couple of Greek philosophers painted entirely by his own hand. When the pictures were finally exhibited, the King and Queen, and the whole court including the fool, the dwarf and the Queen's major-domo, a great expert in the arts, believed them to be originals and were, of course, in their own arrogant fashion, greatly delighted. The Duke of Lerma immediately ordered an equestrian portrait and separate studies of Christ and the twelve apostles, and these trifles Rubens executed with more than usual speed; and having convinced everyone that he was not only the prince of painters but the most gracious of ambassadors, bowed himself out and returned to Italy.

After his return he worked for two years on three big religious pieces celebrating the piety of the Gonzagas, receiving special compensation—when he could collect it—for commissions of this kind. During the rest of his sojourn in Italy, though still in the employ of Duke Vicenzo, he painted but little for his patron. In Milan he copied Leonardo's *The Last Supper*; in Genoa he made 150 drawings of palaces which, a few years later, he published in book form for the improvement of Flemish architecture; in Rome he studied classical literature with his brother Philip, an insufferable Latinist, painted portraits, and hampered by an attack of pleurisy and repeated commands of the Duke to repair at once to Mantua, finished an important altarpiece for the Church of Santa Maria. In the autumn of 1608 he wrote to Gonzaga that "he had received very bad news of his mother's health, and that he was setting out, at once, for Antwerp." He had not seen his mother for nearly nine years; the bond between them was close and he rode hard, only to learn that she had died before he had left Italy. In her will she wrote: "I give to my two sons the cooking utensils and everything else that is present, as well as all the books, papers and writings belonging to me, with the pictures in my possession which are only portraits. The other pictures in my possession which are beautiful, belong to Peter-Paul who painted them."

During his long residence in Italy, Rubens had fed upon many masters: the giant anatomies of Michael Angelo, the classic grace of Raphael, the drawing of Mantegna, the color of Titian and Veronese, and the torrential designs of Tintoretto—all these had gone into the development of his insatiable genius. But he had not lost his identity: the Fleming remained—solidly masoned in a framework that was, as yet, foreign and conglomerate—the individual Fleming, Peter-Paul Rubens. In the pictures of his first period, that is, up to the age of thirty-five, the special virtues of the Italians are obvious, but in looking at these pictures, overladen and experimental, as they unquestionably are, we are not conscious of the borrowings but of the fighting, unformed efforts of a new and mighty personality. Of the countless painters who have followed the precarious and generally suicidal custom of trying to make artists of themselves by dwelling for years in alien environments, Rubens is one of the few who survived the ordeal and returned home a stronger and better man. And let us bear in mind that it was not until he had again warmed his blood at his native hearth and had, after several years of industrious painting in his old haunts, gradually pushed his Italian impressions into the background of his experiences, that he began to produce anything of permanent value.

When he arrived in Antwerp the art of the whole world was in a deplorable state: the Italian tradition had terminated in theatrical profusion, and the painters of his own country, abandoning the tradition of the Van Eycks, were only dull copyists of the rank Italian style. He had the field to himself. There was not a single painter of outstanding ability to oppose him. When he let loose the fecundating, irresistible force of his imagination, the men of his own time were driven before it and the art of the world assumed a new direction. In the succeeding centuries, it whirled through Europe with undiminished vitality, destroying the weak and invigorating the strong. It reappeared, in softer form, in the figures of Renoir, and today artists are still affected by its powerful rhythms.

Rubens, already famous, was welcomed home by his old teachers and friends, and all the worthies of Antwerp who wished to ride to glory in the chariot of their first citizen. Immediately he was made court-painter by the Viceroys, Albert and Isabella, with an annual salary, numerous liberties and immunities, and exemption from the authority of the painters' guild. Spain had finally declared an armistice and peace reigned in the Netherlands; the churches, denuded by Protestant vandals, awaited his brush; commissions poured in; the year after his return he married and settled down to a life of domestic tranquillity, hard work and increasing fame.

His bride was Isabella Brant, not yet eighteen, the daughter of a prominent lawyer, large, handsome and unmistakably Flemish. His brother Philip supplied the epithalamium in Latin, "inviting Hymen to the nuptials, and to the bridal chamber, for which Peter-Paul longed so fervently, and his bride with moderation, though he promised that she would, the next morning, vow that the night had excelled the most beautiful day; eulogizing the ancestors of both parties; personifying Peter-Paul as Adonis; and finally begging that before the sun hath accomplished his annual course, Isabella will boast of a descendant that resembleth her husband." Isabella boasted of three descendants, Clara, Albert and Nicholas; beautiful children they were indeed, and their father painted them many times.

There hangs in Munich one of the earliest of Rubens' great portraits, himself and his wife painted shortly after their marriage. They are sitting, holding hands, in a bower of honeysuckle, splendidly dressed, Rubens in a doublet of yellow-green, black-velvet breeches, orange stockings and a Henri Quatre hat; Isabella, in a black jacket, a blue satin bodice, embroidered in gold, a violet skirt and a yellow petticoat. The picture is painted with a boldness and plasticity and brilliancy of color that shocked his fellow artists and roused them from their empty-headed lethargy.

It is sumptuous and human; a fine, compact, circular design; an invaluable document; a noble tribute to a happy marriage.

His house in Antwerp was a palatial structure in the florid, late Renaissance style, an old place restored and enlarged from his own designs at a great expense of time and money. The house consisted of two parts connected by a portico and a pavilion in which he displayed his collection of old sculptures and smaller antiquities: in one wing he lived with his family in rooms hung with stamped leather and decorated with pictures, his own and those he had brought from Italy; the other contained a vast studio, forty-six feet long, thirty-five feet wide and thirty feet high, and quarters for his pupils and assistants. Peacocks and hunting dogs roamed over the lawns; there were formal gardens, grottoes, fountains and stables for his Spanish horses. On one of the arches of the portico was engraved a quotation from Juvenal, the old familiar exhortation, now an ancient platitude but still fresh and sparkling in those Romanized days, and remarkably descriptive of Rubens' character.

"Let your prayer be for a sound mind in a sound body, a brave heart innocent of fear and cupidity and unacquainted with the terrors of death."

To this house came scholars, painters, politicans, and learned men from all parts of Europe; the vast studio was the art center of the world, sending forth under the master's direction nearly 3000 pictures; and the master, as his wealth and honors multiplied, continued to live simply in the bosom of his family. I say that he lived simply, for his tastes, apart from his strictly aesthetic needs, were modest, and his daily life conducted with conventual austerity. One might think—and such I have discovered to be the popular opinion—from his luxurious establishment, his formal dinners, his nine years in a corrupt Italian court, and the massive fleshiness of the women he painted, that Rubens was a man of omnivorous physical appetites and a self-evident exponent of sensual indulgences. Let us see.

He was up, the year round, at four o'clock, and after hearing Mass, went at once to his studio where he labored as long as the daylight lasted, permitting no one to interrupt him, and painting with a concentration and rapidity that few modern artists know anything about. Late in the afternoon he spent an hour with his engraved gems, his pictures and his marbles, and then went out for a ride on one of his favorite horses. He ate and drank very little, avoiding intemperance in all its forms, and regarded obscenity with an almost prudish abhorrence. His nights were given over to the society of his learned friends and to the study of antique carvings in which field he became one of the foremost authorities in Europe. He had, as Fromentin said, "the most remarkable balance that ever existed in a human brain"; he had no time for and no inclination toward loose-living: though he loved the nude figure with a profound passion, his sexual life found ample satisfaction in the two women whom he married, and not even the most suspicious biographers have succeeded in connecting him with a single intrigue or compromising gallantry.

In 1612, in his thirty-fifth year, Rubens produced his first indisputable masterpiece, *The Descent from the Cross*, in the Antwerp Cathedral, not a characteristic work in color and painted before he had perfected his marvellous skill in "drawing with the brush", but certainly one of the greatest pictorial compositions in art. He was now the acknowledged leader of a new school, and painters realized that it was no longer necessary to go to Italy to study. Instead they flocked to Rubens, and he was reluctantly compelled to turn away more than a hundred pupils, some of whom were friends and relatives. In acknowledging his leadership, painters were persuaded by his urbanity and his personality as well as by his towering artistry. He made no enemies and aroused no jealousies, and the most significant proof of the esteem in which he was held is the fact that all his rivals eventually entered his studio as his assistants, accepted his ideas of composition, and imitated his draughtsmanship and his technique.

The demand for his pictures increased to such proportions that Rubens, with his gusto for painting, his unwillingness to refuse a commission, and his executive ability, organized his corps of assistants into a shop of non-union operatives—he was, remember, independent of guild control—equipped to manufacture everything within the scope of painting; gigantic decorations, religious pieces, mythologies, portraits, landscapes, hunting scenes, and designs for engravers and tapestry weavers. A Danish traveller, visiting Antwerp at this time, pays his respects to Rubens.

"We visited," he records, "the very celebrated and eminent painter Rubens, whom we found at work, and, while he went on with his painting, listening to a reading from Tacitus and dictating a letter. We kept silent for fear of disturbing him; but he spoke to us without stopping his work or the reading, or the dictation, and answered our questions as if to give us proof of his powerful faculties. Then he ordered a servant to conduct us round his magnificent palace and show us his antiquities and the Greek and Roman statues, of which he possesses a great quantity. We also saw a vast room, without windows, lighted by a large opening in the middle of the ceiling. A number of young painters were gathered there, each engaged on a different work, for which Monsieur Rubens had given him a pencil drawing, touched with color here and there. These young people must carry out these pictures in paint, when Monsieur Rubens will finish them off."

Among the staff artists were Snyders and De Vos, animal painters; John Breugel, the florist; Van Uden and Wildens, landscape gardners; and the young Van Dyck, the most gifted of all. Van Dyck was only a boy of nineteen when he entered the studio, but in a short time he became Rubens' right-hand man. "His works soon began to be almost as much admired as those of his master," a contemporary correspondent tells us, "but he could not be persuaded to leave, seeing what an immense fortune Rubens was amassing." An order came in from the Cathedral of Malines for a large altarpiece; the master made the designs and the sketches in color and then sent Van Dyck down to begin the job. The Dean of the Cathedral was exceedingly wroth at the sight of the youthful assistant, fearing that he was not getting what he had bargained for, but some days later, when the great man himself appeared, serene and gentle but no less commanding, mounted the ladder, and with a knowledge of form and a swiftness of execution that reduced his helpers to the ranks of the amateurs, enlivened the color and carried the work forward to the unity indicated by the original sketches; the fears of the Dean were allayed and he agreed that his money had been wisely invested.

Rubens has been severely condemned for his wholesale methods of production, but after all, his methods did not differ materially from those of the Italian fresco painters. Part of the construction of a picture is purely mechanical, a fact which accounts for his ability to paint while listening to readings from the Latin authors, and which explains his scale of prices. He reckoned the value of his works according to the time spent upon them, his income averaging about $100 a day. The design, the truly creative part of a picture, he always performed himself, entrusting the mechanical labors of enlargement and ground painting to his assistants, and then returning to add the color and to pull the work together into its final form. In a desperate rush, he executed the job from start to finish entirely with his own brushes, outspeeding the combined efforts of his subordinates. His factory increased the demand for pictures and gave employment to many competent painters who had no ideas of their own, but it had its objectionable features; it frequently happened that clients were satisfied with copies, or that the master was too busy to put the final touches to a canvas, and the result was that hundreds of studio works in which his great ideas were rendered perfunctorily and without his unique virility were scattered all over Europe and in the course of time attributed to him alone. But the number of pictures painted largely or wholly by himself, and upon which his fame securely rests, exceeds that of any other artist, and we have no reasons to condemn his system of mass-production.

In selling his pictures, Rubens, with punctilious honesty when he might easily have deceived the purchaser, described the work in detail, declaring it to be original or not, and if not, the precise extent of his own labors. He valued originals at double the price of canvases done in collaboration. When he proposed a list of paintings to Sir Dudley Carleton in a transaction which added a notable collection of antique marbles to his gallery in exchange for ten of his pictures, he wrote in his first letter: "the eagle is by Snyders"; "by my own hand, except for a very beautiful landscape by a man extremely clever in this type of work"; "begun by one of my pupils but not yet finished. I shall retouch it entirely myself, so that it would pass for an original"; "by my best pupil (Van Dyck), and thoroughly gone over by myself."

In another letter he said, "Your Excellency has chosen only my original works, by which I am most flattered. You must not, however, imagine that the others are simply copies; they are so well touched up by my hand that it is only with difficulty that they are distinguished from originals; and yet they are appraised at a much lower price." And this frank admission showing the commercial side of his genius: "The reason why I would rather pay for the marbles with my pictures is evident. Although I have not overvalued them, they cost me nothing, and Your Excellency knows that one is more free with the fruit picked in one's own garden than with what one has to buy in the market; besides, I have spent this year several thousand florins in building, and I do not wish, for a luxury, to pass the bounds of wise economy. After all, I am no prince, but one who lives by the work of his hands." The Englishman replied handsomely: "I conform to the suggestions of your last two letters in all things, except that I will not admit the denial you express in the first of them: you say you are not a prince, but I hold you to be the *Principe di pittori et galant huomini*"—(the correspondence was carried on in Italian)—the Prince of Painters and a fine gentleman.

During the fifteen relatively peaceful years following his marriage, the productivity of Rubens was stupendous. His picture factory was running at full blast and all hands strove to rival the terrific industry of the master. Rubens, apparently immune from fatigue, bore the strain without brainstorms or the fitful displays of temperament which characterize the minor artist. His mill was a phenomenon in Flanders—in truth nothing resembling it had appeared in art since Raphael's Roman Fresco Company—and order after order came in from Church, State and the wealthier laity. He filled them all, from the forty huge decorations for the ceiling of the new Jesuit Church in Antwerp to small drawings for the engravers and designs for tapestries which, with his skill in draughtsmanship, he delivered to the weavers in reversed form, ready for use. And in addition to his art business, he found time to write a book on architecture and another on antique gems, and as a representative of the Spanish Regents to visit Holland on a diplomatic mission. For his official services he received from Philip IV "the title and degree of nobility," an honor bestowing upon him a coat-of-arms and other useless ornaments.

The canvases of this interval, for the most part, are composite pieces, which cannot be placed in the first rank, but those done by Rubens alone—or many of them—must be grouped with his best work. Among the masterpieces we may mention *The Miraculous Draught of Fishes* (Malines), painted in one day; *The Last Communion of St. Francis* (Antwerp); *The Rape of the Daughters of Leukippos* (Munich); *The Battle of the Amazons* (Munich); *The Flight Into Egypt* (London) private collection; *The Adoration of the Magi* (Antwerp); *The Triumph of Silenus* (National Gallery); and numerous portraits such as *Susanne Fourment* (National Gallery); and *The Earl of Arundel and His Wife* (Munich).

Small jobs bored him, and he had no patience with the hard costive style of his Flemish predecessors. "I confess," he wrote to King James of England in 1621, "that, owing to a certain natural bent, I am better fitted to do works on a very large scale than to paint little curiosities. Every man according to his gifts. My talents are of such an order that no undertaking, no matter how vast its size and diversity of its subjects, has ever yet daunted my courage." The next year he was elected to a task which in size and subject-matter called for the exercise of all his talents.

Maria de' Medici, daughter of the fat Florentine banker—and not so slender herself—was the sister of the wife of the Duke of Mantua, his first patron. Rubens had met her in Italy when the wealthy Medici, for the sum of 600,000 crowns, had bought the Queenship of France, marrying Maria, by proxy, to King Henry IV. She was a handsome, intriguing, dissolute woman who, after the assassination of her husband, had reigned as regent for four years attended by her Italian lover and her Italian court. She quarrelled and fought with her son, Louis XIII, and Louis, on ascending the throne, promptly sent her into exile, and ordered her lover to be murdered. Mother and son were reconciled but not for long: Maria recruited an army and engaged the royal troops at Pont-de-Ce, but at this juncture, a cunning priest, afterwards Cardinal de Richelieu, intervened and a treaty of peace was signed. As Queen-Mother again, Maria somehow restrained her military passions for six years, and began, after the best traditions of the family, to patronize the arts. She tore down the old Luxembourg hotel and built for herself a grand palace modelled on the Pitti in Florence; and when one of the great galleries was completed, Rubens was nominated to decorate it with episodes from her unedifying career. His appointment was bitterly opposed by the French painters, but Maria knew her man, and agreed with her agent that "no one in Europe except Rubens was capable of so vast a work. The painters of Italy and France would not accomplish in ten years what Rubens would do in four, and would not even think of undertaking pictures of the necessary size."

The subject, as I have suggested, was not inspiring, and the space to be filled was colossal: eighteen panels thirteen feet high and ten feet wide; three canvases thirteen feet high and twenty-four feet wide, and a number of eight-foot portraits. There were disputes to be settled and tempers to be soothed, a preliminary conference of six weeks and three more conferences —and Rubens, remember, had to travel by horse from his studio in Antwerp to Paris. In three years the work was finished, Rubens designing all the pictures and going over them twice—once in his studio, and again when they were hung in the Luxembourg. No one was permitted to see them until the last panel was in place, "so that the full magnificence of the decoration should burst on the public in one clap." The Queen-Mother "was satisfied beyond all expression, proclaiming Rubens the first painter of the world and expressing an unparalleled good-will towards him," and the Cardinal de Richelieu, and even the French painters sang the praises of the Fleming. "Louis XIII was also delighted as he walked through the gallery accompanied by the Abbé de St. Ambroise, who explained the subjects, changing and varying the true meaning with great artifice." Rubens himself was not exactly overjoyed: the procrastinating Court had wearied him and he had not been paid in full. "When I consider the journeys I made to Paris", he said, "and the time I stayed there without recompense, I find that this work for the Queen-Mother has done me little good."

The series hangs today in the Louvre, France, as Rooses says, "having provided the most sumptuous gallery that harbors any collection of art in the world." As allegory in which it was at the time of its unfurling thought to be extraordinarily rich, it has lost most of its significance; as history, except for one or two incidents, particularly the Coronation scene, it was never important; as art it is one of the greatest achievements in painting. Not in its individual portions, for Rubens in his last years painted single pictures surpassing any one of the Medici panels, but collectively, as the overwhelming, and at the same time, the deliberately regulated discharges of a great spirit that was no less profound because it happened to be free from mysteries and gloomy sentiments.

It is the third and last of the complete worlds of the spirit which art has re-created for us, the first being Giotto's Chapel at Padua, the second the Sistine chapel of Michael Angelo. After

Rubens, there is no more mural painting of the first importance—only the little curiosities of the Dutch and the magnified curiosities of other schools.

Rubens cared little enough for the official sins or the shady past of the fat Dowager, and as a consequence loaded his theme with all the resources of his imagination, drawing heavily upon mythology which was in the air and which he genuinely loved. The Queen-Mother is enmeshed in a labyrinth of nudity, pageantry and symbolism: Goddesses of Plenty attend her; nude fates spin her destiny; the Muses guard her education; superb Undines escort her into Marseilles; Jupiter and Juno are her wedding guests. But no one stops to consider the meaning of the symbols, and no one seeks to penetrate the elaborate historical disguises. Rubens, in this series, by means of large, supple bodies consummately modelled and so postured and joined and interrelated as to convey in the highest degree the energy and movement of living forms, by naked figures palpitating with vitality, by the splendor of costumes and scenic accessories rich in color, creates a world which completely satisfied certain human needs, a world in which the frugal, the stunted and the timorous have no place, in which the spirit partakes of the healthy freshness and bracing abundance of organic life.

While occupied with this commission he was pushed into the arena of international politics. The truce between Spain and the Netherlands had ended; the Archduke had died, and his wife, Isabella, chose Rubens as her confidential missionary. The painter had no pronounced affection for politics, but it was thought that his movements would be less suspicious than those of the ordinary agent and he was sent to Holland to propose a new treaty to the Dutch. The power of Spain was declining and she could no longer hope to put down the Dutch rebellion, with the English ready for renewed attacks on her shattered navy, but her terms were not acceptable and Rubens was unable to conclude a peace. He did, however, convince the Spanish King of his skill as an ambassador, and was assigned the difficult task of treating with the English. In Paris he conferred with the Duke of Buckingham whom he at once set down as an arrogant knave, but to whom, nevertheless, he sold a selection of paintings for 100,000 florins. The next year his wife died and he hurried back to Antwerp. "Truly," he wrote, "I have lost the best of companions. I could—what do I say?—I was bound to cherish her with reason, for she had not one of the faults of her sex; no little tempers, no feminine weaknesses, nothing but goodness and delicacy—and since her death there is universal sorrow."

"To ease the sorrows of the heart," as he said, "he plunged into politics," and in mid-summer rode over the dusty mountains to the infernal heats of Madrid. A year passed before the dilatory Spanish monarch could make up his mind on the English situation, and Rubens, as usual, relieved himself by painting. The King, the Queen, and the members of the royal family sat to him for portraits; and without incurring the displeasure of the court-painter, Velasquez, he arranged to decorate entire halls and palaces. In the presence of Velasquez, a much younger man, he copied, or rather made free translations of Titian, giving away whole-heartedly and without condescension his knowledge of the Venetians and the secrets of his own style; and as a crowning act of generosity, persuaded Philip to send his court-painter to Italy.

At last, bearing secret instructions from Philip, he departed for England where he was entertained with great munificence by Charles I, a true patron of the arts. Here again he was forced to endure innumerable delays and evasions. Rubens was too sensitive and too honest to play with scoundrels. "The states today," he cried, "are governed by men without experience, and incapable of following the advice of others; they do not carry out their own ideas and they do not listen to those of others." At the end of ten months, despairing of the ultimate good of his mission, he brought the two crowns together in a makeshift peace. In England he contracted, for the sum of 3000 pounds—an enormous sum in those days—to decorate the ceiling of the banqueting-chamber of Whitehall; the King knighted him, and presented him with a jewelled sword, a diamond ring and a diamond hat-band; and at Cambridge he was given the honorary degree of Master of Arts.

In Antwerp again, after an absence of four years, Rubens opened his factory and returned to his old ways. A lonely widower of fifty-three, he was not the sort of man to live without the companionship of a woman, and soon he married Helen Fourment, the daughter of a silk merchant. "I have married," he wrote, "a young middle-class woman, although everyone advised me to choose a lady from the court. But I was chiefly afraid of finding my companion subject to pride, that plague of the nobility. That was my reason for choosing one who would not blush to see me take up my brush. And, to tell the truth, I loved my liberty too much to exchange it for the embraces of an old woman."

The young, middle-class woman was barely sixteen—the same age as his eldest son—the youngest and fairest of seven sisters, all famous for their charms, and in the opinion of the Governor of the Netherlands, "the most beautiful woman in Antwerp." Helen Fourment incarnated that splendid type of Nordic goddess whom he had first created as the Magdalene in *The Descent from the Cross*. In her he found a wife after his heart's desire—and more a perfect model. Certainly she did not blush to see him take up his brush, for he painted her again and again: as Mary Magdalene, St. Cecilia and the Virgin; gorgeously dressed and bejewelled; with her lovely children—she had six; in the nude as Venus, Susanna, a nymph, and the famous portrait at Vienna. There is no doubt that he loved her with all the tenderness of his great heart, but he did not squander his strength in her huge embraces. His reason, his balance and his imagination did not desert him; the illustrious diplomat became once more the master-painter of the world; he seemed indeed, after his marriage with this strong, blonde burgess, to acquire new virility, and in his last years to paint with the ardency and dazzling power of one suddenly come into eternal youth.

The creative fires of Rubens had never burned so brilliantly. For Charles II he executed the Whitehall designs; he delivered

112 paintings in one consignment to the King of Spain; he designed the triumphal arches and the decorations erected by the City of Antwerp in honor of the new regent, Ferdinand, lavishing all his talents on a transitory political show. And in the midst of these labors he was twice interrupted, once by a flying visit to Holland in a futile attempt to pacify the Dutch; the second time by Maria de' Medici who was on the rampage again, coming to Rubens not as a patron of the arts but as a royal beggar. The painter lent her some money but only after she had pledged her jewels as security. Sick of politics and city life, he bought, for a sum equivalent to $125,000 the manorial estate known as the Chateau de Steen and retired in the summer months to the country where, purely for the love of it, he painted some of the most original and powerful landscapes in existence. The hard work went on. More canvases for Spain and among them his greatest masterpieces—*The Garden of Love*, *The Three Graces* and *The Judgment of Paris*. Concerning the last the Archduke Ferdinand wrote to his brother Philip IV: "All the painters say that it is Rubens' best work. I note but one fault in it, though in this I have found no one to agree with me, and that is the excessive nudity of the three goddesses. The master replied to my criticism that this was precisely wherein one could judge of the excellence of a painting. . . . The Venus in the center is a very truthful portrait of the painter's wife."

But the giant labors were soon ended: Rubens was to enjoy only ten years of autumnal happiness. His old enemy, the gout, which had first attacked him in his fiftieth year, now caused him increasing anxiety and acute suffering. "Never," R. A. M. Stevenson says, "was a man less deserving of this affliction." His left hand was affected, then his right, and he could no longer paint—but he was patient and sweet-tempered to the last. On May 30, 1640, in his sixty-third year, his heart failed him. The religious orders of Antwerp celebrated 700 masses for the repose of his soul.

The influence of Rubens upon painting has exceeded that of any other man; his works have been a source of inspiration for all true and honorable artists. He gave Velasquez lessons in color and drawing; Goya studied his swinging designs; the effect of his landscapes on the English school may be measured by the canvases of Turner, Constable, and Crome; he is the spiritual father of Watteau, and Delacroix's god; he guided the hand of Renoir; and all the modern painters, save those who have been sidetracked by ingenious trivialities, swear by him. Delacroix, the most intelligent of his French disciples, wrote of him: "This prodigious life! This powerful impetus without which there can be no great art! I love his emphasis, his perfectly articulated figures, strained or relaxed, his incomparable draughtsmanship! Titian and Veronese are shallow beside him!"

Yet, despite the example of the artists who, after all, know better than any one else what painting is about, Rubens has never been a popular favorite. Collectors prefer the pallid fashion plates of Van Dyck, the chlorotic delicacies of the French, and the decorated sensuality of the Venetians; while the general public is repelled by the billowy nakedness of his figures. In both instances the distaste may be traced to the conventional aversion of the average person to so honest and uncompromising—yes, even ecstatic expression—of sensuality. There is no cheating in Rubens, no suggestiveness, no evasions; no other painter who suggests so little and expresses so much, who says everything with such lucidity and resplendent candor. Of all the painters of the nude—I mean those emphasizing the fleshliness of woman—he is the only one who faced the subject without blushing, or without seductive intentions or fulsome contempt. The nudes of Correggio are symbols of soft, lascivious desires; those of Titian are unmistakably courtesans; the French ladies tastefully flaunt their naughty charms; the English lasses exhibit a numb modesty that is supposed to be pure Greek; and the Modernist painters, afraid of committing themselves to recognizable sentiments of any kind, convert sullen studio animals into grotesque monsters whom they seem to despise. Rubens painted the naked female as an organic fact. She is neither seducer nor prude,

Rubens: THE THREE GRACES.

Prado Museum, Madrid

neither carnal machine nor sterile image. Once this is understood the approach to his world is clear.

He loved the nude, make no mistake about that, but he was not obsessed by its sexual enticements; nor did he, under the hallowed disguise of art, stoop to the cheap practice of creating creatures of radiant animal fat to burn the imaginations of those who would find in painting a stimulus to their physical desires. The nude is part—perhaps the most essential part—of his philosophical scheme, a system enclosing the health, the ceaseless movement, the rushing generative forces—all the characteristics or organic life. The powerful draughts of organized sensuality that blow through his world are clean and pure; the atmosphere is not polluted by the odors of the studio or the brothel. His passion for life, his love for substantial, sun-warmed nakedness—whatever it was that aroused his imagination—was submitted to the sternest intellectual consideration and reduced to law and order; thus his sensuality was dissolved in the currents of a new synthesis in which no single form protrudes suspiciously. There is no false concentration on faces, breasts, or thighs, no sly beckonings to come and behold salacious poses: all forms beat to one colossal tune. When an artist is engaged in the mental toil of a great composition, his physical yearnings are lost in the struggle and he has no time for sexual blandishments. Most painters of the nude, devoid of legitimate purpose and unable to frame a conception of any importance, busy themselves, like procurers, supplying marketable flesh. When Rubens sinned, it was on the side of redundancy and the flamboyant, but no one is compelled to look at his second-best.

Like Leonardo da Vinci, he loved all natural forms. He painted masterpieces in every department of art except still-life, which was much too tame for his human touch—as an animal painter he has no serious rivals, but the dead game in his hunting-scenes was done by Snyders. His religious pictures, as such, are his least successful works; not that his interest in the subject-matter was forced or artificial or that he failed to achieve great dignity and tenderness—*The Descent from the Cross*, for example, a popular, though none the less genuine religious masterpiece—but his imperturbable, conquering temperament could not reach into the depths of anguish or sorrow. So it happens that his ostensibly religious paintings are now valued for quite other qualities. And here we strike at one of the curious attributes of lasting art. In the subject-pictures of Rubens, religious and mythological alike, the themes were dictated by his own civilization and conditioned by the economic background: it was a time of violent religious contentions and opposing the Protestant reaction against sacred images, he shared with the Jesuits a love for large and arresting decorations; it was also a time when polite learning was under the spell of Italy, and he was a classical scholar. But the illustrative elements of his pictures, which reflect pretty faithfully the tastes of his age and which unquestionably were responsible for his local popularity, have almost, if not completely, disappeared.

I do not believe that anyone today either knows or cares whether his nudes are supposed to represent pagan goddesses or Christian virgins; I do not believe that his numerous Crucifixions will fill any one's heart with the Tragedy of the Cross. What moves us is the expression of certain aspects of humanity which Rubens possessed more abundantly than any other artist: in his mythologies it is the same spirit that circulates through his *Kermis*—that marvellous dance of life, the riot of animate matter, the furious song of heroic energy. In his religious pieces the impulse is more sober but hardly less heroic, and man is a noble animal, even as a corpse.

I have said that artists swear by Rubens. They do so for the reason that he is, beyond all question, the greatest of composers. This with due respect to Giotto, Tintoretto and El Greco. His ability to organize pictorial space into a complex, but at the same time, perfectly lucid harmony of forms cannot be sufficiently praised. We know how prodigal he was with his energies, how his imagination ranged from canvas to canvas until the number soared into the thousands; yet, at his death, his creative powers were stronger than ever, and he felt that his best work lay before him. Only artists can fully understand this ability; only those who have struggled with the problem of relating objects and figures so that the composed forms shall express certain emotions and leave unsaid everything that is distracting or superfluous. What most painters accomplished after months of depressions and sweating trials, Rubens brought to completion in a day or two—and in an infinitely more complicated fashion. But dismiss the notion that he was merely a gigantic talent, a machine that ran automatically and ground out pictures without thinking. He had, of course, a much finer brain—but let us not lose sight of the years of preparation, the constant study, the innumerable drawings from nature, the elaborate sketches in color. He was not harassed by the soul-troubles of Michael Angelo and Rembrandt; in making his designs he worked serenely, but with the intensest concentration. Once the design was finished, he let himself go, spreading his colors with a truly Flemish delight in material richness and with a Flemish pride in beautiful craftsmanship.

"The strong impression exercised on the mind by visible objects," Rubens said, "is the effect of lines and contours rather than of colors." In other words he composed his pictures by the rhythmical interplay of lines and volumes, vanquishing the Florentines on their own ground. What infinite variety he gave to his volumes! What plasticity! What suppleness of articulation! He loved to weave his figures into undulating diagonals, or spirals leading far back into his world of deep space and then returning to complete the movement. But so unimpeded is the flow, so completely are the details subordinated to the basic compositional lines, that the eye follows the action easily and naturally and grasps the design as a single unit. This, needless to say, was made possible by his knowledge of drawing and structure. Rubens is one of the three or four supreme draughtsmen of art. He had what artists call "the profound feeling for form"; in his slightest sketches, his wonderful drawings of children, his portrait-heads done with a few lines, he reveals the essential structure of living matter. In his finished nudes, such as *The*

Three Graces of the Prado, his absolute mastery of the structure of the human figure makes the work of almost all painters noticeably thin and hollow. In comparison the nudes of Titian are painted shells. The difference is one of draughtsmanship. So comprehensive was his knowledge, so extraordinary his capacity to visualize the human body in positions which could not be observed directly that, as Fry points out, "whatever pose of a figure he might require, however improbable or extravagant, he was able to conceive an assured and convincing image of it and to project this on to the canvas."

But the composition is the man. With Rubens it is not a technical device acquired in Italy but the inevitable coördination of the experiences and philosophy of an artist who never lost his sense of values and his love for opulent realities. How could his genius have been otherwise expressed than in a three-dimensional kingdom of boundless movement, muscularity and color? He was none of your little specialists of art; he was a wise man of the world, diplomat and scholar, poet and manorial lord, but always the artist, ingenuous and amiable, an indefatigable worker, free from Bohemian humbug and aesthetic arrogance. To satisfy his universal interests he needed the whole of art—the nude, the saint, the huntsman and the child; the fields and harvesters, historical pomp and domestic contentment; his magnificent vision demanded warmth and color—golden browns, and the lush vermilions which are too strong for less hearty souls. His big nudes, so offensive to dieting moderns, particularly women, are not over-fed animals, not baggy females hypertrophied by nature, but creatures of his imagination, carefully rebuilt to embody his conception of the fulness of life, and so convincing in their vitality as to trouble the consciences of our foolish starvelings.

There is nothing mysterious in his art, and for this he has been called the master of the commonplace. As if it were a commonplace performance to organize with such perfection and finality the healthier and more joyous workings of the spirit! His was the sanest intelligence that ever expressed itself in paint, and being sane and free from profligacy he has been called "the business man of art who gave the people what they wanted." If he gave the people what they wanted, then all honor to the Flemish who loved him, and to the Italians, the Spanish and the French who wanted only the best!

CHAPTER

X

THE DUTCH

WHAT an admirable race! How courageous and intelligent! What human regard for the rights and habits of man! The most enlightened and enviable of modern nations! The Dutch are not living in the past; nor are they capitalizing the past for the entertainment of tourists; nor have they succumbed to the cosmopolitan frivolities created by the Americans. They have the industry of the Americans without the boastfulness; their country is their fortress and their home; they protect it, adorn it and keep it clean. You are welcome there, but you will not be received with any flattery or special ceremony—and you will not be robbed, patronized or exploited. The quaintness of Holland of which you hear so much is but the touch of color and tidiness added to customs and institutions that are worth preserving. Surely there is nothing so confoundedly quaint in white linen and immaculate backyards, in the making of cheese and the cultivation of tulips. The Dutch make the wind and the sea work for them and having an eye for decorative effects, paint the wings of their windmills and the sails of their boats, their fishing nets and even the trees. The country is flat, roads are perfect, distances short, and cycling is not only an excellent means of locomotion, but also a pleasure. The Dutchman prefers a home that is inhabitable—and paid for, a jug of real gin, and a bicycle, to the barren apartment or the ugly, mortgaged house, the automobile and the synthetic poisons of the Americans.

The Dutch are impregnable against wastefulness, ruinous expenditures of energy, degrading standards of living, sham aestheticism, and all the enervating fads associated with modernity. But not against new ideas. They have solved as well as or better than any other state the economic problem of supporting a large population in decency and contentment. They have converted the floor of the sea into meadow lands and flower-beds; their cities have no slums; they are, in many respects, the best of contemporary builders. The new Dutch architecture, in design, is as modern as the American skyscraper, or the French and German experiments in cubical structure. But it is neither fantastic nor sensational—the design is not based upon ingenious pictorial abstractions but upon human requirements; it is an original architecture, solid as the dikes, and taking into account man's need for light and air, color and ornament, and domestic cheerfulness. Truly, the Dutch are a civilized people!

Because Holland has refused to wear the rags of superficial modernism; because the peculiar character of the country has prescribed certain industries—cattle-raising, dairy-farming, fishing and shipping—the Dutch school of painting which passed out of existence in the seventeenth century, appears to be a contemporary manifestation. This, the last of the great original schools, is the most independent and the most completely national outburst of painting in the history of art. I say outburst, for the whole movement was born and buried in a little more than two generations. It began with Frans Hals, whose career as an artist dates from the first years of the seventeenth century, and ended with Hobbema, born in 1638. In this brief period Holland was over-run with painters, hundreds and hundreds of them; more, to tell the sad truth, than she could use, and a good picture would hardly fetch the price of a square meal. There was Brouwer the tramp, who drank beer with Rubens; there was Rembrandt and his ladylike pupil, Gerard Dou, and his imitator, Ferdinand Bol; there was Terborch, and Albert Cuyp; Paul Potter, Jan Steen, Jacob van Ruysdael, Peter de Hoogh; Metsu, Nicholas Maes, Vermeer of Delft, and Van Goyen—names which mean wealth and social distinction to the modern collector, but which meant to the Dutch only the portrait of a canal, a cow, or a ruddy old fish-wife.

Before the formation of the Republic, Dutch painting was an appendage to the Flemish trunk, a barren limb of a dying tree. In the fifteenth and sixteenth centuries, the time of the glorious efflorescence and decline of the early Flemish school, such artists as happened to be born in the provinces which are now Holland were enrolled in the guilds of Antwerp and Ghent; when Rubens returned from Italy to resuscitate the art of Flanders, Dutch painting was indistinguishable from Flemish, and scarcely deserving of mention. It was a bastard Italian product, devotional, Catholic, absurdly pretentious, utterly empty. But, it was so thoroughly extirpated by the Reformed Church that not a shred of it remained. Thus, about 1600, when the northern provinces seceded and constituted themselves as an independent state, the Republic of Holland was born, and with it a new art, an art without ancestry. Not entirely without ancestry—art does not come into the world overnight by spontaneous generation—for in its technical processes, its fine craftsmanship, and its smooth surfaces, it was akin to the work of the Van Eycks, but a unique development in painting, an art without God.

Just why the Dutch who had hitherto been apathetic towards art should suddenly have turned to painting is one of those puzzling questions in social behavior which cannot be positively decided. But devote themselves to painting they did, with the courage and resolution which for centuries they had put forward in reclaiming their land from the sea and establishing their freedom. The immediate impetus sprang from the heroic struggles of Holland to release herself from the noose of Spanish oppression: a part of that energy and of those unparalleled powers of resistance found its way into painting. The final peace with Spain was not signed until 1648; all her important artists were born before that date, and all of them painted to the roar of cannon and the marshalling of troops. It takes courage to paint in such circumstances.

Another factor in the awakening of Dutch painting, one which not only created a demand for pictures but which determined their size and character, was the steadily increasing prosperity. Despite the Eighty Years War Holland had developed a wealthy middle class and had become the leading maritime nation of Europe. And as commerce and manufacture multiplied, so did the riches of the polder. Behind the dikes and the barracks, removed from the congestion of the cities, arose the country house—the large estate of the wealthy merchant, the simple home of the farmer. The country house was literally "a fortress against the climate," and the owner, surrounded by his cows and his poultry, with his store-rooms and his cellar amply provisioned for the entertainment of his friends, passed the long gloomy winters largely within doors. To brighten the dull interiors and to give the illusion of vernal warmth, he hung his walls with pictures, the small intimate domestic things nearest his heart—laughing wenches, appetizing still-life, cook-maids, tavern scenes, and glimpses of the sky and sea. Before long pictures were dirt cheap, and not more highly esteemed than faggots or ale. The artist had a hard time of it.

By some Dutch paradox, or possibly as a mark of his indomitable good sense, the Hollander wanted nothing heroic in his art. One might think that the long struggle for freedom—and where shall we find anything to compare with it in heroic sacrifice?—would have begotten a great school of historical painters or a race of Michael Angelos exalting the abstract qualities of suffering and strength. But not so with the Dutch. Rubens might paint *The Apotheosis of William the Silent*, but the Dutch took no stock in military heroism. War was a cruel business, but the Spaniards were brutes and the Belgians chicken-livered Catholics; and so, like men, they conquered the Castilians and withdrew from the Belgians. But the deed once done, they put it out of mind. They realized that in war one man is as brave as another and they would honor no one for doing his duty. No one but the immortal William, and even him they would not paint. They did not wish to be reminded of agonies and valorous suffering; they loved peace, material goods, comradeship, green fields and the sea—when it kept its distance. They demanded in their pictures, not the fighting, but the things fought for—not the heroic but the homely, not the battlefield but the quiet meadow.

The Dutch did not regard the painter as anybody in particular. "If art is such a noble occupation," they asked, "why is it so easily mastered and why have we so many painters? Why should we pay homage to a man because he works at an easel and not to the soldier or the sailor who works next door to death? Frans Hals, our best artist, paints when he is drunk, and when a man does that, his trade cannot be very difficult. The artist has a soft life." But the artist had anything but a soft life. Old Hals died in the poorhouse and so did Ruysdael; few made more than a bare living and the most famous were forced into odd jobs. Jan Steen kept a tavern; Van Goyen sold tulips; Hobbema was a gauger at the Amsterdam docks; Peter de Hoogh a servant in a family of merchants. And when one man, their only great artist, lifted painting to such a height that all humanity has been ennobled and illuminated by the light of his genius, they let him die in poverty. The Dutch did not honor Rembrandt.

But this very refusal to hail the artist as an aristocrat, this obstinate resistance to the authority of Spain, the Roman Church and the Italian masters, this common-sense notion that art is neither higher nor lower than other forms of human behavior, accounts for the astonishing originality of Dutch painting. For the first time we make our acquaintance with a Protestant, or more precisely, a purely secular art ignoring the kingdom of heaven and concentrating on the ordinary, every-day activities of man in a definite environment; a democratic art conceived and executed by plebeians to satisfy the tastes of the masses; a domestic art appropriate for the garniture of small interiors; a materialistic art dealing with the external aspects of common things; an art without literature, anecdotes or abstractions—in sum, a substitute for nature. In the painting of Italy you may discover facial types and styles in dress and in architecture which are unmistakably Italian, and occasionally a landscape which may be identified with an actual locality, but these local characteristics disappear in the largeness of the design, in the grandeur of forms expressing, to be sure, the mental habits and emotions of the Italians, but comprising a universal record of man's spiritual life. Dutch painting is a mirror of Holland, the most perfect reflection of national life that has ever been thrown upon canvas—so perfect, in fact, in its scrutiny of the appearances of objects, that once the inventory had been taken, the Dutch had no further use for art. Accordingly, the army of painters, having stocked the houses of Holland with pictures, was disbanded and forgotten.

The French critic Fromentin has stated the case in a sentence: "The Dutch, to become artists, only needed to paint the portrait of their country." Whatever subject the artist might select—a child, a consultation of doctors, a side of beef, a picnic or a sand dune—his sole aim was to portray a limited field of vision with minute objective accuracy. To this aim may be attributed both the charming novelty and the inherent weakness of the Dutch school. The painter became a specialist, restricting not only the field of his operations but his imaginative approach to his material. In his search for a more intense realism, he fell into the evil practice of copying natural surfaces from a model—and a new element came into art—the imitated value or tone. And this imitative process, this illusion of surfaces engendered by the expert representation of natural light, was so captivating and effective that it became, later on, the stock-in-trade of minor artists the world over. It is responsible, to a large extent, for the shallowness and the boring mechanical cleverness of most modern exhibitions.

Technically, the rendition of natural surfaces, or in plain speech, the painting of a literal portrait, is simply a matter of concentrated observation. It depends upon one's ability to distinguish values and tones; it requires, not brains, but a trained eye and a ready hand. One looks at an object, examines the fall of light and shade, notes carefully the gradation in atmospheric density from the highest light to the deepest dark; and then, taking brushes and pigment, translates the array of appearances into an equivalent scale of colors. With patience and practice one becomes as unerring in the transcription of slices of nature as the camera. Wouwerman, for example, painted more than a thousand highly finished portraits of ships and of animals, all of them as perfect in verisimilitude as photographs, and, like photographs, as empty of spiritual nourishment as an album of old views. In a country where art was only a substitute for nature, the painter was only a substitute for the camera, and it is no wonder that the sensible Hollander had no exceptional esteem for a mere maker of pictures. Dutch painting is the happy reflection of natural tranquillity; it contains none of "the fever and pain of Italian art"; it does not employ nature as a vehicle to express the spiritual strife of man; it creates no vast scheme of relationships in which physical laws and the accidents of light and shade are systematically flouted, and in which forms are reconstructed to bear the weight of the artist's speculations and experiences; it is a static art, pleasing to the eye, as relaxing as a summer holiday, but it makes small claims upon the mind.

It would be unjust to besmirch all Dutch painting with the name of photography. The work of the rank and file unquestionably merits that opprobrious designation; but if the work of the superior men were as impersonal and as starkly dehumanized as the records of the camera, it would not be worthy of serious consideration. The Dutch loved their country—they had fought too hard for their possessions not to prize them—and while the love of nature and material possessions will not in itself produce art, the honesty and enthusiasm with which the more significant men incorporated this national trait in painting, prompted them to an effectiveness of presentment which is, in varying degrees, creative. The vigorous portraiture of Hals; the taste and refinement of Terborch; the exquisite arrangements of

Vermeer; the seemliness of de Hoogh; the lucid patterns of Hobbema; the grave landscapes of Ruysdael; the compact genre of Brouwer and Jan Steen; these things no doubt called for a certain amount of organizing ability. But the amount, comparatively speaking, is small, and all the Dutch painters, Rembrandt excepted, are more remarkable for their craftsmanship than for their imagination. So fascinating is their craftsmanship that it has led painters into a denial of the value of subject-matter— "it is not what one paints but the manner in which it is painted," they cry—; it has led them to the exaltation of pigments, to the rejection of the social purpose of art, and to the absurd theory of "art for art's sake."

So remarkable is this craftsmanship that Fromentin, one of the pioneers in the appreciation of Dutch and Flemish art, was completely seduced by it, declaring "that no one has ever painted better than Hals and no one ever will." One might as well say that no one has ever written better poetry than Swinburne, or carved better statues than Rodin. And to the great detriment of painting, literary critics, when they speak of *artistic* prose, or of a writer who is "an artist to his finger tips," refer to dazzling technical skill, superficial cleverness, external polish and preciosity rather than to depth of feeling and variety of experiences. Thus Stevenson and Pater, and Poe and Cabell are artistic, but the robust imagination of a Swift, a Fielding or a Mark Twain is something else. Hals is essentially a craftsman, not more extraordinary than Vermeer or John Van Eyck, but more susceptible of imitation. In his ability to capture what is known as a speaking likeness, to map out the features of his model in broad half-tones, adding lights and shadows in swift strokes which seem to hit the mark with drunken good-luck, but which are actually laid on with an infallible sense of fitness, he has never been excelled. His portraits are astonishingly realistic, and display, especially the later ones, a commendable sympathy with disconsolate old women; but having said this, we have nothing more to say of him as a creative artist. His technical mastery which enabled him to knock off a portrait in one sitting, after a night's debauch, and to invest his finished pictures with the liveliness and spontaneity of sketches, has had a bad influence upon painting. Impressionable students and painters who load their canvases with heavy streaks of greasy pigment hoping to conceal a poverty of drawing by a spurious freedom and looseness of handling, are generally the unfortunate followers of the old toper of Haarlem.

So fascinating is Dutch craftsmanship that within the last few years, the works of one painter, Vermeer of Delft, have been appraised in terms out of all proportion to their intrinsic value. If a new and first-class Vermeer should be discovered, it would be promptly acquired by an American collector at a price exceeding a million dollars. I need hardly say that the mad passions of monopolists are not to be taken as a criterion of aesthetic values; collectors buy works of art as investments on which they may be assured of positive returns. Their costly plunder must be not only a cultural asset and a mark of social prestige, but a gilt-edged security that may be sold at a profit. With Vermeer they cannot possibly go wrong: his pictures are among the rarest things in art—only thirty-seven have come to light—and the market will never be glutted. Think of owning a Vermeer when your vulgar competitor has to be content with a Romney or a Raphael! You could not feel more vainglorious if you owned the world's largest diamond, the Rosetta stone, or the Portland Vase! And more: to have your possession unanimously acclaimed by the experts and fashionable aesthetes of every country!

Vermeer, rare as he is in the number of his extant works, is even more rare in that property of paint known as *quality*. His canvases have the lustre of ivory, the texture of enamel, the virginal purity of sunlight on cool water; so delicately fused are his pigments that all evidence of the human touch has disappeared; it is as if nature herself in some precious mood had crystallized her colors in a transparent pattern. His canvases

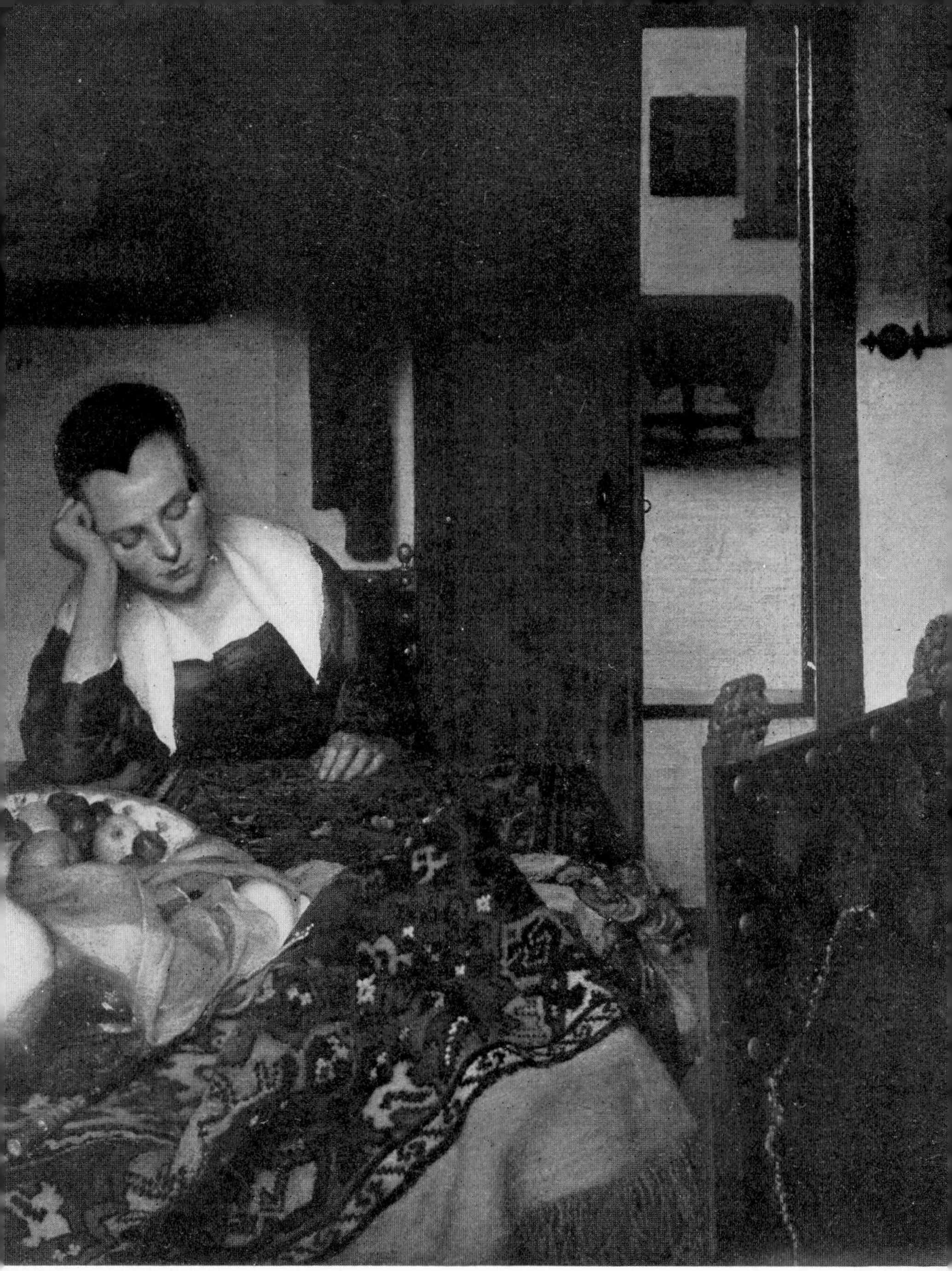

Vermeer: SLEEPING GIRL.
Metropolitan Museum of Art, New York

have that quality of surface described by Proust in his study of a morbid writer who despaired of his art because he could not, with all the resources of language, rival "the perfection of a little patch of yellow on the wall."

Most of his subjects are small interiors: a room with a tiled floor, a grey wall hung with a map or picture; to the left, a window, and in the middle a woman standing at a table, pouring milk or reading a letter. His favorite colors are combinations of blues and yellows; by a command of natural light equalled only by Velasquez and one or two of the Impressionists, and by the fastidious adjustment of tones, he projects his forms into serene space; his textures are so absolutely the replicas of the surfaces that his table covers and stuffs do not impress us as painted illusions but actual materials preserved in amber glazes. The effect is magical, and for such technical attainments Vermeer cannot be praised too lavishly. But the man had no more imagination than a Dutch diamond cutter. Indeed he resembles a diamond cutter in his manner of working and in his finished product, adding globule to globule of pigment to fashion a jeweled object, just as the lapidary, with infinite skill and phlegmatic diligence, adds facet to facet to bring out the splendor of an expensive substance. Try as you may to find anything spiritual in him and you will find yourself talking of craftsmanship and describing precious stones. Vermeer is the last word in Dutch materialism.

But the Dutch painters were honest in their exaltation of materiality. They painted the things they loved, and if they painted them rather literally it was because they were not afraid to rejoice in their possessions; their interest in materials was generous and unaffected; they sold their pictures for what they were—frank pieces of descriptive scenery or human likenesses—and they did not ask any one to find hidden meanings in their handicraft. What a happy frame of mind in contrast with certain modern painters who have nothing to say, who have no interest in any subject on earth, and therefore, who paint meaningless abstractions which they attempt to pass off as profound states of the soul! Dutch painting is perfect within its own limits, but the nature of its perfection is not consistent with an art of the deepest emotions and the richest experiences. Collectively, it may be called a great school; individually it produced but one master.

CHAPTER

XI

REMBRANDT

REMBRANDT is the last of the great spiritual explorers. After three hundred years he is closer to the heart of the modern world than any other painter. He is one of us. His passions, his struggles, his sorrows; his unrelenting contentions with the evils of materialism; his renunciation of popular fame and wealth in order to liberate his soul from the hardening demands of money-grubbers; his solitary splendor in a society of passive traders and cheese-mongers—these bear so intimately on the problems of modern life that he seems a man of our own time. But a man of heroic stature, a rock of refuge for those seeking salvation in the storms of vindictive controversy and shallow skepticism. Who, weary of the empty turmoil and nervous rapidity of contemporary civilization, has not turned to Rembrandt for consolation? Who, in his honest moments, has not coveted the huge Dutchman's strength of character and ability to abandon himself to his noblest impulses? Who does not know that coarse and kindly face; in youth a little proud and cavalier, in old age seamed and bloated, but monumentally direct and at peace with the world? Rembrandt's life is the growth of the human spirit towards complete freedom; in the end he attained that freedom, but at the price of poverty, ostracism and enormous self-discipline. His art is a record of the fundamental experiences of mankind, of things which most deeply concern the groping human race.

He was born at Leyden in 1606. His father was in comfortable circumstances, the owner of several houses and a windmill in which malt was ground for beer; his mother, a God-fearing woman of more than ordinary intelligence, was the daughter of a baker. His four brothers, all older than himself and typical of Dutch mediocrity, were poor cobblers and millers; he had one sister, sad-faced and stout—or so she appears in the portraits he painted of her—to whom he was strongly attached. But he was not like the rest of the family. It was clear from his earliest years that he was not to be a producer of malt or a mender of shoes. He had—I shall not say the temperament of an artist, for the artistic temperament has become a synonym for fatuous eccentricity and defeated egoism—the mind of the independent explorer of human values. He was a sensitive boy, but tough-skinned and vigorously masculine; affectionate but not too sociable to waste his time with frivolous companions; genuinely curious without being inquisitive or suspicious; tender and unselfish, but capable of brusque retaliation when unjustly crossed, and not above temptation and coarseness. He loved his father's windmill with its mysterious depths of shadow, the western ramparts from which he could look down into green meadows and great trees, the Rhine with its procession of colored sails, the little town that had so valorously defied the Spaniard.

It never occurred to the boy, as he wandered along the river alone, poking his broad nose into other people's business, that he should learn a trade; nor, strange as it may seem, did it occur to any member of the family to suggest that he pursue the customary certainties of life. All of them felt that he was destined to some distinguished profession, but it was his mother who understood him best. Night after night, in those long Northern winters, she read the Bible to her beloved son, sensible of his impassioned interest in what were to her the eternal verities, noting with benign satisfaction the light that shone in his sharp eyes as she finished the story of the Prodigal Son or the Supper at Emmaus. The boy would be a great preacher, the scourge of Papists, or if not that, she mused a little sadly, a savant or famous surgeon! So she enrolled him, at the age of fourteen, in the University of Leyden, her husband, Harmen Gerritsz, concurring because he obtained thereby certain tax exemptions.

But Rembrandt, alas for a mother's ambitions! was not an orthodox Protestant—he has even been charged with being a Mennonite! His absorption in the Scriptures was that of a youth in search of unchangeable truths and he found in the Old and New Testaments dramatic stories which stirred his imagination, and, as he reflected on them, which seemed to express certain spiritual states inherent in all races at all times and higher than creeds or established religions. He had no capacity for scholarship and no need for it; books bored him; he knew what he needed most and where to find it—and he knew that it was not to be had from formal training. He regarded Latin as useless; he wrote his own language with a beautiful hand but without ease or correctness; a zoölogical garden nearby lured him from his classes, and the Town Hall with its war trophies and its exhibits of paintings by native artists decided his career. He carried home volumes of sketches he had made when he should have been conjugating irregular verbs, laid the evidence before the family, and notified them of his proper vocation. Reluctantly, for painting was neither a distinguished nor profitable business, his parents allowed him, at the close of the academic year, to withdraw from the University, and apprenticed him to a local artist.

A worse painter than his first teacher could hardly be imagined, but Rembrandt was treated with kindness—a rare exception in the harsh Dutch system of binding apprentices to the strictest servitude, and of the first importance to a sensitive and rather stubborn boy of fifteen—and his ability recognized and encouraged. He was greatly talented, so greatly in fact, that it would have surprised no one had he turned out to be just another Hals, and his life would have been vastly more pleasant, in the superficial sense, if he had been no more than talented. But in his soul dwelt a mighty purpose, and the deepest reverence for the spiritual potentialities of art that had appeared in the world since Michael Angelo. In three years his progress astonished his fellows and he was sent to Amsterdam to study with the famous Lastman.

After six months he returned home to work according to his own inclinations. Lastman, who had lived in Rome, was a learned Italianizer, cold, conceited and destitute of originality, and too full of his own self-esteem to discover the promise of his pupil. But it was through him that Rembrandt was introduced to a novel method of illuminating pictures by startling oppositions of lights and darks, a method known as trap-door lighting which first came into prominence in the paintings of the Italian Caravaggio. This technical expedient he adopted instinctively, refining and modifying it, and in the course of time making it so peculiarly his own property for the rendering of psychological truths, that we are likely to forget that it was, in a violent and theatrical form, well-known in Holland and employed by a number of painters who plumed themselves on their advanced ideas.

Seven more years at Leyden, years overflowing with activity and signalized by the swift development of his technical facility and the relatively slow but consistent growth of his spiritual insight. Rembrandt, in part at least because he was Dutch and Protestant and brought up in a land where religious imagery was proscribed and where the tendency of art ran to portraiture—of man and nature alike—learned more from his own independent investigations of natural forms and less from the concepts and abstractions of the great men of the past than any other artist of the first rank. But this does not mean, as we shall presently see, that he was not an historical student and that so rich and complicated an art as his own could have been conceived without the precepts and examples of the Flemish and Italian masters. He was not an eclectic, but he was certainly not a primitive.

His art, like that of all good Dutchmen, began at home. He made innumerable studies of his own face, his intention being to show how the human countenance reflects the torment and the terror, the sadness and the gaiety, the agitation and the contentment of the soul, but all that we see in those first portraits is a tousled, bull-necked, healthy young man acting before a mirror. He painted his father in military and biblical rôles, but all that we see is a wrinkled little miller absurdly arrayed in a plumed hat or a turban and stupidly wondering what it is all about. He painted his sister as the Virgin or a fine lady in silks and chains of gold, but she is still his sister, plain and staringly self-conscious. But in the portraits of his mother, stern and old before her time, her hands crossed upon the Good Book, there is a touch of majesty that presages his mature genius.

Nothing repelled him. He was headstrong and sensual, ready to weigh the good with the bad, eager for any experience that promised to throw light on the inexplicable wonderings which beset him from his first experiments with paint. Especially did the lower orders attract him. They were less artificial, less likely to hide their true feelings behind the mask of conventionality. He drew and etched and painted the hordes of unfortunates that roamed over Holland, the excrescence of continual wars, the deformed, the halt, the blind, who begged for bread while the merchants got rich and the preachers thumped the pulpits and flung them scraps of theology; he depicted this human scum with strange sympathy for one so young and well-fed, and always to emphasize the infinite variations of individual suffering. He was not, however, an august soul habitually preoccupied with the tragedy of man. There was in him a vein of robust and playful animalism that found, in his youth, graphic expression in a series of jolly drawings and etchings which, the censors willing, would make appropriate decorations for certain modern novels.

At twenty-one Rembrandt was a celebrity in Leyden and the life of a group of local artists. His fame began to travel; a Hague collector bought a picture for a sum amounting to about sixty dollars in modern money, and having tasted the fruits of professionalism, he worked harder than ever. While there was daylight he painted; at night he toiled over his etchings. His first trials with the needle, a number of studies of himself and his mother, date from this period, and though they were done principally as experiments in chiaroscuro, and though they lose by contrast with the grandeur of his later plates, they are superior in every respect to the efforts of all other artists in this ticklish medium. At twenty-two his reputation was such that painters came to his studio for instruction, one of them, Gerard Dou, by virtue of his small-mindedness and his devotion to trivialities, being destined to eclipse the master in popular esteem. He was honored by portrait commissions, honored by ranting theologians who expurgated the churches of religious pictures, but who had no objection to the public display of their own sour visages. He painted them—for money, and the money he spent freely. He helped artists by buying their pictures; stocked his studio with costumes and properties for his oriental visions; bought pretty things for his sister. At twenty-six he followed his fame to Amsterdam.

On his arrival at Amsterdam, Rembrandt, in the externals of painting, in his craftsmanship and his skill in portraiture, seemed to possess precisely the qualities requisite to a continued popular success. But underlying all his work, even his earliest portraits done to order, there was an organic tendency, a central experience which was to carry him farther and farther from a public which expected and desired photographic likenesses and stereotyped emotions. It is difficult to define this central tendency. In a general way, we may say that Rembrandt was profoundly affected by the tragedy of mankind, that whatever he derived from single experiences was assimilated into a common fund wherein it received direction and unifying purpose, and that this spiritual growth colored and controlled his whole point of view leading him to employ the human face, not as a fleshy mask wearing the name of Hendrickje Stoffels or Magdalena van Loo, but as an index to regions of the consciousness dominated by suffering. This tendency, which is after all only the objectification of his personality, as his accumulated sense-impressions coalesced, with time and contemplation, into an organic whole, is but faintly perceptible in his first professional portraits, but in his very earliest biblical compositions, crude as they are in their grotesque pantomime and exaggerated gesturing, it is clearly in evidence.

His propensity towards the tragic aspects of life was not a deliberate acquisition. Indeed, so far as his public was concerned, there was every reason why he should have shunned a form of art which was not merely a substitute for wall-paper, or for the more congenial moods of nature. A man cannot create art, or, at any rate, great art, by projecting in cold blood a certain line of conduct and sticking to it, nor by arbitrarily putting himself in the way of certain experiences: such more often than not, is the delusion of academic minds who hope to become artists by adopting not only the environment but the legendary habits of the masters. Rembrandt's attitude towards humanity, his predilection for biblical themes in an age when everybody was painting canals and cows and things the eye could take in at a single glance, was the result of a natural impulsion which he could no more have escaped than he could have escaped the tide of disfavor that swamped him when he refused to give the merchants and sportsmen what they wanted. But his cultivation of it was deliberate enough. While he was executing the commissions which won him his reputation, he was, in the solitude of his studio, laboring with the greatest energy and the utmost intensity of purpose, to diagnose the inscrutable burdens of the soul.

"He labored," as Blake said of himself, "day and night to create a system," a system to express emotions so deeply rooted within the spirit that they are the despair of most artists and hence are generally pronounced as outside the province of painting. It was not enough that his system should be a plastic architecture of light and dark masses: he was concerned with human beings in dramatic predicaments and the effect of tragic situations on individual characters. Nor was it an accident that the fabric of his visions should have been woven out of concentrated lights that shoot down into the recesses of the soul or glow upon the human face, lifting it out of the mysteries of darkness. His technical method corresponds so closely to the tenor of his career—the brilliancy of his fame suddenly passing into the shadows of neglect—that it was, I think, the only way in which he could have given substance and glory to his imaginings; and he painted, at the age of twenty-five, one picture, the *Presentation in the Temple*, at The Hague, which, in technical boldness, in spaciousness of design and religious insight, holds its own in the company of his later masterpieces. No other painter, I believe, achieved so early in life anything comparable to this canvas. For Rembrandt, you see, did have to borrow his convictions or imitate the religious symbolism of the Italians; he read the Bible, and went to the Scriptures for material, as his confrères went to the docks or the polder.

Amsterdam in 1632 was a free and thriving city that had escaped the horrors of war. Descartes, residing there at this time said of it: "I am the only soul in this vast city not engaged in trade. Everyone is busy making money. I might spend my whole life here in complete solitude." Descartes was right. It was a city of traders dwelling in houses that were scrubbed and refurbished annually, inside and out; an orderly decent people, as a rule, but on occasion given to strong amusements and savage debaucheries. It was the center of painting in Holland, but painting too was a trade, and a very precarious one, the best artists as I have pointed out, having to resort to even less reputable occupations to keep from starving. It was the fashion in those days for young Dutch and Flemish painters, when they could afford it, to go to Italy to study, just as it is the fashion for all modern painters to go to Paris, but Rembrandt went to Amsterdam, much to the disgust of a Dutch scholar who wrote that "the noble youth had only one fault: he held Italy in small account, and through some madness in his temper wilfully neglected to acquire what alone was wanting to the perfection of his art." But Rembrandt was wiser than all the doctors, well aware that the perfection of his art depended upon his understanding of his own environment. He never once strayed beyond the borders of his native land.

Almost immediately he was commissioned by Professor Tulp (contraction for tulip) to paint a memorial for the surgeons' guild. The result was *The Anatomy Lesson*, and Rembrandt, already well-known, became the most celebrated painter in Holland. "I am, thank God, healthy and flourishing!" he wrote home to his mother. But he did not boast that he was happy. *The Anatomy Lesson*, because of its strange theatrical vacuity and the combined pompousness of seven would-be doctors pretending desperately to have an afflatus while Professor Tulip snips the exposed brachial tendons of a waxen corpse, is a repugnant picture. The characters who would be so profoundly awed by the demonstration are all bearded actors. It is a ghastly picture—not in the subject-matter, but in the interpretation. Its impressiveness is offensive. It is the sort of thing that would appeal to Dutch traders and to all doctors. But all the same it is a work of genius, or rather an error of genius: the ghastliness is organized, the imitation of sublimity consistently distributed. Rembrandt was torn between two demands, the demands of his artistic conscience to construct heads revealing more than credible likenesses, and the demands of the surgeons' guild for a galaxy of authentic portraits. The dilemma was too much for him. Ten years later, confronted by a similar situation, he knew exactly what to do. At twenty-six he attempted to reconcile the two demands and produced a striking horror which the world somehow has always found enjoyable.

The Anatomy Lesson marks the beginning of a decade of prosperity. Rembrandt was among the few Dutch painters, if not the only one, who derived a handsome income from the sale of his pictures. In an age when canvases went for next to nothing, he commanded comparatively high prices for his work, and this, with a dazzling talent and a burly constitution enabling him to polish off portraits with great despatch, lifted him into an opulence denied to his less fortunate brethren. But aside from a reckless disregard for the value of money, his worldly rewards did not affect his mode of living. His basic aspirations retained their intrinsic purity, and though he had many years ahead of him before he was to approach his materials with absolute spiritual freedom, he realized the magnitude of his powers and reserved his best energies for their development.

He moved from the house of his friend and dealer, Hendrick van Uylenborch, to a warehouse overlooking a canal where he might study the forlorn wretches who served as models, and where he might retire into his visionary world after his bouts with popular hacks. One of his cronies in this old studio was a tough and shapeless wench whom life had cruelly used. He painted her in the nude, flashing a yellow light upon her scarecrow face, her hanging breasts and her legs cut by the scars of garters, and called her *Diana in the Bath*. This is the earliest of Rembrandt's nudes that have come down to us. It contains everything that lovers of classical art abhor and it would be nothing less than stupid to rank it with the *Woman Bathing*, in the National Gallery, done in his forty-eighth year; physically, it is undeniably ugly, but strange to say we are not repulsed by this ugliness. We look at the picture with a compassionate shudder, disturbed by a quality vaguely defined but sufficiently manifest to link this shapeless naked thing with our innermost selves after its frightening reality has shaken us loose from our false pride and our foolish conventionality.

One day the dealer brought his cousin to the studio, Saskia van Uylenborch, a girl of twenty, fair, sweet-faced, soft and gentle. Saskia was an orphan belonging to a rich patrician family of Friesland. She was living temporarily with one of her relations, a preacher, who watched over her covetously, as even a preacher will do, when his ward is fair and in possession of a considerable fortune. Rembrandt began at once to woo her and in a short time, for he was an ardent fellow in the habit of getting what he most desired, inscribed under a sketch he had made of her, "Saskia, at the age of twenty-one, the third day after our troth-plighting." He carried her off almost as soon as she came of age, amid the angry protests of the preacher and the rest of the self-seeking relatives. It seems that she was marrying beneath her, and while her protectors admitted the talent and the reputation of her suitor, and even his ability to maintain her in the style to which her birth entitled her, they kept repeating that he was only a painter, a low and godless parvenu—and the son of a miller! The notions of the Uylenborches were quite modern. But Rembrandt, in whom snobbery was inconceivable, and in whose scheme of things one man was a good as another, only laughed at their silly aspersions and went about his business.

That he found in Saskia an irreproachable wife and lived with her in entire harmony cannot be gainsaid; that he had for her a deep affection which made him considerate of her rather tender breeding is equally beyond dispute; that he loved her is doubtful. He was in some respects thoroughly domestic—monogamous, easily contented, charitable, unruffled by feminine whims, sedentary, averse to travel and social gadding, and fond of children; a woman was indispensable to him, but not conjugal love. His great and abiding passion was his art; he was approaching a mental condition where nothing else mattered, where the whole of life was a pictorial problem. I do not mean that he was a fanatic smitten with a metaphysical ideal like Balzac's hero in *The Unknown Masterpiece*, or that he was a hermit trying to make pictures out of the unsubstantial texture of subjective maunderings. Rembrandt was solid and clear-headed, frankly sensual, very much a part of his surroundings, but as he assayed his experiences and advanced the borders of his art, he visualized a world in which the inhabitants were counterparts of himself, strongly individualized, mountainous in their palpability, and yet so completely delivered from the bonds of materiality that they exemplify in their radiant bulk the triumph of the human soul over maleficent forces. He moved towards this goal with an iron purpose; nothing deterred him; the loss of his children, his wife and his fortune only strengthened his resolve—and he continued to paint without a whimper.

Saskia was a dutiful spouse. She did not meddle in his painting, never questioned him about his models, never tried to reform him or to make him acceptable to high society. She had a weakness for fine clothes and jewels, but it was more than balanced by his extravagant purchases of works of art—so there was no quarrel on that score. With the large dowry that she brought him, and the income from his pictures and his numerous pupils, Rembrandt was really a man of wealth, and he spent his money with an incautious gusto that prompted the relatives of his wife to tale-bearing and slander. They denounced the painter as a spendthrift and one of them, a close-fisted, spiteful widow, according to a legal document from the year 1638, "did publicly declare that he squandered Saskia's patrimony in ostentation and display, that he dressed her superabundantly, and that she had seen Saskia wearing two large pear-shaped pearls at her throat, a necklace of two rows of pearls, diamond ear-rings and a finger-ring set with huge diamonds." Rembrandt sued the old widow for libel, won the case, and thus stopped the mouths of his envious accusers.

For some years after his marriage, he seems to have felt the necessity of making as much money as possible. The wonder is not that he should have had the desire but that he should have so easily succeeded in discharging it. Great genius, as a rule, is a dismal failure when pitted against popular talent. But Rembrandt competed with the tribe of portrait-servants on their own ground and swept them from the field. The sources of his more lucrative commissions were several: the governing boards of hospitals and charities; the Syndics, or officials of the merchants' guilds; the shooting fraternities, and private traders of means. Most of his paintings executed to order are examples of superlative craftsmanship, a few broad and free, the majority conforming to the glassy tightness so pleasing to Dutch fanciers; some are poor and hurried; all bear witness to his unique method of lighting and modelling. They were done for one purpose—to get money to indulge his wife's love of finery, and his own passion for collecting. His rash bidding made him notorious in the auction rooms. He treasured old armor and oriental gimcracks; he bought canvases by living painters whom he wished to encourage, and Italian masterpieces at prices which only a plutocrat like Rubens could afford. When a painting, or one of his own etchings, was put up for sale, he silenced rival collectors at a single stroke by offering, as the first bid, twice or three times as much as the most liberal of them would have been willing to pay. He did this, he explained, to raise the standard of prices in Holland, a philanthropic gesture, but one ultimately ruinous to himself.

He had no close companions, not even his wife. Aristocratic society he avoided—not for anyone would he alter his plain habits, put on formal dress, or affect the airs of polite breeding. Sometimes men of genuine distinction, scholars, rabbis and connoisseurs, sought him out to listen to his good sense. To a few discerning friends his greatness of mind was taken for granted, but he was heedless of the impression he gave, was utterly impervious to criticism, and never in doubt of his final victory. He seemed to think in terms of light and dark, rarely speaking of his work except in short, ribald remarks such as "Don't get your nose too close to my painting—it smells bad." His marriage did not cut him off from his friends and he was always accessible to artists, boosting the prices of their wares, advising them, and presenting them with his own paintings and etchings—with works which cannot be bought today for love nor money. As a relief from the stench of paint he wandered about Amsterdam, the more sordid quarters by preference where he had many friends. But most of the time he was busy in his studio. He made hundreds of etchings and thousands of drawings—more drawings than any other artist before or since except Turner—studied Holbein and Dürer, Rubens and Brouwer, Correggio and Mantegna, Michael Angelo, Raphael and the Venetians.

During these swift, extravagant years when Rembrandt had outdistanced all competitors as a successful portrait painter, his acquaintance with sorrow ripened with his own direct experiences with death. Three children had been born and each had died in infancy, and Saskia, never very strong, was beginning to decline. These misfortunes had no immediate effect upon his painting, for his art was not a diary of personal tribulations, but they added to his impatience with that side of it which was more or less in compliance with current taste, and heightened his loyalty to his purest convictions. In his restlessness he moved several times, hunting for a place in which he might settle permanently and devote himself exclusively to spiritual issues, to the part of him that could be neither broken nor corrupted. He found such a place in the heart of the Jewish quarter and, in 1639, he bought it, a large dwelling, still known as Rembrandt House, with ample space for a studio and for the expensive plunder he had gathered from the auction rooms.

It was a shock to Saskia's gentle soul, accustomed as she had grown to her husband's extraordinary behavior, to be carried suddenly into the slums, and to see him, at the summit of his popularity, choose an abode in a segregation of refugees from Portugal; but she recovered quickly and despite her delicate health was cheerful and uncomplaining. Rembrandt went to live among the Jews less because he sought isolation and tranquillity of mind than because of his natural sympathy with suffering humanity. Those swarming immigrants whom Holland had welcomed to spite the Spaniards represented to him the children of the Ancient Race; the bearded patriarchs, the learned rabbis, the solemn physicians, the unclean poor in their gleaming rags, the turbans and caftans, the color and mystery of the East—the scene fascinated him like a vivid dream come to life. To him this transported civilization was neither foreign nor exotic; it was the flesh and blood of the visionary world which he had been erecting since childhood; it abounded in pictorial material, affording concrete stimulus to the interpretation of biblical stories to which he alone, of all post-Renaissance painters, was able to give significant embodiment. The year after he entered the Ghetto his mother died and the event, reviving his first scriptural memories, rendered his new surroundings even more congenial.

He painted, during the years of his married life, many portraits of his wife, two of them, the London *Flora* and *Saskia Holding a Red Flower*, at Dresden, brilliant examples of that high property of his work which reproductions obliterate and which no words can fitly describe. It is essentially a spiritual property. Before it we are no more aware of cold pigment than we are aware of the bald type in which a great poem is printed. All distinctions of texture are brushed away; flesh, flowers and costumes, while retaining their objective identity, are transfused into a common substance every part of which is charged with a spiritual content. It is the unfathomable majesty of paint. In this period he also painted four religious pieces of the first rank, *Christ Before Pilate, The Angel Leaving Tobias, The Sacrifice of Manoah* and *David and Absalom*, pictures containing this same majesty but with a psychological injection that has wrought consternation among certain modern critics. These gentlemen, it appears, are spellbound before Rembrandt's plastic mastery, that is, the flowing of the forms one into the other, and the veil of tone that conjoins them, but they regret that he should have portrayed his figures (in one picture even the dog is cowering in awe) in the throes of emotions proper to the theme. It hardly seems possible that anyone could believe that the marvellous plasticity of these pictures would have any meaning if Rembrandt had been concerned only with the scientific aspects of light and the mathematical adjustment of forms, and, after effacing all signs of human expressiveness from his figures had correlated them into groups of classical dummies.

The year 1642 marks a critical point in his career. Captain Banning Cocq, commander of the civic guards of the first ward—Rembrandt's ward before he was enchanted by the Children of Israel—and sixteen of his trusty warriors contributed 100 florins apiece towards a large group picture to hang in the Hall of the Musketeers and unanimously voted Rembrandt as the man to paint it. They received the disappointment of their lives. The artist had little interest in civic guards, less in ordered portraits, and none whatever in the vanity of military men. Heretofore his group pictures had consisted of clusters of small figures stationed in immense space and he was now ready to see what he could do with life-size figures completely filling the canvas. Hence *The Night Watch*, an experiment that pleased nobody. Instead of presenting a company of men responding to a call to arms in military formation, and in broad daylight so that all should be conspicuous, he painted them in confusion and obscurity, several, notably the Captain and his Lieutenant, in a torrent of artificial light, the rest half-buried in nocturnal shadows. And worse: he had no respect for regulation uniforms, and added, free of charge, for the sake of his composition, ten unworthy reservists, and in a pocket where he needed a balancing light, the figure of a little girl. The vain musketeers who had paid their good money for an advertisement of their manly beauty were outraged, feeling, not unnaturally, that they had been hoaxed by an artist capable of doing them full justice had he been so inclined. They ordered Rembrandt to alter it, but this he stoutly refused to do. And so they altered it themselves and hung it, not in their assembly hall, but in an anteroom. To adapt it to a space between two doors, they sawed off three feet of canvas on the right side, eliminating three figures, cutting two others in half, and seriously damaging the composition.

The Night Watch is by no means his greatest work. Its immediate effect is overwhelming but that is because there is nothing like it. Remain with it for any length of time and you will see for yourself that its majesty is not untarnished. It is almost fabulously dramatic in its organized confusion and its red and gold forms blazing out of subterranean murk. Some of the heads are carefully studied and worthy of the hand that made them; but most of them are perfunctory and the whole is thrown together with frenzied rapidity of execution. The nature of the subject was not favorable to his noblest designs, for he worked best with materials into which he entered unreservedly. But he made no compromise with his artistic conscience, as he had done in *The Anatomy Lesson*; in fact his amazingly aggressive indifference to the demands of his patrons was, I am pretty certain, public warning of his contempt for Dutch standards of taste.

After *The Night Watch*, the tide of popular favor, as he had anticipated, turned against him. But he did not care. He was

Rembrandt: CHRIST HEALING THE SICK.
(Courtesy of M. Knoedler & Co., New York)

faced with a far more desolating situation. In the preceding year his wife had given birth to a son whom she had named Titus in memory of her sister Titia, and to his unbounded delight the boy had lived. But the mother had wasted away, and while the injured musketeers were haggling over a great work of art which they had not bargained for, she died. Rembrandt was profoundly hurt but he was not crushed. He made a drawing of a sad, old man feeding an angry baby with a big spoon and under it he wrote in his exquisite handwriting, *A Lonely Widower*. It is a mere sketch—done, we might almost suppose without once lifting his reed pen from the paper—but it shows in its curious blending of pathos and caricature the detachment with which he was able to ponder his vicissitudes. His imagination soared into new fields. From the melancholy atmosphere of the studio he turned to the out-of-doors, painting vast mountains and ruined castles—he had never seen mountains—and miraculous windmills that rise up from solid masses of shadow to gather the winds of heaven with their golden wings. At night he strained his eyes over his copper plates, etching old Hebrews and now and then a faithful friend, and pulling from the metal a set of designs so rich in pictorial effects as to fill all subsequent etchers with secret shame and confessions of incompetence. Again he reverted to his Bible, and the stories which had never failed to excite him now moved him to his loftiest religious utterances and he painted *The Holy Family*, in the Hermitage, and *The Supper at Emmaus* in the Louvre. He was entering the period of his greatest productions.

Rembrandt seemed rather to welcome than lament the loss of his public. But he was not, as has been frequently asserted, a broken recluse living in the world of his dreams. More and more he explored the Ghetto, counting among the Jews some of his staunchest admirers; the more intelligent artists, regarding him as the fallen monarch, were still happy to be admitted to his studio; and he was on close terms with a few decent collectors and amateurs. His mother had left him a small legacy, his wife a large one, and he had, as yet, no need to think about money. The place formerly occupied by his wife, or more accurately, the bed occupied by his wife, was now taken by his son's nurse, Geertje Dircx, a grinning hulk. Old Geertje was insanely devoted to Titus, but she was quarrelsome and ill-favored, and when Rembrandt brought home a young woman to keep house for him, she made a scene and quitted his service.

In an incurable rage, the old nurse, who was really half-cracked, appeared before the matrimonial court and swore that "Rembrandt, the painter, had promised to marry her, had given her a wedding dress, and had repeatedly had sexual intercourse with her." She demanded marriage or maintenance. The painter ignored the charges until he had been twice fined, whereupon he denied the promise of marriage, declared that he was not required to admit misconduct—that the plaintiff must prove it—and that the wedding dress had been stolen from his deceased wife's wardrobe. The court ordered him to increase the plaintiff's allowance. Shortly afterward the old woman died in a private asylum, where she had been maintained at Rembrandt's expense, leaving her little property to the boy Titus.

While involved in this sordid affair he was pouring the light of his genius into the cavernous spaces of the soul. "What I want," he said, "is not honors but freedom!" He was getting his wish. Freedom from the claims of the moneyed rabble; freedom to pursue his art into the regions where his own beliefs commanded the marvels of his craft! It was the year of the great etching of *Christ Healing the Sick*, known universally as *The Hundred Guilder Piece* from its record price at a sale a century later. Rembrandt's etchings are almost the sole excuse for the existence of the finical and laborious process of scratching smudged pieces of copper. What is with other artists seldom more than an idle craft—even Whistler's plates are only cautious renderings of picturesque scenes or delicate heads failing, for all their suggested poetic charm, to conceal his feeble draughtsmanship—a stilted and oblique method of arriving at effects which an ordinary pen gains freely and directly, becomes in Rembrandt's hands an instrument rivaling the scope and power of the medium of paint. Whether he worked with a few lines and coarsely hatched shadows, or with intricate folds of chiaroscuro, the results are transcendent.

The Hundred Guilder Piece is such a baffling mixture of lights and darks that etchers are wont to shake their heads over it and say, "It is contrary to the spirit of the medium!" What spirit, I wonder? The spirit of hidebound obedience to limitations which none but the mighty can over-rule? Christ, a Portuguese Jew, stands between two groups of sufferers, those on his left hand tumbled on the ground in prayerful attitudes, but enclosed in a solid unit by the impenetrably subtle use of strong lights leaping out of utter blackness or flowing gently into scattered half-tones; those on his right standing in a line which fades off into a knot of unfinished old men. There is a plastic dog and a plastic baby. A few outlines, apparently careless and indeterminate but actually set down with masterly knowledge of their structural value; lights merging into deepening shadows —and a form has its being. First, from studies made in the Ghetto, he builds up his figures, giving them the peculiar limpness of the sick and helpless, and the convincing, living stature of men, women and children; next, he undertakes to reveal, and does reveal, by gestures, facial expressions, and the essential magic of his genius which defies analysis, the light of a divine presence. One does not have to be a Catholic, a Mennonite or a Fundamentalist, to perceive this. The picture presents, without a glint of sentimentality, a section of humanity, a pitiable lot, invested with spiritual glory. If this be illustration, let us be thankful that Rembrandt had beliefs worthy of such illustration.

His young housekeeper, Hendrickje Stoffels, was, like the wife of William Blake, a perfect companion for a man of genius. And like Blake's wife, she could neither read nor write. She was modest and soft of speech, her complexion fresh, her eyes large and sad, her figure well-rounded; and she had, in addition to her physical gifts, a character of the finest grain, a noble sympathy with his art and an indissoluble loyalty to him in his adversities. Rembrandt's first child by her died at birth and the unhappy circumstance precipitated the wrath of the council of the church where she was a communicant. She was summoned before the elders and publicly reproved "for living in concubinage with Rembrandt the painter" and ordered to mend her ways. She saw no error in her ways and when a second child was born, the sanctified elders forbade her to partake of the sacrament. The infant was taken to another church for baptism and named Cornelia after the painter's mother, a name which, on two similar occasions, had been given to Saskia's unfortunate daughters. Rembrandt treated Hendrickje as his wife and she was loved as a second mother by young Titus—but he never married her. Possibly because the terms of Saskia's will granted him the income from property held in trust for her son as long as he remained unmarried; more probably, I think, because of his increasing carelessness in everything not directly bearing upon his painting.

He dressed in a slovenly fashion, not intentionally, as many painters do, but because the formality of dress meant as little to him as the formality of a marriage contract. The obloquy attached to his irregular ménage fetched from him not so much as a round oath of resentment against the best people: he was painting some of his greatest portraits, himself, a battered and immovable giant; Hendrickje, his peasant consort, a symbol of sovereign dignity—all told he was fulfilling his life-purpose, and the consciousness of the fulfilment induced a serenity of mind and a formidable outward composure that made him proof against the dwarfs and snobs who prattled about his immorality and his crumbling art. But he was careless in matters of a much more disastrous nature. Commissions had practically ceased and he made no effort to recover his lost prestige. And he persisted in his old habits of extravagant collecting, spending whatever funds he could get hold of, and thoughtlessly drawing on his son's inheritance. He borrowed money right and left and could not repay it; his brothers were destitute, his sister in distress, and he came to their rescue; notes fell due and he could not meet them. The storm descended upon him in his fiftieth year and Hendrickje was powerless to prevent it. She did not understand these financial tangles; nor had Rembrandt ever paused to enlighten her. There was a sparkle of joy in the master's tired eyes—his work was going well; her own child was properly fed and clothed; the frail Titus was growing stronger: the peaceful household seemed immune from designing creditors.

He had forgot that his house was encumbered, allowing not only the payments to lapse but also the interest and the taxes. The mortgage holder threatened foreclosure and at this point the relatives of Saskia stepped in, had a guardian appointed for Titus, and obtained a second mortgage to indemnify the son for the loss of his fortune. A general row ensued and, in 1656, Rembrandt was declared bankrupt. His creditors were merciless. An inventory was drawn up and in the following year a public sale announced. All his possessions—his own paintings, his Italian and Flemish acquisitions, his smaller treasures—were knocked down at prices which must have made the painter's heart ache; and the house passed into the hands of a shoemaker. He was spared but one item, the plates of his etchings. Hendrickje succeeded in getting a court order to clean out an old cupboard in which she had secreted a little money, some pieces of linen, and shabby wearing apparel.

The eviction did not embitter him. He seemed indeed, as he thought it over in a neighboring inn to which he had moved his family while the sale was in progress, to accept it as the natural consequence of his mismanagement. And to show that he harbored no ill-will against his prosecutors, he invited the auctioneer to the inn, drank his health, and honored him with the gift of an etching. But once the mischief was ended and the old creative problems began to crowd his brain, he realized to what extremities his art had led him. He could not paint in a tavern, yet paint he must: that was his only salvation. There remained his etchings, his sole means of subsistence. He borrowed the use of a press, pulled off a bundle of impressions, and disposed of them to dealers who, seeing how hard up he was, made as if they were doing him a favor by paying him starvation driblets for masterpieces. He moved again to an unfrequented quarter at the end of the Ghetto where the lowest of Jews trafficked in second-hand goods. This was his last residence. For reasons of economy he resumed work in black-and-white, but the excessive demands he had made upon his vision had so weakened his eyes that he was forced to abandon etching altogether. He was awarded a decoration for the Town Hall—but only because the painter originally chosen had conveniently died. When he delivered the picture, it was rejected. Two of his oldest friends died—he helped to bury them, and went back to his painting.

Through the influence of a wealthy dyer who, in his youth, had been one of Rembrandt's pupils, and gratefully remembered the association, he was commissioned to paint a group portrait of the *Syndics of the Drapers' Guild*, his last work of this character, and the greatest work of this character in existence. But it netted him nothing—the money was immediately seized by creditors in satisfaction of old claims. It was plain that he could no longer support his family. The family, however, was equal to the crisis. Titus, by a legal abridgment of his minority, came into his inheritance, and together with Hendrickje set up shop as a dealer in art. Rembrandt was retained as official advisor, the firm advancing him moneys for his immediate wants, and holding an option on such pictures as he might produce in the future. This last was an obvious measure to keep his earnings within the family. The shop started slowly, for business was none too flourishing in Holland and the market was overstocked with paintings, but with the most careful management it began to pay its way, and in the second year showed a small margin of profit. But it was not to last. Hendrickje fell ill and soon was carried to the grave. Rembrandt sold the family vault in which Saskia and his children were buried to provide a resting place in his own district for the good woman who had served as mistress, model and mother. He was now wholly dependent upon his son.

Let us not offer this man our pity. To do so would be a mockery of his immense self-discipline. Let us not offer him our condemnation; such would be a denial of his right to put his life and his art at the service of his convictions. He was no mere eccentric blindly following a destructive whim; no fanatic like Van Gogh whose mad passion for reforming the world led to the asylum and to suicide; no saint whose love for the humblest of his brothers impelled him to restrict his experiences to the hard fare of asceticism. From first to last he was an industrious, amiable Dutchman with none of the conceits and none of the delusions of the minor artist who prefers starvation to honest toil—but with powers of clairvoyance far exceeding those of any other painter. If, at the end of his life, he was clad in rags, it was only because he had nothing finer to wear, and not because he believed with St. Francis that only thus could he purify his soul. Why then, it may be asked, when he saw the material world slipping through his fingers, did he make no move to avert it? This question, I believe, has already been answered. He had outgrown his public and he preferred the consequences of his own aesthetic rectitude to a life of shameless compromise.

It is not the easiest thing in the world to forfeit a large popular fame and a handsome income in order to preserve a clean conscience or to gain freedom of speech. We, in America, where the sacrifice of the smallest material extravagance for the sake of common decency is regarded as an act of stupidity, know that only too well. And it must be remembered that Rembrandt did not wilfully seek to alienate his public: he was astonished, not to say dismayed, that his best work—the superiority of which has been recognized by generations of artists and laymen alike—should have been cried down by a public which he felt was not unprepared for a spiritual shock. But why did he work so hard after his markets were gone and his public grown hostile? To prove his competence as a man and as an artist; to prove that his ideas were worth living for; to hold his human relationship with the small friendly audience that needed his art;

for those moments of indescribable joy which come only to the conquerors of great difficulties; for the sweet relief that settles on the soul of man when he has given utterance to his burdens and thus put them from him.

Rembrandt was not a happy man. I do not mean that he was a lugubrious nuisance to his friends, or that he lay awake racked with morbid broodings on the mystery of death. But the peculiar quality of his imagination could have developed only in a mind perpetually occupied with experiences which were certainly the opposite of those springing from happiness. Among all his characters there is not one who is filled with exuberance, or animal spirits. You may have observed that his faces, without exception, are old faces. Even his children seem to have lived a long time and to have had glimpses of the eternal reality of sorrow. He was not concerned with the hopes and dreams of youth but with man after he has been sorely tried; in the marks that suffering has left upon him; in his majesty and his imperturbable repose, after he has mastered his afflictions. The loss of his public was incidental to his development. If anything, it hastened the day of his emancipation. For certain it is that after his financial collapse he was one of the pure in heart, without pride, resentment, servility or avarice, a free man, if ever one lived.

It was now possible for Rembrandt to approach his subject-matter with unconditional freedom of the spirit, a state to which he had attained once or twice before in his religious pieces, notably *The Supper at Emmaus*. Which is to say, that if he were to paint a portrait of Hendrickje Stoffels or himself, or Hendrickje as a *Woman Bathing* or as *Bathsheba*, or his son, or six bourgeois *Syndics*, he would paint them with the same fervor and disinterestedness that he would bestow upon a conception of Christ. He would not be dominated by immediate sense-impressions; he would ignore the ephemeral appearances of the face and figure under the accidents of natural light; he would paint into them the full force of his experiences after he had bound them into a single, unalterable conception of a noble human being. He would create them in his own image, or, as Vasari said so often of his beloved Italians, "he would paint them in the divine light of his own genius."

This becomes clearer if we bear in mind that Rembrandt's light is neither sunlight nor candlelight but his own created illumination, unique and inimitable. When employed by men without his conviction, it is hardly more significant than the incandescence of the spotlight. In its sources, distribution, intensity and quality, it is but remotely related to the light through which we behold the visible world. The effects of ordinary daylight might suffice for an enameller like Vermeer or a scientist like Velasquez—painters absorbed in "things as they are." Rembrandt had had enough of things as they are. He was born into a population of painters whose notion of art was to duplicate the skin of the human face so that butchers and bakers might be spared the necessity of looking into a mirror. The only art that he believed to be worth living for was an art in which man, the actual, familiar fact, was transfigured into a spiritual agent, into a being retaining its essential connection with the familiar fact, but relieved of everything that emphasized the purely physical.

This transfiguration, of course, was accomplished by technical means. But the greatest master of tone in the history of painting applied his knowledge to the integration of his lights and darks—and not to their objective accuracy. His world is a synthesis of forms immersed in a sea of marvellous tone. He understood, as no artist has understood before or since, the architectural value of light and dark masses, the sequences of the planes receiving light, and the structural wholeness of forms composed in tones, instead of contours and precise outlines. With a few colors and tints, reds and browns, greys running into blacks, deep golden yellows and olive greens, he created pictures of supernatural luminosity. His heads seem to be scooped out of unfathomable mixtures of radiance and shadow. The most massive heads ever painted; no misshapen jaws, no loosely hinged parts; no weaknesses anywhere. And made of a film of ground earth and oil! Yet these heads would avail us nothing if they were only painted illusions of weight, plasticity, perfect articulation and massive structure; if Rembrandt, as Taine pointed out, had not revealed through them the concentrated history of the soul.

But a technical analysis of Rembrandt is not very edifying. Before his pictures formal criticism is helpless. For the criticism of our Modernist painters who, in the absence of any spiritual content in their work, have composed an esoteric mummery to the God of Structure, we have an appropriate technical apparatus; but this formal instrument, theoretically capable of probing into the vitals of all art, barely scratches the surface of Rembrandt's painting. To get at the meaning of his pictures we do not have to trench our way through devious technical barriers: what he has to say is expressed with such manifest directness that to estimate its value in any terms of structural hocus-pocus is to expound the religious experiences of man by means of a diagram of the human skeleton.

The great works of his later years are symbols, pure and simple. Their appeal is straightforward and fundamental. They are not portraits of this man or that woman; nor is their appeal based upon allusions to external characteristics or events in themselves affecting by virtue of pathetic associations. That which is merely local or Dutch has been translated into a universal language, and in this sense Rembrandt's masterpieces are independent of time and circumstance. They are not records of touching episodes or suggestions of tender sentiments—they embody emotions as old as man. To know them is to add a new experience to one's life, an experience so fresh and vivid and powerful as to sink to the very bottom of one's soul and to leave therein its imperishable register. I have said that Rembrandt deals with emotions as old as man, with things of fundamental concern to the race. He does, but the magical freshness, the depth, and the wonder of his canvases comes from the new and individual valuations which he puts on the old human stuff. And from the fact that he accepts nothing at second-hand: his experiences are his own, and when we encounter them we understand the profoundly authentic speech of an artist who faced the world, reflected on it, and created emblems of tragic majesty out of the rags of common suffering. And from the peculiar quality of his experiences after they have passed through his vision, taken the color and the very substance of his personality, and entered the medium of paint.

It would be a fruitless task to attempt a psychological analysis of these symbols or to identify them with specific emotions—fruitless because they do not represent specific emotions. Rembrandt, in his final works, is not interested in the particular feelings of his models, or in displaying his own reactions to special circumstances. He makes each of them a carrier for all that he has learned and felt and accumulated in his harsh journey through life, and each of them is a spiritualized version of himself. If it were otherwise he would be no better than the thousands of Dutch face-painters. It is admissible to say that his great pictures reflect the general tone of his heroic later years, and even to say that in the faces of those superb *Syndics*, or in the studies of himself and Hendrickje, we may discern the curious wisdom and the gigantic serenity of the artist for whom life no longer holds mysteries or terrors. Further we cannot go and remain intelligible. But it does not follow that because his symbols are indefinable, they are vague and ambiguous. Containing the sum-total of his experiences condensed into forms of enormous simplicity, they become emotional stimulants of incalculable force. They flush the spirit of everything that is trivial, temporary and ignoble, heighten our perceptions, extend our capacities for contemplation, and create within us a new vision of humanity.

In his last years Rembrandt was the most enviable of mortals. His wants were few: paint and gin; cheese and pickled herring; a box of coals to warm his fingers. He was at peace with the world—the peace that comes upon a man when he has finished a great work. Fat, debt-ridden and friendless, he sat at his window above the Rose Canal and painted. His son married and went away. He painted a portrait of the pale young man and his bride, two of his finest things. He worked on with unremitting discipline, pushing the medium of paint farther and farther, laying the soul bare with a few strokes of the palette knife. The next year his son died, and as he followed the body to the grave, wearing his best rags, a fur-lined coat smeared with many colors, he kept his head erect and the loafers of the quarter marvelled at this old man's composure. He painted himself again—the last of a long series of self-portraits which have made his face familiar to everyone—a mask of colored mud laughing at the world which had tried so many times to beat him. One year more of life and work. When death came, in 1669, it brought him no greater peace than the peace he had already won. His funeral was attended by his nurse, his daughter Cornelia, his son's widow and a number of inquisitive Jews who had heard that he had once been a famous man in Amsterdam. When the grave was sealed, his son's widow ran back to the house to see if he had taken the gold coins—half of which belonged to her—from Cornelia's money-box. He had not taken them.

CHAPTER

XII

THREE SPANIARDS

THE SOUL OF SPAIN

THE curious fascination which Spain has exerted on the imagination of the world for three centuries has not been founded on her contributions to humanity. It is a more subtle fascination than anything rising from mere achievement; it has its roots in an insensible rigidity of temperament which writers, with one accord, have been pleased to call the soul. We have heard so much about the soul of Spain that we might, with reason, assume that no other nation has ever been similarly blest. Precisely what constitutes this national possession it is difficult to say. We read that Lope de Vega with his thousand and one plays—all alike, all cloak-and-sword claptrap, all affairs of honor—is the incarnation of the Spanish soul; but we read the same of Calderon and Tirso de Molina, the creator of Don Juan, and even of Cervantes, the only writer who has crossed the Pyrenees. We are informed by Castilian critics that El Greco, an adopted son, "mirrors the true soul of Spain—noble, mystical and pious"; but these critics, forgetting themselves, award the same honor to the court servitor Velasquez, and again to the peasant Goya.

To the outside world Spain is the only country in Christendom that has devoted herself, at the cost of everything that is modern, decent and enlightened, to the preservation of her romantic soul. Robert Louis Stevenson, ill abed in the bleak city of Edinburgh and longing for the sensual heats of the South, wrote a story which illustrates to perfection the romantic notions of the foreigner. But he had not seen Spain. Travellers in the Peninsula have had a different story to tell. Borrow and Mérimée, both genuine explorers, discovered that the Spain of romance existed only among the Gypsies; and Gautier, with as keen an eye for such matters as one could wish for, returned to Paris completely disillusioned. He found much that was singular and exciting, but no romance. "Old Castile," he said, "is so named because of the preponderance of old women there. The women of Spain age rapidly and all of them have beards like mouldy cheese." It is the fabulous, romantic Spain that has ensnared the rest of the world: the legends of Don Juan in the versions of Byron and Zorilla; the rendezvous of Gypsies; the land of pale, thin-waisted, small-footed beauties smouldering with savage passions; the home of the grandee and the hidalgo, of Carmen, dancers and bull-fighters, of blood and pride and stolen gold. In justice to Spain, I must add that she has never encouraged this popular conception of her national character. With her cast-iron contempt for foreigners, and also with a certain consciousness of her disintegration, she has regarded the outside world—when she has noticed it at all—as incapable of understanding her grand and contradictory soul, and has sullenly resented criticism, praise as well as censure.

Spain, as one of her modern poets affirms, "won the whole world and lost the whole world"—lost it through her arrogance and brutal selfishness. No other power occupying so conspicuous a position in the affairs of mankind has been so uncreative. All that she can lay claim to was produced in the hundred and fifty years following the accession of Charles V. Since the death of Philip IV she has sunk lower and lower in slothfulness and ruin, silent, immovable and illiterate, decaying with a distinction that makes the adolescent energy of America a little ridiculous, content to bask in the artificial splendor of the past, clinging to ancestral diseases and vices rather than educate her women or cover the bones of her beggars and cripples. But even in the heroic age the bulk of her wealth was not created—it was stolen wealth. Her foot soldiers, the finest in Europe and the most cruel, were organized bandits and executioners who strangled the Low Countries, sacked Italy and drained the New World of its deposits of gold and silver. Naturally, when it was easier to plunder than to work, her own resources were neglected; her weavers, it is true, were fairly industrious, but the manufacture of cloth in the entire kingdom in the most flourishing period was not equal to the output of Bruges alone. By means of piracy and conquest she maintained the most extravagant court in Europe and supported an enormous number of shiftless and vicious aristocrats. It was the ambition of every Spaniard to gain a title, and at one time half the population were nobles of one sort or another, and every noble was a slaveholder. The other half were slaves, priests, picaroons, smugglers, dwarfs, bull-fighters and material for the autos-da-fe.

The Spanish soul is filled with ferocious hatred of life. Search this soul closely, in the time of its most fruitful expansion or at any moment in its stagnant complacency, and you will find therein no love of nature, nor of art, nor of humanity. The great wave of Renaissance humanism could not sweeten its brackish hatreds, fertilize its harsh vitality or modify its intolerance. In the blood of Spain flow the perverse cruelty and savage contempt for life born of the deadly mixture of the old Roman and African strains, and this cruelty and this mutilating antipathy to everything redeeming man from barbarism, sharpened instead of being allayed by seven hundred years of warfare against the Moors, resisted the Reformation in the most monstrous system of torture on record, a system instituted by her Catholic Majesties and enjoyed by the masses. Enjoyed is hardly the word. The Inquisition brought to Spain a fiendish satisfaction in the realistic and ingenious application of her genius for premeditated cruelty. There is no joy in the Spanish soul; none of the inspiriting intellectual curiosity of Florence; no pleasure in refined voluptuousness, such as characterized Venice; none of the friendliness, the healthy wantonness and the simple delight in material abundance that made the Flemish so glad to be alive.

The pride of Spain which, since the collapse of her empire, has been no more than a tenacious scorn for everything beyond her borders, was, in the short season of her glory, a synonym for fantastic cupidity and destructive arrogance. It was her pride, as thus defined, that led her to squander her energies and her wealth trying to bleed and dominate the world; that led her to safeguard the purity of her blood—as if it had ever been pure!—and to defend her mediaeval religion by expelling the Jews and Moors, her only producers, and by burning heretics; that led King Philip and his royal counsellors to debate in all seriousness the advisability of challenging the Pope to a duel because a Spanish cardinal had been punched in the face by an agent of the Vatican; that led her to declare that no one, in any circumstance whatever and under pain of death, should touch the person of her Queen, not even to save her life, and to borrow from the Arabs the custom of keeping her women indoors; that led her, in her abhorrence of the Moors who were inveterate bathers, to renounce the ancient custom of scrubbing the body and to remain to this day unwashed. It was her ineffable pride in her soul that prompted her to take such gruesome liberties with the body: to spatter the walls of churches with the blood of penitents; to practice flagellation; to create invalids; to collect dwarfs, buffoons, idiots and deformities; to reverence insanity; to deny the importance of the material life, to starve and suffer, and thus to purify the soul into a pathological state of ecstasy so that it might enter the divine presence.

The soul of Spain is at once sensual and puritan, mystical and realistic. The famous Spanish dances are explicitly sensual, but rigorously controlled, and always checked this side of obscenity by a fanatic sense of prudery. Spanish puritanism is far more obdurate and restricting than the killjoy righteousness of the Anglo-Saxons. There are, for instance, only two nude women in Spanish art—Velasquez's *Venus*, painted during a momentary lapse of the prohibitory laws, and Goya's *Maja*, the defiant stroke of a bold rogue—and both have never ceased to offend the tastes of a nation so justly renowned for beautiful women. While the Inquisition was in force, a painter was thrown into jail for representing the Virgin in an embroidered petticoat. Puritanism de-

El Greco: VIEW OF TOLEDO.
Metropolitan Museum of Art, New York

creed for women a form of dress designed to deny the existence of the body below the waist, and distrusting the equally strong instinct of sensuality, forbade a lover a moment of privacy with his betrothed until after the marriage. The novels and poetry of Spain deal, for the most part, with lust subtilized into declamatory mysticism, with endless justifications for disturbed chastity and seductions "in which women are taken as besieged towns, whose defenses have never been in good order." The sexual instincts of the male are allowed pretty free play: he keeps a *querida* or a dancer, marries early, but once married, loses all interest in his wife save as the mother of his ten or twelve children, seduces a servant or factory girl, "and then, after she has been turned out of her home and gone to the public lying-in hospital, takes her to a brothel and deposits her there, promising to visit her occasionally and to send her wealthy patrons."

When Spanish sensuality is transferred to mysticism, it becomes a devouring, intolerable passion for the intoxicating raptures of the spirit, affirming, in the words of San Juan de la Cruz, that "by contemplation man may become incorporated with the Deity." There is today, and always has been in Spain, an extraordinary amount of this sort of contemplation—it is indeed all that most Spaniards, particularly the women, have in life. We see it in the eyes of old men who sun themselves day after day in the plazas or patios; we see it among the women, the peasants in the arid fields, the shrivelled dueñas guarding amorous couples, and mothers old before their time gazing out into the world from behind an iron grating, as from a cell. But to the foreigner it is only a form of indolence—a proud and sinister and cultivated indolence that is responsible for the backwardness and misery of modern Spain. This mysticism, however, is generally balanced by a stern sense of realistic values, a condition which would seem to be a union of opposites, but which is no more inconsistent than the co-existence of poetry and practicality in the British nation. El Greco, the most mystical of Spanish painters, was also a shrewd business man; and Santa

Teresa, the flower of mysticism and the greatest woman of Spain, if not the world, was by no means blind to the ways of secular life. She was contemplating the evil destiny of the average Spanish girl when she wrote, "I would not have my daughters be, or seem to be, women in anything, but brave men." A Carmelite nun, she referred to convent life, as "a short-cut to hell," and went on to say that "if parents took my advice, they would rather marry their daughters to the poorest of men, or keep them at home under their own eyes."

Yet Spain, in the face of all that may be earnestly said against her, continues to charm intelligent travellers. A large part of this charm is, I believe, of a negative order: the relief experienced by those whose minds and bodies have been racked beyond endurance by the forces of modern industrialism when they encounter a race opposed to material advancement, or at least to the desperate struggles accompanying it. But this opposition is not necessarily advantageous to the life of the spirit, as has been too frequently assumed. Unamuno, one of the few Spaniards who have had the courage to attack the vicious obscurantism of their country, has been banished for his honest criticism. Unamuno pleads for a new Spain, a Spain delivered from "sterility and empty impracticable dreams." But gentlemen adventurers like Cunninghame Graham love Spain above all countries and would not have her otherwise than she is. Convinced, as they seem to be, of the failure of the capitalistic culture of the more progressive nations, they uphold Spain for her uncompromising attitude towards materialism, an attitude which, though it has admittedly bred squalor and decay, is compensated by spiritual qualities not to be found elsewhere. They claim for Spain the finest courtesy in the world, an ingrained and genuine dignity of speech and bearing, and affections based upon a fundamental need for the responses of companionship and not measured by the recognition of wealth or position. They acknowledge the superiority of the women—their intelligence and fascination, their warmth, wit and loyalty—despite the fact that they are virtually slaves to the men, forced as swiftly as possible into one of two careers, motherhood or prostitution. All this is soothing to gentlemen adventurers, but of small comfort to those having the future of their country at heart, to the few public-spirited men who would rescue Spain from what seems to be her inevitable fate—total dissolution and spoliation by foreign capitalists.

Strictly speaking, Spain has had no national art, no school of painting. Her best architecture was Moorish, which, in its decline, was submerged in the Gothic tradition to form the plateresque, the closest approach to an original style. Plateresque architecture, named from its fantastic and delicate ornamentation borrowed from the silversmiths, was temporarily set aside by Philip II who mistook a barren ascetic style for classicism and ordered that awful gridiron, the Escorial. Popular taste, however, soon reasserted itself, and cultivated the baroque tendency with excessive enthusiasm and ingenuity, plastering the façades of public buildings and stuffing the interiors of churches with an insane profusion of decorative trumpery which strikes the reasonable mind as the sad orgy of a soul suddenly released from mad repressions, and amid this profusion one is likely to see an excellent piece of sculpture, usually in wood, the muscular structure simply and admirably managed, but as revoltingly realistic as the wax effigies one sees in the religious processions in every town during Christmas and Holy Week. Spain produced a number of good carvers but none of importance. She had little use for sculpture as a mural or architectural art, demanding it only as a stimulus to her hideous piety. For the Spanish soul at the one extreme tropically sensual, was, at the other morbidly ascetic and long-suffering. Lope de Vega is typical of this duality. An incorrigible lecher, he would, when his soul needed disciplining, turn priest and lash his body until the walls of his cell were red with blood.

The glory of Spanish painting is confined to three men, all accidents of genius, and one of them a Greek. There is no primitive painting of any significance, and when Rubens went to Madrid on his first diplomatic mission, he was unable to find a single artist of even ordinary competence. El Greco and Velasquez had no successors and after Goya there is silence: a good illustrator, Vierge, and two painters who made a fortune in America solely because they happened to be Spanish. One of them, Sorolla, is dead and forgotten; the other, Zuloaga, sold to American aristocrats a cargo of canvases in which he had brought together all the Carmens, dancers, duchesses, mantillas, fans, and bull-fighters in Spain—all the properties of theatrical romance—and then retired into the obscurity of his own country. I have not overlooked the bewildering Picasso, but he has turned out to be a Frenchman, and we shall have more of him hereafter. There is nothing romantic in the three great painters; there is mysticism, dignity, brutality, realism, and much besides that reflects the most memorable treasure of Spain—her soul.

EL GRECO

We have now to consider the strangest of painters and in the narrower sense, the most original, a man without honor while he lived, who filled an unknown grave for nearly three centuries, and then rose from the dead to become the Messiah of Modernism.

The first question that confronts us is how to account for the resurrection of this extraordinary figure: how did it happen that El Greco, permanently interred, so it seemed, in Spanish darkness, should have emerged, at the close of the nineteenth century, from his long sleep to dispossess Velasquez, to mount higher and higher in the esteem of modern men, and finally to become the most discussed of the Old Masters? The question is difficult, involving many issues historical and technical alike, but it is possible, I believe, to answer it in civilized language.

In the history of the race there will be certain individuals called artists, generally groups of men under the leadership of one or more strong personalities, whose business it is to assess the spiritual and psychological values of their age; but if these men are to be useful members of society, they must express themselves in terms intelligible to their contemporaries. Although it is true that the art of a given period is always conditioned by the social forces prevailing during that period, there are times when the correspondence between art and life-between art-forms and styles and the characteristic social tendencies—is much happier and closer than at other times. In Italy, for example, where painting was better understood and therefore in greater demand than in other nations, the Renaissance culminated in a body of great artists whose work is a perfectly consistent expression of the temper and ideals of the Italian people. Even more obviously does the prolific Dutch school attest the economic law of supply and demand. But rarely does the historian encounter such harmonious connection between artist and society. What happens, as a rule, is this: a fortunate age produces one or more significant and influential artists whose technique is organically sound, that is to say, appropriate to and determined by environmental needs; the influence of these artists continues on into the succeeding age when the tide of affairs has turned, when new modes of thought and different spiritual tendencies imply a new technique and fresh forms, and we have a class of ineffectual minor artists aping their predecessors, instead of referring directly to life and operating from first-hand experiences.

In such periods of maladjustment the connection between art and life seems to be broken; art becomes stale and unprofitable, in other words, academic, and continues to be so until some man of genius rises to smite the parasites, restore the balance and create a technique of his own. The important thing to remember is that the usefulness of the artist is variable: he may, in his own day, be a man of tremendous prestige and power, and then be completely forgotten by the second generation, lingering on, a mere name, highly revered no doubt, but without function, into the distant future until a propitious moment brings him into prominence again. A product of certain conditions, he will be of service to humanity only with the recurrence of such conditions, or since that is not altogether possible, when similar spiritual needs force the world to recognize his message. Thereupon revaluations come thick and fast; artists imitate and praise him; in time the public follows the artists, and everyone exclaims, "How modern El Greco is!"

To be more specific. In the second half of the nineteenth century the lord of painting was Velasquez. Greater he was than Leonardo or Raphael, than Rubens or Rembrandt. In England the little despot Whistler paid tribute to one greater than himself, and those who peddled the crumbs of his wit, the Stevensons, Henley, the amateur scribblers and the gentleman cognoscenti, all worshipped the Spanish god and the holy ghost Whistler. In France it was much the same, though more and better painters were involved in the squabble. Through the influence of two men, Courbet, a fire-brand of a fellow who had studied the Spaniards—but not El Greco—and advocated the painting of *facts*, and Manet, who had traveled in Spain and had formed his style on Velasquez and Goya—but not on El Greco—the young men of France removed the scales from their eyes and observed the world as it is, or as they fancied it to be after they had seen the marvellous illusions of real life painted by Velasquez and his disciples. Why it was that the times were favorable on both sides of the Channel for the Spanish vision can only be mentioned here; it must suffice that both countries were ripe for a return to realism with Velasquez as the authority, the guide, and the master.

Realism triumphed, and for some thirty years painting throve handsomely, especially in France: one should paint only what the eye could see, without imagination, knowledge, or preferences for one subject above another. Then came the reaction. As the century closed, the Velasquez boom collapsed with a detonation that still rings with anguish in the hearts of those who had been taught to believe in the invincibility of Spanish realism. Painting only what the eye could see had developed into a dreadfully boring pastime. The leader of the revolt against the literal acceptance of nature was Paul Cézanne, seconded by Van Gogh, Gauguin and a veritable army of international Modernists whose aims and heresies we need not discuss except to point out that they believed themselves to be vastly more important than their models, that, as creative artists, they were entitled to take liberties with the facts of life, to do violence to them, to distort and reconstruct them in order to enhance the emotional force of their designs.

In this turbulent reaction the radical painters produced their champion, El Greco, another Spaniard, and an Old Master. Nothing is more comforting to the pioneers of a new movement in art than to turn loose an Old Master upon their enemies. El Greco was precisely the weapon with which to kill Velasquez. He contained a mine of technical resources that had never been touched; and more, a frenzied, shocking, religious subject-matter which the Modernists, theoretically repudiating such irrelevant baggage, were very happy to offer to a public unable, as yet, to swallow their naked abstractions. Who discovered El Greco is an open question. While in Spain, Gautier had looked him over, but what he had written about him did no credit to his usually excellent judgment. Certainly Cézanne was among the first to appreciate and, in a measure, to use him; and credit must be given to the German critic Meier-Graefe who went to Spain expressly to confirm his admiration for Velasquez, lost all respect for the painter he had been schooled to admire, fell madly in love with El Greco, and wrote a book in which the greatness of El Greco was solidly established, and the weaknesses of Velasquez exposed without compunction or fear of reputations. The artists needed him, needed him in their technical disputes and in their twisted spiritual embarrassment; and after they had incorporated him, body and soul, with their own works, and had proved the modernity of his style, the public, no longer repelled by the sensational departures of the new art and ready for any powerful stimulus, contracted the El Greco habit. The collectors also needed him and would have despoiled Toledo of all her masterpieces but for the persistent antagonism of several valiant Spaniards. So at last El Greco has come into his own, and now that he has been made the hero of a lurid romance, we may say with the painters that he has arrived.

Let us examine more closely the distinction between the two

Spaniards, for an understanding of the whole trend of modern painting turns on this distinction. El Greco belongs to the classic tradition, the old current of art that runs back through his master Tintoretto, to Michael Angelo and Signorelli—and much further, if you care to pursue it. Velasquez stands for what we have called, in default of a less ambiguous term, *realism*, a more direct method of painting anticipated in the last canvases of Titian—when he was palsied and half-blind. In the hands of the little Dutchman, realism, you will remember, was carried to the last pitch of manual perfection; in modern times, under various disguises, it becomes the life of painting, winding up in its derivative Impressionism, as a demonstration of the laws of chemistry and optics. Preeminent in the classic tradition was the insistence on *knowledge*: the old painters were absolute masters of the architecture of forms, as distinguished from the realists who rely upon their immediate visual perception of things. Following the procedure of Velasquez, painters devised an effective substitute for knowledge: instead of presenting the essentials of an object as gained from a patient and exhaustive study of its structure, they fell into the habit of depending on the momentary appearance of the model, mimicking with a clever technique its values, tones, and external characteristics.

Let us not suppose, however, that this distinction is merely one of the numerous technical problems over which painters are continually bickering; it is equally valid in every department of organic activity and defines the diverging courses of human behavior. In common speech, it is the difference between seeing and knowing. Most of us, bound to the same environment day after day, imagine that we know our own world pretty well, only to discover, to our shame, when called upon to describe our closest friends or objects with which we are habitually associated, how defective is our observation and how limited our knowledge. We do not even know our own faces; we see clearly, perhaps, but only in swift generalizations. Our heads are filled with blurred impressions of objects imperfectly apprehended; we retain only faint images of things, only so much as is useful for purposes of recognition. Objects are thus no more than instruments to action; we hold in mind a confusion of shreds and patches, a visual memorandum enabling us to transact our business, avoid accidents and enjoy life or complain about it. If you wish to be convinced of your total ignorance of a fact which you should know more intimately than anything else, try to draw your own face, not from memory but before a mirror. I do not mean to draw it with the finesse of an artist but merely to indicate in outline the general proportions. Try to put the ears where they belong; to join the nose to the forehead, to establish the proper relationship of the features. You will quickly perceive that what you actually know about the structure of your head is practically nothing at all.

With the artist it is different. He is, perforce, a trained observer, a specialist in seeing. Even the poorest when he looks at an object is immediately conscious, if not of its integral framework, at least of certain lines and areas of light and shadow which, when carefully reproduced, will bear a superficial resemblance to the original. But there are, of course, grades of artists just as there are grades of laymen. Ninety-nine out of every hundred, being lazy or unintelligent, or both, are content to use their eyes and not their heads. The classic artist, I must repeat, was trained in a tradition of knowledge-seekers; he was an indefatigable student; he knew his subject matter through and through. No classic artist ever painted directly from nature. The final product was invariably composed from drawings. The reason for this procedure is simple enough: there is no single situation that will reveal the essential structure of an object. A model posed in any scheme of lighting presents but one aspect—one "front", and if the artist is to paint it as a solid body with all the parts convincingly related, he must have studied it from every point of view. Furthermore, natural light and shade play the devil with true structure, filling up cavities, and smoothing out projections. The artist must correct these falsifications from his past experience, painting not what he sees but what he knows to be present, employing lights and darks as he needs them and not where they happen to fall in a single instance. If he is without knowledge, he will attempt to dissemble his ignorance by technical jugglery, painting a figure in the artificial arrangement of lights and shadows which is taught in art schools instead of functional drawing. Compare a portrait by El Greco with some of Sargent's faithful masks and you will readily grasp the difference between knowing and seeing.

In preceding chapters I have purposely underlined the boundless industry of the Renaissance artists in order to show that drawing, in the classic sense, is just about the hardest thing in the world to master. Primarily occupied with the human figure, which was proper, the classic painters were anatomists; they knew the origin and course of every muscle; its function, and its change of form in every circumstance of repose or movement. Thus equipped they were able to communicate life, energy and reality to their forms; and when they had occasion to picture a figure in a position in which it could not possibly be observed—a flying angel, for example—they did so convincingly by means of their knowledge of bodily structure and movement. There are no immutable laws for classic drawing—only precedents; nor will the acquisition of knowledge make a man an artist unless he has imagination and creative purpose.

Velasquez was a man of rare intelligence, but a true Spaniard, and temperamentally lazy, trusting in his incredibly accurate and penetrating eye. Painting largely by eye, he had the wisdom, as you will probably have noticed, to paint figures in the stiffest repose, and to avoid the embarrassing complications in which the artist who paints by eye finds himself the moment he undertakes to portray moving bodies. Two or three times he was obliged to paint galloping horses. Now you cannot capture the true action of a horse, or any other galloping animal by photographing its attitude at a given point in its flight. What you get is a fractional view, a snapshot which appears monstrous and impossible because the eye does not register a separate instantaneous position but the sum total of all the positions. We must have then, in a picture, a single attitude representing a synthesis of the whole movement, and this demands knowledge and study. Velasquez had not studied horses; he could not synthesize their movements; his horses, for all their exquisite surfaces, look like stuffed velvet; they are as awkward as dogs standing on their hind legs.

But why so much talk about seeing and knowing? What place have these psychological questions in the study of art as a carrier of spiritual values? The answer, I believe, has already been given: to enable us to estimate the fundamental humanity of a work of art and to explain the connection between the emotional elements and the technique in which they are expressed. If the artist is a man of power, a Leonardo or a Rembrandt, with a wide range of experience and a searching knowledge of life; if he is to appeal, not to a select coterie at a particular moment, but to all mankind from one age to another, he must command a large and complex instrument of expression; he must know all the potentialities of the human body; how to adapt it to his own purposes; to enlarge, alter and reconstruct it into a new entity impregnated with his own personality—into a new form which shall be without weaknesses or inconsistencies, thoroughly possible and of far greater reality than any image of which the eye alone is conscious. If he lives in a narrow environment, as did Velasquez, and is satisfied to commemorate the visages of a decadent royalty, then his appeal is likely to be confined to historians and to connoisseurs who prefer brilliant craftsmanship in painting to more imaginative qualities. But we must remember that the distinction between seeing and knowing is relative; it is not humanly possible "to see things as they are." The meanest of painters whose highest aim is to copy what is in front of his nose brings to his task a certain amount of knowledge which, in spite of himself, enters into his work, differentiating it from the photograph and from the work of other artists. The gulf between the average portrait painter and Manet is as great as that which separates Velasquez from Michael Angelo.

We may now understand why El Greco distorted the human

body; that his distortions were based upon knowledge and made for a special purpose; why he shocked and still shocks people accustomed to a realistic vision; why so sane a man was charged with insanity by his contemporaries and why the same charge has cropped up in our own times among those who should know better.

Today Spain is glad to claim him, and none need dispute her rights; for more profoundly than any artist of her own blood does he express the ghastly passions and interpret the tragedy of her mystic soul. But while he lived and worked and quarreled in Toledo, she watched his movements with suspicion, eager to bring him before the Inquisition, never thinking of him but as a foreigner, and calling him *The Greek*. He, in turn, was neither soft-spoken nor agreeable; prouder even than the Spaniards, he did not fear them, but held them off with high indifference and scorn, telling them they were below the Italians, and adding that the Italians were inferior to his own people, the Greeks. He was, he said, descended from the greatest of all races, and to remind the Castilians of his classical origin, retained his eastern name, Domenikos Theotokopoulos. Thus, in Greek characters, did he sign his pictures.

El Greco was born in the island of Crete about 1550. As a youth he went to Venice where he is mentioned in an old document as a pupil of Titian, but it is clear from his early paintings that his master was Tintoretto. Next we hear of him in Rome studying Michael Angelo whom he described "as an admirable man but with no idea of painting." In his twenty-fifth year, for what reasons we do not know, he left the semi-pagan culture of Italy and journeyed to Spain settling in Toledo in the heart of Catholic intolerance. Apparently Spain satisfied his exotic tastes; certainly she transformed and inspired him, and though his life there was anything but peaceful, he never chose to return to the more humane civilization of the Italians. From the few existing references, we learn that he was an extraordinary personality, scholarly and aristocratic, unusually sane, astute in practical affairs, and not at all modest in his opinion of his own attainments. The Spaniards called him bizarre, a word which with them signifies brave, gallant, and high-spirited, and allowed him more freedom of speech than was their custom with strangers. He had no hesitation in fighting his battles in the courts, once appearing to argue that painting should be exempt from taxation—and winning his case—and on three other occasions in suits to collect the relatively large sums which he asked for his pictures.

He was admired by a few intellectuals like Góngora but not by the King, and he had no popular fame. Yet he knew how to dispose of his works, and is reported to have lived in elegance in a house of twenty-four rooms. We know that he sent to Venice for musicians to entertain him while he dined, and that he was proud of his discriminating tastes and his erudition. His library contained most of the Greek classics, a large number of Italians, and many volumes on architecture. It has been ably contended that he wrote a treatise on painting and that he was a practicing architect, but these facts have yet to be proved. We know that he was an extremely deliberate, scrupulous and systematic painter, working from clay models and making smaller and carefully finished versions of all his pictures. And we know that Doña Jerónima, his sole heir, was not his wife but his mistress, and that she bore him one son, Jorge Manuel, a painter—and a poor one. He died in 1614, an infirm and solitary old man, as Cossío tells us. No one has discovered his burial place, and no authentic portrait of him has come to light. Nothing more is known of the greatest of Spanish painters.

After Domenikos Theotokopoulos, the Cretan, arrived at Toledo, he wandered no more. Manifestly he was at home there, and though he was always looked upon as an uninvited guest and nicknamed with a tincture of Spanish snobbery, the Greek, he was, one might almost say by foreordination, to express certain states of the Spanish soul in symbols so frightfully true and of such high-pitched intensity as to be offensive even to a race steeped in melodramatic immolation. Some years later the young Rubens, also fresh from the courtesan city of the Adriatic, came to Spain and departed as soon as the dilatory courtiers would relieve him of his cargo of political gifts, unmoved save for a tart remark or two on the incompetence of the painters and the indolence of the aristocrats. With El Greco the reverse was true. He could not get enough of Spain; he loved and hated the country, and Spain, reciprocating, punished him by indifference, and turned away from the mirror of her soul which he so loftily held before her.

What Spain did to El Greco may be seen in the change that came over him after his arrival. It was more than a change—it was a transformation. During his sojourn in Italy, he was nobody in particular—only a young man well-grounded in the styles of Tintoretto and Veronese; in Toledo he embarked suddenly into the most audacious and individual style of painting that has ever been affected. I do not mean that he sloughed off his old self as a snake sheds its skin—it was his classic heritage that served as a point of departure for his Spanish investiture—but that he was suddenly impelled towards the technique suitable for the objectification of his peculiar vision. Gautier attributes this transformation to the fact that El Greco was nettled at being called an imitator of Titian and deliberately plunged into the wildest extravagances to win fame. Granting the notorious jealousies of artists, this opinion becomes untenable when we bear in mind that if El Greco were seeking a short-cut to fame, he could have found it in continuing to paint like the Venetians, since the great patron Philip II cared only for Venetian art and was enamored of the sensual loveliness of Titian.

It is not to be denied that he was, at least in his first years in Spain, ambitious of fame, but only on his own terms: he would compromise with no one, not even the King. At pains to announce his abilities, he was recommended to Philip, and in 1579, was commissioned by that monarch to paint a picture of Saint Maurice and his companions for an altar in the Church of the Escorial. The picture was rejected by His Majesty and assailed by the critics, one of whom wrote as follows:

"Of a certain El Greco, who now lives and does excellent

things in Toledo, there remained here a picture of Saint Maurice and his soldiers, which he did for an altar of this saint; it did not content His Majesty (it is no wonder) because it pleased few people, though some said it was great art, and that its author knows much, and that this is seen in the excellent things by his hand."

The picture presents two aspects of his genius, one looking back into the classical past and observing the heroic proportions of the figure, the other looking far ahead into the intricacies of modern geometrical design. At thirty El Greco had the new style well in hand. We need not trouble ourselves further about the whys and wherefores of this style: it was, in a word, the outcome of a new environment, and it was less singular than the wilful posture of his friend Góngora who, after writing lucid verses that brought him no renown, declared that "he would write only for *los cultos*," the cultivated, and forthwith launched into the most nonsensical conceits that have ever been put forward in the name of poetry. With the Saint Maurice he forfeited royal patronage, but made no effort to regain it, satisfied to paint for the few in his house at Toledo into which he withdrew with the contempt for the herd that so endears him to the modern artist.

Breathing the rank religious air of Spain as naturally as any Spaniard, El Greco devoted his art to the service of the Church, but in addition to his religious pieces, painted several landscapes filled with thunder and lightning and zigzag terrors, and a gallery of portraits done for personal reasons and not on commission which, with those of Rembrandt, must be placed among the greatest things attained by mental toil. As I have said, his methods were deliberate in the extreme and his medium, a tempera base with an admixture of oils, was more conducive to careful planning and forethought than the pure oil technique of Velasquez. The final perfection of his work was the result of repeated experiments beginning first with small sculptures in clay and continued through a series of studies in color. Hence the many extant versions of the same subjects showing the growth of his designs and how he worked them over and over again, pruning, transposing and accentuating until he had arrived at the maximum of expressiveness. His prepossession with movement in design and with the human body attenuated and strained into fluid rhythms increased with time and emboldened him, in his later years, to take unheard-of liberties with natural shapes and contours; and there can be no doubt, as he surveyed with delight the wonders he had performed, that his own created forms reacted upon him and urged him, in a measure, to view the world around him, the Spanish world, as a counterpart of the volcanic life of his own kingdom. Just as in the modern world the instruments of locomotion created by man to conquer space have in turn reacted upon him and modified his perceptions of time, distance and dimension, and for that matter, of all moving things; and those Modernist painters, living with the images of El Greco and his disciples constantly before them, have trained upon the world of today a vision which to the ordinary eye is disconcerting, if not incredible.

The world of El Greco is a furnace in which the soul, hating the heat of the body, struggles in an unearthly passion to release itself. In the convulsive duel, the resisting body is pulled out of joint and elongated into a fiery apparition. His gaunt figures, suffering from some burning malaise of the flesh, are preternaturally tall; their eyes are fixed on God; they throw their arms upward, in the agony of living, to clutch at the celestial throne. He paints portraits of men, never of women, lest his stern penetration be relaxed by the appeal of sentiment; he paints bulging eyes streaked with highlights and bearded skulls in divine meditation; the *Cardinal-Inquisitor*—Satan in sanctified vestments. He paints the *Christ Embracing the Cross*, serene and forgiving, happy to die, or triumphant in death in *The Crucifixion*. He paints *The Baptism*, and six times, *The Agony in the Garden*; Francis, the saint who renounced the material world, figures in twenty of his canvases. He paints apocalyptic dreams and *The Coming of the Holy Ghost* in which the ascending movement of the Virgin and the Apostles is accelerated by jets of flame placed over their heads instead of halos. He paints figures upside-down, stretched by violence into service of his designs; he paints them soaring in the air with the certainty of one who has called down the angels to pose for him; his backgrounds are stormy and dramatic, overhung with greenish clouds and illuminated by spectral flashes; his harsh and unexpected colors reinforce each other with sinister intensity, and in one picture, *The Dead Christ* of the Prado, he floods the background with lemon-yellow lights, annulling the so-called laws of the spatial positions of colors.

He paints the burial of a Spanish nobleman and produces a masterpiece rivalling *The Last Judgment* of Michael Angelo. Here again he is concerned with the separation of soul and body: St. Augustine and St. Stephen bend over the lifeless count; behind them is a row of Spanish cavaliers, each head carefully individualized; the upper half of the composition discloses a vast amount of heavenly business—an angel bearing aloft the soul of the Count in the shape of a vaguely defined infant; musicians folded in the bosom of a cloud; St. Peter with his keys; St. John the Baptist, the Virgin, saints, apostles, a multitude of the blessed, and at the highest point of the vault, the figure of Christ in a white robe. Señor Unamuno, commenting on the mystical side of El Greco's art, has said of this picture:

"These men whom El Greco paints, fortified within themselves, severe and rigid, seem to say 'I for the Lord and the Lord for me, and nothing else in the world!' These cavaliers are silent, as silent as the Count of Orgaz who is to be buried. Only their hands speak. They speak, the winged hands El Greco painted. One can call them 'winged', as Homer called the word. One must listen to them, those winged hands, poised on the breasts of the saints or fluttering in fantastic foreshortenings. There is one, above all, that seems a mystic dove, a messenger of the secret of death. It is the hand which belongs to one of the cavaliers in the *Burial*, and appears in it, ascending, enclosed in a wristband of lace, out of the shadows above the corpse of the Count of Orgaz, as if to salute it in its departure from this world."

So much for his subjects. According to his own statement, El Greco elongated his figures "to make celestial bodies appear large, however small they be, just as we see lights when we look at them from a distance." I have, improperly perhaps, referred to these elongated forms as distortions; it would be better to call them reconstructions, for they do not impress us as bodies pulled out of proportion by whim or incapacity, but rather as distinct types, harmonious throughout, created on a new scale as parts of a spiritual context in which they function to perfection. That such exaggerated recastings of nature, and of the human figure especially, can be utilized in designs embodying experiences radically different from the experiences of El Greco is a question the Modernist painters have not successfully answered. Since the rebirth of El Greco a mass of literature has accreted around him, most of it in praise of his technical innovations and his marvellous designs. We read of his "vividly apprehended units of form" and of "his pushing pictorial expression to its uttermost boundaries"; we read of his arbitrary handling of lights and darks, and his colored shadows, his expression of movement, his figures that leap and twist and turn like flames, his "subordination of natural appearances to his peculiar vision," that is to say, his conversion of clouds, rocks and draperies into geometrical space-fillers; of his compositions every part of which, from his triangular rocks down to his winged hands, is essential to the movement, unity and vitality of the whole. All of which is true, and I suppose, to painters, useful; but let us not lose sight of the significance of his personal mechanism.

To create the illusion of movement, force, power or any other abstraction dissociated from a human context, is not, and has never been the aim of the genuine artist. The purpose of art, if it can be compressed into a sentence, has been flawlessly defined by Coleridge: "the subjection of matter to spirit so as to be transformed into a symbol, in and through which the spirit reveals itself." There is not more movement, as such, in

El Greco than in Rubens, but the two painters are poles apart. The Fleming congratulated God on the success of His earthly experiment; to the Graeco-Spaniard life on this earth was hardly an improvement on the fires of hell. Both reveal the adventures of the spirit in and through moving symbols, and El Greco, ruthlessly violating the normal proportions of the figure, never strays so far from the norm as to destroy the specific character of his subjects. Thus he retains the strong Spanish savor of the environment that preyed upon his spirit; thus he saves himself from the emptiness of abstractions, communicating his experiences in forms which are not merely mathematical units of design but receptacles of human meanings.

The hysterical religiosity of Spain flares through El Greco's world in a conflagration, wiping out earthly joys and anaesthetizing the soul against the attacks of the flesh. We may, without incurring the risk of being called fanatics, hear the crackle of the Inquisition in this riot of flames. El Greco hated the flesh as vehemently as Swift hated all life, but he affirmed his hatred with a creative enthusiasm that amounts to curious devotional joy—the joy of conquering the body, of a great job done superlatively well. And he affirmed his hatred with as much vitality as is possible in paint. But at times, and we may as well admit it along with our admiration for his genius, in straining after tragic effects he warps expression beyond endurance, and becomes morbid, neurotic, blatant, and absurd. For there is a point, as Thomas Hardy, who also worked on the borderland between tragedy and melodrama, once testified, at which the sublime, if pushed a step further, overshoots the mark and passes into ghastliness. El Greco frequently passes into ghastliness; his cock-eyed saints and his weird conceptions, similar in vulgarity to those of Poe, send a shiver of revulsion up our spines.

There is, for example, in the National Gallery, one of the variants of *The Agony in the Garden*, a late work and very famous for its startling design. Ignore, if you can, the subject matter of this picture; I, for one, cannot—it is much too declamatory to be ignored. However perfect the picture may be as a unified structure, it fails of its tragical purport by reason of an absurdity in the conception. El Greco, partly for the sake of his design, partly because his febrile imagination could not always distinguish between the tragic and the ridiculous, reduces three apostles to the size of manikins and stuffs them, in the proximity of figures larger than life, into the pocket of a cloud resembling a huge and unhealthy oyster. The effect verges on the comical. William Blake, in his hypnotic moods, is guilty of fatuities of exactly the same sort. I know of no picture that demolishes more convincingly the theory that the design is independent of the subject. It is sometimes said, in defence of these pictures which make us shudder, that he reflects the Jesuit vulgarity of his age. True enough, but if the artist reflects the sentiments of the herd, he must subject them to his own personal intelligence—by profound pity, as Daumier did, by satire as used by Hogarth and Goya—else he convicts himself of harboring the same ideals. No artist, of course, can entirely escape the common evils of his time, and if El Greco falls into the lurid religiosity of Spain, reminding us of the gruesome effigies in the churches, he also rises to a height where he reminds us of no one, a great artist, like Rembrandt standing alone.

When the flame burns clean and pure, it lights up a region of the spirit over which he remains the greatest master. It is a mystical region lying, in most of us, on the margin of the consciousness and controlling religious experiences which, it would seem, were much more common to mankind in past epochs than in the present, but which, I suspect, are of more general occurrence today than rationalists will allow. In El Greco this region extends over the whole consciousness, fusing all his experiences into a mystical vision. It is no wonder then that St. Francis, who also held communication with the heavenly powers, was his favorite saint. If ever the restrictions of matter have been abolished; if ever the mystical vision of life has been expressed in graphic symbols, it is in the pictures of El Greco. It is hard to describe this vision in words, for it is concerned with a form of knowledge gained through a spiritual union of God and man, and not through the normal channels of the senses. Roughly speaking, it is knowledge of the infinite possessed by certain minds in a marked degree and before which scientific procedure is helpless. In strong intelligences it may be of immense practical service, as in the case of St. Joan obeying her "voices", and St. Teresa's acute understanding of human passions. In intelligences not sustained by ordinary commerce with realities it leads to derangement and despair: it drove Blake into theosophical nonsense and Van Gogh to lunacy and self-destruction. All of us possess this mystical sense, though most of us, fortunately no doubt, in a very moderate form. All of us have inchoate yearnings to dissolve the bonds of the flesh; a dim perception of metaphysical states, an awareness of the supernatural which is generally held in check but which occasionally flares up bringing a strange feeling of relief from life, or as likely as not, unbearable torments. With El Greco, the vision is intense and pure and magnificently articulate.

His portraits of men, what noble works they are! Spaniards unmistakably, but how much more! Drawn by a master of the structure of the head, with asymmetric variations to enunciate individual character, they are heroic souls. They have great strength, but it is the strength of the spirit, not of the flesh. The flesh has been burnt away; the cheeks are hollow; the skin stretched tight over the skull; but in the eyes set within deep bony sockets burn the fires of the life beyond death. These men are conquerors, and in their gaunt poetic faces, we may see the traces of a great weariness; it is the weariness born of victory, the final exhaustion of the body in surrendering to the mystical vision. They have not the serenity of Rembrandt's characters, for the great Dutchman won the battle by a complete acceptance of life; the Spaniard must destroy all things in order to win spiritual freedom. In his larger pictures the battle is still waging, and not man alone but all nature is transformed and thrown into an ecstasy of movement to symbolize the hostile elements of the Spanish soul.

Now that El Greco has been rescued from Spanish oblivion,

there is little danger that he will again be forgotten, or that he will become in time a museum curiosity. Surely no one will again risk the opinion of Pacheco, the pedant who tried to teach Velasquez: "El Greco set his hand to his canvases many and many times over, working upon them again and again, but left his colors crude and unblent in great blots, as a boastful display of his dexterity. I call this working to no purpose."

But the future does not matter. It is sufficient that he is very much alive and that he has at last been useful to humanity. Part of his present vogue, however, is the faddish raving which follows every movement in art, after public opposition has been undermined by the artists; and those painters who have borrowed his technique without sharing his convictions are already looking for other masters to plunder. With such, El Greco, like Cézanne, has been only a means to notoriety. But the real excuse for the Modernist revolt was not technical—it was a genuine disaffection with naturalistic standards; and El Greco, standing alone, heroic in his superiority, contemptuous of the ruck, the champion of individualism, ascetic, mystic, trafficking in experiences regarded by the generality as dangerous or inadmissible to art, has been a spiritual brother to a large body of outlaws whom modern society has refused to sanction, and who have, therefore, painted solely to please themselves, speaking to one another in a language of abstractions.

VELASQUEZ

The descent from El Greco's far-flung visions into the matter-of-fact world of Velasquez is sudden and refreshing. It affords a solid exhilaration such as we should experience in turning from the soul-troubles of Dostoievsky to the pellucid objectivity of Ernest Hemingway's novels. There are no soul-troubles in Velasquez, no troubles indeed of any sort: the overwhelming religious tragedy of Spain, the decaying glory of the Empire; rebellion in Holland and Portugal; the sickening society of the Hapsburgs—none of these caused him a moment of uneasiness.

Velasquez: MARIANNA OF AUSTRIA.

Prado Museum, Madrid

Cooped up in the King's closet; painting, at the King's pleasure, the abortions of the court; compelled to bow to the criticisms of His Majesty, himself a dabbler in paint, he lost neither his distinction nor his independence, never shirked his job, never complained of the monotony of his servitude. If he was bored or lonely, if he was light-hearted or oppressed by his confinement, he kept his feelings buried within himself. His work is abnormally free from passions and philosophies; he is the most reserved, the most disinterested of men—and for those to whom art is the scientific statement of the facts of the visible world, the faultless painter.

Velasquez was a Portuguese aristocrat born in Sevilla in 1599. His father, desiring him to enter one of the learned professions, had him carefully educated, so an old Sevillian informs us; but his education could not have been very extensive, for he determined at an early age to become a painter, and having proved his skill, was apprenticed in his thirteenth year to Herrera, an artist of some prominence in southern Spain. The association did not prosper: Herrera was half-mad and given to spells of inexcusable cruelty, and his pupil soon left him for the more amiable and scholarly Pacheco in whose house he lived for five years. Pacheco was not much of a painter, but he was a man of superior tastes, of estimable ambitions, and a charming companion. Furthermore, he had a daughter. He was strong for Raphael, but Velasquez did not take to Raphael, nor to any of the Florentines, and while the master proclaimed the sublimity of classic art, the young hidalgo painted Andalusian peasants—and made love to Juana. At nineteen, fully grown and the best painter in the South, and in all Spain save for the Cretan at Toledo, he married the girl, "moved thereto," Pacheco says, "by her virtue, beauty and good qualities and his trust in his own natural genius."

He was spared the privations, the long immaturity, and the dark introspections which so many painters have had to suffer. He was as void of idealism as the peasants whom he preferred to paint because their negroid faces were as expressionless as *calabazas*, or pumpkins, by which name they are politely designated in Spanish; without religious convictions, he was immune from the excrutiating mysticism of his time; having no imagination, he confined his brush to things embraced by the eye alone. His aim, and he had but one, was verisimilitude: to see clearly and to record convincingly. This aim is as definitively stated in his first canvases as in his last. There are fewer influences at work in his art than in any other painter of importance. Rejecting, so far as his own needs were concerned, the art of the past; too slothful to submit to the hard labor exacted of classic draughtsmen, he began by studying Caravaggio, one of the first painters to break with the religious tradition and to portray naturalistic scenes. Aroused by Caravaggio, he tried his skill at *bodegones*, or tavern pieces—rustics at table, servants cooking, water-carriers, and vagabond musicians—studio pictures, obviously, but in their way admirable. In the disposition of the figures and in bringing the various parts of his pictures into satisfactory relationship, always his weakness, he is a novice; his color is crude and dingy; but in some of the heads and more markedly in the bits of still-life which he could examine closely under a strong lighting, he shows the phenomenal powers of observation which were, at a later date, to dazzle the world in the portrait of *Pope Innocent X*. He also painted, possibly in emulation of El Greco whom he had the good sense to appreciate, a number of religious pictures, the only worthless things he did. When he represents Christ and the apostles as Spanish beggars, his work has the astonishing optical truth of his other genre pieces; when he attempts an imaginary conception, that is, to construct a situation which he could not possibly have observed with his own eyes, he is worse than Murillo. He is so literal-minded that he must not only paint what is before him, but he must paint it as an actuality, not as a symbol.

Such a talent, so direct and perspicuous, is not likely to go abegging, and it comes as no surprise to learn that Velasquez, when only twenty-four, was appointed painter to the King. He went up to Madrid seeking this appointment, through political pull was presented to Philip, a knock-kneed, new-born sovereign of eighteen, won the young King's favor by a single painting, an equestrian portrait, and for thirty-six years, or the rest of his life, was a fixture at court. The emoluments were precious little, the honors presumably abundant. He was classed with the dwarfs and the idiots, and was paid the same salary as the buffoons with whom he was constrained to associate, notwithstanding his noble birth. To serve the King in whatever capacity was, in itself, honor enough, though I dare say that with Velasquez the honor must have worn pretty threadbare as he painted day after day the long yellow hair, the underhung jaw and the dead fish eyes of His Majesty, and the stunted Infantas with their bloodless, green-sick faces. It must have been a dismal existence even for a man in whose eyes there were neither living things nor dead—only material substances absorbing or reflecting light.

There were, of course, perquisites. He had a studio in the royal palace—rent free; he wore the King's cast-off clothing, and proudly, I assure you, for that too was an honor; from the royal kitchen came baskets of bread and onions and wine for his wife and daughter; his renown as court painter gained him the more coveted and more lucrative office of Valet to the King's Wardrobe from which he was promoted to the position of Valet to the King's Bedchamber, thereby adding a few pesetas to his little income; twice he traveled in Italy at Philip's expense; and in his last years, after a lifetime of painting and valeting, he was created, as a crowning honor, Marshal of the Palace, with jurisdiction over festivals, tournaments and weddings; but the burdens of the post—an important one in Spain—were too heavy for him, and he died under the strain of preparing a nuptial fête for the Infanta Maria Teresa. His faithful spouse, Juana, having nothing more to live for, was buried by his side, eight days afterwards.

Never was an artist more contented with his environment, or less open to new experiences. His world began and ended at the court of King Philip. His travels in Italy had no effect on him unless it were in the modification of his color, but even that, I am inclined to believe, came to him as it came to the modern Impressionists, from his marvellously acute perception of atmospheric values. On his first visit, undertaken in 1629, at the suggestion of Rubens who recognized at once his great natural gifts and his Spanish immobility, he studiously avoided Florence, and in Rome, as if to affront the memory of Raphael and Michael Angelo, he painted *The Forge of Vulcan*, which in conception is identical with the kitchen scenes of his youth. On his second visit, travelling as curator to the royal museum, he resolved to leave the Italians a monument to his artistic supremacy, to reveal to them the true elegance of painting to which none of their innumerable masters cradled in the oldest and most refined of traditions had ever attained. So he painted the Pope, and the Italians were astounded, exclaiming, "It is made out of nothing—yet there it is!" But when His Holiness, in testimony of his affection and high approval sent a chair to the painter, the artist in him yielded to the Spanish nobleman, and he returned the gift with the answer, "My master always pays me with his own hand."

The Venetians alone called forth his admiration, and in his *Memoria De Las Pinturas*, a book unknown to all his biographers, he records, in Spanish as clear and pure as the language of his brush, his praise of Tintoretto and Veronese. His notes on Tintoretto's *Washing of the Feet*, might well be a description of one of his own canvases, and show us exactly what he expected of the art of painting. "It is hard to believe," he writes, "that one is looking at a painting. Such is the truth of color, such the exactness of perspective, that one might think to go in and walk on the pavement, tessellated with stones of divers colors, which, diminishing in size, make the room seem larger, and lead one to believe that there is atmosphere between the figures. The table, seats—and a dog which is worked in—are truth, not paint. . . . Once for all, any picture placed beside it looks like something expressed in terms of color, and this, therefore, seems all the truer."

Despite the apparent simplicity of Velasquez's point of view, it is not a simple matter to explain the conjunction of his impassive personality with the facts of life, and harder still is it to describe the peculiar satisfaction derived from his paintings. He scrutinized his models with the neutral eye of the scientist. I use the word scientist with due caution, having used it once before with reference to Michael Angelo. The difference between the two men is incalculable. The Florentine, while carrying art to the uttermost limits of which individual expression is capable, was haunted by an ideal of beauty that is on the one hand a Platonic abstraction, on the other, a system of scientific relationships—scientific in that the harmony of its forms is based upon a comprehension of the organic structure of the human body. And having coerced the human body into the mightiest harmonies ever conceived by man, Michael Angelo directed his knowledge into architecture and thence into all the arts, seeking universal principles of unity, obsessed by gigantic dreams of a created world in which beauty, "absolute and everlasting" is implicit throughout all its forms. But alas! growing older, he relied more and more upon science, as one who had solved the great creative riddle, and his work, as it approximates abstract purity, loses correspondingly in vitality.

The science of the Spaniard is more transparent and mundane, and incidentally, more modern. He knew very little about the organic structure of the human body, and was as ignorant of the universal aspects of art as was his wife, Juana. His is the science of externals, the logic of light and shade. He approached his subjects in what might be termed the spirit of scientific purity, examining them in the atmosphere of his studio with truly spectroscopical precision. He is responsible for the theory inscribed defiantly on the red banners of Modernism, namely, that *it is not what one paints but how*. His attitude towards his subjects, borrowed by the French, became the staple of the Impressionists and was pithily expressed in a remark commonly fathered upon Cézanne: the artist should have as much respect for a cheese or a cabbage as for a human head. Wherefore Rembrandt's study of the guts of a slaughtered ox should be as moving as his great heads under the stress of the profoundest emotions. Whistler, slyly pilfering from the Spaniard and arranging wisps of tone with impeccable delicacy, malignantly flung the challenge of the "inhumanity of art" into the faces of Philistine sentimentalists. Asserting that the reading of character was the business of the confessional—or the police court, he said, "The truth remains, solid and irrefragable, that the sitter is an accident; his whims and humors may torment his family or puzzle the psychologist, but the painter looks not below the surface and portrays no more character than the skin suggests."

In the case of Velasquez, the sitters were indeed accidents, and the truth remains that he did not pry into their characters. The notion that he was psychoanalyst in ordinary to the Hapsburgs is not only beside the mark but an aspersion of his singular merits as a painter. Those who tell us that Philip, in the portraits of his conscientious valet, is "every inch a king," and that the legless Infantas, inserted in their crinolines like marionettes, are personifications of aristocratic *hauteur*, have looked at the pictures casually and filled in their hasty impressions with romantic lore of Old Spain. No more unkingly wretch than Philip IV ever sat to a great painter; the little princesses are fit companions for their freakish playthings; but Velasquez considered neither their birth nor their arrested development. The secret of his art lies in the fact that he was not swayed by sentiment or conviction, that he was interested in objects as things and painted them for their own sake.

The royal family was not more agreeable to his brush than the indentured morons of the court; he regarded them all as so much still-life, and if they possess a large measure of dignity, it is an extrinsic quality engendered by the sobriety of his arrangements and the perfection of his style. He brought neither the sensual nor the spiritual to his high-born rubbish, and in consequence his figures are lacking in vitality. They are collections of particles moulded into human shapes but drained of human attributes. We cannot say that they are dead—they are inert, or rather, the bodily forces are suspended; we cannot call them inanimate—they are insentient; to say they have repose is misleading for repose implies the power of motion. They were created as stationary objects, and so they must abide like the stones of the earth. And yet, somehow, the absence of organic properties does not invalidate their existence. They are concrete and real, standing before us as things actually seen, as isolated specimens of glorified matter.

Velasquez's method of painting was comparatively simple. Relying entirely on his eye for just proportions and the accuracy of values; concerned only with the appearances of objects; posing his models in rigid attitudes and avoiding all attitudes which, for plausible representation, presuppose exhaustive study of the figure; using his sitters as receptacles of light and shade, and not as material to be remade into new organisms emphasizing certain experiences; he dispensed with preliminary drawings and painted directly from nature like the Impressionist that he was. He never formed the habit of drawing which to most artists is indispensable. He made, so far as we know, only a few sketches, the three or four that have been preserved betraying a flaccidity of draughtsmanship hard to believe in a painter of his reputation. Draughtsmanship in the classic sense—the relating of line to line and of mass to mass, the organization of one or more figures into a compact unit—was foreign to his talent; his dominion was that of tone. Naturally then was he the first painter to adopt an exclusively oil technique, this medium allowing swift stroking, freedom of handling, easy corrections, lightness of touch, and the realization of a single aspect of his model in an atmosphere of shifting lights and shadows. With an instinctive sense of placement, he divided the space to be covered and arranged his areas of tones, almost invariably—when dealing with single figures—contriving a dignified balance of parts. If, on the first trial, a figure seemed to occupy too much space, he did not repaint it, but had the canvas enlarged, and then expanded the background.

None but a scientist could have maintained such unjaded interest in light and air. Rembrandt was forever experimenting with light but only as a means to illuminate his conception of humanity. Velasquez, abjuring human problems, merely observed and recorded the physiognomy of objects as changed by the changing flux of daylight. Every day, when the ungainly King entered his studio, a new problem in the visual aspects of matter presented itself. That was all. The King, as I have said, was treated as still-life. Time and again he painted him, but we know no more of him in the last pictures than in the first, and no more of the artist, save that his eye grew more searching, his handling of pigment more dextrous, his tones more silvery and enchanting. He painted the King's face in precisely the same spirit as his modern kinsman Monet painted haystacks—the same old stacks twenty times over to prove that the atmosphere is colored and the color varies with the march of the sun.

When we open our eyes on the world, objects appear before us in varying degrees of visibility, those in the center of the field of vision standing out clearly and in full detail, those at the edges blurring out into indistinct fragments. As the field recedes, objects grow smaller and smaller until the vanishing point is reached. This is a matter of common observation, a part of our daily experiences, and this is exactly the way in which Velasquez looked at nature when he began to paint. It was scientific; it was logical; but neither science nor logic may be accepted as a criterion of artistic excellence. With single figures it worked well enough; he painted, we might say, from the face outward, concentrating on the features in the center of the field of vision and painting the rest of the figure very lightly against a plain background. The effect is startling: a modelled head on a silhouetted body, a simplified illusion of reality, an object isolated from its blurred surroundings.

But with groups of figures he scarcely knew which way to turn. Men like Rembrandt and Rubens, artists depicting human forms not as they actually were but endowed with special characteristics, did not paint on the dead level of optical law, but violated perspective and visual appearances freely and confidently. Cognizant of the fact that if an artist depends entirely upon what is before him, he must cluster all his important figures in the foreground in order that they may be clearly seen, and that such a plan is inharmonious and unconvincing, they distributed important figures through the several planes of the picture space, and united them by sequences of lines and balancing lights and masses created to suit their own ends. Velasquez's large pictures, strictly speaking, are not compositions at all. In combining figures, he was almost as helpless as Sargent. *The Surrender of Breda* and *The Maids of Honor* are all foreground: the first, as many soldiers as possible crammed into the front line of the picture; the second, less involved and more convincing photographically, a little group of actors, at the front of the stage, taking a bow. It is often said, on behalf of these canvases, that they are so *natural*. They are, but if we are to judge art by its naturalness, which is only another way of saying that it shall display no signs of imagination or of the activity of the mind, then we might name a hundred Dutchmen who throw Velasquez into the shade. The Spaniard is a painter of single figures, and his large works have no value as units but as assemblages of brilliant patches.

It is difficult to discuss this man in any but a technical language, difficult because his fame and influence, for the most part, rest upon his ability to handle paint. Technically, he is generally acknowledged to be the greatest of painters, although a good case might be made for Vermeer. But it does not matter. Let us concede his preëminence, not forgetting, however, that by technique we mean craftsmanship and not the inevitable form evolved by every artist who has anything to say. Velasquez's eye was practically unerring; his hand obedient to his eye; his touch inexpressibly sensitive. When he fixed that eye on a head, he envisaged lights and shadows merging one into the other to form a spheroid; these lights and shadows he translated into paint—in his later works into delicate tones of grey and silver tinted with rose—and so remarkably just was his reading of values that the tones on the canvas contain precisely the same amounts of light and dark as the equivalent planes on the model, hence taking their proper position in space to produce a facsimile of the sitter. When nature was favorable and offered a reasonably clear transition of planes, he wrought such marvels as *Pope Innocent X*, whose head seems to have been fashioned without drawing, an image compounded of spots of color, exquisitely clear and so deftly joined that the Italians, beholding the solid likeness and the impalpable thinness of the pigment, cried out, as I have told, that it was made out of nothing.

When the lighting was less propitious, he got into trouble. Seldom do we find in his portraits any structural connection between head, neck and torso, a condition arising from his inability to paint what he could not see and to grasp forms concealed in shadow. His Pope, you will notice, has no neck; the faces of his princesses are masks stuck into grotesque wigs; and the head of the *Infanta Margaret* of the Louvre, is a curious deformation—solid down to the eyes, below the eyes without volume. These objections would be irrelevant if the pictures had been conceived as flat decorations, but where the intention was to convey the illusion of bulk-form, and the result is a form solid in one part and flat in another, we cannot remain blind to the discrepancy. The celebrated *Venus*, purchased by the National Gallery for 45,000 pounds, might be stricken from his works without serious damage to his fame. It is plainly a studio piece, a tour de force painted for no other purpose than to please a duke, the sort of thing Velasquez was least fitted by temperament and training to bring off—a meaningless picture, for all its cleverness, neither a "harmony from nature," nor a realistic nude, and in parts, deplorable, the drawing of the arm, for instance. The longer we look at the *Venus*, the less does it impress us as a new creation—a work of art—and we cannot help feeling that the painting is less interesting than the model who posed for it.

Goya: SELF-PORTRAIT.

Smith College Museum of Art, Northampton, Mass.

Connoisseurs, seduced by his "beautiful painting," praise his charms in the cadences of a lover doting on a fresh mistress. They smack their lips over the rose and grey stuff, extol the purity of tones blended with the lightness of water-color, grow eloquent over the caressing softness of brush-strokes that twist a little blob of paint into a lip or a bit of lace, talk of the "muted melodies" of his color, and shout in adoration of his infinite tact when he drops a touch of color into a shadow—the final fleck to define the tip of the nose. All of which is fine and rare and delightful to the eye.

In analyzing Velasquez's straightforward approach to life, I have, perhaps, over-emphasized his literalness. His heads are not the emotionally flat images recorded by the camera; his harmonies do not exist ready-made in nature. It is true that he added little to his subject—less of the spiritual than any other notable painter—but he removed the confusion of details impinging on the retinal field. One has only to compare him with the Dutch painters, men of similar aims but so thoroughly in love with little things that they crowded their pictures with trifles, to see with what magnificent simplicity he renders costumes, how he eliminates the insignificant, and focuses attention on the essential features of object or scene. What he gives us is an intensified version of the visible world, an harmonious resolution of appearances. I have spoken of the peculiar satisfaction of his paintings, a satisfaction, as we now see, deriving from his perfectly normal point of view. Here is a man unencumbered by a heavy burden of distressing ideals and annoying philosophies, neither classic nor romantic, reserved, self-sufficient and discreet; here is an artist who gives us, not the dignity of man, but the dignity of matter.

In Velasquez this is refreshing; of his followers we cannot say as much. After him there is no further need for architectural painting; he made it easy for non-thinking artists to usurp the field; he directed attention to the dignity of material things by suppressing the spiritual, and his disciples, completing the ruin of the classical edifice, have taken the mind out of painting altogether and reduced it to the level of barren processes.

GOYA

More powerful by far is Goya, the peasant. He arrived on the scene nearly a century after the death of Philip's painter, lived beyond fourscore years, and throughout his long career, from the day when, as a child, he was discovered—so the story goes—by the village priest drawing with a lump of charcoal on the walls of Fuendetodos, to his exile in Bordeaux where, a dark old man, gouty and stone deaf, he drew from memory those great lithographs of the bull-ring, he drenched the decaying soul of Spain with a torrent of vitality. It was the time of Voltaire and Rousseau, of Byron and Shelley, of the French Revolution and Napoleon Bonaparte. When Goya was born, the whole of Europe, led by France, was preparing a battle-royal for the new freedom. He lived to see the battle fought and won, to see the *Ancien Régime* wiped off the earth. How much he contributed to the destruction of the old iniquity is debatable—neither patriot nor reformer, he was at heart an anarchist and adventurer—but in the energy and range of his attack on art and in the vivid recklessness of his imagination and the invigorating assertiveness of his life, he was the forerunner of the new freedom in painting. After the débris of the Revolution had been cleared away and France had put her house in order, his example inflamed the courage of Géricault and Delacroix in their fight against the sham classicism of David; and as the rapid modern current hurried onward, he exerted, as much by his use of contemporary themes as by his method of painting, a powerful influence on Daumier, Courbet and Manet.

Spain was rotten in body and soul. There was no background of appreciation and no tradition of painting—only a shattered civilization, bankrupt mentally and physically, and in the aristocratic circles degraded by the imitation of French frivolity. Art was dead. Since Velasquez there had not been a name worth mentioning; the court painters, except Tiepolo, were cheap Italians or nondescript wastrels of Fragonard lineage. The morbid Hapsburgs disappeared for want of issue, and in their stead ruled the Bourbons of more active viciousness. Charles IV, a brawny, ursine scoundrel without character or intellect, divided his time between the peasants of the field and the less robust lewdity of the court, brawling, gambling, and shooting rabbits. His wife, the harlot Queen, Maria Luisa, was the real sovereign, and the foulest woman in looks and habits alike, that ever wore a crown. Any young officer or groom was by royal decree—only thus could she compel her servants into action—her bed-fellow, and one of them, the most diligent, she appointed Prime Minister of Spain. The Bonaparte fiasco brought the rabid Ferdinand VII to the throne and upon the land new shedding of inquisitional blood. "Every heretic," announced this despicable boor, "shall have his tongue bored through with a red hot iron." Jesuit spies herded in their victims; the Holy Office worked night and day; and Spain sank into irredeemable lethargy and ruin.

Goya was part of all this, and a very conspicuous part: Goya of the bull-neck, the sensual lips and devastating eye; the father of some twenty legitimate children, sufficient evidence, I think, of the virility of the man of the soil which pallid duchesses preferred to the effete lechery of the aristocratic buzzards. But he differed from his rivals in another respect: he had an intellect—the only intellect in Spain. And when this intellect was finally silenced by a stroke of apoplexy, it had wrought the most comprehensive history of a period that has ever been written in graphic form, an inhuman comedy comparable to the system of Balzac. "One of his sketches," declares Gautier, "consisting of four touches of his graver in a cloud of aquatint, tells you more about the manners of the country than the longest description." As a historian of manners, he fulfilled one of the most useful offices of the artist, an office which so many painters, sequestered in the ivory towers of humanism, cautiously evade to protect their pretty dreams from the gross realities of life.

The past had no charms for Goya: a greedy participant in the crumbling violence of his time, he ransacked the soul of Spain of its mysteries and ignoble terrors, turning his experiences into works of art. If the ironic sisters had not given him the magic of the artist, he would not have grieved—art for its own sake did not appeal to his raging temperament—but would have won fame as insurrectionist or toreador, or any other strenuous profession calling for courage and decision.

Goya was not a religious force like Shelley, but a dare-devil and a libertine of Byronic cast. In many ways he bears a close resemblance to Byron: in his skeptical insolence, his antinomian looseness, his penchant for the brutal and obscene, his hatred of respectability, his physical excesses, and in his uncontrollable craving for new scenes and sharper excitements. Both were blackguards; both endowed with a talent for intrigue and a capacity for scandal; both overbearing egoists lacking in finer sensibilities. Like the Englishman, he was extraordinarily prolific, staking everything on the force of the first attack, working at top speed and guilty of many works that do him no credit. But Goya was more masculine, more genuine, and more profound than Byron. He was not a poseur; his hypochondria was an honest affliction and he did not advertise it; he took no interest in, and derived no perverse pleasure from the effect of his conduct on the world. Coming from the humblest stratum of society, and climbing to the top of his profession by brute strength and the audacity of genius, his struggle was long and hard, and if he portrayed the woes of the downtrodden in horrible symbols—foetuses, apes, cats and corpses—it is a truthful symbolism, truthful because he had been an underdog himself in Spain and had found the life abominable. But it cannot be said that he portrayed this life, or the high life of his later years, with any sympathy—the stamp of scorn lies upon everything he did. Life afforded him many experiences but few satisfactions, and it is fortunate for us that his energy found an outlet in art.

He was born in 1746, in Fuendetodos, a wretched mountain

village of a hundred inhabitants, in a stone hut which, through the generosity of Zuloaga, is now a public museum. As a child he worked in the fields with his two brothers and his sister until his talent for drawing put an end to his misery. At the age of twelve he painted a curtain for the altar of the village church, and on his return to Fuendetodos, sixty years afterwards, found the church unchanged and the curtain still hanging. "Don't tell anyone I painted that," he said to one of his companions. At fourteen, supported by a wealthy patron, he went to Saragossa, about six leagues away, to study with a court painter, and here, in the capital of Aragon, foot-loose and free, he begins his picaresque journey through a disordered world. He did nothing by halves, feared nothing, had no self-respect, lived for himself alone. Confident from the first, he rushed from one department of art to another, learning readily but loathing the precious and sedentary aspects of the business. Not less boldly did he enter into the affairs of the crowded town. He had a fine singing voice, was an excellent swordsman, boxer and dancer, and a gang leader of parts. In a fight between his men and a rival faction, several combatants were murdered, and warned that the Holy Office was moved to action, he fled to Madrid. He was then in his nineteenth year.

Goya made himself known in Madrid but it was his ruffianly behavior and not his art that brought him before the public. A gangster again, the chief of the Aragonese colony, he frequented the bull-ring and consorted with roving thieves, and one morning was picked up out of the gutter with a dagger sticking in his back. A company of bull-fighters spirited him away to the coast and he took ship for Rome. How he subsisted in Rome is a mystery—probably by his wits and by the proceeds from Spanish scenes which he sold to the French residents with whom he associated as a free lance painter and man of the world. He painted only for profit in Italy and had no particular reverence for Italian art. But the life of Rome—the processions, the carnival, the prostitutes, the gay and dangerous underworld—was a constant lash to his impulsive animalism, and he is credited with many foolhardy adventures, such as carving his name in the lantern of St. Peter's and entering a nunnery by night with the intention of abducting a young lady who had resisted his advances. But he was a Spaniard and a man of strong family affections, and two years later was home again, faced with the necessity of making a living and relieving the poverty of his father and mother.

He sought work immediately, submitting designs for the decoration of a church at Saragossa, received the commission, and executed it in six months. The decorations are not very impressive; first, because he was not a religious painter and could do little with ecclesiastical themes when not mocking the hypocrisies of the clergy; second, because his originality developed slowly, coming forward after he had discarded all the spurious influences of his erratic training. With a little money in hand, he married, in his twenty-ninth year, Josefa Bayeu, sister of a well-known painter. His wife remained at home, after the Spanish custom, in a state of chronic pregnancy, while Goya continued his old life among the Bohemians of Saragossa, the favorite of gypsies, dancing girls, musicians and matadors. Sad and exhausted, his wife bore a sickly brood of children, only one of the twenty, proponents of birth-control will be glad to know, reaching maturity. But despite his carousing irregularities among the Bohemians and his indulgences in the fast life of the court, Goya was a man of plain tastes, hating display and furnishing his house with peasant simplicity—even when he made large sums of money. He collected nothing, least of all pictures, and could not tolerate connoisseurship in art. He was addicted to the Spanish vice of over-eating, and this, together with his immoderate concentration on his work, rendered him, as early as his thirty-fourth year, subject to periods of ill-health and morose debilitation, during which he could do nothing but stay at home and play with the children.

Shortly after his marriage, having been recommended to the King by Mengs, the principal court painter, he was attached to the royal tapestry factory, and in the next four years, designed

Goya: DON MANUEL OSORIO DE ZUÑIGA.

(*Courtesy of Jules S. Bache.*)

thirty cartoons for the King's weavers. With these he leaped into fame. Instead of falling back on the artificial languors of mythology, in the manner of the French imitators of Rubens, he boldly drew upon Spanish *genre* for his subjects—stilt-walkers, boys climbing trees and playing *pelota*, gallants and their wantons dining *al fresco*—things snatched out of his own experiences. At this distance we should say that his choice was the obvious one, but in his own generation, in a court dominated by imported vendors of the trappings of misunderstood classicism, it was an innovation that would have occurred to none but a parvenu—and a genius—like Goya. But it was not only the subjects that irritated his envious competitors: it was the unheralded decorative quality of the cartoons, the superb mixing of mass and silhouette into strangely oriental designs, the germs of which Goya's eagle eye might have detected in the Sassanian decorations of Spain. Though done with extreme rapidity, the tapestry series illustrates, for the first time, the electrical vitality which his brush imparted to everything that invited unforced attention, and which distinguishes his naked *Maja* from Velasquez's corpse of Venus.

Being famous, he made enemies. His tactlessness and insulting candor tried the patience of his closest friends. But neither whispered slurs on his character nor the political manoeuvering of his rivals could check the momentum of his fame. As an artist there was no longer any doubt of his superiority; as a personality, he was dangerous and masterful, and hence irresistible to the voluptuous ladies of the court. He quarreled with his brother-in-law and with everyone who endeavored, however gently, to restrain his unceremonious tactics. The death of his father so depressed his spirits that he could not paint—and what is more remarkable, could not eat; and he sat alone in a bare room, etching plate after plate to allay his nervousness. He was besieged with commissions—portraits, altarpieces, and murals—and unhesitatingly attempted anything that came his way. He moved to Madrid and was soon a boon companion of the King's brother, but Charles III could not stand him, and twice refused his petition for a court job. When he was forty years old, he was made President of the Academy, and when Charles IV ascended to the throne, he was without delay named as one of the King's painters.

Up to his thirty-seventh year, if we leave out of account the tapestry cartoons and five small pictures discovered by Professor Rothenstein, Goya painted nothing of any significance: but once in control of his refractory powers, as if to make amends for his late maturity, he produced masterpieces with the speed of Rubens. His court appointment was followed by a decade of incessant activity—years of painting and scandal, with intervals of bad health. At forty-two, surviving a terrible attack of indigestion, he had the face of a profligate old man, but he recovered his strength, and unchastened, went on with his intemperate habits. The most famous man in Spain, he disdained to run after anyone: the great ladies came to his studio—and got what they wanted. Duchesses quarreled over his favors, the victorious Alba, in all probability, posing for the two *Majas* in the Prado, in one, nude, in the other even more seductive in her thin, skin-tight breeches—*Maja* meaning gay lady, harlot or duchess, or both, there being little difference in Goya's time. The Spanish scholar, De Beruete, more interested in renovating the honor of an ancient and dishonorable family than in verifying the conquests of an upstart painter, discredits this likely bit of gossip, offering a mass of chronological data to remove one stain from the name of the godless Duchess. He may be right—but the chronology of Goya's intrigues is an inextricable affair.

We know for certain that the Duchess of Alba visited the artist's studio to be rouged, powdered and properly caressed; we know that she sent little remembrances to his family—delicacies delivered in dishes of silver, the dishes, according to etiquette, being presented as well as the contents, just as the hospitable Spaniard gives his house to his guest but does not expect his guest to take title; and we know that Mrs. Goya neglected to return the ancestral plate. We also know that the Duchess, determined to monopolize the painter, comported herself so brazenly that she was obliged, at the Queen's suggestion, to retire temporarily to her estate in Andalusia. Goya applied at once to the King for leave of absence, and the King, enjoying the sport and so filled with admiration of Goya's rapacious deeds that he would gladly have offered him the Queen, had his painter been equal to so unsightly a partner, willingly granted the request. The pair set out together for the South, but on a rough mountain road the carriage broke down with a sprung axle. Goya kindled a fire and with great strength forged the steel into shape again, but the heat and exertion brought on a chill which affected his ears and eventually led to total deafness. Life in Madrid was dull without him; the King needed him; and at the end of a year the Duchess was recalled.

Sick and exacerbated, Goya took up the needle and executed the first of his wonderful groups of etchings, *Los Caprichos*, in which the throne, the Church, the law and the army are held up to ridicule and satirized with contemptuous ferocity. In this series he exposes the weaknesses of women he had known and maliciously caricatures his evil friends. One plate containing a hideous figure, presumably the Queen, bears the title, *She Says Yes to Anyone*. The prints were sold on subscription to his wealthy admirers, many of whom, strange to relate, were the objects of his spleen. Why they should have paid for the exhibition of their crimes and vulgarities is a vexatious question—anyhow, they liked it and clamored for more. Occasionally, in the annals of human audacity, we come across a man the brilliancy of whose sins and the magnitude of whose insolence excite the admiration of his compatriots, even though they be the victims of his wrath. Such men, as we say, get away with murder. Goya was one of these. But when he levelled his satire at the impostures of priests, the Church decided to call a halt, and the King hearing of vengeance, called in, or pretended to call in, the plates which, he said, "had been done at his command," thus saving the artist from the Inquisition.

In appreciation, Goya decorated the church of San Antonio de la Florida, situated on royal property near Madrid, "a coquettish little church with a white and gold interior, more like a boudoir than a shrine." He finished the undertaking in three months without assistance and without missing a day—100 figures, all larger than life. The decorations are more suitable to a high-class brothel than to a place of worship. For angels he painted the comely strumpets of the court—his favorite Duchess among them—insidiously rouged; he painted naked children climbing over railings, ballet dancers, recognizable beauties stretching out their legs, and alluring women ogled by dandified men. Compared to the great murals of Italy, the frescoes are pretty flimsy—dazzling sketches of riotous characters rather than transformations of nature into monumental order. But in sheer liveliness, in spontaneous agility and careless animation, there is nothing in Italy, or in any other land, to compare with them. They are the gayest church decorations in art.

Returning the compliment, the King rewarded Goya with the coveted post of first court painter, gave him a seat in the royal coach, and talked with him in a language of signs and gestures. And the Queen, no less pleased, sent him a picture by Velasquez, the only painting, save his own, that he possessed. As the century closed, he entered into the period of his best portraiture: *Doña Isabel Corbo de Porcel*, the eyes of which are modelled (Manet, though a staunch supporter of Goya, regarded the modelling of the eye as the lowest of pictorial crimes); the *Portrait of His Wife*, which will stand up with the late Rembrandts; *The Family of Charles IV*, characterized once for all by Gautier as "the grocer's family who have won the big lottery prize."

The Duchess of Alba died in 1802—"before her beauty had faded"; his wife died in 1804, exhausted and forlorn; his son was a weakling. Surly and unmanageable, Goya lived on, alone as much as possible, self-absorbed, painting because he could not help it, or perhaps because there was nothing better to do. But his work suffered no decline. In fact, it got better with years, as is usually the case with good painters. The French came and slaughtered the populace at the city gate. He painted the massacre—with a spoon it is said—and bequeathed to mankind, not the most tragic nor the most touching commentary, but the most frightening curse ever uttered against the horrors of war. The ragged, cowardly populace frozen with fears of death; men with their hands sticking up; men hiding their faces, clenching their fists; dead bodies in pools of blood—impotent civilians before a firing squad. A picture which should be reproduced in full color and hung in the council chambers of the war lords of every nation.

Yet Goya, with the curious turncoat soul of the artist, caring not whom he painted for so long as he was free to paint, welcomed the Bonapartes and clung to his office at the court. When the scene shifted again, restoring the Bourbons and all the tortures of the Inquisition, he took the oath of allegiance to the new King without a qualm. "You deserve exile," Ferdinand told him. "You deserve hanging, but you are an artist, and I will forget everything." But he felt that he was not wanted at the new court and his etchings on the calamities of war hardly confirmed his avowed loyalty to the King. Despite his failing health, he journeyed to Sevilla to paint in the Cathedral there, and in his sardonic fury, used as models for angels two celebrated demi-mondaines. "I will cause the faithful to worship vice," he said, as if he had played a great joke on the church.

In Madrid again, in 1818, he withdrew to a house on the outskirts of the city. To amuse himself he decorated his dining-room with gigantic fancies, one of them, now in the Prado, representing Saturn devouring his children. This, however, was not the conception of a disordered mind; his head was as clear as ever and his hand as steady. Here he etched his thirty-three plates on the bull-ring, and painted many portraits. In his seventy-eighth year, he obtained permission from the King to visit France, and traveled for two weeks in a stage coach, in the burning Spanish summer. He arrived in Paris eager to see the world, but he was too old and rheumatic to enjoy Paris. He made the rounds of the studios, applauded Géricault and Delacroix, invariably praised the art that was destined to last, and then bade farewell to the young Frenchmen and went to Bordeaux.

Goya was a character in Bordeaux as he hobbled about the town, half-blind and deaf, always wearing his huge Bolivar hat, and attended by a little girl, a distant cousin for whom he predicted a distinguished future as an artist. (His protegée turned out to be a poor copyist in the Prado.) He continued to work, painting with rags and brooms, drawing on stone, and on everything within reach. "I lack strength and sight," he remarked, "but I have an abundance of good will. I shall live to be ninety-nine like Titian." He journeyed back to Madrid again, had his leave extended, and returned to Bordeaux to die, in his eighty-third year.

From this headlong seizure of life we should not expect a calm and refined art, nor a reflective one. Yet Goya was more than a Nietzschean egoist riding roughshod over the world to assert his supermanhood. He was receptive to all shades of feeling, and it was his extreme sensitivity as well as his muscular temerity that actuated his assaults on the outrageous society of Spain. And when ill-health forced him into quiescence, he brooded long and deeply over his art, and in such strange interludes, accomplished his best work—his etchings. Classicism, humanism, academic erudition, he ridiculed with a devil's sneer. "My masters are Velasquez, Rembrandt and Nature," he said. From the first he learned how to use his eyes; from the second, his head; and the third, he maintained, "was a much better guide than Raphael." Nature, not culture, supplied the materials for his art.

"The professors," he said, "are always talking about lines and never about masses. But where does one see lines? I find that neither lines nor colors exist in nature—only light and shade. I see only illuminated bodies, planes in relief and planes in recession, projections and hollows. I will paint your portrait with a piece of charcoal."

These remarks notwithstanding, he wields a mighty line, and in his etchings demonstrates a draughtsmanship of the first rank. In paint, like Velasquez, he is more or less dependent on the model, but not in the detached fashion of the expert in still-life. When the sitter does not interest him, he knocks off a likeness as swiftly as possible, and if the likeness is literal, or the handling slovenly, he refuses to worry. But when the subject appeals to him, the results are astounding, not only as psychological studies, but as carriers of his own ideas of mankind. Of all painters dealing so directly with the facts of life—with celebrities and obscure wretches, mountebanks, scenes of violence and persecution—he maintains the most perfect interaction between the circumstances he depicts and the effects of those circumstances upon himself—introduces us to a person or a scene, shows us what the object or event does to him, and then in turn, what he does to the object as a thinking artist. Thus his art becomes more than the graphic record of actualities.

If a woman is ugly, he makes her a despicable horror; if she is alluring, he dramatizes her charms, giving her feral eyes, a piercing wanton glance, and a figure that swells amorously to fill her flimsy clothing; Charles IV and his family are a beastly lot—he does not spare them; he loves children and paints them from unlimited paternal experience—with wise, tender, credulous faces, and firm small bodies suggesting the round belly of the child, and tapering down to delicate feet and ankles. He prefers to finish his portraits at one sitting and is a tyrant with his models. Like Velasquez, he concentrates on faces, but he draws his heads cunningly, and constructs them out of tones of transparent greys. The costumes are composed of summary patches of broken colors, sometimes—in *Charles IV and His Family*, for example—in very high colors. Mean faces, cruel, hideous, tragical, seductive faces, all Spanish and all instinct with life. "Vitality!" he cries. "Ideal proportions and classic beauty be damned!" And in all these faces we read not only the soul of Spain but the unconsenting scornful soul of Goya himself. He scours every layer of society for his faces, and yet they all belong to the same family. He transforms his models into creatures of an imaginary world. They haunt him and turn upon him, and he begins to visualize Spain as a nightmare of his own creating. In his old age, the medium of paint—the colored earth in which he must embody his imaginings—infuriates him: his hand and eye can no longer obey the unbroken will. In the end, "the dream of reason," he tells us, "produces masters."

Monstrous forms inhabit his black-and-white world: fiends with bat's wings; great birds croaking and flapping over the earth; a colossus sitting on a mountain top; animals performing like silly humans, as in Swift; shrivelled naked idiots huddled among bags of gold; grinning giants dancing ponderously. A corpse rising out of a grave leans on its elbow and writes, with a bony finger on a piece of paper, the artist's black agnosticism in one word—*Nada*—or nothingness. These are his most profoundly deliberated productions. They were not done in mad haste, as were most of his oils, but from closely reasoned studies in red chalk. Unfortunately in reproduction, owing to the worn condition of the plates, the cutting effectiveness of the original designs is not fully conveyed. Writing in the catalogue to *Los Caprichos* Goya says:

"Painting, like poetry, selects from the universe the material she can best use for her own ends. She unites and concentrates in one fantastic figure circumstances and characters which nature has distributed among a number of individuals. Thanks to the wise and ingenious combination, the artist deserves the title of inventor and ceases to be a mere subordinate copyist."

This, I think, is all that need be said of the personal allusions hidden within the etchings. Much time and ingenuity have been wasted in the attempt to uncover specific references and to identify the objects of satire with Goya's friends or enemies. Unquestionably some of the plates were made to satisfy the artist's private malice, but the slanderous elements no longer interest us. The satire still burns, and we cannot escape it. Nor should we try to escape it. It burns so fiercely that Ruskin, aghast that an artist should use his great gifts to scathe the world, is said to have destroyed a set of reproductions of the *Caprichos* presented to him, I daresay, by some one with a sense of humor. Within the compass of a small piece of copper, Goya focuses his choleric antipathies, his understanding of evil, his universal scorn; in one small ghost story he exposes the superstitious rubbish of Old Spain. Not a single plate that is tranquil, tolerant, or good-humored! He weaves his angry spirit into lines that "live and give life"; into attitudes that quail and sag and die; into masses that move and spin and shudder. His fantastic figures, as he calls them, fill us with a sense of ignoble joy, aggravate our devilish instincts and delight us with the uncharitable ecstasies of destruction. And all this neither wild nor disarrayed, but pressed into design as compact as a bullet!

His genius attains its highest point in his etchings on the horrors of war. When placed beside the work of Goya, other pictures of war pale into sentimental studies of cruelty. I do not believe that Goya should be called "the first deliberate opponent of militarism"; it is by no means certain that he disapproved of war as an institution; he had no sympathies with causes or movements, but instead, an insatiable curiosity in life and the energy to indulge it, and through his own hardships, a far-reaching knowledge of the feelings of the poor and of the cannon-fodder. He saw horrible things and his blood boiled, but in expressing his experiences, his purpose was not to show the iniquity of war but how men and women behave in circumstances of tragedy and suffering. And he shows it! He avoids the scattered action of the battlefield, and confines himself to isolated scenes of butchery. Nowhere else does he display such mastery of form and movement, such dramatic gestures and appalling effects of light and darkness. The body of a man dangles from a tree—lynched: we choke as the noose tightens round our own throats. A soldier, shot to death, raises his arms as he falls; we not only see the arms in one position, but feel the pull of the whole movement. A woman, clasping a naked baby against her hip, drives a lance into the groin of a uniformed brute: her lunging figure is composed of a few lines, but every line is a living nerve. And when we have recovered from the first shock, and look at these pictures more soberly, we can hardly believe our eyes. With the evidence before us, it does not seem possible that an artist, working so summarily, can call to life such vivid characters and such dreadful condensations of human misery.

Goya is perhaps the most approachable of painters. His art, like his life, is an open book. He concealed nothing from his contemporaries, and offered his art to them with the same frankness. The entrance to his world is not barricaded with technical difficulties. He proved that if a man has the capacity to live and multiply his experiences, to fight and work, he can produce great art without classical decorum and traditional respectability. In an age of unsurpassed sterility, he proved that a man of genius, single-handed and suspect, rising above all obstacles, can make himself the most feared and the most famous character of his times, even though he is an artist.

CHAPTER

XIII

ENGLISHMEN

IT IS said that the theory and practice of British art are subject to the influence of the British school-girl, and that he is unworthy the name of artist whose achievement is of a kind to call a blush to the cheek of youth.—*Henley.*

In England, to have a sense of art is to be one in a thousand, the other nine hundred and ninety-nine being either Philistine voluptuaries or Calvinistic anti-voluptuaries.—*Bernard Shaw.*

English civilization, or what passes for civilization, is so smug and hypocritical, so grossly Philistine, and at bottom so brutal, that every first-rate Englishman necessarily becomes an outlaw. . . . As for artists, they, unless they happen to have achieved commercial success or canonization in some public gallery, are pretty sure to be family jokes.—*Clive Bell.*

The history of English painting, from the destruction of its ancient nurseries, the monasteries, down to the second quarter of the eighteenth century, is the history of a struggle against foreign invasion.—*Sir Walter Armstrong.*

The British public dearly loves an imitation: a man who can make a noise like a bus changing gear is sure of a warm place in Britannia's bosom.—*Anthony Bertram.*

The tradition that all public British art shall be crassly mediocre and inexpressive is so firmly rooted that it seems to have almost the prestige of constitutional precedent.—*Roger Fry.*

Give a nation a bad name and the name sticks, in art as well as in other assertions of racial tendencies. The Turk, the most charming and hospitable of Europeans, has been so maliciously misrepresented as a cut-throat and a traitor that no Christian will credit him with having a single humane impulse; and the Englishman in the field of art has been so perpetually ridiculed that he has come to be regarded as an object of common contempt. But it is the English themselves, you will have perceived, who are responsible for the evil repute of their artists. From Hogarth, who had to contend with the harsh prejudices of Walpole, and the confections of the rising host of fashionable face-painters whom he called the *portait manufacturers*; through Ruskin's endless and biblical scolding, down to the present generation of Anglo-French aesthetes, the Englishman has been warned by his arbiters that he has no aptitude for art, that when he attempts to paint he does not approach the medium in the pure creative spirit of the artists of other nations—America excepted, of course—but as a shopkeeper who "goes in for painting."

There is nothing so humiliating to the contemporary artist as to be told that he paints like an Englishman, unless it is to be told that he paints like a woman. And if we take the Englishman's word for it, there is little difference. To paint like an Englishman means to be insipid and spongy and sentimental; to view life with a disobliging moral bias, or, instead of dealing directly with hard facts, to approach nature through a mirage induced by an overdose of poetry; in short, to be a modiste or a fabulist. Sir Walter Armstrong, one of the most generous of British critics, whose monograph on *Art in Great Britain and Ireland* is an argument against the skeptical, patronizing attitude of his countrymen, after pointing out in his book "the impossibility of denying the aesthetic gifts of a people which has left behind it the early Christian art of Ireland, the exquisite churches which stud the whole of Britain, the manuscripts and needlework of the twelfth, thirteenth and fourteenth centuries, the perpendicular style of Gothic architecture, the countless numbers of miniature portraits, the Renaissance architecture of Jones and Wren, the great portrait painters of the eighteenth century and the landscape painters who followed them," does not even mention the names of Blake and Rowlandson! The British do not deserve their great artists.

No one, I imagine, would wish to extenuate the villainies of the Philistine environment, so noxious to sensitive natures, and the tight, unchangeable culture of the "Island Pharisees" against which the voice of every great English artist, poet and painter alike, has been a ringing protest. It is no wonder that the English painter, when he has not been a purveyor to His Majesty and to an insufferable aristocracy, has returned to nature for his inspiration, or has fled to the more congenial atmosphere of the Continent. The average Anglo-Saxon is a sober person, undemonstrative, without much imagination, and inclined to expect no more from his kingdom than the dole of commonplace, uninterrupted cheerfulness. Let him rise out of his class; let him inherit a little money from some unknown uncle who has conveniently died in one of the colonies, and he immediately adopts the standards and pleasures of the landed gentry that has done its best to keep him in his place. When confronted with spiritual issues, he becomes self-conscious, preferring to leave such matters to schoolmasters and specialists, but if the greatness of his country is called in question, he awkwardly invokes the assistance of the ancient cultural fetish and employs traditional beliefs to bludgeon his antagonist into silence. He cites with pride the vast literary glories of England—the greatest literature in the history of the world; like the British navy, the greatest in tonnage, variety of craft and in cruising range. That his knowledge of his literature is next to nothing does not embarrass him; he falls back on the body of consolidated opinion, on a national superiority taken for granted, and repeats what he has been taught by the custodians of culture.

But he does not use his art as a cultural weapon: it never occurs to him that England has any art. Poets, being as numerous as lords, and with the immortal fame of Shakespeare echoing in every land, as indispensable to the prestige of the Empire as colonial cooperation, he accepts as a necessary evil. But those "artist chaps" are upsetting to his sense of security and his ingrained morality. They remind him of Frenchmen, and that, in itself, is enough to condemn them. If, however, he chances to meet an Academician who has been knighted for his portraits of royal seadogs, he is duly awed; and he cherishes a certain measure of respect for the comic illustrators who make their art pay. As Roger Fry puts it, "the Philistine hates any art of which he becomes aware. He is only contented and peaceful when, as he jogs his way, he can pass public monuments and statues without having any sensation at all." But when his serenity is challenged, as happened on the unveiling of Epstein's Hudson Memorial, one of the few decent monuments "among the hundred thousand horrors to which the streets of London expose us," and more recently on the exhibition of the best work of the modern Frenchmen, he "carries on like an hysterical woman in the lift."

Although the lower classes have produced, without exception, the painters to whom England is indebted for her distinguished position in the development of modern art, they have always been insensitive to painting. If they have thought of it at all, it has not been as a means to a richer emotional life, but as a luxury for lords and plutocrats. And so in truth it has always been in Great Britain. When the early religious art was destroyed by the Puritans, painting, as a collective expression, ceased to exist, and surviving in the form of portraiture, became the adornment and the plaything of the throne and the leisured rich. Under the patronage of the kings, beginning with Henry VIII, foreigners, to the discouragement of native talent, did a thriving business—first Holbein, then Rubens and Van Dyck, and later on, Lely and Kneller. Of these, the most influential was Van Dyck, flatterer by appointment to His Majesty, Charles I, and the pet of all London. How the King's milliner conducted his fashionable shop is thus described by one of his customers:

"He gave the day and the hour to persons who wished to be painted, and never worked for more than an hour at any one portrait, whether sketch or picture. At the stroke of the hour he rose, bowed to his sitter to signify that it was enough for that day, and proceeded to give the day and hour for the next sitting. While his assistant cleaned his brushes and set his new palette, the painter received the next person who had an appointment. In this manner he worked on several portraits the same day with extraordinary rapidity. After he had made a slight sketch, he made his sitter take the pose he had decided upon, and in a quarter of an hour he drew the figure and costume in black and white on grey paper. This sketch he handed to skilful assistants, who then painted in the dresses from the costumes themselves, which the clients sent to the studio at Van Dyck's request. After the assistants had got the draperies to the best of their ability, he worked over them lightly, and in a short time gave them the truth and art we admire in them. For the hands he had persons of both sexes in the house who served him as models."

Here we have the genesis of British portraiture, the form of painting, I am loath to say, by which England, to the prejudice of her noble artists in landscape, is popularly remembered. Not the continuation of the early religious expression uniting men in a common faith; nothing of the mural art of Rubens, the Whitehall decorations upon which he lavished all his gifts in order to set a shining example to the Anglo-Saxons; not the compositions of Hogarth, nor the illustrations of Blake; but an extraneous pattern of artificial elegance whereby swells might appear before the world in all their glory. The standard established, the native painters, as the English critic Manson has it, were "little simpletons working for the benefit of a maudlin society of painted jades and pampered pimps." Hogarth, a man of high courage, a loyal Britisher with the finest qualities of heart and mind, resolved to "wipe the foreigners off the earth," and by the light of his own genius to guide his pettifogging countrymen away from degrading flattery to the consideration of the realities of English life. But his pugnacious campaign against the charlatans was not more welcome to polite society than the unorthodox honesty of his art, and although he reclaimed the Island for Englishmen, his successors, whatever their intentions, were intellectually too effeminate and morally too subservient to the vanity of their clients to build up a school of painting on the foundations he had so firmly planted. And so it came about that in the eighteenth century, when the first British school appeared under the leadership of Reynolds, it was not the solid humanity of Hogarth that called it into being, but the formula, the tone and the sleazy artifices supplied by the courtly Van Dyck.

Reynolds and his associates won a triumph for British art, painting thousands of porous fashion-plates, and securing for art the official protection of the Royal Academy of which Sir Joshua was the first president. It is admitted by every enlightened Englishman that the influence of the Royal Academy has been pernicious and stultifying, that it has been the refuge of muttonheads and obscurantists, that no genuine artist has ever been at home within its dreary ranks; and yet it stands today as impregnable as the throne and the right of primogeniture. And more: it is the belief of the average Britisher that once a man has submitted to the deadly routine of academic training, and has gained the right to append the coveted R. A. to his otherwise honorable name, he is, of necessity, an artist. Such is the authority of tradition and official sanction.

I trust I have made it clear that the upper classes are no fonder of art than the lower: they go in for it just as they travel and ride to the hounds—because it is the correct thing to do. It is the hall-mark of snobbery, the sport of the idle rich. After Reynolds had discovered the aristocracy of the Renaissance Italians, and had, with the collaboration of his numerous disciples, presented the British nobility in a style which, to the uncritical egoist, was the genuine thing and not a pompous imitation of Venetian splendor, the gentleman became a fancier of pictures. To proclaim his superior birth, he filled his baronial halls and castles with portraits of his family; as insignia of his superior tastes, he collected masterpieces of every school and period. In these collections one may see many of the greatest pictures ever painted, though it is best not to inquire how the

Hogarth: SELF-PORTRAIT.
National Gallery

British came by them. The British are justly proud of their art treasures and guard them as they guard all their possessions—as if they owned them by divine right. And when the weary traveller, after tramping the galleries of the Continent, where the good is jumbled with the bad and often indistinguishable from the bad because of dirt and criminal negligence, enters the black pile at Trafalgar Square, he enters the most notable of picture galleries. Here is a museum purged of dry rot. Here are the choicest paintings of practically every school, displayed to their fullest advantage and groomed with all the care that science and vigilance can give them. Feasting his eyes, the excited traveller forgets his weariness and exclaims reverentially, "God save the King!"

The affectation of painting as a badge of snobbery is not confined to the upper classes. In watercolorists and etchers, Great Britain outnumbers the other nations, five to one, most of the practitioners being men and women of bourgeois origin who go in for art on the side, as a means to social advancement. They go in for watercolor and etching because these mediums lend themselves to passable results without demanding any talent whatever. And it is precisely this spirit of aspiring snobbery that attracts rich American collectors to eighteenth century English portraiture, that urges them to pay huge fortunes for stunt pictures like the *Blue Boy* and for tenth-rate canvases by Romney, Hoppner and Lawrence. They would fain be aristocrats and the best they can do is to surround themselves with emblems of a higher caste. They buy Gainsboroughs as they buy castles; they change their accent, get presented at court and ride in the Grand National; they love that part of England which her portraits so perfectly reflect. The royal England that Shakespeare loved:

"This royal throne of kings, this scepter'd isle,
This happy breed of men, this little world,
This precious stone set in the silver sea—
This blessed plot, this earth, this realm, this England,
This nurse, this teeming womb of royal kings,

Feared by their breed and famous by their birth—
This land of such dear souls, this dear dear land,
Dear for her reputation through the world."

This dear land of kings and Philistines, of standards and inflexible conventions, of royal portrait-manufacturers, Academicians and dabbling amateurs, has not received her original painters with noticeable cordiality. But original painters she has bred, not in shoals, but in men of independent genius, individualists of true artistic character like Hogarth, Blake, Turner and Constable, to say nothing of Rowlandson, Wilson, Gainsborough, Bonington, Girtin, Cotman and Crome. To these England owes her reputation in modern painting. Let us give the shopkeeper his due.

HOGARTH

In one of his self-portraits, Hogarth was at pains to include three books bearing the respective names of Shakespeare, Milton and Swift. He rightly felt that he belonged in the company of the great men of England, and was not too modest to remind the bigwigs of his time that he was more than a plebeian storyteller with a sense of humor. He was Shakespearean in his conception of painting as a dramatic art: "My picture is my stage," he wrote, "my men and women my players." Like Milton he was constantly occupied with aesthetic speculations which, being expressed without cant or classical humbug, were not taken seriously by his contemporaries. As a satirist of a bawdy, gin-drinking age, he joined hands with the author of "Gulliver's Travels." To this company we might add the names of Fielding and Newton and many others combining coarse-fibred practical strength with intellectual faculties of the highest order—men who have carried the name of England into the corners of the world.

But Hogarth did not ally himself with painters, British or foreign. He was so roundly disgusted with fraudulent connoisseurship that he pilloried the Italians—the "Black Masters" he labelled them—as a matter of self-preservation. As for native painters, before him there had been none; and those of his own day were not worthy to clean his boots. Knowing his own merits and the illegitimate reputations of the painters who had profited by his example only to pay him back by reviling him, Sir Joshua along with the rest, he chose as companions in immortality artists with whom his kinship would one day be recognized as incontestable. His place among the great Englishmen has never been more secure than at the present. He stands first in the list of English painters, above and apart from all others. It is time these acknowledgments were made.

Hogarth was born in London in 1697, the son of a poor schoolmaster who had come up from the country in search of a better living and had failed to find it. His education, if it may be so dignified, was scant and irregular, but the lack of academic training was no disadvantage to one suspicious from infancy of conventional schemes for improving the mind. He educated himself, resembling in the scope of his attainments and in his independent thinking, another distinguished Englishman—Samuel Butler, not the author of "Hudibras", for which he made illustrations, but the Victorian satirist. Like Butler, he had a great stock of good humor, the habit of looking at life through his own eyes and observing it closely, a sharp tongue and a devilish talent for getting under the skins of his countrymen, a sly contempt for stereotyped judgments, and an irritating disloyalty to established reputations. "Genius," he said—and the words might have been uttered by Butler, "is only labor and diligence."

"I cut a poor figure at school," Hogarth remarked in later life. "Blockheads with better memories could surpass me. I was fond of shows of all sorts; I had a good eye, and I was always drawing." He was apprenticed to a silver-plate engraver, and in his twentieth year, on the death of his father, struck out on his own hook as a commercial artist, designing arms, shopkeepers' signs, tradesmen's cards and formal invitations to sprees and funerals. When his two handsome sisters went into business, he engraved their advertising cards, one, an interior of a shop with an announcement below it, reading as follows:

> Mary & Ann Hogarth
>
> from the old Frock-shop the corner of the Long Walk facing the Cloysters, Removed to ye Kings Arms joyning to ye Little Britain gate. Sells ye best & most Fashionable Ready Made Frocks, sutes of Fustian, Ticken & Holland, stript Dimmity & Flanel Wastcoats & Bluecoat Boys Drawers. Likewise Fustian, Tickens & Flanels in Ye piece, by Wholesale or Retale, at Reasonable Rates.

The London of the first half of the eighteenth century was probably no worse than the London of George V—surely it was less dreary, and it could hardly have exceeded the modern city in poverty and commercialized vice—but if we are to trust the words of Swift and Fielding, and the line of Hogarth, its corruption was more open, its vices filthier, its amusements more beastly. Cock-fighting, bear-baiting, dueling, whoring and gaming were gentlemanly recreations, with the seduction of servant girls—still the gentleman's privilege—not less to the fore. In several of Hogarth's pictures our attention is drawn to the distent middle of a young girl who points sadly to her condition, while the rake, callously preparing to abandon her, holds out a shiny coin to pay for her shame. It was a rough-and-tumble age. The upper classes, devoid of taste and culture, were duped by foreign adventurers—Italian tenors, French dancers and ballet masters; the crowds were preyed upon by political sharpers, exotics and quacks of all kinds. At night nobody was safe. Leaky oil lamps flared dimly in the fog; and Irish bullies and drunken watermen, armed with shillelahs, lurked in the shadows of Covent Garden and Temple Bar, ready to waylay straggling revellers and to beat them to death for the sheer pleasure of hearing their bones crack.

Starving hacks and prostitutes inhabited the garrets of Grub

Street. Art was in the hands of auctioneers and pirates. Gin was the national beverage. But in this rough world were coteries of intelligent men justly appreciative of one another's talents and with a large sense of conviviality. Hard drinkers they were, and hard fighters, asking no quarter from anyone, and joining forces in the interests of good work and masculine decency. Most of them were writers now of classic fame; but one, a short, stocky, blue-eyed man with the keenest wit and the tenderest heart in the entire company, was Hogarth, painter and engraver.

From his twentieth to his thirtieth year, Hogarth diligently pursued his trade, training himself for the great works which were shortly to astonish his friends and expose his enemies. He went about his tasks in a thoroughly business-like manner, made a fair living, and very early brought himself into public notice. A true metropolitan, he loved London despite its pimps and coxcombs, and there was no form of life, high or low, that escaped his critical intelligence or offended his artistic sensibilities. He knew his London; he loved English women and the beefy men whom he drew and painted with the bulk strength of sculpture. He frequented fairs and taverns, sideshows and cock-fights, dances and all-night supper parties; watched parading Redcoats, and election riots, and followed the crowd to executions. But contrary to general opinion, he made practically no drawings from nature—did not observe the comedy of English life, sketchbook in hand. He observed it first as a man, a Britisher who was part of it, studying its significance and the character, expressions and behavior of the players composing it. When it came to the making of pictures, he had his own method, a novel and very difficult method—one, it seems to me, that few artists would be willing to recommend.

"I discovered," he informs us, "that he who could by any means acquire and retain in his memory perfect ideas of the subjects he meant to draw, would have as clear a knowledge of the figure as a man who can write freely hath of the letters of the alphabet, and would consequently be an accurate designer. I therefore endeavored to habituate myself to the exercise of a sort of technical memory, and by repeating in my own mind the parts of which objects were composed, I could by degrees combine and put them down with my pencil. Thus with all the drawbacks, I had one material advantage over my competitors, viz.: the early habit I thus acquired of retaining in my mind's eye, without coldly copying it on the spot, whatever I intended to imitate. Sometimes, I took the life for correcting the parts I had not perfectly enough remembered, and then I transferred them to my compositions."

One side of his genius—the critic of life, which proved to be his most popular and lucrative vein—blossomed in his early twenties, and fetched a hearty laugh from the town. In a series of engraved burlesques of current follies called *Masquerades and Operas* he aimed a couple of shots at one William Kent, knave-of-all-trades, who, through the patronage of Lord Burlington, had seized a number of art commissions which he was carrying out with ludicrous incapacity. Hogarth exhibited him posed on the top of Burlington gate in a comic attitude, supported by Raphael and Michael Angelo, with the dwarfish Alexander Pope vigorously whitewashing the gate and bespattering the passers-by. Burlington House he prophetically called "Academy of Arts." In addition to this he broadcast a print purporting to be an exact copy of an altarpiece which the impostor Kent, for all his brash confidence, could not finish. The engraving was, and is, a masterpiece of burlesqued bad drawing and the garbled machinery of religious decoration, and the explanations accompanying it are still fresh and witty. William Kent was ruined, but young William Hogarth was made.

During these years of experiment he undertook book illustration, supplying prints for the *Beggar's Opera*, *Don Quixote* and *Hudibras,* but with indifferent results. Illustration, besides being unprofitable and in low esteem, circumscribed his invention, for he could not work freely when dealing with borrowed ideas. For a stipulated sum he agreed to engrave a set of tapestry designs, but on the delivery of the plates, his client, for some reason or other, objected to the terms and withheld payment. Hogarth, with characteristic decision, promptly sued for the full amount and won the case. Between jobs, and in his own way, he taught himself to paint, producing conversation-pieces—little scenes from metropolitan life—which show that he had already given much thought to the structure of pictures. His first canvases are admirably designed and unlike anything that had hitherto appeared in the British Isles. Technically, so far as they are derivative at all, they are founded upon the Dutch and Flemish masters: the Italians he stubbornly avoided, and the French whose fripperies he mocked with an invective that has nettled Gallic critics from Diderot to Faure, he said were ignorant of the use of color. After painting his pictures, he copied them with his graver, a practice followed throughout his life for pecuniary reasons. The engravings became popular, and after the scurvy ethics of the times, were pirated without delay.

The success of these small oils—in his own mind, at least—furthered his deep-laid plans for a cycle of dramatic compositions, but in a moment of uneasiness, feeling that his self-instruction was not, perhaps, quite adequate for so ambitious a program, he enrolled in the classes of Sir James Thornhill to have a fling at the nude. He found just what his natural distrust had counselled him to expect: that drawing as taught by Thornhill, and Sir James was well above the average, was but a species of copying, and "copying," he said, "was like pouring water out of one vessel into another." The venture, however, ended happily. Hogarth won the love of Jane Thornhill, his master's only daughter, twenty and very lovely, and proposed marriage. His master frowned on the match, skeptical of the engraver's ability to support the girl. The young couple immediately eloped and had no cause to regret it. Nor had the father, after the enormous popularity of Hogarth's first important work.

The important work was begun soon after his marriage. Impatient to put to a practical test his ideas of "composing pictures on canvas similar to representations on the stage," he took a house in Leicester Fields which he occupied till his death, and bent all his wits to a study of the career of a loose woman. In

1731, *A Harlot's Progress* burst upon London. This, the first of his social dramas, relates in a sequence of paintings the story of Moll Hackabout, a pretty country girl of easy virtue: she arrives in London; she becomes a kept woman; she quarrels with her rich Jew; she is apprehended by a magistrate; she beats hemp in Bridewell prison; she dies; she is buried. In the funeral scene her little son is perched on the coffin winding his top, "the only thing," according to Lamb, "in that assembly that is not a hypocrite." There are no Magdalens or repentant sinners in Hogarth's dramas. As Austin Dobson says, "harlots are harlots to the end of the book." He sees things as realities, offering no apologies for his characters and no moral sop to his audience. He is an artist from first to last, never a hack like Defoe who itemizes the coarse appliances of seduction to tickle the pornographic itchings of his readers, and then attempts to conceal the trick under a veil of perfunctory sermonizing.

A Harlot's Progress was received with instantaneous and universal applause, netting the author, by the sale of engravings, £1260, a snug fortune in those days, and reinstating him in the good will of his wife's father. The plates were freely pirated and Hogarth, tired of this evil, petitioned Parliament for protection. A bill granting the privileges of copyright to engravers and designers was passed and piracy was gradually extinguished. Poor Moll Hackabout was the rage of London. She was put into pantomime and opera, sung in street ballads, painted on fans and tea services. Her only detractors were the auctioneers—"the dealers in dark pictures," to use Hogarth's phrase—and the highbrow painters of the grand style who grudgingly allowed that she was an appealing wench, but let it be known that she was not art.

The public did not pause to consider her artistic pretensions. They recognized her as one of their own kind, frail but not without charm and the lust for easy living, one of the most familiar ladies of the town, who, had she not been Moll, would have been Jane or Phyllis, or but for her birth, the good Queen Anne of fragrant memory. Nor can I believe that they were more than lightly touched by the morality of her fall which the divines, never satisfied to let a picture explain itself, harped upon so approvingly. Her fall was not unexpected—that was one of the chances one took in such a sport—and they were delighted with Hogarth's unsparing realism. Certainly his poetic justice did not affect the prestige of Moll's profession any more than the wholesale hangings discouraged the pursuit of crime. That the pictures contained well-known haunts of rakes and portraits of well-known characters—the "harlot hunting judge," for example—contributed, no doubt, to their sensational success; but the principal reason for their popularity is the love of all mankind, from the most primitive to the most cultivated social groups, for dramatic representation. The truth is that Hogarth revived the oldest and most appealing form of art, the art of story-telling which had been lost to the world since the early Italians. And all art, as Meier-Graefe points out, has its origin in illustration. Rubens, Bruegel, and Rembrandt, I need hardly say, had painted marvellous representations of Flemish and Dutch life, but in the form of single scenes. Hogarth brought back to art the connected narrative, and the British, having had no art, drank it in like children at a circus. By presenting in dramatic form ideas close to the imagination of his people, he established kinship with the greatest of all story-tellers in paint, the master who converted the Arena Chapel into a picture book; and the British welcomed his social fables as whole-heartedly as the Italians of the fourteenth century welcomed the religious fables of Giotto.

Hogarth did not rest on his laurels, nor did he allow the shouting of the mob to turn his head. He was pleased with his success, of course—it was among other things a blow at the auctioneers; but he was too excellent a critic to overlook the shortcomings of his work and too wise a man to accept the verdict of the majority for more than it was worth. Before proceeding to the companion piece to Moll Hackabout's vagaries, he went up the river with two of his friends on a holiday, junketing from tavern to tavern, drinking beer and playing practical jokes with the irresponsibility of a truant schoolboy. As a record of this jolly excursion, he made a group of drawings called *Five Days Tour*, memorable technically for the free and wavy line which he was soon to use with a strength and grace unrivalled in British art and in all art, until it was resumed by Daumier; and spiritually, as an example of his talent for gross clowning and nonsensical extravagance. His clowning, a playful strain indigenous to Anglo-Saxons, kept his mind healthy and in perfect combative trim, and kept his satire, however cruel it might seem, within humanitarian bounds, as distinguished from the Mephistophelian visions of Goya.

His next satire was *The Rake's Progress*, a play in eight scenes picturing the career of a spendthrift: the miserly father is dead and the young heir, Tom Rakewell, takes possession; he is surrounded by fashionable parasites; he revels; he is arrested for debt; he marries an old maid for her money; he gambles and loses; he is sent to prison; he dies in Bedlam. A better work in every respect than its predecessor—in characterization, draughtsmanship, color and in the relation of the actors to the rococo settings—*The Rake's Progress*, though greeted with enthusiasm, did not set London on fire as did the story of the lowly Moll Hackabout. The picture-drama was no longer a novelty and mobs are fickle; but perhaps the best explanation of the diminished popularity of the second series is given by Dobson: "the artist was now working in a higher genre of English life, and dealing with a man instead of a woman."

But Hogarth did not grieve over fluctuating public tastes. He had been well repaid for his efforts, and if he was snubbed in certain art circles as a bourgeois anecdotist, he was everywhere recognized as a man with whom one would not care to quarrel. He had, moreover, many labors to perform before he had finished with life. He took an active part in the erection of a Foundling Hospital—the first in England—and with his wife, an active interest in the welfare of the inmates. He painted for the office of the hospital a portrait of his friend Captain Coram, the founder of the enterprise, refuting in fine style Wal-

Hogarth: STROLLING ACTRESSES DRESSING IN A BARN.

pole's dictum that "as a painter Hogarth had slender merit." It was Hogarth's turn to laugh. "If I am so wretched an artist," he remarked, "how is it that my *Captain Coram*, my first life-size portrait, is better than the best of the first painters of the kingdom?" When his father-in-law died, he assumed control of the art school, endowed it and supervised the curriculum, hoping against his suspicions that he might discover a method other than his own "whereby talent might be developed freely and not shaped to copy the dead for the dealers." The dealers were his special abomination. "The connoisseurs and I are at war, you know," he said. "They think because I hate them, I hate Titian—and let them." When they condemned a picture of Thornhill's because of a minor defect, he denounced them publicly in a letter which bears so beautifully on the swindlers of today that I must quote it at length.

"There is another set of gentry more noxious to art than the local connoisseurs—your picture-jobbers from abroad, who are always ready to raise a great cry in the prints whenever they think their own craft is in danger; and indeed it is to their interest to depreciate every English work as hurtful to their trade of continually importing shiploads of dead Christs, Holy Families, Madonas (*sic*) and other dismal dark subjects neither entertaining nor ornamental; on which they scrawl the terrible cramp names of some Italian master, and fix on us poor Englishmen the character of universal dupes. If a man, naturally a judge of painting and not bigoted to these empirics, should cast his eye on one of their sham virtuoso pieces, he would be very apt to say, 'Mr. Bubbleman, that grand Venus (as you are pleased to call her) has not beauty enough for the character of an English cookmaid.' Upon which the quack answers with a confident air, 'O Sir, I find that you are not a connoisseur! That picture, I assure you, is in Alesso Baldovinetti's second and best manner, boldly painted and truly sublime, the contour gracious, the air of the head in the high Greek taste—and a most divine idea it is!' Then spitting on an obscure place and rubbing it with a dirty handkerchief, he takes a skip to the other end of the room, and screams out in raptures, 'There is an amazing touch! A man should have this picture a twelvemonth in his collection before he can discover half its beauties!' The gentleman (though naturally a judge of what is beautiful, yet ashamed to be out of the fashion in judging for himself) with this cant is struck dumb, gives a vast sum for the picture, very modestly confesses he is indeed quite ignorant of painting, and bestows a frame worth 50 pounds on a frightful thing, without the hard names on it not worth as many farthings."

His other abomination was the French whom he eviscerated at the smallest provocation—sometimes with more passion than judgment. Hogarth was not much of a traveller, but in his fiftieth year, he crossed the Channel and was unjustifiably arrested while sketching at the gate of Calais. The outrage stung his pride and his British sense of justice; and happily for posterity, led to the painting of *The Gate of Calais*, one of his unquestioned masterpieces. He shows us a little scene at the entrance of the city: a porter struggling under the weight of a joint of beef which a fat priest is about to embrace with salacious gusto; two haggard guardsmen grinning pitifully at the sight of food; and in the background, by the gate, the squat form of the artist engaged in the criminal act of sketching. It was my pleasure to examine this picture in the company of a Frenchman, an artist of high repute among the Modernists. "'Ogarth, 'Ogarth!" he exclaimed. "What a master!" He praised the consummate design, the drawing, the color, and the exquisite handling of paint which the French love. His eloquence came from the heart and his insight into the structure of the work was admirable. Then, suddenly, his enthusiasm turned into anger and he began to scream as if in great pain. The ragged, bony, starving soldiers had destroyed his aesthetic pleasure and recalled his patriotism. "It is a lie!" he cried. "France has never starved her soldiers!" His behavior was most instructive. Here was a man who argued, by his painting which was a suave modification of Cubism, and by his writing, an example of French logic at its best, that it was the design, and only the design, that provoked an emotional disturbance in the beholder—if the beholder were an artist; and yet who was thrown into a spasm by the Englishman's masterly characterization of the French. After 150 years Hogarth's humanity was capable of creating an emotional storm that made havoc of preconceived theories of appreciation.

In the second episode of *The Rake's Progress*, Hogarth raps another type of Frenchman, the strutting, ceremonious Parisian so repulsive to British reserve. He gives the center of the stage to an undersized ballet-master—a head shorter than the other actors—a conceited little fool, dainty and half-woman, amusing and yet thoroughly detestable, and so charmed with his own importance that he fancies the whole world revolves round his lifted toe. He trips a gay measure, his right foot artfully poised, his right hand swinging a baton like a fairy flourishing a magic wand, his little fingers affectedly pointing, his face simpering with self-satisfaction—the quintessence of factitious refinement as seen through British prejudice. The French deplore these cutting sallies, but ungenerously, I fear. Compared to his treatment of his own race, Hogarth's handling of the French is flattering. The French have always been hysterically afraid of criticism, from their own wits and ironists as well as from outsiders. When an outspoken Englishman finds his country too hot for him, he goes to France; when a Frenchman speaks his mind, he goes to jail or into exile.

Three times in his life, Hogarth, annoyed by the slurs of his enemies on his incompetence as a painter, embarked into the field of religion and history. "I entertained some hopes," he said, "of succeeding in what the puffers in books call the great style of painting, and without having had a stroke of this *grand* business, I painted a couple of pictures for a hospital to prove how easily it could be done." These grand conceptions add nothing to his fame. They are not without distinction and they do not deserve the ridicule in which he afterwards held them. We have every reason to believe that Hogarth's genius was particularly adapted to large scale compositions and that he might have attained great honor in this department had he chosen subjects related to his experiences instead of hastily deciding to outpaint his rivals. Where he showed up his enemies in their own sphere was in portraiture, but the returns from portraiture were small because he was not a flatterer and because he would not paint, for any consideration, a person who did not appeal to him. He portrayed a deformed and decrepit lord so truthfully that his lordship, expecting to be refurbished into a handsome cavalier, rejected the picture with all possible indignation. Whereupon Hogarth sent him a note saying: "If his lordship does not send for the canvas in three days, it will be disposed of, with the addition of a tail and some other appendages, to Mr. Hare, the famous wild beast man, Mr. Hare having promised to buy it on condition of his lordship's refusal." The deformed gentleman sent for the picture at once. When some chafferer reproved him with the remark, "You must think you are a better painter than Van Dyck"; he replied, "I am. Give me my time, and let me choose my subject." And who, save the dealers, will disagree?

Garrick, his best friend, paid him £200 for a portrait, at the time the highest price ever received by an English artist for such a commission; but there was only one Little Davy, and Hogarth was forced to admit that "I found this branch of my art not sufficiently profitable to pay the expenses of my family, and being unwilling to sink into a portrait-manufacturer, I dropped my expectations and returned to prints and to my former practice of dealing with the public at large." He announced a third dramatic performance, a study of high life in six scenes, entitled *Marriage à la Mode*. There was considerable speculation on his ability to depict high life, some maintaining that he knew nothing about it, others, better informed, anticipating the worst. The third cycle tells of the scandals of a titled pair: the contract; the dissipations; the adultery of the Countess; the killing of the Earl by the Countess's lover; and finally, the death of the Countess. It is a brilliant achievement, the high-water mark in his work in this genre; brilliant in all things distinguishing the creator from the scene-painter, the spokesman of humanity from the raconteur of eighteenth century tattle. But the patrons of art did not rush forward to bid for it—not with Reynolds and his minions supplying the irreproachable garniture for aristocrats. What, besides shame and resentment, could they have got from paintings which not only disclosed the seamy side of high life but which, in the absurd classic nudes disfiguring the backgrounds of *Marriage à la Mode*, had burlesqued the tastes of would-be connoisseurs? Hogarth kept the six paintings in his studio for five years rather than entrust them to the dealers, finally disposing of them at public auction. The whole set brought the insignificant sum of £126!

The last decade of his life was enlivened by controversies some of which caused him more trouble than they were worth. His best work had been done, with the exception of the great Election series, and his health was failing; but a "good quarrel," he said, "always restored him." And being a public-spirited Englishman whose art, in one direction, was a merciless criticism of manners, he had plenty of opportunities to quarrel, if only to defend his integrity. He painted on order, *Sigismonda*, his last essay in the ideal style, working it out with the utmost pains. The picture was rejected by the patron, hooted by the critics, hated by the dealers. Walpole called *Sigismonda* a strumpet, a stupid criticism, for the lady is the purest of cook-maids. Hogarth was hurt: he knew that the picture was a creditable job, better, to tell the truth, than anything manufactured by the bigoted guardians of the great style; and he knew that, in attacking it, his adversaries were indirectly attacking the character of the man who had painted it. But the hurt did not kill him. He pitched into his foes with redoubled vigor, matched his graver against the pen of a political rogue in a heated duel, exterminated him, and called for more battles.

In his last years he wrote *The Analysis of Beauty*, the first treatise on the aesthetics of painting in the English language, and one of the most profound and remarkable books on the subject in any language. "I found," he says, "that literary men set you down where they first took you up, amusing their readers with amazing (but often misapplied) encomiums on deceased painters." Accordingly, after a lifetime of thinking, and what was equally pertinent, of painting, he undertook to formulate his theories. Instead of employing the stale obscurities of philosophy or the lofty jargon of Sir Joshua, he spoke in plain Anglo-Saxon, without a single allusion to the Greeks or Romans or anybody else—in the same style that Defoe would have used in explaining the principle of the Immaculate Conception. "When a vessel sails well," Hogarth writes, "the sailors call her a beauty." That was his idea of art: it should be judged by what it accomplishes. He argues for the curve as the basic compositional line, calling the double curve, the letter S traced on the palette included in his self-portrait, "The Line of Beauty." His own paintings, however, do not bear out this notion, being compounded of many varieties of lines. He discusses the static elements of symmetry and regularity; analyzes the structure of natural forms; distinguishes with marvellous clarity between artistic movement and the suspended action of literal copies; and arrives blithely and independently at the grand postulate laid down by Father Aristotle—that true composition is variety in unity.

Shortly before his death, he remarked, "I have gone through the principal circumstances of life pretty much to my own satisfaction, and in no respect injuriously, I hope, to any other man." He died in his sixty-sixth year from enlargement of the arteries, and was buried—so a clergyman editor of his works tells us—"beneath a plain but neat mausoleum with an elegant inscription by Davy Garrick."

Hogarth is called a moralist. He is—in the same way that Molière is a moralist. He is called an illustrator. He is: a creator of epics like the first of the Italians. He is stigmatized as a humorist. He is that too, with Aristophanes to keep him company. Is art so poor a mistress of mankind that she cannot afford to shed a little mirth in a naughty world? Is the human spirit, as it somehow gets itself expressed in paint, to be denied the luxury of a smile? Let us be grateful to England for giving us a man who purified the gloomy house of art with his blasting laughter.

Hogarth is all these things at the same time—and more. Were he a moralist of the stripe that the Rev. John Trusler, his editor, makes him out, he would have less claims on our regard than a prohibition agent. Not being a sot or a procurer, he had no more love for the baser instincts of his race than any other decent Englishman. He hated white slavery, bribery, vote-selling, hypocritical art dealers, sponges on society, French fops, and drunkards rolling in the gutter, as intelligent men today hate these evils. But unlike Shelley, he had no mad passion for reforming the world, no plans or philosophies for a vegetarian Utopia cleansed of gin and Philistines. His raillery against shams and his "ridicule of life"—the phrase is Sir Joshua's—never soured his art. His laughter was proof against all ills, and while exposing the world, he got a vast amount of fun out of it, and discovered more materials for his pencil than he could use. In attack he was happy; in reproof inimitable; but his main concern was in applying the imagination of the artist to subjects which, once his mind began to work upon them, were neither vices nor virtues, but realities. He needed satire for the release of his creative energy, just as Giotto needed religion, El Greco Spanish mysticism, and the Venetians women of sumptuous charms. That his men and women behave rather badly does not lessen our enjoyment in them as distinctive characters.

He never sacrificed his art to cheap sentiment or sobbing parable. The story is present, though more anecdotal in the first dramatic series than in the last; and time and change have not dried up his capacious satire. There is no cogent reason why such things should not exist in art and no reason why one should not enjoy them when they do exist. We are not so rich in righteousness or so dissimilar in the consumption of gin that we can coolly dismiss the illustrative side of Hogarth's art as the obsolete depravity of intemperate Britons, and pass at once to more aesthetic considerations. His passions and prejudices, his satire and his scorn, are so inextricably bound up with his aesthetic designs that we could not ignore them if we would—as the French painter learned to his public discomfiture.

I do not say that his satire strikes us with the crushing force with which it fell upon his contemporaries. His age is dead and gone, surviving for us in the heroic forms of Tom Jones, Captain Lemuel Gulliver, and Hogarth's gallery of able-bodied men and beautiful women. Nor would I pretend that we should translate the engravings of *Beer Street* and *Gin Lane,* into the homiletic sentiments of the Rev. Mr. Trusler who wrote of the first that, "in this print, Mr. Hogarth has thought proper to show the advantages almost every individual receives from the drinking of this valuable liquor," and of the second, that "this abominable liquor is, among the vulgar, very justly called by the name of *Strip-me-naked*—not leaving them, at least, the bare necessaries of life." We enjoy in the one the bloated jocularity of the scene, the huge tradesmen quaffing their foaming steins; the open love-making so typical of the English lower classes, and the sign-painter, placed above the crowd on a ladder, appraising his art with great satisfaction. We enjoy in the other the movement and the maudlin horrors; the gouging pawnbroker; the scorbutic hag, beyond redemption, her face contorted into the leer of a death's head, her screaming brat holding by its feet to her naked breast as it falls over the rail; and the inscription on the arch of the gin cellar—"Drunk for a penny; dead drunk for twopence; clean straw for nothing." And we enjoy in both the coherent whole into which Hogarth has woven the many details and simultaneous incidents.

Hogarth is the most various of British artists. Not for him the puling introspections of the men of little faith and less knowledge of life—the small-size painters who catch hold of a trifling theory of color, or a subjective notion of form, which they endeavor, in bitter solitude, to hang upon the dull facets of their empty world. The whole of England sweeps through his imagination: the grim and the sweet; the coarse, the cruel, the lusty and the tender. He has so much to say that his pictures—portraits and dramas alike—are full to overflowing. Before he learns to control his energy, he cannot find room for all his ideas, packing his scenes with a multiplicity of forms. Nor is he, as one might well suppose from his continual knocking of the Old Masters, so removed from his predecessors that he is under no obligations to the past. So complex a structure as he reared could not conceivably have been born without antecedent examples. But his technique is so firmly wedded to his personal vision, so thoroughly conditioned by his environment, that we may pronounce him one of the most original of painters.

He is far and away the greatest of Anglo-Saxon composers: in other words, the greatest of Anglo-Saxon artists—the only one, in fact, who will stand comparison with the Continentals whose black shadows, he said, lay so densely on the British manufacturers. It is not at all necessary to the appreciation of his art to compare him with Rubens, or Rembrandt, or anybody else—what he would have said against this critical habit we may readily imagine—but it is instructive, in passing, to note that traditions in painting, like traditions in architecture, are handed down from generation to generation, affording beginners a point of departure in the making of new things. Art, with Hogarth, was not a trade, but an adventure. When he conceived a picture, he did not say, "Well, I think I'll make a composition today"—as if a composition were an irrelative plant conjured up in a vacuum—and then, with an eye on Rubens or Tintoretto, proceed to juggle lines and masses until he arrived at an harmonious balance. His compositions grew out of his experiences—were, we might say, dictated by his experiences. Each was a new and distinct creation, demanding a different approach and a different plan of attack. Hence the freshness, the variety, the organic oneness of his pictures. In finding the true, the appropriate, the inevitable form for the objectification of his ideas, Hogarth has perhaps never been equalled, certainly never excelled. His figures never seem to be striking attitudes; his groupings never to be studio models lashed together arbitrarily to exhibit a taste for arrangement, with supernumeraries here and there to fill up holes or complete a rhythm. They are all combatants, all necessary to the action; and they transmit the intended action so perfectly that we think of them as living characters involved in dramatic difficulties.

On account of the plausibility of his compositions, the ease and fitness of gestures and the spontaneous communication between characters, Hogarth was called an illustrator by his competitors, the term being used censoriously to spread the impression that he had only a knack for describing situations which he had observed in real life. This libellous notion still tells against his significance as an artist. It is pretended today by painters who would pull him down to their own level, that his aim was merely to amuse the public by reproducing timely foibles. If his monumental figures and his scenes of concentrated activity had existed in real life, there would have been no need to repeat them in art. Nor would any man of sense have faced the labor he bestowed upon his pictures merely to amuse people. It was Hogarth's conception of painting as a vessel freighted with a spiritual cargo and his ability to sail his craft truly that entitle him to a seat among the master-mariners of art.

He possessed the true creative instinct, without which no amount of labor and diligence would have made him an artist; the instinct to perceive, one might say to feel, in a given experience the outlines of a new structure. To put it a little more technically, subjects that moved him suggested immediately abstract relationships—schemes for designs consistent with the material at hand. He did not go out in search of something to paint; his subjects pursued him demanding expression. First he abstracted from nature the working graph of an orderly structure, the skeleton of a new body. This is the way of all true artists, individual experiences and variations determining the development of the organism. All his life he pondered on the abstract, or constructive side, of painting, exploring the potentialities of lines and colors, of shapes and rhythms. We have sketches showing the evolution of his pictures; how they grew like plants, the final form implicit in the initial stem; how with foresight and knowledge he added branch to branch, pruning and grafting, until he had reared a great tree deeply rooted in rich soil, strong and sappy, and laden with the fruit of his experiences. It is because the finished work is so plausible and convincing that Hogarth has been charged with having taken his compositions ready-made from real life. No one else ever found such things in real life. They are Hogarth's unique property, containing the mind and soul of the man who made them.

His genius is most comprehensively embodied in the *Election* series of Sir John Soane's Museum, London. These magnificent compositions illustrate the political system of England at the height of its corruption. As illustrations they are still enjoyable, and the world must needs have outlived its greediness before the political methods satirized herein shall have become extinct. But after the topical interest has been exhausted, the pictures carry us beyond politics into a little Hogarthian universe organized in four movements, the beat of humanity accelerated from scene to scene, and culminating in a furious concentration of energy in which the heat of the artist's imagination boils over in a riot of savage forms. There is enough material in any one of these movements for a dozen pictures: plays within plays; design within design—all related and all subordinated to the central action. It is a far cry from the divine magic of Leonardo da Vinci to the Saxon graces of Hogarth, but the Englishman has his own magic—less elevated than the Italian brand but more human, and of magnetic pungency. He gives us the whole complexion of the bourgeois mind, the texture and color of the carnivorous bourgeois soul; he makes us feel the heaving madness of crowds; he presents figures in panoramas and in clusters of threes—a pair of agents offering money to a vulnerable fellow for his vote, the three rogues composing a marvellous unit in which attitude and emotion, form and expressiveness, are one and the same; and in the group serving as the nucleus of the fourth scene he surpasses himself, creating out of a commonplace and essentially brutal episode a design in which rabid men clubbing one another become the engines of superhuman vigor. And in these swarms of peculiar Englishmen, in the fat and the lean, the stately and the gauche, in their faces and in their rough antics, we feel the wise and witty mind of Hogarth, who fashioned them with benevolence and with humor, laying bare their lawless passions and their brute strength but, at the same time, gracing them with the irresistible magic of his personality.

When an artist gives us so much, to ask for more is extortionate. But more there is: the portraits—himself; his sister *Ann*; *Quin the Actor*; *Garrick and Mrs. Garrick*; *Peg Woffington*; *George Arnold*; his six servants; *Lord Lovat*, and many others hardly less distinguished. Where and how, we are moved to wonder, as we stand before these men and women, did Hogarth learn to paint the human head so truthfully, bringing out the quality and condition of the sitter, and while so doing, informing each head with his own qualities of mind and heart? The question is tempting, but out of respect for Hogarth let us refrain from genealogical speculations. Here is the flower of English portraiture, everything that constitutes fine painting: a sure and accurate touch; exquisite color; superb draughtsmanship; variety of design; and each work a new and subtle construction of nature. Hogarth painted the loveliest English women, combining health and intelligence with sweetness of character. And the sweetness is authentic—not the stagey, tailor-made stuff of the Reynolds school. With even greater effectiveness he painted men, rugged, unbending types solid as rocks, yet, thanks to his sense of design, noble and decorative.

His *Lord Lovat*, painted the day before the famous rascal was hanged, is a masterpiece of characterization and powerful modelling. The smiling face is the personification of artful wickedness; the heavy-set body crouches forward and seems to settle down through its own weight into a position of substantial comfort; the figure is as corporeal as a piece of sculpture, yet flexible and meaty,—the overnourished Englishman in all his stodginess. And as a bravura piece, he painted *The Shrimp Girl*, his most popular work, a thing so dazzling and skilful, that

MEMOIRS

Hogarth: LORD LOVAT.

the French, prostrate in admiration, are almost willing to overlook the starving soldiers and fops for the sake of this delicious performance.

Since we have agreed to call Hogarth a moralist, it is fitting that we conclude our account with a moral of our own, a precept intended for all modern painters, but especially useful to Americans: *Hogarth found art in Gin Lane and Beer Street.*

BLAKE

William Blake died in London a hundred years ago, and was buried together with three other paupers in a grave which to this day has remained without an identification stone. He died as he had lived, in obscurity, totally indifferent to temporal rewards, and in his last illness, expressing his indifference with characteristic pride:

"I should be sorry if I had any earthly fame, for whatever natural glory a man has is so much taken from his spiritual glory. I wish to do nothing for profit. I wish to live for art. I am quite happy."

The earthly fame, however, has slowly accumulated without impairing the spiritual glory, and today he is accepted by the land that reared him and by all the world as the foremost, if not the only genuine symbolist produced by the Anglo-Saxon race. His fame has grown in three directions: first, he was hailed by Swinburne, Rossetti and Yeats as the founder of the romantic movement in English poetry; next, with Bernard Shaw as trumpeter, he was given the title of artist-philosopher, to separate him from and also to shame the British sheep who go in for art because it is the thing to do and cultivate letters as a belletristic game of style; and finally, with the turn of the century, a sect of radical painters generally designated as Expressionists, discovering in him a symbolical affinity, spread his artistic claims far and wide, and by preaching the doctrine of intuitive knowledge and individual freedom as opposed to traditional authority, opened the way to a more liberal understanding of his designs. Like El Greco, he is now one of the prophets of Modernism, an object of worship among cults and amateurs, and in consequence, his most delirious obsessions are put forward as eternal truths, and valued more highly than his sanest utterances. And incidentally, he is the sport of collectors, his colored drawings for Dante's "Divine Comedy," made shortly before his death for practically nothing, recently selling for £7665 at Christie's.

Blake was a born visionary. At the age of four he saw God's face against the window, and turned away in terror, this being his first experience with the supernatural. When still a child he came upon a flock of angels sitting among the boughs of a tree; and one summer day met Ezekiel in an open field, "and was beaten by his mother for bringing home so unlikely a story." His father, a poor hosier and a Swedenborgian but a man of some discernment, approved of his son's imaginative bent and would have had him study painting, but the boy protested that the heavy premium would be too great a burden on the family—there were five children in all—and as the next best thing took up engraving. His apprenticeship was hard and long, lasting seven years, but in time he became a master craftsman, inventing new processes of reproduction, his relief-etching, for example, which still puzzles the experts.

At twenty-five, he married the daughter of a market gardener and set up housekeeping in Leicester Square. His wife, Catherine, was illiterate, signing the register with her mark, but under Blake's teaching learned to read and write, to copy his manuscripts, color his illuminated books, and even to see visions. By the unanimous consent of all married artists, she has gone into history as "the perfect wife." To his great sorrow she bore him no children, but Yeats forgives her in these words: "She repaid her husband for the lack of childish voices by a love that knew no limit and a friendship that knew no flaw. In the day she would often take long walks with him, thirty miles at a stretch being no unusual distance, and having dined at a wayside inn, return under the light of the stars; and often at night, when the presences bade him get up from his bed and write, she would sit beside him, holding his hand." Sometimes her devotion was sorely tried but she did not complain. When one of his memorable fancies bade them undress and sit in the back garden as Adam and Eve, she complied willingly; and thus, naked and unashamed, they were tempted by Satan.

Save for three years at Felpham, a little village which seemed to him "entirely beautiful, beloved of God and of the spirits" until the worldliness of his patron made it unbearable, Blake's whole life was passed in London. It was a noble, and leaving out an interval of dark unproductiveness, a happy life. He wrote lyrics—the purest verbal imagery that ever came out of England. Listen to this, a song *To the Evening Star*:

Thou fair-haired angel of the Evening,
Now, whilst the sun rests on the mountains, light
Thy bright torch of love: thy radiant crown
Put on, and smile upon our evening bed!
Smile on our loves: and, while thou drawest the
Blue curtains of the sky, scatter thy silver dew
On every flower that shuts its sweet eyes
In timely sleep. Let thy west wind sleep on
The lake: speak silence with thy glimmering eyes,
And wash the dusk with silver.

He engraved, printed, decorated, illuminated and bound his own books—justly described as "the most wonderful books ever made by one hand"; he composed vast prophecies that nobody read, or reading, understood; six or seven epics as long as Homer and twenty tragedies as long as Macbeth; for a livelihood he was dependent on his illustrations for old and new books—Job, Milton, Gray and Cowper—and on his woodcuts and commercial engravings. It was a thin living he got from his hard and unremitting toil; his art, if it was known at all, was an enigma and a nightmare to a public nursed by fashionable face-painters. And besides, Blake was a poor business man, misled by patrons and cheated by collectors.

At times he lived on ten shillings a week in a flat of two rooms—in the same flat for seventeen years. But surroundings mattered little to one who was, as Catherine Blake said, "incessantly away in Paradise." He was childlike and gentle, though bursting, once in a while, into irascibility at some scoundrel who had tricked him; at Reynolds, his arch-enemy; at the misery of the London into which he returned after his wanderings in the Paradise of his imagination. He loved his wife and a handful of friends, children and green meadows; he loved his work, his explorations into the spirit world, and the relaxing joys of fine craftsmanship. He did not expect riches from an art that was a vehement denial of every canon of popular taste; nor did he sit and whine over the failure of the world to recognize his genius. He chose deliberately to trust his visions and took the consequences. His work brought him the rewards he desired most; day in and day out he labored at his creative business, running downstairs periodically to fetch a pot of beer from a neighboring public house.

Blake is perhaps the oddest figure in the history of art, assuredly the least conventional. He had in one compartment of his brain a mind of phenomenal lucidity—the power to see far into the soul and to see clearly—to condense in a single trenchant sentence truths that have occupied thinking men since the dawn of time; to express himself in prose, verse, or line with crystalline intelligibility; the other half of him was teeming with fanatical stuff, with mystic dreams and theosophical fragments which he spun out into the volumes comprising his *Prophetic Books*. He has been called mad, but madness is too cheap an indictment to fling at the opaque side of genius. He was a man of infinite wisdom, conducting his daily life, on the whole, with fine sanity and with something of Rembrandt's honest acceptance of his anomalous position in art; and it may be that ultimately the cabbalistic elements of his art will prove to be of profoundest value to humanity. But of this I am doubtful. Those temperamentally closest to him—interpreters of the occult and initiates into the mysteries of the oversoul—have forged no key to his

Blake: WHEN THE MORNING STARS SANG TOGETHER.

(*Courtesy of the Metropolitan Museum of Art*)

world beyond the world, a life more real to him than his beef-and-beer existence as engraver and print seller. There have been many attempts to unlock the door, most of them esoteric or silly, one or two, notably S. Foster Damon's *Philosophy and Symbols*, written with a cool head; but all these, I find, are more mysterious than the subjects to be explained. And for an obvious cause: Blake, the transcendentalist, dealt with things rarely visualized, and his symbols are too remote from the normal moods of man to carry any meaning to any one incapable of hallucinations. There is no better evidence of the cryptic nature of his thought than the fact that he could arrange the pages of the *Prophetic Books* in various sequences, the order making no difference to his own sense of continuity.

It is hard to reduce his ideas to plain speech. The art of his own day he denounced as violently as Hogarth had denounced it, and fundamentally on the same grounds, holding that Reynolds and Gainsborough were literal copyists of lifeless corporeality—"the blot and blur method of imitation," he termed it; he attacked the sources of their methods and condemned in wholesale fashion all Venetian and Flemish painting, though unfamiliar with the best work of either school. He said, "A man puts a model before him, and paints it so neat as to make it a deception. Now I ask any man of sense, is that art?" Again: "No man of sense ever supposes that copying from nature is the art of painting. If the art is no more than this, it is no better than any other manual labor; anybody may do it, and the fool often will do it best, as it is a work of no mind."

Certainly this is plain enough. But Blake carried his ideas much further than Hogarth would have allowed; beyond the objective world into a region of inflammable abstractions. With the audacity of supreme conviction he hurled the lightning of his visions against the giant corpus of art erected by the Italians, Rubens and Rembrandt, and fancied he had destroyed it. He believed in inspiration unreservedly—inspiration as the act of divine revelation. He denied absolutely the value of referring to the ordinary business of life for artistic material. "Nature," he exclaimed, "is the work of the devil! Is it not reasonable to suppose that one can create by the workings of the mind forms stronger, clearer and more moving than anything produced by nature? If not, what is the imagination for? And what, in heaven's name, is the use of art?"

Imagination and intellect, passion and inspiration—the terms are interchangeable. These induce the active, the creative state. To the opposite condition he gives the name of reason, identifying it with the dull, the dead, and the natural. Better evil that is active, than good that is mechanical and non-productive. Imagination, or passion, is the sixth or spiritual sense; spirits are organized men; the body of God the only reality. Far from curbing our passions, he advocates that we should be mastered by them, taking care, of course, to be mastered by the noblest passions—Mr. Shaw's philosophy in a nutshell. Work up the imagination to the state of vision; transcribe the vision; and behold the true divinity of art! This, needless to say, is mystic doctrine. We might set against it the practices of a hundred realists, or blast it to pieces with the dogmas of Behaviorism, but to what end? The concrete expression remains intact. For Blake's visions, unlike the vague and dreary effusions of most mystics, are clear-cut and carefully put together, "the indefinite," he said, "being circumcised away by a firm and determinate outline," and more powerful than things seen with the naked eye. Do you doubt it? Then look at his *Job* and his *Dante* and be converted to his system. "I labor day and night," he wrote, "that enthusiasm and life may not cease. I must create a system, or be enslaved by another man's. My business is to create."

Thus, in the rising industrialism of the England of Farmer George, Blake became a tempestuous solitary apart from all tradition. Undoubtedly he had some knowledge of primitive forms, particularly the Byzantine—he was remembered by the print-sellers as "the little connoisseur"—but of the art from which he was directly descended, not temporally but intrinsically, the iconography of Babylonia and Assyria, he was completely ignorant. But a man does not build form out of nothingness. He grasped this commonsense fact and spoke of it with penetration: "Form and substance are one—an original invention cannot exist without execution organized, delineated and articulated—man can only compare and judge of what he has already perceived." Early in life he learned to regard art, not as a stimulus to erotic sensations, but as a medium for visionary truth; and it was second nature for him to look within himself and to express his ideas in symbolical language. As a poet he was extraordinarily sensitive to the phenomenal world; but as a painter he remained sublimely aloof from external motifs, and drew his inspiration from the subjective materials tormenting his soothsayer's brain.

His art, like its ancient Babylonian prototype, is essentially anthropomorphic: he delineated God and the angels and ordered heaven and earth in a living cosmography. But he seldom went directly to life, that is to say, he did not "work from nature" and used no models for his figures. At war with prevailing tendencies, he traveled his own road, picking up figures and attitudes where he could find them, out of the Gothic tombs of Westminster Abbey, out of Michael Angelo, Raphael, and the old engravers, and investing his trees and rocks with curiously human attributes. In due course he had invented his own representational devices, casting aside the fancifulness of youth and clarifying his visions, and his forms took their place in a new system which to him was the true reality of art. He employed the same types over and over again as hieroglyphs; turning the world into an arcanum in which physical life was transubstantiated into his own conceptions—fiends, angels, singing stars, and illimitable oceans, all brought together to personify the ecstasies of the spirit.

Since art is based upon experience, most painters, and indeed the very greatest, have had to refer continually to nature in order to vitalize their forms and to prevent their knowledge from lapsing into an academic method. Without formal knowledge and refreshing relations with the objective world, art leads exactly where Blake and the modern Expressionists have taken it—to symbolism, and most symbolists are worthless. Blake is one of the rare exceptions. His visions happened to be so tremendously intense and creative that physical shapes—friends, enemies, animals, and what-not—and figurative impressions from old prints, were reconstructed by his imagination and projected into the world again as ghosts or "presences"; and these presences were vivid and embodied—he seemed actually to recognize them as the ordinary man his fellow creatures, and to see in them messengers of divine wisdom or wrath—and when he came to portray them, they trooped before his eyes as "spiritual models," so he insisted, and he held them fast in hard, wiry outlines.

In the main his labors were applied to literary texts, but the text was incorporated with the design and enforced by minutely consistent adornment. His pictures therefore are exemplifications of mystical states rather than illustrations, the poetic side of his genius lending impressiveness to his drawing. Light-and-shade painting he abhorred, and all portraiture which he maintained was the opposite of the spiritual. For Titian he had only the harshest criticism, arguing that he was a sensual copyist, that "his men were made of leather, his women of chalk"; and Rembrandt, he said, evaded the issue in a fog of chiaroscuro.

He lived, as he put it, in "the flat world of the imagination," and his designs have the flatness of the Eastern masters, but they are, in the light of aesthetic analysis, magnificently constructed. He cared little for the human form as such, and his knowledge of artistic anatomy amounted to almost nothing; his figures bear a superficial resemblance to Renaissance draughtsmanship, but taken from their context are no more than stock forms—lay figures drawn from memory, and poorly drawn. An engraver by training, he adhered to the "determinate outline," and while he relieved the vacancy of his forms by delicately toned washes of luminous color, he had no skill at modelling. I mention these things, not as deficiencies, for he triumphed over them one and all, but to show that in spite of his meagre equipment, he completely realized his conceptions and delivered his dreams with amazing certainty and precision.

Writing and painting incessantly, and often when his mind was far from its moorings, Blake produced a quantity of meaningless exercises: fatuous drawings such as the *Ghost of a Flea*, eccentricities no better than the nonsensical flights of queer children; and long prophecies dangerously close to the drivel of table-rappers and psychic charlatans. In his most fortunate moods he is sublime, his mind clear and rational, his memorable fancies issuing processionally, and guided by a firm hand into graphic order. He had no formula, no science, and no background—his sense of harmony was original and instinctive. His best designs are flawless: nothing is discrete or superfluous; the figures are secure, perfectly related and supremely appropriate. That they shrink considerably when compared with the monumental art he condemned does not rob them of their perfection: they are not wall decorations, but illustrations conceived as such and intended for the pages of books. He knew the value of the long, flowing frieze to establish a rhythmical sweep of line, and how to balance his waving sequences with a giant oak, a stretch of ocean or a screaming god. His pictures are never static; the forms glide and circulate—sometimes in a complex universe of monsters with flying arms, and legions of angels; again in a little woodcut of a shepherd watching his flock. In either case we are conscious of the reality of his strange world, are held by the striking energy of his forms, drawn into his fervent moods—his moods of supplication, almighty wrath, celestial joy, tenderness, freezing terror, dancing mirth, implacable scorn—the overwhelming ecstasies of the spirit.

As is characteristic of Expressionists, Blake was incredibly productive. After his death, one Tatham, a theological ass, devoted two days to the burning of what he considered the inventions of a heretic. More than a hundred volumes! Notwithstanding this villainy, it is probable that his best work has been preserved—certainly we have abundant and glorious evidence of his genius. On the strength of the *Job* illustrations alone, he may be called a great designer, but his art, a symbolism of his own making, defies imitation. His work is the crowning accomplishment of isolated conviction. Blake came of no school and left no disciples.

FACE-PAINTERS AND ARTISTS

It is recorded that a functionary with more courage than discretion once endeavored to interest George III in the paintings of Blake. The King allowed the watercolors to be set before him, looked, and threw up his hands. "Take 'em away!" he shouted. "Take 'em away!" The inability to appreciate Blake does not necessarily imply the want of sense or taste: Farmer George was one of thousands, and there are many of the same mind today. Meier-Graefe, one of the wisest of living writers on art, can see nothing in the English mystic but "the obscene hallucinations of a fever-stricken dwarf obsessed by the figures of Michael Angelo," which, to my way of thinking, is egregious misapprehension. But the stupid and refractory sovereign was as callous to the fine arts as any Philistine churl. His cry against Blake expresses his attitude exactly, "Take 'em away!"—the landscapes of Wilson, Gainsborough, Crome and Constable. Take away everything good—the possessions across the sea; the poetry of the young revolutionaries; everything but the obvious business of portraiture.

Yet the long reign of George III embraces all the great names in the history of British art; and after this astonishing fruition of national genius, there is no more painting of importance. In the second half of the nineteenth century we have the Pre-Raphaelites, earnest men and intelligent, but as artists, sickly and ineffectual—swooners for school-girls; and at present the wholly futile efforts of the Modernists to counteract the tyranny of the Royal Academy. Hogarth, who had still four years to live when George III came to the throne, had laid the foundations for a national art of the amplest proportions; but unhappily, his successors were weaker vessels carried along by the currents of fashion. They followed, perhaps unconsciously, his example in turning to nature for their subjects, but further they were unwilling or unable to go: none seemed to study his pictures, and none had the strength of character to stand uncompromisingly against academic convention. It was easier to play the game according to Van Dyck's rules: to paint the face; dress up the doll, and pocket the fee. Hogarth, in a man's country, had made an art for men; those whom he branded the portrait-manufacturers softened painting into a ladylike affair of modes and artificial graces.

England, despite her wars and her muddle-headed King, was growing rich and arrogant. Plunderers, returning from India laden with gold, became social leaders; profiteers, emerging from the misery of the Industrial Revolution assumed the airs of born aristocrats; politicians made fortunes at the expense of the government just as they do in America today. And having money, the Englishman began to travel. The Grand Tour was invented, and young gentlemen, before settling down to the more serious business of gambling and fox-hunting, carted their tin bathtubs up and down the continent under the protection of the Red Ensign. They acquired a smattering of Italian culture and collected Italian pictures, that is, Venetian painting glorifying the splendor of Adriatic traders. All that was needed to round out their smug routine was a native school of painters who could be counted on to praise and please—to mould the most overbearing face into a mask of refinement and charm. And before long they had called such a school into existence. The Royal Academy was founded, with Reynolds who had, of course, taken the Grand Tour, as first President. Thus the painter was promoted to an official status in society, with set obligations to England, with standards, and all the rest. Scholarships and subventions sent young students to Italy to prepare themselves for Sir Joshua's grand style; the Dilettanti society kept the Italian fires burning at home; and the boom in painting was on.

In fifty years the output of portraits in Great Britain exceeded three centuries of Continental production. Reynolds painted more than 2000; Gainsborough at least 1000; and Romney boasted of 9000 sittings in twenty years, the entries in his notebook reading like this: "Mr. Pitt at 12, Lady Betty Compton at ¼ to 2." And Lady Hamilton at all hours. The brush took the place of the modern camera, but with this difference: the British face-painters aimed not at a close likeness but at effective prettiness. Unquestionably Sir Joshua's great vogue lay in his ability to cover Anglo-Saxon plainness with a veneer of counterfeit dignity. He was so notoriously free with his sitters that Gainsborough, a genuine artist, "wondered that the President had the nerve to send out such faces." Lawrence went mad trying to paint a woman's blushes; and Hoppner, a pupil reports, "frequently remarked that in painting ladies' portraits he used to make as beautiful a face as he could, then give it a likeness to his sitter, working down from this beautiful state till a bystander should cry out, 'O I see a likeness coming!' Whereupon he stopped and never ventured to make it more like."

Prices were comparatively low, Reynolds and Gainsborough charging two to five guineas a head for their first commissions and 75 to 100 for choice things done at the height of their fame. With the court to be served and every family of means clamoring for portraits, a condition arose in art the recurrence of which would cause modern painters to rejoice: the demand was greater than the supply. On the face of it this condition would seem to denote a time of health and legitimate prosperity, but unfortunately, the demand for pictures was based upon a faddish and competitive yearning for attractive furniture rather than upon a spiritual awakening or a disturbance of the sensibilities such as inspired the romantic poets. When only secondary things are required of the artist, it is not likely that the artist will exert himself. The British portrait painters were clever and gifted men whose patent shortcomings should not blind us to their just attainments. They did what was asked of them and did it with the thoroughness we call British. Their purpose was to heighten gentility, to contrive patterns of superiority, to make the Englishman, his wife, and his children—and his mistress too, if he happened to be Lord Nelson—pure and enviable, the most charming people in the world. But saying this, we have exhausted our praise.

Reynolds, the most famous, is a disappointing figure: as a man resentful and disingenuous, as an artist afraid of his natural propensities. His *Discourses*, which must have been a liberal education to his pupils at the Academy, may still be read with profit; they show his veneration for classical art, his knowledge of the Italians; his restless observation. He was ambitious and immensely talented; he sought to discover in Raphael and Michael Angelo principles upon which he might build a lofty structure of his own—the beginnings of a national art in the grand style. "A painter," he said, "should form his rules from pictures rather than from books or precepts. He who has his mind filled with ideas, and his hand made expert by practice, works with ease and readiness, whilst he who would have you believe that he is waiting for the inspirations of genius, is in reality at a loss how to begin." To this Blake replied, "He endeavors in this Discourse to prove that there is no such thing as inspiration, and that any man of plain understanding may, by thieving from others, become a Michael Angelo." But Sir Joshua did not practice what he preached. He debased the Venetians, and Rembrandt whom he publicly aspersed as vulgar; he courted favor as Van Dyck had courted it and his waiting rooms were filled with sitters to whom he doled out samples of "fancy poses." The fancy poses are conspicuous in his paintings, his characters always trying to be something which they emphatically are not—goddesses or kings. His men are faked heroes drawn by rule; his women belong to the feathered tribe. In sum, his work, we feel, is theatrical and insincere when it might, with his equipment, have rivalled the vitality and charm of Hogarth. When he forgot his classical paraphernalia and let himself go, he painted *Dr. Johnson*, a noble characterization and a distinguished study of the human head. Children unhorsed him and brought him down to realities; and impelled him to paint with the ease and readiness he talked of so glibly. His grandiose contraptions are interesting only as social curiosities; his artistic fame reposes on his portraits of children.

The glory of the school is centered in Thomas Gainsborough who did not seek it. For he was a landscape painter without a market. "I'm a landscape painter," he explained, "and yet they will come to me for portraits. I can't paint portraits. Look at that damned arm! I have been at it all the morning and I can't get it right." A self-trained artist with an abiding admiration for Rubens, Van Dyck and Dutch genre, he was lured from the Suffolk lanes which he loved so well into the fashionable circles of Bath and London. He was everything the imperious Sir Joshua was not: a true Bohemian, fond of music and tramp fiddlers, oblivious of the Italians, generous and light-hearted—an enchanting personality. The figure was not his forte and his drawing will not stand close inspection; but he was one of those rare souls whom the polite world takes into its bosom, and to the great discontent of the President of the Academy, he entered the lucrative field of portraiture. As a creator of unadulterated charm, Gainsborough has a place of his own in the history of art. In him the quality is the real thing, neither strained nor mechanically concocted; not the trumped-up prettiness of Romney nor the stilted, quasi-elegance of Reynolds, but the pure and spontaneous emanation of the man's character. Charm is seldom the property of the greatest painters; nor can it be bought by diligence, as his rivals discovered. Many valuable qualities the artist may acquire by forethought and labor—but not charm. To attempt to filch it from the model, when it does not exist in the heart of the painter, is perjury. Hence the difference between Gainsborough and the rest of the school.

In his gay and passionate nature flowed a spring of delicacy which was decidedly feminine; and this feminine trait pervades all his portraits. He was best with women, portraying not only Lady this or that—he was a dead shot at likenesses—but sensitizing the lady with his own fascinating personality. The combination is a picture of irresistible charm. He was withal a splendid executant. Against his inclinations, it was ordained that he

Constable: VIEW OF SUFFOLK.

Metropolitan Museum of Art, New York

should express to perfection the quality which the British prize almost as highly as maritime supremacy. No wonder Gainsborough was as beloved as a prince! No wonder his canvases are coveted by Yankee millionaires who foolishly would obtain by money what has been denied to them by nature!

If the face-painters swam with the tide of fashion, the landscape artists, moved by the same strong impulses that summoned the lyrics of Wordsworth, Coleridge, Shelley and Keats, followed nature—and were utterly neglected. Why they should have been neglected is not altogether clear. Granted that faces are more impressive to the average person than landscape; granted that the social atmosphere was exceptionally favorable to the trade in portraiture; there remains the Englishman's love of nature, a trait so genuine, so distinctive and national, that it should have made him peculiarly receptive to a form of art the appeal of which was essentially poetic. But it is a cruel fact that the nature painters, with the exception of Turner whose father, he confessed, "taught him to lay one penny upon another," were less prosperous than greengrocers, and until Turner, in consequence of Ruskin's majestic praise, was enthroned as the god of light, not more highly regarded. Wilson carried his pictures from door to door like a common peddler; Old Crome, the father of twenty-four children, was a carriage painter; Bonington went to France for recognition; Gainsborough's house in Pall Mall was strewn with landscapes which his vainglorious clients deemed unworthy of his brush; and Constable's wife inherited a little money.

The love of nature will not, in itself, produce artists; it may produce botanists or pedestrian watercolorists; a great scientist like Darwin; a great critic like Ruskin; or Impressionist painters. But in the Englishmen, this love was so intense and intimate, so joyous and unaffected, that it brought them into communion with things they knew best, the glorious rural world which was their birthright. And this love became more than a local devotion: fanned by the rising winds of philosophy, it developed into a cult—with the poets into a pantheistic religion—

and uniting with the contagion spread by Rousseau against the enervating and destructive forces of kings, a panacea for an afflicted civilization. There had been, of course, landscape painters before the British: Poussin and Claude—but they had seen nature from afar: Rubens, the greatest of them all—but Rubens was a whole cosmos; the Dutch—but the men of Holland painted indoors. It was the English who took painting into the open air, under God's—and Ruskin's—great blue sky, who, in peace and freedom, explored the soul of nature, revealing her secret moods and mysteries, her infinite variety and her blessings. The English, painting directly from nature, observing atmospheric vibrations and the fugitive blendings of colors, originated the modern landscape which as it passed through the hands of the French from Corot to Monet, lost its significance as the expression of man's ideas and feelings aroused by and projected into natural forms, and ended in scientific meddling with optical effects.

Richard Wilson, who lived for many years in Italy and returned home to beg and starve, has been named "the father of English landscape," an honor belonging, I think, to Gainsborough. Wilson, a successful portrait painter, under the influence of Claude, turned to landscape—artistically a correct move, but financially disastrous. His pictures witness a calm and reflective, but limited mind—a man of one mood. He has breadth and dignity; his canvases are nicely balanced and cautiously thought out, but the dead atmosphere of archaeology hangs over them. His trees are pasted up; his buildings stage settings. In short, his work lacks vitality. But his influence on the young English nature-lovers was timely and beneficial. An intermediary between French classicism in which natural forms were employed as piles of lumber in the construction of a lifeless mechanism, and outdoor painters inclined, through their training in watercolor to depend too literally on the objects before them, he warned them that a work of art, to afford lasting satisfaction, is not the record of a single impression, however fresh and captivating, but the resolved and deliberated statement of a consistent point of view.

Gainsborough's landscapes are among the most affecting things in British painting. Nature was his first and greatest love, and though his wayward soul was sidetracked into the fashionable art of portraiture, gaining him wealth and renown, and absorbing his best energies, he remained faithful to his first mistress and continued, amid the distractions of London, to sketch from memory the ineffaceable scenes of his early years in Suffolk. Faces and costumes he painted lightly, throwing round them his iridescent charm; nature he painted from his deepest sensibilities, as a true artist under obligations to his most cherished experiences. As a youth, he roved, like the young Shakespeare, the fields and woods, observing for the first time in British painting, not groups of trees and general shapes, but individual forms with all the minutiae of foliage and bladed grass. There was, he said, "no picturesque clump of trees, nor even a single tree of any beauty, no, nor hedgerow, stem, nor stump, in his home that he did not know by heart." Extraordinarily sensitive to the poetry of his native surroundings, he began to paint familiar scenes, not, let us understand, as simple portraits or souvenirs of nature, but as conveyances of the feelings nature had evoked within him. It was hard work and he had no one to help him—nothing but a few Dutch pictures which he saw on the walls of the country houses. But he succeeded, and there is no telling to what eminence he might have traveled had he consecrated his life to landscape. In after years he developed far more facility and more harmonious color, but in the essentials of art—the power to play upon the emotions—he never surpassed his earliest efforts. Weary of his fame and the formalities of his metropolitan establishment he said, "I'm sick of portraits and wish very much to take my viol-da-gamba and walk off to some sweet village, where I can paint landskips and enjoy the fag-end of life in quietness and ease."

One of the first to appreciate him was Constable. "The landscape of Gainsborough," he wrote, "is soothing, tender and affecting. The stillness of noon, the depths of twilight and the dews and pearls of the morning, are all to be found in the canvases of this most benevolent and kindhearted man. On looking at them, we find tears in our eyes and know not what brings them. The lovely haunts of the solitary shepherd—the return of the rustic with his bundle of wood—the darksome lane or dell—the sweet little cottage girl at the spring with her pitcher—were the things he delighted to paint, and which he painted with exquisite refinement."

The tears that welled, Constable knew not how, were probably drawn by the melancholy tone of the landscapes, the romantic loneliness of Gainsborough which those attracted by the brightness of his portraits had not suspected. Always the pathos of the lonely soul come home, after his frolics and dissipations, to secret converse with his faithful mistress. Deep twilight in the shadows; consoling tranquillity in the trees. Not the dramatic harmonies of Rubens—the hurryings of storms; the pull and toss of heroic winds and clouds; the whole world swimming in a golden harvest—but a chord of sadness. This mood Gainsborough conveys with the subtlest art. His landscapes touch the emotions with the voice of a stringed instrument. The key is low, the volume slender but the tone is perfect and the composition stainless. Natural colors he changes to browns, olives, and silver-greys; his shadows are dark; his trees enclose a winding road or a nook in which he places a couple of woodmen or a few rustics in a cart. His world, compared to that of Rubens, is only a little corner of nature, but more lyrical and delicate, and within its range, as finely constructed; nature reshaped; colors modified; trees and earth conjoined—the mood restrained and gentle—a melody that soothes the spirit.

For Constable I have an affection that goes back to my earliest recollections. In the first years of my childhood, there hung in the hall of my father's house a large steel-engraving of *The Cornfield*. Often, in the long hot summers of the Middle West, I used to lie on the floor, gazing for hours into this English landscape, carried from the dry and burning world around me into a vista of blessed coolness, thick verdure, dampness, and everlasting peace. I lived in that picture. To me it was more beautiful than a dream: the boy, flat on the ground drinking from a running brook; the sheep dog waiting patiently with turned head; the ambling flock; the old silent trees; the fat clouds reeking moisture. But the picture sometimes puzzled me. Where was the cornfield? Corn, as I knew it, grew tall and rank in the Spring, and then was shrivelled into rows of mummies by the hot winds of late July. I did not understand the British use of the word, and it would never have crossed my mind to associate the small stretch of grain running back from the center of the landscape with a wheat field. My State was famous for wheat: yellow seas of it surrounding the town. But there were no trees in Kansas wheat. And so the patch of corn in the coarsely engraved print I took to be a broad stream of water flowing quietly uphill, and never bothered my head more.

Some years later, when I went to London to study pictures, I saw *The Cornfield* and many others by Constable, and my first impressions were confirmed. The absolute repose, the ineffable calm of his canvases, was not an ambiguous languor, but a strong and positive quality which I had never dreamed of in my childish reveries. In his grasp of the stable, one might almost say formidable, repose that man feels in the presence of nature, and in communicating the spiritual contentment induced by companionship with nature, in his day a form of worship, Constable is the master of the English school. This solid tranquillity was the life of the man. When he lived there were many great men in England, but none other whose brilliancy was not blemished by aberrations or lurid egoism.

A miller's son, he was himself a miller for a while, and thereafter a painter. His road to fame was long, but his faith in nature and in himself, and the help of his intelligent and kindly wife sustained him throughout. His patience was infinite; he worked and waited and eventually enjoyed all that the wise and healthy man requires. He waited five years for the woman he loved; fifteen or more before he had dug his way through Claude, Gainsborough, Rubens and the Dutch, to the roots of his own genius; and such as bought his pictures came after his wife's legacy had made patrons unnecessary. In the *Salon of 1824*, in Paris, his pictures were the sensation; Delacroix hailed him as "the father of modern landscape," and Gautier raved sweetly; but during this portentous event he stayed at home and painted. He attended a royal banquet, watched the strutting Reynolds, and a pair of actors—Lord Byron and Mrs. Siddons—shook his head, and returned to the country. But he bore no one envy or ill-will. His praise of his fellow-painters was as generous as it was just; and when he addressed himself to analytical problems, he wrote the best art criticism of the time. From his biographer, Leslie, we might easily infer that he was too good to live, an impression which has been corrected by recent investigations. His spiritual serenity was leavened by a strain of Saxon coarseness; he was given to over-eating and loose conversation; and when the occasion warranted it, defended his pictures against the curt journalists with unexpected and stinging sarcasms.

Constable's contribution to painting is twofold—poetic and scientific. In the first he has been overshadowed by the more varied and powerful art of Turner. His imagination was active within a small sphere; he was habitually concerned with a single aspect of nature, or rather with the same terrain used again and again to illumine an invariable experience. Working and reworking a fixed theme, he frequently painted when his inspiration was napping, and produced not the poetry he intended but drowsy prose. His aim was to build landscapes as scientifically charted as those of Claude and Rubens, but to enhance their vividness and intimacy by a more searching scrutiny of natural forms. In other words, to put as much observation as possible in a picture without reproducing the scene that lay before him. He was too intelligent an artist to suppose that because a certain view of Suffolk had stirred his inmost feelings, he could arouse the same feelings in others by the simple process of copying what he had, in one circumstance, observed.

The effect of nature, at any given moment, was the effect on a man of many experiences, a poetic mind enriched by countless imaginings and sharpened by a thousand reflections. He

Turner: SELF-PORTRAIT.

Private Collection, London

must, therefore, put himself in the picture, with the sum-total of his emotions interwoven to carry the fullness of his poetic soul. This may sound like quibbling, but if it were not so, why then the differences between Constable and Gainsborough? Both were artists; both lived in Suffolk and painted the same face of the world; and yet each remade nature after his heart's desire.

Constable's naturalism has provoked much controversy, his opponents preferring against him the charge of methodical imitation, his admirers, insisting on his "art to conceal art," that his landscape "with its marvellous combinations of objective truth and aesthetic unity, requires a finer instinct for selection, for seizing upon the things which tell and neglecting those which do not, and for design, both at large and in detail, than anything carried out on more idealistic lines." The truth, I think, lies somewhere between the two extremes. That he is much closer to nature than his predecessors no one would care to dispute. He was the first to paint in the open air, to restore the color of grass from the brown of an old Cremona fiddle to its natural green, the first to paint the wetness of water; he gives us the freshness, the sparkle, the shimmering richness of the outdoor world; his sky is not a background but an enveloping atmosphere of light and color; his clouds move; before his canvases we seem to be in the presence of nature herself, and not looking at a picture of nature. It may be objected that such matters are not intrinsically artistic. They are not. But Constable did not stop with objective accuracy—the word science was always on his lips. By science he meant construction, architectural building; he planned his effects as systematically as his teachers had planned their own, adding observation and direct painting to knowledge gained from Rubens and Claude. To say that he is more literal and less creative than Rubens or Turner is not to declaim against his methods or his accomplishment: he painted what it was in him to paint without stammering, always with freedom, sometimes with power.

Constable's influence, for the most part, has been scientific, and for the most part, French. The British did not need him;

to the young Romantics of France he introduced a method of painting with which to kill the lingering disease of antiquity. The method was Impressionism: he flooded his landscape with natural light and air; he used bright color—but his color, I am compelled to report, has lost its original brilliancy—and divided his tones, which means that what appears at a distance to be a patch of vivid green, is at close range, a collection of separate tones of green, laid on, smear by the side of smear, with a palette knife; and he took his easel into the country, bringing to landscape more of nature and less of mind. These are commonplaces today, but to the men of 1824, they were revolutionary.

TURNER

Turner was a professional artist at the age of ten, an excellent draughtsman at twelve; when, in his fourteenth year, he was admitted to the classes of Reynolds, he had already studied with seven masters, earning his way from the proceeds of drawings exposed in the shop windows of Maiden Lane; at fifteen he was an exhibiting painter at the Royal Academy; at eighteen an independent artist with a studio of his own; he was famous at twenty-five, an R. A. at twenty-seven; during his three score years of strenuous and indefatigable artistry, he traveled, mostly on foot, twenty-five miles a day, rain or shine, over a large part of the British Isles and Western Europe, exploring the face of the earth, the heavens above the earth, and the swathing atmosphere—the stratified growth of mountains, the tenacious vegetation, the interfering work of man, the anatomy of the sea and the architecture of the clouds, the lives of rivers and tides, storms, sunsets, splendor and decay—with the eye of a naturalist and the soul of an artist.

Endowed with the constitution of an ox and a nervous system that nothing could derange; fortified with intellect, a lusty animal satisfaction in labor and in living, and an unparalleled capacity for new experiences, he was the most completely educated man who ever addressed himself to the art of landscape.

His working knowledge of natural forms was as comprehensive as Michael Angelo's knowledge of the human figure, and in the amount of work done he surpasses all other painters, not excepting Rubens. For his work, every stroke and stain of it, was done by himself alone, and he toiled while others slept. Besides a fortune of 140,000 pounds he left 2000 finished pictures and 19,000 drawings, sketches and watercolors. And these last, take notice, are not the collected débris of incorrigible industry, but drawings full of purpose and meaning, there being among them hardly one that does not attest an immensely acute observation painstakingly directed to an artistic end. Think these things over. Then examine the fruits of his toil, the second and third best as well as the best, for Turner must be received as a whole, and at his poorest, contains more nourishment than most men at their best; take Ruskin's multitudinous apology with as much salt as you like; bring on your specialists—your proud Vergilian echoes, your little Dutch domestics, your dabblers in smug repose, your dealers in transitory impressions and granulated scenery; set them against this one man and try to measure the difference between painters who have looked at nature through a peep-hole, and a master of the elements, between the makers of single scenes and the creator of a whole drama.

Turner was secretive and mysterious, holding that his private life was his own business, and guarding it with elaborate artifices. Nobody ever saw him paint; nobody knew where he lived; and when, at last, overborne by work and illness, he was tracked down to his lair, the world marvelled at his life, as it had marvelled at his canvases, and could not understand why such a man, rich beyond telling, and infinitely sensitive beneath his hard exterior, should have chosen to live in squalor. The squalor was fortuitous. He was born in ugliness, and the ugliness of personal negligence, grime and disorder clung to him like an incurable disease. As his fame increased, his ambitions grew proportionately, and he worked incessantly, to the abandonment of all standards of decency and the amenities of the social life into which, as a distinguished figure, he was obliged occasionally to participate. He hoarded money as he hoarded his pictures, with the cupidity of a miser, but he had no use for riches. When he might have had luxury and the homage of fashionable admirers, he lived meanly and alone, in sordid quarters that would have been death to a man of less will and purpose. His knowledge piled up; his imagination took wings; his vision broke terrestrial bonds; step by step he removed himself from realistic contemplation, soaring in his dreams to the sun which, he said, was God. No other man ever surrendered so unconditionally to art. Turner severed all social ties and steered away from all diversions and conventional obligations, protecting his ecstasies and his fiery dreams by a barrier of sordidness. As to what happened on the other side of the barrier, he kept silent, mystifying the curious and offending the polite, knowing that the wise would gain access by way of his pictures.

His devious career contains much that has not been and probably never will be satisfactorily straightened out, but the trend of it is clear enough. He was born in Maiden Lane, April 23, 1775, the son of a barber. The circumstances of his birth and childhood were ever a source of shame and humiliation, shaming him into secrecy and inordinate rivalry where rivalry was uncalled-for, humiliating him because, being proud and not too personable, sensitive to everything noble and poetic and on the reverse side, tough and sensual, he felt, we may say absurdly, that his mind and art—and he had no doubts of the greatness of either—could never atone for his inferior origin. In a land where gentility counts for more than attainment, the Cockney in him would not down. His mother was a masculine type, vicious and ungovernable, and subject to spells of insanity. When death charitably disposed of her, there were no lamentations. Turner never mentioned her to a living soul. His father was no better and no worse than most barbers, windy, greedy, and eager to advance his son's education when he discovered that the boy could make money by drawing. "Dad never praised me for anything except saving a halfpenny," Turner once remarked. If the painter had little affection for his gossipy sire, he had loyalty and kindness, taking a house in the country when the barber's trade was ruined by the powder tax, and allowing the old man to potter about as he pleased. Here his father stretched and varnished canvases, dug in the garden, and served as watch dog and man of all work. Every morning he came to London in a market gardener's cart to save the price of a carriage, tipping the driver a glass of gin.

The inheritance was low and mortifying, the environment confused and far from lovely, but Turner developed swiftly, resourceful from childhood and remarkably energetic. His schooling was brief but sufficient. Until lately it was commonly believed that he was an ignoramous in matters outside of art, so poorly trained and so dull of wit that he could not write his own language. Armstrong, his most trustworthy biographer, disproves this notion, adducing letters to show that Turner, at least in early life, expressed himself correctly, with reasonable fluency, and with fewer mistakes in spelling than Reynolds committed, and that he was better educated than the average youth of his station. It is true that he read little—he had more important things to do—but he had the Englishman's superstitious reverence for the classical authors, knew them in translation, and was strongly influenced by them. It is also true that words were uncertain and cumbrous instruments for his rapid thoughts, and as time went on, he ceased to use them, thinking almost entirely in images. It was then that he shed his command of English like a wornout garment, and writing, when he attempted it, became hopelessly inexpressive. All his life he had the habit of throwing overboard superfluous cargo, deciding values by experience and not by precedent.

Culturally, he remained the son of a barber, but his education in the true meaning of the term was gigantic. His interest in nature is scarcely to be described: it was omniverous and encyclopaedic, reborn each day, a mingling of scientific curiosity and poetic contemplation. He never counted the cost of labor, or regretted the hardships imposed upon him by his ambitions. There was always some new thing in the world to hearten him, some phenomenon to be investigated. One who knew him remembers an instance of his self-absorption. This friend, strolling along the Embankment of the Thames, encountered "a little Jewish-nosed man in an ill-cut, brown tail-coat, striped waistcoat and enormous frilled shirt, with feet and hands notably small," squatting on his heels in the sand, and peering into the water with a fixity of attention that betokened an unbalanced mind. For a full half-hour the little man crouched there immovable, arose, and was recognized as the great Turner. He explained that he was observing the progress of the tide and the action of waves on the sand!

This astounding spirit of inquiry came out in the first years of his childhood, and he attached himself ardently to the life of London, the foul and commercial, the picturesque and haunting. Three minutes from his father's shop ran the great River. He was always near it or upon it. He saw the endless warehouses and factories, the smoke drifting over it; the sooty fogs; the bridges and boats, and the backwash of wretched men and women crushed by the pestilent breath of coal and steam. He saw the watermen and barges, fishmongers and ships of all denominations—freighters laden with exotic wares, men-of-war in full dress. As often as he could steal aboard, he rode down to the sea in ships, got the hang of them, mastered them, every rope and spar, made himself a sailor. An illness sent him into the country to live with an aunt, and with the same insatiable interest, he observed English parks and meadows. In these years of learning and wondering, he thought of his environment as neither beautiful nor ugly, observing it with an eye for the structure and shapes of things and their effect upon man.

At the same time he was learning to draw; first, coloring engravings for fourpence a plate, after his eleventh year with a number of teachers who profited him but little. At the Royal Academy he drew from the nude, and drew exceedingly well, but his genius, from the beginning, was at home in landscape, and on the sea, and in the course of time, he seemed to forget the structure of the human figure, as he forgot the structure of the language of words. His facility was not more prodigious than his industry, his patience and his memory. Ruskin describes a watercolor of a man-of-war taking in stores, a drawing about 16 inches by 11 and fully finished. "The hull of a first-rate occupies nearly one half of the picture on the right, her bows towards the spectator, seen in sharp perspective from stem to stern, with all her port-holes, guns, anchors, and lower rigging elaborately detailed; there are two other ships of the line in the middle distance, drawn with equal precision; a noble breezy sea dancing against their broad bows, full of delicate drawing in its waves; a store-ship beneath the hull of the larger vessel, and several other boats, and a complicated cloudy sky. It might appear," Ruskin adds, "no small exertion of mind to draw the detail of all this shipping down to the smallest ropes, from memory, in the drawing room of a mansion in the middle of Yorkshire, even if considerable time had been given to the effort. But Turner took a piece of blank paper one morning after breakfast, outlined the ships and finished the drawing in three hours."

His first painting was in watercolor, a medium which, in its effects of transparency and purity of tone, the English may be said to have invented, and which Turner practiced inveterately, proving all its capacities, and developing its resources with incomparable dexterity and imagination. In comparison with his work, other watercolors appear to us as vague or flashy impressions or tinted topography. I have heard it said that he has his superiors—Constable and Cézanne to name but two—but the efforts of these men, brilliant in the one, experimental in the other, are, after all, only sketches. Turner produced pictures in watercolor, complete works of art, not merely provocative studies. He learned the medium from Girtin, a heavy-drinking, consumptive youth, who died at twenty-nine, already a master. Turner spoke of him with ironic sympathy. "If Tom Girtin had lived I should have starved. I never in my life made drawings like his—I would at any time have given one of my fingers to have done as well."

From his fifteenth to his twenty-fifth year he did an endless amount of topographical hacking, washing in fancy backgrounds for architectural designs, drawing recognizable portraits of estates, cathedrals, castles and manor houses for the albums and walls of country gentlemen. When asked if he did not regret those years of drudgery, he replied, "Why should I? What could have been better training?" During this period he made frequent walking tours through England and the lake district of the North, alone or with his friend Girtin, sketching continually, and studying rural life as hungrily as he had studied shipping and the sea. He was a born tramp. With his luggage in a handkerchief at the end of a stick, he roamed and worked. Every day a new landscape, new vistas of rain and cloud and sunlight, more knowledge of the natural world. Nothing upset him. He could eat anything, sleep anywhere, work in all kinds of weather. If there was no water at hand, he spat in his powdered colors and made the best of it. But he insisted on absolute privacy while painting, though quite willing to spy upon others if he thought he might learn from them. Before sitting down to draw, he hunted out a spot near a convenient ditch, and the moment intruders appeared, dropped out of sight. He would devote hours to a study; and having satisfied himself of the way in which leaves unfold or light breaks through the morning mist, would double the paper twice and stuff it into his pocket for future reference. Towards the end of the century we find him, with Girtin again, spending his evenings with Dr. Monro, one of the King's physicians and patron of the arts, at whose house he copied, for money, engravings of the Old Masters, and discussed and studied his forerunners in landscape, particularly Claude. His reputation was now established: he was an Associate of the Academy, confining his exhibits to oil-paintings; a celebrity with vast ambitions at an age when most young men are trying to decide what to do with themselves.

The year 1800 marks the beginning of his bewildering program which, at its completion, had carried him through all the prospects of the earth and the sea, into experiences, lyrical and tempestuous, with the more prevalent operations of nature, into mythology and the Old Testament, an invader and the conqueror of the special provinces of the founders of landscape, and finally, away from the objective world into a realm which none before him had ever penetrated. Turner from 1800 to 1835 is so fecund and diversified, so constantly in motion, that we can only indicate the general lines of his attack. First, affected by everything and in possession of unprecedented knowledge of nature, he must learn to compose his materials, and it was not, therefore, irrational for him to turn to his predecessors for help. Such is the way of all painters. There has been too much loose talk about his competitive spirit. In some respects it was absurd—the continuation of his persistent battle to remove all obstacles from his route—and in his duels with Rembrandt and Titian he was badly beaten. But on the whole, it was the legitimate challenge of a greater mind. He admired Vandevelde, but the Dutchman was limited and passionless. "I know more about the sea," Turner told himself. "I know what waves do to ships and what storms and ships do to men. I have taken in more and I have more to give out." Soon he had outdistanced the Dutch.

There was not an iota of jealousy in his rivalries. "My dear Sir," he once said to Ruskin, "if you only knew how difficult it is to paint even a decent picture, you would not say the severe things you do of those who fail." His affection for Wilson and Gainsborough moved him, a taciturn soul, to the warmest praise—praise based on understanding; but as an artist, a friendly adversary, he matched the antique blandness of the first and the gentle melancholy of the second, with works of dramatic force and fatalistic grandeur. It was Claude who goaded him to protracted, unnecessary and, sometimes, unscrupulous competition. The Frenchman, in Ruskin's words, "first set the pictorial sun in the pictorial heaven," and Turner worshipped the sun. For years he painted large classical machines, and least of all was he fitted for such things—a golden sunlight falling on a litter of second-hand ruins; and it was not until he had returned to his own sun and his own heaven that he outshone the Latin baker.

Thus it happened that while he was painting masterpieces of a more or less realistic character—landscape and the sea in which the strength of nature, as he had experienced it, animates simple things dark in tone, but firmly composed—such pictures as *Calais Pier, The Shipwreck, The Frosty Morning* and *Bligh Sand*, he was also confounding the public with huge and riotous fantasies: Old Testament melodramas, inspired by Poussin; and in emulation of Claude, mythological panoramas clogged with details and properties interesting in themselves but without order or continuity. Slowly the two tendencies began to coalesce. After a visit to Italy the darkness went out of his pictures. Retaining the solid structure of the natural world, he set out to transform it with the iridescence of light and color. The change is conspicuous in the *Bay of Baiae*, exhibited in 1823; and six years later bursts out in gorgeous array in the famous *Ulysses Deriding Polyphemus*, wherein design prepared with the utmost care and deliberation binds together sea and land, ships and sky, in a fiery atmosphere of gold and scarlet shot with blue.

From 1807 to 1819 he was busy with *Liber Studiorum,* a collection of drawings, etchings and mezzotints conceived in his irrepressible passion to conquer Claude Lorrain. In this case the rivalry was hardly to his credit: Claude's *Liber Veritatis* was merely a bundle of incomplete sketches compiled after his death as an index to the classification of his paintings, whereas Turner's book executed in the years of his fullest vigor, was an independent project calculated to display, in black and white, and in sequence, the immensity of his powers as a landscape artist. The work comprises a hundred illustrations, only seventy of which were published, the rest remaining in various states of incompletion. Turner made all the designs—the layouts—in sepia and turned them over to the engravers whose labors he supervised with an eagle eye. He changed his assistants frequently, partly because of the hard bargains he drove, partly because of his dubious notions of business ethics. In a pinch he worked through all the processes himself, etching and mezzotinting in masterly style. To those who prefer the early Turner—

and they are increasing in number—the great draughtsman, the architect of all the emotions aroused by nature in man, from lyrical delight to tragic shame and humiliation—*Liber Studiorum* epitomizes the best that he had to give.

His life during these years, industry aside, was shapeless and erratic, with a steady drift towards solitude and indecent relaxations. Turner was not an anti-social man; he was, in fact, until the final period, a rather jolly companion among a few cronies, but his inheritance and upbringing held in check and finally extinguished his social propensities. He desired respect, friendships, affection, but did not know how to obtain them; and his preoccupation with his art kept him in isolation until the desire was gone. He enjoyed the Academy dinners, unconscious of his undisciplined table-manners, and at the councils, when called to the chair in the absence of the president, felt immoderately honored. Though irritable and difficult to approach, he was kindhearted and, in spirit, generous, giving to the poor without ostentation and assisting fellow-artists to his own disadvantage. When he was chosen, for some unaccountable reason, Professor of Perspective, he was unspeakably proud, adding P.P. to his signature as well as R.A. As a speaker he was an abysmal failure, but apparently he thought himself a great success. Thrice he left his notes in a carriage and could not, in consequence, utter a word; and when equipped with elaborate papers he muddled his ideas incommunicably. His audience, it seems, came solely to see the marvellous drawings with which he illustrated his lectures. The poetry in him, which he expressed in paint with such magnificent skill and dramatic emphasis, he once essayed in words, in a long poem called *Fallacies of Hope*, quoting it liberally in a catalogue of one of his exhibitions, after the practice of British painters. It is perhaps the most execrable poetry ever penned by a man of genius.

About 1800 he began to live with a girl of sixteen, his housekeeper, and continued to live with her until his death; in 1802 he traveled on the Continent and returned with hundreds of drawings—Swiss peasants, Alpine scenes, French dancers, fishermen, cows, buildings, still-life—and when wars closed the Continent to travellers, he wandered all over England. He sailed up and down the coast in colliers; he made a voyage in the North Sea with a fishing fleet, and in a storm, stood for four hours lashed to the mast so that he might observe the elements in their angriest mood. The first years of the century were the happiest of his life. As often as he cared to come, he was a welcome guest at the mansion of Walter Fawkes, a Yorkshire squire, one of his best patrons, and the only man, it seems, who loved and understood Turner, and put him at ease. In 1812 he purchased two adjoining houses in Queen Anne Street, thenceforth his permanent residence, where he maintained, free of charge, a private gallery of his own pictures. It is not known how much affection he had for his housekeeper or whether he really loved anything but nature and his work. The youthful romance, repeated by most biographers, rests upon such flimsy evidence that we may disregard it. It is known, however, that he was a man of strong sexual impulsions, "the sultan" as Sir Walter Armstrong discreetly phrases it, "of various illiterate domestics," and the father of four natural children whom he neither acknowledged nor provided for. As life wore on, the sordid and secretive habits triumphed over the healthy and decent. He drank more than was good for him; he would work for days like one possessed, after which he would disappear, with a five-pound note in his pocket, on a long debauch in the brothels and dives of the East End.

After 1835, Turner is a friendless old man buried in paint. His father was dead; Fawkes and Monro were dead; exorbitant exertion of mind and body had compelled him to reduce his working hours, and he could not endure the misery of repose. But his great strength was by no means exhausted. His principal concern now was with light and color, and to confirm and further his own observations, he sought out, with his usual thoroughness and curiosity, everything that had been recorded on the subject. He read Goethe's speculations on color and Field's theories, disappointed in both; when photography made its appearance, he was the first painter to examine and reject its thefts from nature; and convinced that de Loutherbourg had a secret method of lighting pictures, he hung about the studio of that worthless painter until Madam de Loutherbourg had him thrown out. He went to Italy again, to Venice, and on his return, embarked boldly into what is generally called "his period of free expression," producing the *Fighting Temeraire*, the *Sun of Venice*, the *Slave Ship, Petworth Interior*, and *Rain, Steam and Speed*, brilliant examples of luminous, broken color which, thirty years later, filled the eyes of two young Frenchmen, Monet and Pissarro, conscripts escaped to London during the war.

These are his last masterpieces. The light dimmed with the decaying body, and by 1845, so far as art is concerned, he is ready to depart. In his last years his actions betray a mind unhinged by over-work, an imagination disintegrated into channels of dirt and drunkenness, but leaping out occasionally with flashes of old majesty. His house was a monumental ruin; the rain beat in; the furniture fell to pieces; the pictures rotted and suffered in the damp and drawings, watercolors and engravings, 30,000 of them, lay in heaps on the floor, eaten by mice and worms. The housekeeper, old and decrepit, was not permitted to touch a thing. The master was away most of the time, now, and she had no idea where he hid himself. One day, in 1851, he vanished for good, and discovering his address on a letter, she traced him to a house in Chelsea on the banks of the river, where he was living with a cancerous old woman named Mrs. Booth. In the neighborhood Turner was known as "Puggy Booth," or Admiral Booth," from his habit of studying the heavens. He died some days after his strange menage was discovered. Ruskin says that the "window of his death-chamber was turned towards the west, and the sun shone upon his face in its setting, and rested there, as he expired."

For many years Turner's art was the subject of malignant disputes and hot antagonisms on the part of the foes of Ruskin. Never before had a great painter been championed by a writer of such eloquence and power, of such insight, enthusiasm, and integrity, and the combination inflamed the hostility of a rising faction of aesthetic showmen regimented by Whistler. They hated Ruskin, his scholarship, his poetry, his irresistible English, his moral and ethical valuations, his proselytizing solemnity, and hating the critic, they must also deny the painter. They were angered that he should have got so much from art, that he should have found God in Turner, and the English death—"life trampled out in the slime of the street, crushed to dust amidst the roaring of the wheel, tossed countlessly away into howling winter wind along five hundred leagues of rock-fanged shore." As if a man were not entitled to get from art all that his faculties enabled him to discover! And so they undertook to demolish Turner and Ruskin by dilettante quips and spiteful sophistries. That both have survived the shower of sparks hardly needs to be mentioned. And now that Whistler, whose *Nocturnes* are but the shadows of Turner, and the Impressionists, who more chivalrously acknowledged their parentage, have fallen into desuetude, we may approach Turner in a more equable spirit.

Turner's greatness consists of a number of things any one of which would distinguish him in art. He had, to begin with, the painter's gift, or shall we say, the special equipment, the restless apprehending eye of one dealing in visual images. Added to this was his technical mastery—the born painter who takes to his medium as other artists take to words or notes. His interest in the natural world I have already brought out. It was stupendous. Everything engaged him from the shingle on the beach to the clouds in the sky; calm water and the turmoil of the sea; pastoral England and the Alps; rains and winds; and always light, the sun that reveals and illuminates all. But he was not a collector or curio-monger who picked up odd facts and specimens of earth and weather, and displayed them on canvas. He was a poet, and by that I do not mean that he was trying to duplicate in paint the emotions aroused by ballads and mediaeval song. Such were the Pre-Raphaelites, but not Turner. He worked directly from his experiences, that is to say, from contemporary things that moved him, and his experiences were universal. I question whether anyone, even Shakespeare, was so profoundly and so variously moved by nature. He observed nature passionately, considering forms in their relation to each other and their effect upon man. In his most hurried sketches he is never the botanist describing external characteristics: his forms develop according to his own creative laws, expanding in proportion to their effect upon him, in his smaller things growing with the most exquisite delicacy, yielding to his sensitive touch to express his feelings of delight and wonder; in his large works, uniting with one another to incarnate the abundance and power of life and the extension of nature into the regions of the infinite. And being a man of his time, he gathered together all the poetic tendencies sweeping the world—revolt, discovery, romance; the beneficence of nature as opposed to the wrecking activities of man—organized them, projected them into a thousand forms of grandeur and mystery, of sadness and peace.

In substance, Turner—and it is the same with all artists—gave out what he had taken in, but having a better mind and greater industry than the plurality of painters, he received more from the world, and hence had vastly more to say. This accounts not only for the number of his pictures but for his range and versatility: his sins, like those of Shakespeare and Rubens, are on the side of abundance. It is commonly objected that he "forced the limits of painting." I do not know what this means. The boundaries of art are set by men of genius, not by critics nor by precedent. If it means that he shattered classical elegance and propriety, reserving for sketches and watercolors effects which Claude and Poussin could only achieve in large canvases, then he did indeed force the limits of painting. But if it means that he brought to landscape the vitality of a sharper and more receptive mind, that his knowledge and reactions impelled him to enlarge the scope of landscape, to conceive and introduce new ideas and unheard-of combinations, and innumerable avenues of enchantment, then he only advanced the boundaries of painting to fit his own experiences. To condemn

Turner because he cannot be cramped in the mould of Poussin is as unjust as to condemn Shakespeare because he is not Racine.

Man against nature! Such is the burden of Turner's art. In the end he lost, dying as he had been born, in dirt, but as close to the infinite as man has ever come—infinite space, light, despair. First, the foundations of nature: the solid earth, the sculptured plastic sea; broad plains and hills, ships and squalls; waves rolling in as no other painter has made them, piling higher and higher like masonry—but all these in human terms. Everything is drawn sharp and clear; the light coming from one source and playing upon the forms with the low tones of tragedy.

Nature becomes a human organism, yielding up strong feelings of terror, hopelessness, and impotent decay. In Turner's major work there is neither joy nor composure, but dramatic strife and the eternal quiet of death—splendor perhaps, but the splendor of noble ruin. This sense of desolation he expressed again and again by contrasting the glory of nature with a crumbling castle, or some other ruin made by man. Ruskin attributes to Turner a lifelong bitterness against the evils of steam and the new Industrialism—the universal desecration of Nature. That Turner was sensible of this there can be little doubt, and to all the destructive agencies of his time, but not, as Ruskin fancied, in the prophetic or economic sense. Did he not make a work of art out of a Great Western express train? It was rather the expression of the fatality of human life, a state of mind appearing again in Conrad, who, the more he learned of nature, the less faith he put in man and in man's handiwork.

Next he discovers the sun and the ruins glow. The Yorkshire hills become sunlit mountains, and the misty Thames a river of light. Nothing now but the magnificence of illumination. White light and scarlet shadow. The sun bathing the wreck of ships and the wreck of nature with blood and fire. And at last objects themselves are ruined, dissolving in a fluid radiance of gold and white, of scarlet and emerald. But even in his last phase, the old alchemist never relinquishes his grip on design and his knowledge of structure, never forgets the human relation-

Turner: ROCKETS AND BLUE LIGHTS.

Charles M. Schwab Collection, New York

(Courtesy of M. Knoedler & Co., New York)

Ryder: TOILERS OF THE SEA.
Phillips Academy, Andover, Mass.

ship, and those final works, at once so close to Impressionism and yet so far, are neither sensual impressions of nature nor jugglery of abstract forms, but the efforts of a master to express by material means the infinity and mystery of life into which his passion for nature had inevitably carried him.

CHAPTER

XIV

RYDER: AN AMERICAN MASTER

As a boy, standing before my easel with its square of stretched canvas, I realized that I had in my possession the wherewith to create a masterpiece that would live throughout the coming ages. The great masters had no more.—*Ryder*.

ON THE western shore of a fair harbor looking down into Buzzard's Bay lies the city of New Bedford. It is a poor sort of place, a New England mill town with foundries and textile factories in which sullen youths, prematurely old, and shabby girls hammer and spin to uphold the material position of the remnants of Colonial culture. At night the mill hands swarm the streets hunting for sensual excitement to relieve their pinched-in souls; and the survivors of the old aristocracy are driven into the gloomy seclusion of their distant Georgian abodes. The picturesque waterfront serves no maritime purpose, and the fair harbor is empty of craft, save the ancient New York boat, the Martha's Vineyard packet, and an occasional barge or coastwise schooner.

In the year 1847, three important events occurred in New Bedford. The town, numbering within its limits more than 15,000 inhabitants, was incorporated under the laws of the Commonwealth of Massachusetts, as a full-fledged city; ships were despatched for the first time into the Arctic zone, and the city, by extending the field of operation, became the greatest whaling port in the world; and on March 19th Albert Pinkham Ryder was born.

The greatest of American painters was descended from a long line of Cape Cod folk—mechanics, shopkeepers and seafaring men. His ancestors were typical Yankees, taciturn, narrow-minded, God-fearing, and undistinguished. His father, a petty customs-house official and fuel dealer, belonged to an offshoot of Wesleyan zealots who dressed and behaved like Quakers. Pinkie, as the youngest of four sons was nicknamed, inherited a large measure of traditional piety, but oddly enough, piety blended with extreme gentleness, tolerance, and good-will. Two of his brothers followed the sea, and the third, journeying to New York, opened a small hotel which, shrewdly managed, soon developed into a moderately profitable business. Pinkie Ryder, having no practical ambitions, submitted to the dismal routine of the New Bedford grammar school, but his academic education was suddenly curtailed by a severe attack of vaccine poisoning. The illness weakened his eyes and troubled him throughout his life. It has been said that his predilection for moonlight scenes and allegorical fantasies was the consequence of his early disability, but this, I think, is a critical error. The technical excellence of Ryder's canvases, and his delicate perceptions of balance and minutely harmonious color-values, are sufficient proof of a keen and unimpaired vision.

At an early age, this large-framed, smiling, silent boy began to draw. There is nothing unusual in the fact. Most children have a talent for picture-making, and draw astonishingly well until crushed by pedants or put to work by close-fisted parents. Ryder, fortunately, suffered neither of these cruelties. Though docile and unaggressive, he was, in his own way, as independent and determined as Thoreau. He believed that he had a great work to perform, and approached the task with religious fervor, with the passionate faith which, in violent form, harrowed the soul of Vincent Van Gogh. There was more than a little of New England transcendentalism in Albert Ryder, but his spiritual struggles were regulated by good sense and humanized by happy contacts with the realities of life.

The elder Ryer was baffled, but to his credit, acquiesced in his son's queer proceedings. When informed by an artist that Pinkie possessed a unique talent, he exclaimed, "I don't know! I'm glad if you think so! I don't understand him!" In the studio of a local painter named Sherman, young Ryder was apprenticed to the drudgery of copying poor engravings of the Old Masters. After a while, without any sign of remonstrance, he quietly threw his worthless efforts aside, and pursued his own course, painting from nature and experimenting with color. "As I worked," he wrote later on, "I saw that it was good and clean and strong. I saw nature springing to life upon my dead canvas. It was better than nature, for it was vibrating with the thrill of a new creation."

In the studio of his first teacher he came under an influence which unquestionably helped him to discover the true direction of his gifts: he was introduced to the work of Albert Bierstadt, a popular painter of the day who looked at American landscape through the eyes of Hobbema and the Düsseldorf school. Let me say at once that there is no comparison between the mature Ryder and the bombastic Bierstadt: with the possible exception of Thomas Moran, Bierstadt is the worst of all the post-Colonial nonentities hanging in the Metropolitan Museum. But to a boy who had seen few original paintings, those huge theatricalities must have been strangely impressive and romantic. He did not imitate them—Ryder did less imitating than any painter I know of; he studied them, puzzling his head over the towering crags and misty waters which, to his inexperienced eye, bespoke the grandeurs of nature, and trying to analyze the effulgent light-effects which, as he subsequently found out, were but sentimental dilutions of Rembrandt's methods. Just as Ossian, the Celtic impostor, cast his weird spell on a host of English bards, so did this Bierstadt inspire the devout Yankee to test his powers on the abundant material surrounding him.

Ryder's attitude toward life was fixed at an age when most boys are irresponsible savages. From his solitary habits it has frequently been assumed that he was indifferent to the ordinary affairs of the world. It is true that he was alone the greater part of the time, but his work demanded it. He had none of the grand assurance of the ringmaster which enabled Rubens to paint in the presence of visitors and assistants; he must work in secret, bestowing upon a single canvas months and even years of toil and concentration. Crowds amused him, and he was fond of wandering about unaccompanied, reflecting on the curious antics of his fellow men. But in the main he was a non-participant, refusing to get excited over the general run of events.

Above all he loved the sea—the majesty and terror of the Atlantic, the procession of whalers that rode proudly into the harbor. The sea was in his blood. New Bedford was a tough and boisterous town, the rendezvous of smugglers and the pleasure ground of hundreds of sailors who affectionately called it the bawdy house of America. Ryder observed the swaggering effrontery of those reckless fellows, some of whom were his kinsmen; they made a great show of themselves and bragged gloriously of their deeds to their hired wenches. The young artist noted the fact and smiled. He watched the ships put out to sea and months later awaited their return. Some of them never came back. He noted that too, but found it hard to smile. He was constantly haunted by the terror of the waves, by the mystery of the cradle endlessly rocking. Again and again he painted the sea—in *The Flying Dutchman, The Smuggler, The Wreck, Pirate's Isle, Jonah and the Whale, The Lorelei*—but always in its tragic moods, always to emphasize the pitiable insignificance of man. Sometimes, in a more poetic mood, he created a fabulous drama of sinister waters, opaque as slate and crossed with wan lights, but even here, in the small sketchy figures, one catches the inescapable cry of human anguish. However symbolical the sea became with him, however deeply he strove to make it the emblem of the mysterious forces of life, he invariably painted it as a hard reality, as the destructive agency that had awed and fascinated him as a boy in New Bedford.

In his native town Ryder was perfectly content. At his feet lay the subject-matter that interested him most, and he was slowly learning to put his experiences into intelligible form. But his father's business dwindled away, and the family sadly departed for New York in a final stand against poverty. The painter was then in his early twenties, without means of support and not in the least perturbed by his indigence. Few painters have possessed his iron conviction, and few, if any, have borne themselves with such quiet dignity and fine masculine honor. For more than ten years he was dependent on his brother, resolved to have his say as an artist rather than follow a trade after the New England tradition.

First he studied with a painter named Marshall, from whom he seems to have learned nothing. Tired of his teacher's continual references to the neo-classical art of nineteenth century France, he enrolled, in January 1871, in the classes of the National Academy. Hereupon, for the first time, his tranquillity gave way to despair. He was compelled to forego his dreams, to forget his ships, the storm clouds and the turbulent sea, and to apply himself to the incredibly absurd process of drawing dusty casts of Jupiter and the Graces. One evening, in his dejection, he tramped through Canal Street, and thence toward South Street, at that date one of the busiest thoroughfares on the waterfront. Approaching the wharves, he was confronted suddenly with the rigging of scores of ships—the sailing vessels that he loved most—and his eyes followed the masts and spars outlined against the sky. From that moment he was a free man again. He never returned to the poisonous atmosphere of the Academy.

As an exhibitor he was affiliated with the Academy for many years. It was then the only channel through which pictures could reach the public, and he was not averse to recognition. In 1873 his first canvas was accepted and hung. It was not a good picture: he was consciously emulating the authorized romanticism of the leaders of the American school—and he was far from clever. During the next fifteen years he was an annual exhibitor, sending some of his most distinguished work and receiving in return little intelligent response.

Contemporary critics set him down as inferior to the maundering Blakelock, and informed him that he had no imagination, that "he painted marines without knowing the sea, and landscapes without observing the facts of nature." This against a man who had lived in perpetual contact with the sea, and in whose landscapes one may discern not only the general characteristics of the New England scene—sheepfolds, bits of Georgian architecture, dunes with beach plums and stunted oaks—but also specific localities such as the Gay Head cliffs! In 1902 he was voted an associate academician, and in 1906, a member in full standing, the second honor carrying the dubious tribute of a portrait executed by J. Alden Weir. Save for his occasional contributions to a dissenting group known as the Society of American Artists, there is nothing more to be said of his official career.

Ryder's genius, so exceptional in our own painting, so startlingly individual in all nineteenth-century painting, was nevertheless substantially American, as we shall see by examining his relation to the civilization that produced him. He arrived in New York shortly after the close of the Civil War. The country was groaning with moral pains and economic depressions. The financial panic of '69 wrought devastation everywhere: the provinces were prostrated and the cities demoralized by riots and suffering. The reconstructionists refused to meet the situation realistically, and the people were duped by the nostrums of romantic hypocrites, shysters and prophets. In literature the Puritans were still in ascendancy—Whittier, the rustic ballad-monger; Longfellow, the fireside troubadour; the introspective Hawthorne; the platitudinous Bryant and the transcendental Emerson. To this group we must add the rising crowd of drivelling fictionists bred by the war and extolling its chivalric glories.

In painting there was an analogous condition. The French romantic movement, of which Delacroix was the fiery avatar, spread to the New World, where it was impregnated with parables, sweet sentiments and uplifting anecdotes. In America the revolt split into two factions, though the divisional line was never sharply drawn. On the one hand were figure painters such as Chase, Duveneck, Thayer and Blashfield, all of whom compromised between Delacroix and the academies of Paris and Munich; on the other were Innes, Tryon, Wyant, Daingerfield, Hunt, Blakelock, and Martin, all disciples of Corot, Millet, Rousseau and the Barbizon school. Ryder naturally was more at home in the second group. He was not a figure painter, and he found in the transplanted Barbizon school an approach to nature somewhat akin to his own. He was a groping student largely self-taught, and from his carefully trained associates he gathered confidence and technical hints which facilitated the solution of his own problems. In a brief time he had taken all they could give him, and henceforth he stood alone. Looking back on his earlier New York pictures, he said, "I cannot but feel that I have gone a little higher up the mountain and can see other peaks showing along the horizon."

He was not then a miraculous figure untouched by the drift of American art, but his resemblance to his contemporaries must not be carried too far. To the idle spectator he belongs with Wyant, Blakelock and Daingerfield, but the similarity is all on the surface. The intrinsic difference is inestimable. Ryder does not paint a scene for its own sake—merely to render the effect of moonlight on water, or sunlight bathing golden fields; he reduces his favorite forms—his trees, clouds, and waves—to the barest essentials, throwing out everything that might encumber his meaning. He makes the forms of nature his own language, turns them into magical elements, puts them together in a design that is, notwithstanding its limited range, extraordinarily dramatic. The others are inarticulate dreamers. They paint solemn nightmares which fill us with the sort of nausea churned up by Poe at his worst; their experiences are shadowy and indefinite, and their vaporous conceptions derived from bookish lore and the conscience-stricken Barbizons. "What avails the storm cloud accurate in form and color, if the storm is not therein?" Such was Ryder's poetic way of asking why painters should go to so much trouble to reproduce the details of objects when they have nothing to put into them.

New York afforded Ryder all that his soul desired. "A rain-tight roof, frugal living, a box of colors, and God's sunlight through clear windows keep the soul attuned and the body vigorous for one's daily work." This was his credo and his answer to painters advising him to travel. From the day of his arrival till his death in 1917, except for a flying visit to New Bedford, he seems to have left the city but twice, his attachment reminding us of Blake's devotion to London. His first venture was a voyage to England as a guest of his friend Captain Robinson, from whose account we learn that the artist spent most of his time observing clouds, or trying to paint while stretched out on the floor of his cabin. In the summer of 1903, he traveled through Europe with Warner, the sculptor, but the Continent made little impression on him, and he was glad to return. He loved the old art but remarked, "It is not for me. I cannot use it. If I am to do anything worth remembering, I must paint my own experiences in my own way."

Ryder's life was devoid of excesses and external adventures. His best work was done between the years 1875 and 1898 in an attic room in Fifteenth Street. Here, in a strong south light, amid dirt and disorder contrasting strangely with his pictures and the cast of a Greek head, he labored with his imaginings. He took life as he found it and made no effort to reform, astonish or conquer the world. At rare intervals—mainly because it took him so long to finish anything—he sold a canvas, and his income therefrom was enough for his meager wants. In one unlucky hour of prosperity he moved to better quarters in Washington Square, but could not accommodate himself to luxuries, and soon returned to his old nook. "Sumptuous studios," he said, "are for business men who paint pot-boilers, and upon the pot-boiler is inscribed the epitaph of art. I have two windows that look out upon an old garden whose great trees thrust their green-laden branches over the casement sills, filtering a network of light and shadow on the bare boards of my floor. Beyond the roof tops sweeps the eternal firmament with its ever-changing panorama of mystery and beauty. I would not exchange these two windows for a palace."

His painting garb was a sailor's blouse and overalls, but on the street he was a correctly groomed gentleman of the old school, with a silk hat, frock coat and gold-headed cane. His habits were as simple and almost as regular as those of Immanuel Kant. At the close of his day's work he would go down to the

Battery to study the ships, sometimes sketching the harbor from the decks of ships commanded by his friends; at nightfall he would walk back to his room, cook his dinner, and read or paint again. He was fond of music and occasionally attended concerts alone. He loved to "soak in the moonlight," as he said, and on clear nights would walk for hours in the parks or the Jersey woods. On his excursions into lower Manhattan he strolled through some of the vilest parts of the city—the Bowery in those days was gang-ridden and dangerous—but he was never molested. "People aren't so bad as they are supposed to be," he remarked. I daresay his venerable appearance was disarming. According to Frederick Fairchild Sherman to whom I am indebted for many biographical facts, "he looked like one of the old apostles . . . a great, rugged, bearded figure, with nobly symmetrical features, radiating kindliness and peace." He seems never to have been in love, although there is a story to the effect that he was enchanted by the playing of a woman fiddler who lived next door to him in Washington Square, and that he proposed to her on short acquaintance and was rejected. During the last decade he was incapable of original work, and devoted himself to finishing or repainting old ideas. In 1915, after a severe illness, he was taken to Elmhurst, Long Island, where he lingered on for two years more under the care of friends.

It is consistent with the restricted scope of Ryder's genius that he should not have been greatly productive, that is, in the manner of Rembrandt and Turner whose creative powers were stimulated by an endless variety of experiences. His contribution to American art consists of less than 150 small pictures. He painted exclusively in oils and carefully destroyed all preliminary studies. He cared nothing for drawings and unfinished canvases; and it is precisely the completion of his work, the perfect realization of his ideas, that transforms the encrustation of pigments on a piece of linen measuring fifteen by twenty inches into a haunting reality. Unfortunately, owing to his singular painting habits, many of his canvases are in bad condition. He used inferior pigments and cheap varnishes, and worst of all, he would spread thick patches of color over a ground that was not thoroughly dry, and the unequal contraction of the two layers has resulted in cracks and fissures. His palette is a sombre scale of grays, neutral blues and greens, and siennas, but his surfaces, glazed again and again with transparent colors, shine out with the hard brilliancy of enamels.

Ryder called himself a dreamer, and such perhaps he was; but let us not confuse his dreams with wish-fulfilments or the manias of neurotics who resort to the "substitutive gratifications" of art—the "phantasy-pleasures" of Freud—as compensation for frustrated desires. No man, not even Corot, was happier or healthier in his life and in his work. He was, in the things that appealed to him, a sharp observer; and in his most visionary pictures the phantasy subject is submerged in his love for and his knowledge of ships, barnyards and rocky coves. Upon this solid objective foundation he builds his dream which is, after all, his visionary penetration—his glimpse into the world beyond the world—which invests his New England themes with a magical or supernatural quality.

And let us not confuse his dreams with the abstractions of the Modernists. That Ryder is a great designer is plain to anyone who has seen his paintings, or reproductions of his paintings; but the value of his design does not lie in the pattern of his lines or in the abstract arrangement of his black and white masses. With him design is a means to give dramatic emphasis and human significance to his experiences. He was fortunate enough to feel certain aspects of life more profoundly than most people, and artist enough to seek out the proper symbols for his moods and responses in order to present them with the utmost clarity. To do this he kept his pictures by him for years, correcting them, altering the lights and shadows, and refining upon his conceptions with the methodical industry of an early Fleming or a New Bedford cabinet maker. Hence the extreme simplicity of his works, the avoidance of detail, the absence of everything that might lead to contradictory emotions. In his own sphere his art is perfect. His imagination, even in the most slippery themes, never gets out of control. He is never capricious, never forces himself into theatrical effects; he objectifies a mood with marvellous intensity, and with a painter's eye for the exciting shapes and values peculiar to the visual arts.

The boundaries of the field in which Ryder is incontestably a master are a little difficult to define. Puritan he was born and Puritan he remained. A rich, full-blooded anthropological inquiry into the life and habits of man was as foreign to him as it was to his compatriot Hawthorne. Not that he was abnormal or exotic: the path of his emotional journey lay along the horizon of the world in which the reckless human comedy is played. Wine, women and song did not move him—always it was pity, terror and the sea. The rarer, the more elusive and fleeting states of the soul—strange fears and dangers, premonitions of death, the intoxication of moonlight, the mysterious power of the sea, the witchery of the Forest of Arden—dominated his whole life. But his dreams did not disorganize him, as so frequently happens to those preoccupied with the less common emotions. His composure, his excellent good humor and the diligence with which he painted, saved him from superstitions and absurdities. Ryder stands out today as one of the noblest figures in modern art. He was an American with good sense, a fine passion for paint, and the ability to discover dramatic material in his own country.

CHAPTER

XV

THE FRENCH

WHEN the creative energy of the Italian Renaissance was exhausted, the lamp of enlightenment passed into the hands of the French—and by French hands it has been tended to this day. For upwards of three centuries, France, or more precisely, Paris, has been esteemed as the centre of all that is intelligent, gracious and civilized, maintaining her supremacy less by outstanding individual genius than by a nationalistic attitude towards art, by the production of a culture universally acknowledged as a mark of the highest distinction. In the annals of French painting you will find few men capable of standing up with the masters of other nations; you will find instead an army of talent laboring for the glory of *la patrie*. One might say that the aim of the French has been the suppression of individuality for the prosperity of the national tradition. Certainly individuality has never been tolerated when it happened to contravene—as genius usually does—cultural and academic standards. In no other country has art been so systematically propagated, so thoroughly professionalized, so powerful an instrument for the preservation of national prestige.

In 1648 the French invented the Academy, and since the foundation of that overwhelming menace, French art has been, in varying degrees, and so far as independent minds will submit to the authority of politicians, a patriotic industry. This official recognition and control has not been without its advantages. It has ensured a high standard of skill and competence, a uniformity of taste, elegance and refinement unmatched in any other modern nation. It has encouraged and supported artists, given them something to do, made them useful citizens. It has kept alive the language of painting in periods of warfare and economic depression, harmonized art with the social order, and raised the artist to a position of self-respect and public importance which he has not elsewhere enjoyed. It has, by continually drawing upon the past, helped to bring about that remarkable solidarity of French ideals, the loyalty to France and the belief in her greatness—in her descent from the classical civilization of Greece and Rome. Napoleon got at the root of the matter when he said, "What the French want is Glory and the satisfaction of their vanity!" Accordingly, he put the architects to work, ordered David to paint historical compositions in the Italian style, and plundered Italy of her masterpieces to embellish his capital. And it has made France the most orderly and beautiful of modern countries, French the language of *la politesse*, and Paris the most enjoyable of cities where one breathes, in spite of the intrinsic conventionality of the architecture and the unimaginative cleverness of the public monuments and decorations, the air of culture, where one feels the presence of art in all things—in gaiety, good living, good wines, seductive women, and the general emancipation of the senses.

The negative side is not so alluring. The Academy—and the Academy is but the official device of the provincialism and conservative spirit of the French at large—with its honors, emoluments and prestige, has formalized art, has prescribed, in place of the dramatic and creative, style, eclectic combinations, and ornamentation. From Poussin to Fragonard, from Ingres to Renoir, the main body of French painting has been ornamentation in one form or another: pompous, frivolous, pseudo-classical, or sensual; but always with the distinguishing accent of style and graceful measure. In nothing have the French been so triumphant as in their aesthetic adaptability. With taste, impeccable tact, and ingenuity carried to the pitch of genius, they have foraged every field of art—Italian, Flemish, Dutch, Spanish and English—have made their borrowings their own and converted them into new forms impressed with the unmistakable stamp of Gallic culture. This in contrast with the Americans who for fifty years have been going to Paris to acquire the "cosmopolitan touch," and have succeeded only in losing their identity among the miscellaneous fads of cultural experts.

The academic system, the salvation of the popular and fashionable artist, has been the mortal enemy of originality. Whenever a powerful artist has arrived in Paris, generous, hospitable Paris has tried to cry him down or emasculate him with academic honors. So unrelenting is this hatred of originality that men of the highest intelligence have solicited official sanction in order to avoid exile. During the nineteenth century practically every new movement, every new idea in painting, had its origin in France, but the opposition of the guardians of tradition to the insurgent forces was appalling in its ignorance and brutality. The storm of ridicule and insult which greeted Delacroix, Daumier, Courbet, Manet and Cézanne, is disquieting to those who have been taught that France is the home of art, liberty, and enlightenment. The conflict between the elaborately entrenched academicians and the intelligent minority is described by Balzac in his tale of a stupid painter, who, by doing what he was told to do and painting what was expected of him, rose to wealth and fame, while his confrères, worthy and genuine artists but insubordinate, were despised and rejected.

The academic machine, operating through storm and calm for three centuries, has extended its jurisdiction into every department of French life. It has disseminated among the people not a knowledge of art, not indeed an appreciation of the best art, but a chauvinistic point of view forming a cultural implement that functions easily, naturally and profitably. Thus culture enters into routine affairs, lending them grace and distinction, and the simplest transactions—overcharging an American for a bottle of perfume, for instance—become ceremonies performed in *la grande manière*. Doubtless it is true, as French critics assure us, that the inclusiveness of their cultural program has bred familiarity with the nature of creative work, and a peculiar respect for artists; but it has done more than that. It has tended to degrade and cheapen art. When the emotional intensity attached to the consideration of genuine products of the imagination is transferred to national interests of every description, it becomes a matter of business, and neither charm nor ceremony can conceal the underlying commercialization. On this account philosophy, science and the fine arts are not more important to the prestige of France than are cookery, cosmetics and prostitution; and the French genius, in essence materialistic, has been preëminent in the field of ornamentation—in fashions, salon art, interior decoration, furniture and cheap jewelry. On this account the practical French have sedulously protected the tradition of painting and have established in Paris, as a source of revenue, a picturesque Bohemia for romantics, misfits and pretenders of all nationalities.

We find, then, that French painting seldom rises to the imaginative heights attained by the painting of other countries; that it is, in the aggregate, orderly rather than imaginative, stylistic instead of dramatic, nationalistic instead of original. Though it illustrates to perfection Taine's theory that art is a racial reflection; though it has, at all times, expressed the will and temper of the French people; it has known no periods of exuberance, no moments of ecstasy. Its history is a succession of adaptations—of revisions of old styles, borrowings, and inventions—to keep in pace with changing social conditions. It has been called forth by official decrees, by the concerted efforts of patriots to satisfy materialistic needs and to perpetuate the tradition of intelligence and good taste. Save in the primitive, or Gothic period, when it was subservient to Flemish and Italian influences, French painting has never been religious. Nor has it been concerned with the more human issues; nor exhibited a delight in simple things, a curiosity in natural objects, such as characterized the Dutch. For these reasons, Fromentin, one of France's most brilliant critics and a practicing artist, said, "France has shown a great deal of inventive genius but little real faculty for painting." From the earliest beginnings, as far back as the twelfth century, the French have effected a disinterestedness towards objects, an inclination to consider objects as still-life, or geometrical forms

Cézanne: STILL-LIFE.

Chester Dale Collection, New York

separated from emotional associations. This disinterestedness used to be called classical; of late years the name has been changed to intellectual, or more fashionably to abstract. It is, in reality, the academic approach to art. Even in the most glorious days of the Academy, the reign of Louis XIV, when Colbert, the King's minister, dictated the choice of subjects, the artists obediently did as they were told, painting and carving not from their experiences with things that interested them, but to decorate the vanity and glory of the State with the pompous bones of classicism.

It is no exaggeration to say that French painting has been kept alive by intellectual differences—the disputes among Academicians for honors and subventions; the variations of taste accompanying social reconstructions; and the hostility between the academic crowd and the independent few to whom we owe all that is fine and significant in Gallic art. To simplify matters we may divide French painters into two classes: the preponderant, or Academic; and for want of a more acceptable term, the Impressionist. These divisions are not absolute. They overlap and mingle, but that they are valid enough we shall see as we proceed with our analysis. Throughout all their vicissitudes and quarrels the two have had this in common: the presence of the eclectic mind; the converging of all the streams of European painting into one channel distinctively and undeniably French. In the first manifestations of French painting we discover this nationalistic bias: we discover it in the efforts of the Primitives to refine upon the Flemish influence; in the intentions of Francis I to rival the Italian Renaissance, summoning to his court Leonardo da Vinci, and Andrea del Sarto; in the magnificence of the Grand Monarch; in the Revolution, the Empire, and in every mood and movement of the Republic.

The academic tendency begins with Poussin, the first French painter of importance; is consolidated by LeBrun and the servants of Louis XIV; is strengthened again by David and his pupils; corroborated by Ingres; reinforced by Chasseriau; inculcated into mural design by Puvis de Chavannes; and within the memory of most of us rendered intolerably odious by a multitude of salon panders and dissembling portraitists too numerous to mention, and unworthy of mention. The Impressionist tendency dates from Claude Lorrain, a contemporary of Poussin; it reappears in Watteau and the followers of Rubens, and in the work of Chardin; battles fiercely for life under the valiant leadership of Delacroix who was supported by the English landscape painters; is ennobled by Corot; given a realistic turn by Daumier, Courbet and Manet; a pagan touch by Renoir; and ends exhausted in Cézanne. Let us now examine more closely the meaning of the two tendencies.

The term academic, in its official sense, derives from the Royal Academy of Fine Arts, chartered and brought under state control by the minister of Louis XIV. The purpose of the Academy was to monopolize the arts; not only to organize and administer art as a national industry, but to specify the nature of the product and to force into starvation and contempt all artists dissenting from the ideas and the authority of the directors. And it attained its end to the satisfaction of an absolute monarch, reducing French art to a state of vassalage from which it has never recovered, and standardizing it once for all. Its spiritual mission was not more lofty than the ambitions of Colbert who wrote to his King: "I consider it essential to refrain from all sorts of expense so as to have millions wherever it is a question of promoting your glory and that of France." Millions were bled from the masses and thrown into art, and there ensued a frenzied recrudescence of antiquity which is still one of the attractions of Paris. The neo-classical orgies in architecture, sculpture and the crafts; the bastard Graeco-Roman majesty of Versailles; the furniture and tapestries of the Gobelins; the collecting of Italian deposits and the grandiose imitating of the same, we shall have to leave unsung. But the bureaucracy of painting contains the whole story of the sublime absurdity of the academic scheme.

Pupils of the Academy were treated as if they had no minds of their own—which seems more than probable. Had they been children or convicts, they could not have been guarded more rigorously. The regimen included, besides the daily copying of classical pieces, the hours of getting up and going to bed, the selection of proper companions, habits of living, and the consecration of the soul to the sun-king and the sungod. They were crammed with high thoughts and noble ideals, that is to say, as such thoughts and ideals were supposed to exist in the heroic Greeks and Romans. And if they were made of the regulation stuff, they were accredited to the branch Academy at Rome, where, at the expense of the State, they received graduate instruction in antiquity.

The aesthetic credo was based upon the maxims and practices of Poussin, and appropriately embalmed in Latin hexameters. The main articles of the credo were in brief: Art should deal with grand and important subjects, never with the familiar things of life, and all grand and important subjects are to be found among the ancients; art should serve the State, not the individual; nature is low, common and vulgar, and must be used sparingly; the safe course is to trust the old poets and sculptors who have selected from nature all that is dignified and inspiring; observation is degrading—rely upon the classic artists for your themes; drawing is the thing, not color; painting should imitate the grandeur and severity of sculpture; the judge of painting is not the artist, nor the public, but the infallible King. The testament ended with a scientific code of light and shade that would make one's head swim. Painters complying with these tenets could not go wrong. Fame and fortune were guaranteed by the State. The custom of exhibiting pictures was established, first at the Palais Royal, later at the Salon Carré of the Louvre, whence the term salon picture. So much for the official side of the Academy.

We are now prepared to understand the psychological meaning of the term academic as exemplified by the mind and art of Poussin, and by all subsequent painters of similar proclivities. The academic artist is one whom contemporary life excites to no healthy or independent action. He is held in bondage by the productions of his predecessors, by accumulated art-forms bearing little or no relation to his own perceptional experiences. He attempts in an altogether different civilization to recapture the inspiration of men who are dead and gone, to make pictures by sifting, measuring and reassembling forms evolved by other artists from direct communication with the world. He believes that the value of art is absolute and immutable, existing intact from one age to another, irrespective of human needs modified by changing social conditions. He endeavors by an act of will to live in the past. His point of view is not creative, but historical, or more correctly, archaeological. He is the exponent of learning for its own sake, art for art's sake.

Of such was Poussin, the first Academician. A Frenchman by birth, he preferred to live in Rome far away from the monarchical enterprises of his fellow academics, where his dead soul might rest among the dead, where, with grave and sentimental regrets, he deplored the passing of the pagan past, where he lived in perpetual contemplation of old monuments and disfigured relics, weeping daily over a Bacchic torso which he said contained all the principles of art. Poussin was a Neo-Platonist—as cruel an epithet to fasten upon a painter as upon a philosopher. By his mental habits, his sterile intellectualism, his mode of living, and by his art, he denied the human side of life—the emotions, feelings, and the everyday experiences out of which the true artist makes his pictures. The life of the senses, so far as it afforded him first-hand knowledge of the passions and actions of man, he sternly ignored, extolling the life of pure thought, of passive reverie. His intellect, of course, had to work upon something; and so he filled himself with memories and the dimensions of tombs. Thus, in his quest for ideal combinations and "ultimate realities," he painted abstractions: his Bacchanalian pictures, which of all themes should be characterized by fire and passion, are no more than lifeless stageplay, nicely regulated but emotionally null.

Poussin believed that art is a form of organized knowledge and in some respects it is; but being a neo-classic, he confused knowledge in the abstract with knowledge that is living and useful.

For knowledge has a dual nature: it is both static and dynamic, if I may be permitted such ugly terms—the accumulation of facts, and the *knowing* of things. The first is a matter of labor rather than intelligence, and may be acquired in retirement without commerce with the world. It is the scholarly, the professorial, the academic brand. Without the leaven of direct experiences and under no necessity of putting its store of facts to *new* uses, it settles into moulds, deifies precedent, and distorts a realistic view of life. Going further, this atrophied learning—for it is no more than that—declaims against and finds unsatisfactory all conditions of life which do not square with traditional observances. We see the academic mind in our inflexible systems of jurisprudence the purpose of which, it would seem, is to serve precedent, not justice. By simplifying the problem of right and wrong, by codifying ancient practices and constantly citing obsolete opinions, our jurists twist the obvious facts of life into strained and impossible relationships, into arbitrary constructions devoid of meaning except as they refer to precedent, and devoid of sense to all but legal minds. But the prestige of learning—of knowledge of facts—compels acceptance of academic judgments. This authority of erudition is the vestigial remnant of the primitive veneration for astrologers and medicine-men whose stock of recipes and amulets is analogous to the hoardings of the civilized academicians.

The other form of knowledge, the knowing of things, is the life-blood of art and of humanity. Such was the knowledge of Leonardo, Rembrandt, Goethe and Turner, to whom facts were not an accumulation of fossils picked up on a dead seashore, but a procession of living things intrinsically related; living because directly experienced; related, not through any conformity to precedent but because of their bearing upon one another, a unity determined solely by the creative insight of the artist. Here precedent may be useful if it facilitates technical procedure. I have already told how Turner, for years, could not keep his eyes off the canvases of Claude, but he did not go to Claude for his facts—

his subject-matter. He had more ideas and more material for landscape in a single day than the Frenchman had in a lifetime. His interest in Claude was purely technical. He felt that the situations confronting him were similar to those with which Claude had successfully contended, and that Claude's method of solving difficulties might be of assistance to him in his own problems. I must qualify this statement: there was a period in which Turner, actuated by gauche rivalry, did attempt to introduce some of Claude's classical trumpery into his English backgrounds, and the collision between borrowed facts and forms truly his own is painful to look upon.

The cardinal weakness of the academic mind is the inability to separate the technique of procedure from the things affected by procedure. Poussin recognized and admired, yes, even loved and worshipped, the classic organization of things, but he could not dissociate the organization from the materials under its control. Inasmuch as the subjects he meditated—Vergilian heroes, Roman gods, nymphs and Sabine women—were vicariously experienced, that is, through the classic structures, they could only be employed academically, as scholarly facts. Living among tombs and excavations, he fondly imagined that he was one of the old Romans in daily converse with gods and heroes, but unfortunately the environment which had produced the classic forms had passed into oblivion. In consequence, Poussin was left to deal, or elected to deal with dead things. He was an architect who collected fragments from the ruins of antiquity—a column here, a cornice there—and pieced them together to build a Roman temple. The temple is consummately joined but it is neither a new building nor a copy of an old—it is a curiosity of art.

While scholarship of this sort may be defensible in certain fields, defensible even as a "way of life," it has no place in creative art which, whatever its subject may be, is occupied wholly with the organization of experienced things. When knowledge is divorced from current activities, from new needs and new experiences, it becomes the tool of the historian and the archaeologist.

Nevertheless, Poussin, to his countrymen, has always been one of the masters. French taste apparently is not disturbed by the poverty of his color, nor by the fact that his canvases have the appearance of copies rather than originals, a general drabness in which faulty execution plays no part, but which is the true reflection of his colorless mind. They find in him the perfect expression of their cultural fetish that art, not man, is the measure of all things; his compositions, so obviously inspired by art, not by life, with their predetermined notions of the significant and grand, establish consanguinity with the ancient rulers of the world. They do this literally as well as symbolically. For Poussin collected his facts from the Renaissance masters, particularly Raphael and Titian, as studiously as he quarried in Roman sculpture, and by rearranging forms and reducing murals to the scale of the easel picture, adapted Italian painting to the French salon. This, in French eyes, is a great achievement, invaluable service to the patriotic ideal, the more so since it is effected with the precision, the avoidance of excess, the characterless ingenuity which the French prize above all things in art.

Of late years Poussin's glory has been diligently restored and polished, and today his name is perhaps the most sacred in the pantheon of French painting. There are good reasons for this canonization. In part, it is political: the indigence of official art —its mediocrity and utter worthlessness—has gravely imperilled the prestige of the academic tradition; and to bolster up this prestige, as well as to conceal its organic decay, the French have invoked, once more, the incorruptible art of Poussin. The other chorus of praise—the homage offered by the claque of Parisian Modernists is, on the surface, a reactionary outburst. For the Modernists originally were anything but academic. But whatever they may have been, they represent at the moment, a body of painters who, by removing themselves from contemporary affairs and by their refusal or their incapacity to find in life anything but abstract relationships, have ended in a wrangle of neo-classic theories. Their admiration for Poussin is a case of like calling to like. They admire the lack of hesitancy, the absence of effort in his pictures—qualities to be found in all good machines; they care nothing for his subjects, satisfied with the consciousness of his organizing faculty. To respond purely and absolutely to his art, that is to say, to recognize and diagram his technical rhythms, is enough.

This is a strange state of affairs. Poussin's rhythms, examined in the light of Modernist doctrine, are automatic beats, square masses and horizontal lines, uniformly repeated, curved lines recurring with monotonous and geometrical accuracy. His rhythms are analogous to symmetrical friezes. They are lifeless patterns imposed by an adept and scholarly artificer on second-hand materials. His compositions, flawlessly articulated, gracefully dimensioned, sterilized of every detail and gesture, every costume and occupation connecting art with the workaday world, will never move anyone to strong emotions or set one's soul atremble. His mind, aroused by no preferences for one thing above another, proceeds on a dead level and arrives at no conclusions. As a result, his compositions do not get anywhere. They are mechanisms, the most convincing evidence we have that pictures, in their formal structure, may be above reproach, and yet carry no meaning whatever. This is not the true rhythm of art—it is repetition, mechanical adjustment. In contrast we have the rhythms of Rembrandt, El Greco and Hogarth in which preferences are active to the point of violence, causing monumental accentuations, dramatic concentrations of energy in prominent forms, variations in size and type; in which static uniformity is abolished and we feel the beat of living materials, of knowledge used creatively to induce the deepest emotions. In Poussin's pictures—and this is limited to his drawings—the only things not conventionally felt and delineated are his trees. For once he seemed to forget his antiquities and to experience his subject-matter directly. It is a mistake to call his pictures museum pieces: they are museums in themselves—impressively appointed and in good order, but museums none the less.

We turn now to the more estimable side of the French temperament—the non-academical or Impressionist. I use the term Impressionist with some reluctance, inasmuch as its usual connotation is restricted to a group of nineteenth century painters who, under the leadership of Monet and Pissarro, carried to its logical termination, and only yesterday under the spell of Cézanne, carried to its inevitable extinction tendencies originating as far back as Claude Lorrain. But I know of none other so apt and inclusive, none other which will serve as a common denominator for the various departures of French painting when at war with academic practice. Impressionist! The word, in a measure, explains itself. The man for whom, in the famous utterance of Gautier, the visible world exists. One receptive to stimuli from every source; roused to action by the force of immediate circumstances; staking all on the dramatic freshness of the new experience. The original as opposed to the conventional; personal freedom rather than traditional safety. Color instead of form, and instead of absolute space, atmosphere, luminosity, and tone. Not objects themselves, but the *effects* of objects as seen through sheaths of tone. The abolition of fixed contours; not the hard and determinate outline but the blurred edge and the fusion of patches of tone. Let the eye be the judge, the innocent eye which forgets all and knows nothing, the eye which does not see the rigid shapes and indissoluble forms existing under the ephemeral aspects of light and shade, but which follows the disconnected facts of vision and loses contours in impertinent shadows.

These distinctions, of course, are relative. The Impressionist, like Claude, Corot, Seurat and Cézanne, may hanker after the divine serenity and the inhuman composure of classicism; he may, like Delacroix, be an exotic drugged with oriental dreams; a messianic visionary like Van Gogh; a sophisticated outcast like

Gauguin; or like Courbet, a noisy sensualist. But whatever his particular creed or folly, he is always a liberator standing for the truth of his sensations, always an artist seeking for some general formula in which to enclose his impressions of the visible world. He will serve his country as eagerly as the most stupid of academics, but only upon his own terms; often we hear his pathetic wail for official honors and medals, but that is merely a just complaint against the tyranny of the organized gang. Once and once only he discovers the golden mean between sensation, or direct experience, on the one hand and abstract thinking or contemplation on the other. Then his provincialism becomes monumental, his glory truly classic. Then he is Daumier, the great French master, a man of power and grandeur, in whose art we find neither good taste nor the glittering fool's gold of culture, but the new and profound valuation of old things, whose solid humanity, let us hope, has finally given the death-blow to the fancy breed of stereotypes and ornamentalists.

The first Impressionist is Claude Lorrain, an unlettered pastry-cook born in 1600 and, by preference, passing his whole life on Roman soil. It is customary to call him a classicist, and if you like the word, you are at liberty to hold on to it, remembering however that it is a superficial designation descriptive of the false and conventional elements in his style which have had so baneful an influence on his academic admirers. Claude was a tame and languid soul ambitious, on his weaker side, of the antiquated scenery, the gimcrack ruins and degenerate mythologies which his friend Poussin laboriously pieced together into stationary landscapes. He went to Rome as the modern pilgrim of art goes to Paris, for in those days the sun of ancient culture, though low in the heavens, had not yet set, and the French Academy was a thing unborn. His efforts to be noble and heroic, after the manner of the ancients, are ludicrous and naïve; and the desiccated classicality of his oil paintings with their burning theatrical lighting, their faked marble edifices, their puny, ill-shapen, ill-placed figures, their idle waters, and the feeble nostalgia for creeds outworn hanging over them in lethargic vapors, is as foreign to the art of painting when founded upon first-hand experiences, as the artificial solemnity of Poussin. There is nothing to be gained by further discussion of his oils. They have indeed one merit, and a signal one—the new use of space and atmosphere—but that is in the nature of an innovation rather than a pictorial achievement. For his real contribution we must seek his wash-drawings and sketches, clean, exhilarating stuff containing all that is important in his canvases, and certain far-reaching discoveries expressed without the impediments of a trumped-up grandiosity.

At heart Claude was a simple, lyric poet. His impressionable mind delighted in the sunny pastorals of Italy. He had no more aptitude for epical thought than Keats had for classic drama. We must pardon his aspirations to an intellectual art; it was the thing to do, and even the lordly Rubens was not above current fashions, offering his meaty Flemish nudes as Roman goddesses. That Claude was able to remove his head from the classical halter and return to the things he really loved is sufficient proof of the depth of his convictions. He loved nature only this side of idolatry, and observed it with the curious disinterestedness that is one of the characteristics of the French artist. If he could distinguish one kind of tree from another; if he knew the varieties of grass, the different formations of clouds, the shapes of waves and the behavior of winds, his pictures do not show it. What interested him was not the growth and structure of natural forms, but the effects of light and atmosphere on vegetation and water. And these effects he generalized, using trees and hills as component masses held together by the consummate blending of the atmospheric divisions. So working, he made pictures displaying little knowledge of natural facts, and having little value as representations. They are valuable, however, as impressions, as statements of his feelings, or more exactly, the single state of bliss induced in him by the languorous country of his adoption. The mood is invariably soft and peaceful; an idyllic world lit by the golden rays of the declining sun; the season of mists and autumnal laziness; a world undisturbed by the grime and toil of man; pagan happiness, pleasant shade, bucolic sentiment.

Like a true Impressionist, he went straight to nature, probably the first painter to work extensively in the open air. He did not paint from nature as Constable did, and all the modern Impressionists, but noted twilight shadows and the degrees of atmospheric density in rapid sketches, mixed his tones, and hurried home to organize his observations while they were still hot in his mind. This was not the way of the Old Masters; it marked instead the beginning of the great schism in painting—seeing vs. knowing—which I have outlined in the chapter on Velasquez and shall discuss fully later on. Here a few general distinctions will suffice. We find in Giorgione and Titian indications of the presence of natural light and in Titian hints of colors resolved into patches of tones; Leonardo in his notebooks formulates Impressionist theories in a language but little altered by modern science, but he did not put his theories into practice; we have seen that Velasquez was dependent on optical truth, painting wholly by eye: and while Claude was alive, Rembrandt was modelling in tones as a sculptor models in clay. But Claude was the first painter to put the sun to work, the first to make us feel the presence of the outdoor atmosphere, to introduce into pictorial space the light and air of nature. Today such things are taken for granted—we might wonder how a painter could avoid them if he tried—but in Claude's day they were momentous discoveries.

The old painters—Raphael and the Umbrians, Piero della Francesca, Signorelli, Tintoretto—were masters of space composition. But it was absolute space, space without time, circumstance or atmosphere. There is no sunshine in the classical world—just light arriving from nowhere, encompassing all. Looking at the pictures of Raphael, Michael Angelo, and the Florentines big and little, we are conscious neither of the out-of-doors nor of the subdued interior, but of forms occupying space. The old masters had no time and no use for the fugitive effects of atmosphere; nor were they more than moderately concerned with external nature. They were interested in man; and they worked, I must repeat, from knowledge, modelling their forms in black-and-white, and adding color as a decorative garment. Let me make this clear. They were primarily draughtsmen: they used sharp edges to limit forms, defined contours firmly and precisely, modelled the enclosed spaces in neutral colors—colors equivalent to black-and-white—to build up solid objects, and last, tinted the whole with local colors—the natural hues of flesh and stuffs. In short, while they studied the model, they rose above it, never pulling objects out of shape into arbitrary distortions, but making new things based on the old, revising and accentuating organic structure to suit their own purposes. Quite properly they subordinated landscape to the human figure, but it is reasonable to assume from the backgrounds of their canvases, that they could have done marvellous things in pure landscape had they been so minded. The sea they let alone, and trees, rivers and rocks were used sparingly to decorate distant spaces. It is not, however, the natural landscape of Claude and Constable, but landscape made indoors and made with no more respect for the accidents of light and atmosphere than enters into the construction of the classic figure.

With Claude, Velasquez, Rembrandt and, to a certain extent, Rubens, the old procedure was abandoned; strict contours abolished, edges blurred; and the consideration of the effects of atmosphere introduced into painting. Henceforth the history of painting in western Europe is the warfare between the adherents of the two methods; and in the nineteenth century the battle is fought out in France. What happened there I have already pointed out: the classic tradition, academicized from its very beginning by Poussin, ended in insufferable salon nastiness; the Impressionist in pseudo-scientific reporting. At present the Modernists have won a negative victory by compromising, by performing a surgical operation on nature and redistributing the particles with something of Poussin's skill at synthesis; but what this experimentation will bring forth in the shape of useful pictures remains to be seen. It were a waste of time to try to decide whether an artist should belong to one party or the other—that is his own business, and if his convictions cannot decide for him, cannot naturally align him with men of kindred sympathies, he is lost anyway. Delacroix never could make up his mind to adopt the classic contour or the looser weave of Rubens and Constable, and his work, remarkable as it unquestionably is, is full of indecisions and violent lurchings after the styles of others. Daumier knew instinctively where he belonged: he stood with Rembrandt, Michael Angelo, and Hogarth—but he did his work in his own way. You may call him anything you like, classic, romantic, Impressionist, anything but academic. There is no label big enough for greatness. And Rembrandt, though working in tone, with planes absorbing or reflecting light, and with wavy outlines, may be denominated, by virtue of his immense store of directly acquired knowedge and his ability to organize that knowledge, a classic artist. Wherever there is first-hand experience, searching, passionate interest in things, and the translation of the experience into new and coherent forms, the shapes and colors of which are determined by the unique personality of the maker, there is art.

Claude was a poet carried away by the luminous vistas of the South. He was also an artist with a sound sense of design—I mean that he consolidates his impressions into a general statement which rouses within us feelings of exquisite satisfaction: the wonder and the unexpected thrill of a spacious landscape flooded with the golden light of the friendly sun, stretching far away through shining vapors into a world of infinite distances. His effects of light and air, being closely observed, he manages beautifully; having little interest in the particular forms of nature, he has difficulty in relating details to the basic rhythms, and we find in his best works, cluttered foregrounds and bits of disconnected débris deposited here and there for no good reason. But the important masses are nobly planned and joined. His handling of tones—the diluting of pure colors to increase or diminish their black-and-white values—is thoroughly modern and astonishing. He divides his space into three planes—now an academic habit: the dark foreground, half-tones in the middle distance; and a waning background filled with light, and these divisions he blurs and dissolves one into the other, thus establishing unity of form and mood. It was Claude's constructive ability, his playing of line against line, and tone against tone, to achieve rhythmical balance, as well as his original interest in natural phenomena, that made him the master of Constable, Turner and Corot. He is the first significant French painter.

During the seventeenth century, in the long reign of Louis XIV, the Academy held undisputed control over art, but after the death of the Grand Monarch, official tyrants and the followers of Poussin came in for a bitter and unexpected struggle for existence. This was due to a number of things: the frivolous reaction against the stern absurdities of Louis XIV, the cult of gallantry expressed by Watteau and Fragonard who brought to French painting the warmth and color of Rubens; the widening of the circle of patronage. Though art remained, as in England, a luxury for the rich, patronage was extended from the king to the court, and the body of courtiers was oppressively large, including besides the indolent sycophants, scientists, writers, important citizens, financiers, and not least, pretty women. Such a society, urbane and pleasure-loving, not to say wanton, demanded for the adornment of its salons and boudoirs a more intimate and representative art than the bloodless concoctions of the classicists, and the demand was met by the popular nondescripts of Flemish extraction. But this was only a temporary irritation to the academic bigots.

The paintings of Watteau, Lancret, Fragonard and Boucher, though far more genuine than the official trash, were not taken seriously, were not regarded as "high art," but as delectable furniture. In the end the polticians won out. For France had never really lost faith in the antique, and continued to educate her artists in the Greek and Roman tradition founded by the master Poussin. Thus the unconscionable outburst of neo-classicism in the Revolution and the Empire was but the reaffirmation of French ideals which had been interrupted by the licentiousness of the age of Louis XV. As a matter of fact the sturdy French people were sick of scandals and bedroom art before the Revolution broke, and we call to witness the alarmist Diderot preaching the cheap moralities of Greuze and the kitchen-wares of Chardin. To be exact, the restoration of the Graeco-Roman ideal dates from the middle of the century, from the excavations at Pompeii and Herculaneum, and the mighty eloquence and logic of the Germans—Winckelmann's plea for antiquity in his *History of Art Among the Ancients;* Lessing's *Laokoön,* and the Olympian pose of Goethe. And when the storm descended shattering the foundations of the old society, it could not shatter France's love of the heroic and classical, and art, heedless of the voice of Rousseau crying out to his people to return to the wilderness, followed the Rationalists with David as its prophet.

There is something vastly ridiculous in the spectacle of those indomitable French Republicans acting the rôles of the old Greeks and Romans, and something vastly courageous in the intensity with which they abandoned themselves, drenched with the blood of slaughter, to the job of creating a new government based upon the dictates of pure reason. It was a perfectly natural undertaking, and to call it play-acting is perhaps to be unjust to the spirit of French nationalism. It was the last fermentation of the noble Roman blood, France's most heroic effort to rise to the grandeur of her republican ancestors. But still, I insist, the spectacle of an incendiary, eighteenth century bourgeoisie wearing togas, speaking Plutarch, reviving pagan ceremonies, and discussing absolute ideals in rooms furnished in Pompeiian style, is not without its humorous aspects. A democracy regulated by the intellect, classic in its origin and pagan in its forms! The union of art and politics! What a program, and who, save the French, would have dared it? The experiment did not work, but it produced modern France and sentiments of liberty now current in every civilized country. And it produced an art which, while consistent with French culture, has been a target for the execrations of every modern painter of liberal sympathies, French or foreign.

It was all very exciting for a band of frenzied politicians to wear Roman skirts; to lay down laws for Liberty, Equality and Fraternity as derived from a study of the ancients; to attempt, by the syllogisms of Rationalism to subdue the passions of a democratic mob; to govern by calculation and ideology; to arrive, by the processes of reason, at the dogma that art is an "absolute harmony of forms to be attained only by knowledge of the antique, that true beauty is untouched by changes of fashions because it is founded on reason, that it was realized once for all by the ancients," and the best we can do is to imitate the Greeks and Romans—and it did produce art, if one cares to call it art. For there came to the Republican cause, by predestined arrangement it would seem, a painter, politician and antiquarian all in one. His name was Louis David.

In quieter times, David would have been the feared and hated master of a boy's school beating Greek and Latin into helpless youth. Winning the Prix de Rome, he went to Italy when the worship of the dead was raging as a universal religion owing to the excavations at Pompeii and German idealism, and was converted at once to neo-classic doctrine. Extraordinarily industrious, he exhibited in 1784, five years before the Revolution, *The Oath of the Horatii.* This picture, a perfect reflex of the tastes of his compatriots, was welcomed with an hysterical clamor rarely accorded to a mere work of art. It was a solemn fraud, a mockery of the ancients, but the Republicans, engaged in a national mockery, saw themselves in its austere figures, and applauded excessively like true Frenchmen. Immediately, with unanimous approbation, David became the leader, and with the Revolution, the Caesar of painting. Never before or since, has art been so completely dominated by the iron hand and the narrow, inflexible mind of one man. For imagination he substituted a set of fixed and exhausted forms taken from late Roman bas-reliefs; instead of convictions he had Jacobinical prejudices; instead of sensitivity, the passions of an omnipotent bully. Furthermore, he had a certain kind of hard competence in paint, and the fearlessness of blind and self-destroying egoism. Give a Frenchman authority, asserts Romain Rolland, and he becomes if not a lunatic, a dangerous fanatic. David was a fanatic of the worst kind, one with executive ability, using art to illustrate academic knowledge and to gratify the insane pretensions of politicians.

He abolished the old Academy and instituted his own with principles similar to those of Poussin, only more pedantic and stifling, and with an authority so despotic that his enemies were compelled to imitate him or lose their heads; he organized the fêtes of Regeneration and the Supreme Being, designed costumes, is said to be responsible for Empire furniture, and when the Republic fell, having no sympathy with contemporary life, unhesitatingly covered his papier-maché nudes with imperial robes to please the vanity of Napoleon. The terrible events of the Revolution made no impression on his metallic mind; heartless and soulless, he painted not one picture—even the *Marat* has the antique mould, a hideous bas-relief or a bad Poussin—of which we may say, as one must say of the true artist, "Here the subject has moved him, forced him to build, to unburden himself of his feelings; to transfer to nature the intensity of his experiences, the flavor of a rare personality, the joy, the deeper interest, the sharper tragedy of one afflicted with living."

But David's greatest crime is not in his paintings, bad as they are: the spurious Roman legends and the colossal Napoleonic space-fillers which no one honest with himself can endure, except as museum relics of fanatical self-confidence. He completed the evil started by Poussin, put the French curse on the teaching of art, and fixed the tradition of the plaster-cast figure and the manufactured nude ruling all modern academies. To him we must ascribe the system of drawing the figure by precedent and rigid prescription, without reference to its true structure and with no specific purpose in mind—simply to make a "beautiful nude," tight, sleek, and conforming to arbitrary or ideal proportions supposed to be pure Greek, but actually handed down from

Graeco-Roman copies by French academicians. David boasted that he drew nothing without a model. Nobody disputes the fact. So did Ingres, and so do most academicians. But he used the model only as a means to recover the poses of antique statuary, to lend a touch of realism to stolen attitudes and memorized forms, just as the thousands of little Davids use the model in the traditional fashion to make art for art's sake. The popularity of Davidian drawing is not hard to explain: it is within the reach of any student, provided he is obtuse enough to yield to meaningless discipline; and among politicians and official juries, it still passes for art. Except in his portraits, where the surface facts of nature could not be eluded, David's art is sham-classicism of a pernicious variety.

The successor of David was his pupil Ingres. Not that Ingres was an imitator of his master, but like David, whom he called "the only master of his age," he was an academician of the first water. He too won the Prix de Rome, lived for a score of years in the Eternal City, and had circumstances permitted, would have buried himself there for the rest of his long life, making art or trying to, out of Raphael and Leonardo. He was first drawn to Giotto and Masaccio, but the early Italians had no discoverable effect on his essentially Parisian talent. Having no interest in humanity, he turned his sensual gaze on Raphael, and his cultivation of the abstract qualities of the Italian gained for him, among the French, the title of the great modern classic master. While in Rome he executed, entirely for money, his fellowship paying only a pittance, a large number of pencil portraits of travellers, little sketches distinguished by exquisite taste and astounding craftsmanship, but otherwise no more than harmless miniatures in which heads are drawn quite literally and costumes described by outlines of microscopical fineness, lines so dry and inexpressive as to suggest the costume drawings in the advertisements of modern newspapers. In the *Salon of 1824* where Delacroix and the English provoked a hullabaloo that has not yet subsided, he made a noise with his *Vow of Louis XIII* which, by virtue of the subject, fooled the young Romantics into thinking he was one of them. But Ingres soon showed where he belonged: he was of the school, petty, unimaginative and overweening. He insulted Delacroix and every other painter of intelligence, regarded himself as the sole heir of the great age, and like most men without ideas, hated the ideas of his rivals. He lived to be eighty-seven, growing, if possible, more intolerant with years, and suffering to the end from an uncontrollable itch for young girls.

Ingres painted portraits, nudes and a few compositions in the nature of classical allegories. The last are particularly fatuous. Least of all was he capable of the noble and heroic, and his seraglios of prettified nudes, if they express anything, express only the senile eroticism of his unhealthy mind. So self-abasing was he before Raphael that in practically all his heads, men and women alike, we may recognize at once the features of the sentimental Madonna. His portraits are so many pieces of still-life drawn with a razor and tinted with harsh repellent colors; his nudes boneless houris with swollen thyroids and faces as vacuous as those of Greuze. He despised his age and it is not surprising therefore that his work is devoid of vitality—and without vitality there can be no art of any importance. Next to Raphael he loved nude girls, but in painting them, he was so servilely absorbed in improving on Raphael that his boorish sensuality was vitiated into chic emblems of sterilized desire. Unable to conceive of anything new in art, or to experience anything worth while, he expended his energy—and he had plenty of it—on academic processes, on fiddling with sinuous lines, on fining down his lines until they lost their strength, their tension, and their relation to living materials.

Ingres fancied himself a Greek. He is the finest type of cultivated Parisian, of the mind which demands in painting, not character but cleverness, not the spiritual but the chic and tasteful, not conviction but craftsmanship. Out of the painting of Italy he fabricated a characteristically French product—let us give him credit for that. He set the standard of nudity in French painting—the sleek, naked animal which, like adultery in the novel and on the stage, has become so boring and meaningless. Of late, he has been admired by Picasso and others for his abstract qualities, that is, for his skill in depicting the human body as a flat pattern from which the organic and emotional life has been completely emptied. In other words for making a picture resembling a man or a woman, but before which we feel nothing but cunning arrangements of flattened forms, flowing lines and stuffs rendered with photographic accuracy. Let us give him credit for that too, and say no more of him.

The decadent painting of Ingres is continued in Bouguereau, Gérôme, Cabanel and Lefebvre, and with an admixture of false romanticism, in Delaroche and Couture. We need not pursue it. These men are beneath contempt; yet their influence rules the French Salon of today and survives in the canvases of hundreds of facile quacks and caterers whom nothing can destroy—not even the depredations of the Modernists. The bourgeois Frenchman loves his cheap ornamentation, but he does not, I think, take it as seriously as the Englishman takes his Leightons, his Albert Moores and his Alma-Tademas, or the American his Coxes and Blashfields. There is nothing to be done about it. The poor in painting, as in the other arts, we shall always have with us. Did not Michael Angelo, in a moment of despair, cry out that "the times were unfavorable for art?" Did not Blake declaim bitterly against the portrait manufacturers? And old Cézanne go back to the farm?

The last academician of prominence is Puvis de Chavannes. His aim was commendable enough: to bring mural painting and architecture into harmonious conjunction and to use as subject-matter French legends and poetic genre. But his mind was dull and prosaic, without force or personality. A pinch of Raphael, a little of Ingres, more—of all things!—of Burne-Jones, and very much of Giotto; not color or movement, or anything positive, but dead neutral tones, petrifaction and silhouette; not a living attitude, not an attitude of his own, but conventional gestures lifted from the early Italians—so he made murals. He has been called a master of space composition. A foolish judgment, for he avoided all complications, arranging his figures in sparse patterns as one would lay out a formal garden. His rhythms, such as they are, resemble the monotonous repetitions of Poussin. He has no sense of co-ordination, emphasizes nothing, can conceive of no plausible action for his figures. That is because nothing in life excited him to original constructions or convincing preferences. He must achieve style—style in the abstract, dignity in the abstract, poetry in the abstract. Instead of arousing poetic emotions by plunging his characters into some fundamentally human predicament based upon his own eagerness, sympathy and experience,—almost any one of Giotto's frescoes will bear out my point—he attempts to create a concept of poetry by tastefully placing his figures here and there, and posing them in passive attitudes. Such works he calls *The Sacred Grove*; *Peace and War*; *Work*; *Play*; *Art* and *Nature*. He might as well call them anything, so vague are they.

We have recently seen an identical manifestation of abstract art in certain Modernists who would symbolize the dynamic energy of a machine age by combinations of lines and planes having no specific reference to machines themselves. At his worst, *The Poor Fisherman*, for example, Puvis de Chavannes is simply stupid; at his best he obtains a pallid dignity that is not unpleasing. But his greatest merit is his modesty and discretion. His unobtrusive murals are not artistic assertions but backgrounds, like wall-paper, sinking quietly into the general flatness of the plaster. Unfortunately, being so easy to steal from, they have killed the gallant efforts of Delacroix to establish a genuine mural art; and in America are father to most of those hideous academic decorations which in the name of Industry, Commerce, Labor, and what not, disfigure the walls of our state capitols and public halls.

It is a relief to have done with official art and to enter the little world which Watteau erected outside the walls of the Academy. Watteau, of Flemish blood, formed his art on Rubens and the little Dutchmen, wandered to Paris in his youth, went through ten lean years and ten more of increasing prosperity marred by ill-health and melancholy, and died of consumption at the age of thirty-seven. Thrown between two civilizations, he viewed the dying majesty of the old with some regrets and ushered in the new to the sound of lutes and the murmuring of lovers. No other artist has rendered so truthfully and enchantingly the old Parisian spirit. I say old because the most cautious French critics assure us that the spirit of gallantry is gone forever, having been usurped in the reign of Louis XV by licentiousness which, weathering the storms of the Revolution, and the social changes of the nineteenth century, exists today thinly disguised by stage manners and affectation. But this, I fear, is the verdict of those who would warn their compatriots that Paris, through her very generosity, is sinking into cosmopolitan indolence and depravity. To others less disheartened by the commercialized Bohemia of Paris, and to outsiders privileged to enjoy what is affectionately known as "the fine old French society," the world of Watteau is a living reality, and such persons, standing before his canvases, infallibly express their sentiments in the exclamation, "How French it all is!"

A Fleming, Watteau was not smitten with visions of French glory, nor did he trouble himself over the grandeur of the ancients. The world of the senses, the visible Impressionist world, was sufficient; indeed more than sufficient for his diseased body and afflicted soul. One would hardly expect a robust and healthy painter—say his master Rubens—to devote his art to the etiquette of love-making. He has but one idea: men and women, not playing at the game of love, but whose lives are dedicated to love. They are dressed for the part; they exercise restraint lest the passion burn out; they avoid everything gross and uncultivated, displaying their seductions with the greatest delicacy and charm. A frivolous preoccupation? Perhaps, to this workaday world, but a little of Watteau's gallantry would not hurt the coarse mating of American lovers. The *Embarkation for Cytherea* summarizes all that he had to say: here his assembled couples prepare to sail away to the blessed isle where there is no death, where love-making is prolonged into eternity. The Frenchman's idea of heaven!

Watteau's technique is a frail instrument, but one thoroughly adequate to his art, which is all that matters. He retains the ambers, blues and cherry tones of Rubens; his draughtsmanship is the light and shade drawing of the Impressionists; he had little knowledge of the structure of the body and seldom painted the nude, training his eye to observe the fluttering effects of light on faces, costumes and landscape. But his attitudes and figures are never borrowed—they are his own, and observed from life. His way of working was to fill his notebooks with sketches of heads, figures, and costumes of his own invention, and to compose his pictures from his stock of drawings. Natural forms he seems never to have studied closely, his trees being banks of plumage in fanciful landscape designed as an ideal setting for his courtly lovers. He is a poor hand at grouping his figures, scattering them thoughtlessly like flowers strewn upon the grass, and holding them together by a magical atmosphere of tone. In this he resembles Claude, but advances a step closer to modern Impressionism in the shimmering mists, the transparent curtains of gold hanging over his mountain tops.

Watteau's characters may not have a thought in their heads; they may, in Rolland's branding words, have "whipped-cream souls," but how seriously he handles them! The mood is real. Here is romantic love created by an artist. In Boucher the theme becomes vulgar boudoir decoration—too mechanical to be seductive; in Fragonard it fades into flashy artifice, the dexterous mummery reproduced by the modern cinema.

Chardin, who was just beginning to paint when Watteau died, was little esteemed by the connoisseurs of his licentious age, but today the vogue of still-life painting created by Cézanne has revived his art and attached to it the extravagant values of fashionable enthusiasm and belated discovery. A plain man, the son of a carpenter, without culture, living happily among the bourgeoisie of Paris, he painted kitchen utensils, loaves and bottles, and domestic occurrences which, seen with sympathy and rendered with art, are transfigured into poetry. He was trained in the Dutch tradition, and in his choice of homely subjects he resembles the Dutch. But in essentials he is French: in his Impressionist method, and in his scrupulous search for style. You will not find in his pictures the sharp edges and the clear atmosphere of the Dutch interior—everything is blurred, immersed in atmosphere, "as if reflected in a dull mirror." He loved his subjects—his fruits and game, his children saying their prayers, his neighbors and servants—no doubt of that, but not in the Dutch fashion, as good things to see and to possess, but in the French, as good things to paint. He spends hours posing his models and days arranging his pots and pans; honest workman that he is, he paints slowly and with great pains, touch by touch, removing every useless detail and gradually building up little units of solid form. But his interest, remember, is directed less to revealing the character and individuality of objects, than to the presentment of forms, the appearances of solids in special atmospheric conditions.

I do not mean that he paints abstractions, but that his work, in comparison with Dutch painting, is French Impressionism. His technique, in fact, is strikingly modern. "His painting is singular," remarked a friend; "he places his colors one against the other, rarely mixing them, in a way that reminds us of the mosaic-like effect of tapestry done with a needle. Look closely, everything is blurred, flattened out and lost. Go farther away and everything comes together again. All the objects are unified one with another, and from this results a transparency of color which vivifies everything his brush touches." Chardin worked with the model before him, simplified what he saw, and composed, without resorting to distortions, pictures of more substance than the Impressionists of the Manet type. He is an admirable but not a great painter. Those who say he "evoked the secret soul of fruits and vegetables" are speaking in hyperboles. His mind was pretty literal; he could not imagine anything that lay outside the field of vision. But he wrought, in a small way, magical effects from plain things; and his little masterpieces touch our emotions with the appeal of minor poetry.

Chardin died before the Revolution had flung painting into the power of David. But in the midst of the upheaval, in 1796, Corot, the happiest of painters, was born. The classical paroxysm left no mark upon him—nor did the fight to the death between the partisans of Delacroix and Ingres, nor had he the faintest notion of what went on in 1830, 1848 and 1870. In politics, a Conservative; in religion, a staunch Catholic; in art, a believer in the best French tradition, that of Claude; this simple-hearted, generous man lived his four-score years in that blissful state of nature apostrophized by Rousseau. Only he was ignorant of Rousseau, and for that matter, of all the French writers. Reading put him to sleep—he was a painter and nothing more. He loved nature and women, loved them chastely, and nature and women were his true religion despite his professed Romanism. His worship was compounded of poetic fervor and adolescent sentimentality; he never grew up, wandering through life without a care, and without an enemy, a gipsying dreamer—and incidentally, a terrific worker,—and when, at last, the happy journey was over, he said, with a devout faith in "the good Lord" that always amused his Bohemian friends, "that he hoped to go on painting in heaven." When he was not working in the fields, he was by the fireside chatting with old ladies, or in his studio painting bathing girls and pretty milliners.

Corot never married and never, so far as I know, had any sexual experience, preserving throughout his life his naïve belief in the purity and divinity of all women. Hence the virginal quality of his landscape, and the absence of sex in his women. To save his soul he could not paint a man, and when we consider that he painted almost everything else with the greatest readiness and distinction, the fact becomes psychologically telling. There is more of the feminine in him than in any other painter of equal rank—and more that is nobly feminine. Physically, however, he was as robustly constituted as Turner, rising before dawn to observe the morning twilight, a ceaseless worker, producing some 2500 canvases, and like Turner again, covering most of Western Europe in his travels. To him the antique was a closed book, and he set little store by the Renaissance masters. Thrice he journeyed to Italy, but only to study landscape, shutting his eyes on the celebrated wonders, and refusing to enter the Sistine Chapel. He traveled to discover picturesque materials which he painted with a song on his lips, for the joy of it, striving neither to be great nor astonishing.

It has been the misfortune of Corot to be remembered by his worst things, to acquire enormous posthumous fame on the strength, or rather on the weakness, of pictures not entitled to live. Always the agent of the softer emotions, he is, when bad, intolerably spineless and vulgar, and also, it has happened, extraordinarily popular and high-priced. In early life he painted, for the most part in Italy, classical landscapes so-called by reason of their firmness of structure, their fine tranquillity, and the dignity with which they communicate his strongest feelings before nature. These are masculine conceptions ranking among his best works, but having been hidden until very recently in private collections, are not generally known. In his middle years he painted innumerable scenes in the popular or silvery-grey manner, the filmy, fuzzy scourings of tinsel and sentimentality which have made him, among Americans, a household favorite. It is estimated that 3000 of these gutless reflections, some genuine, the majority faked by starving French Impressionists in their salad days, have been purchased, at fancy prices, by American collectors. At the age of sixty he took a new lease on life and painted worthily again. In all three periods he worked steadily at figure pieces: portraits, virgins painted indoors and then inserted as sylvan goddesses into leafy backgrounds, and finally, clothed women in studio settings. Today Corot, the figure painter, has come into sudden fame, astute buyers paying fantastic sums for anything put on the market.

Why a man who painted so many good pictures should have painted so many more that are unqualifiedly bad is a puzzling problem. And the bad are not ambitious schemes that do not come off, but perfect expressions of trivial moods or the same trivial mood. The English critic Wilenski lays it to the influence of the camera, and it is undoubtedly true that Corot, as he approaches modern Impressionism, is guilty of photographic flimsiness in his drawing and in his effects of light and shade. It may have been the inheritance from his mother, a Swiss milliner, or that he was willing to knock off salable stuff in order to get money to indulge his lavish generosity. But the main reason, it seems to me, is to be found in his femininity to which we owe the best and the worst of him. When present in the proper amount, this ingredient invests his work with a stainless purity of conception that is Corot's special property in painting; a cool purity analogous to the incorruptible cleanliness of Willa Cather's fiction. When predominant, it dissolves his structure entirely, leaving a filmy mess which induces in the beholder illegitimate emotions of no higher grade than the sniffles aroused by a precocious child singing sentimental ballads in an old ladies' home. Corot lacked, Meier-Graefe shrewdly observes, the grain of poison which is the preservative of greatness. Yet a first-rate Corot is a good thing to own. It speaks softly but the tones are clear. The landscapes have the saintliness of Madonnas, conveying a religious devotion to nature; the figures, nude or draped, show the same devotion, a worship of women expressed in clean modelling, noble attitudes and chaste forms.

CHAPTER

XVI

DELACROIX

DELACROIX is a spectacular figure. Enormously gifted, he seemed to possess all the preliminaries to great painting: he had intellect, energy, and ideas; he had courage, one of the finest critical minds of the century, extraordinary facility, and he had temperament. He was born into an age of revolt, a world of political insurrection and unparalleled discord among the artists; the time had come to slay the academic monster, and having strong convictions and the fighting courage that goes with them, he found himself, when a very young man, the leader of the radical forces. He did not seek the command, but standing head and shoulders above the embattled Romantics, he accepted the responsibility and became the champion of individual freedom in painting. The French critics, with their talent for scurvy epithet and their flouting of unofficial art, insulted him to his dying day but the men of intelligence—Balzac, Gautier, Musset, Baudelaire, Daumier—were with him, and he bore the attacks of his enemies with the superb loftiness of the true aristocrat. Today, in France, he is a national glory, and by common acclaim, the hero of modern painting.

In the history of painting I dislike the word romantic—it is a verbal hack with repulsive implications—but I can find no substitute. It has come to signify almost everything that is contemptible in art: Bohemian corruption, temperament instead of good sense; the sensational and precious, the extravagant and disorderly, the exotic and picturesque, the unbearable effeminacy of poseurs, the mountebank of opera and fiction. And I am bound to admit that the worst features of Romanticism are caricatures of Delacroix's febrile temperament; for he was a pale, Byronic dandy whose weaknesses were precisely of the sort which inferior minds seize upon as manifestations of greatness. But he was no poseur, and he despised the little creatures who dragged his ideas of historical decoration into the gutters of drooling sentiment and silly anecdote. After all, there are only two classes of painters, the intelligent and the unintelligent, and Delacroix belongs in the first. His merits, usually described as peculiarly romantic, are common to all good painting. His exaggerated forms are not more exaggerated than the giants of Michael Angelo or the enlarged anatomies of Rubens; his subject-matter is not more dramatic than that of Leonardo or Tintoretto, not to mention a dozen others, and not more exotic than Rembrandt's oriental themes; and his color, while brighter than the color of his predecessors, is employed after the method of Rubens, with superficial splashes borrowed from the English and the Spaniards.

Let us remember then that when we call Delacroix a Romantic, we do so to distinguish him from the pseudo-classic or academic painters of France, and to identify him with the worldwide revolt of youth against official tyranny in government and in art. In England the movement was no longer new, nor was it new in Germany; but in France it took the individualist Napoleon to jolt the artists out of their traditional subservience to the bureaucratic system. The romantic upheaval occurred a generation after the Revolution, a curious phenomenon. I have already told how the Republicans, while engaged in demolishing the old régime, patterned their state on the ancient Roman model, and how the academic painters, to a man, swallowed the doctrine of the antique. France, it seemed, could not produce an artist capable of thinking for himself. At length, assailed on all sides by rebellious forces, her fighting spirit was aroused; and the fiery example of foreigners burning in the minds of young artists reared in the turmoil of the Revolution, and the Napoleonic wars supplied the fuel for the great romantic victory of 1830.

Before this date there had been notorious romantic performances by Dumas, Balzac, Géricault and Delacroix himself, but in 1830, the year of Hugo's *Hernani* and the overthrow of the Bourbons, the movement was organized, and the French, with their partisan habits, their rabble instinct for taking sides on all questions, arrayed themselves into two parties: in one, the exponents of free speech in art; in the other, the conservatives fighting desperately for academic authority. The Romantics drew their fire from many sources: from Scott, Byron, Constable and Bonington; from Goethe, Schiller and Beethoven, and from Goya; the Academics clung to the dreary tragedies of Corneille, Racine and Voltaire, and the bleak platitudes of Poussin and David. I have said that the Romantics were victorious. The statement is true, but it was a moral victory. They were the founders of modern art and letters, but officially and popularly they were unmercifully beaten. In the mad excitement of 1830, Racine and Corneille continued to pack the theatres, and the academic painters received all the commissions, as usual. The French business of excoriating good painters was first practiced on Delacroix; in the succeeding generations Manet and Courbet were flayed; and what happened to Cézanne and the Modernists is familiar to everyone.

Delacroix came into notice in 1822 with his *Dante and Vergil*, an impressive work for a student of twenty-three. The old guard, caught by the classical subject, remarked it favorably and invited him to come into their fold "to learn how to draw." He declined politely and went on his way, influenced by the masters, particularly Rubens, and by his friend Géricault, a man of power, and the first to bring movement and color into the degenerate still-life ornamentation of French painting. Géricault, an Anglophile, went to England to live, was thrown from a horse, and fatally injured in his thirty-first year. The burden of leadership was shouldered immediately by Delacroix. In the *Salon of 1824*, dominated, you will recall, by the English—he exhibited the *Massacre of Scio*, an episode taken from the struggle of the Greeks against the Turks. It is a matter of history that Delacroix, proud and impressionable, was bowled over by the brilliancy of Constable's *Hay Wain*, and that he repainted, some say in three days, others in two weeks, the entire background of his canvas in the luminous broken tones of the English masterpiece. The academic scribes and Pharisees, trembling for the safety of the French tradition, screamed with indignation, and proclaimed the work the "Massacre of Painting." Never perhaps was a man of integrity and intelligence so insanely calumniated. But Delacroix was a dauntless soul. "I became," he said, "the abomination of painting. I was refused water and salt—but I was delighted with myself." He did not waste his energies throwing mud at his vile accusers; he aggravated their spleen with more paintings, and for the benefit of those having the sense to understand him, kept a journal in which he expressed, in the most exquisite French, his ideas of art.

The abuse lavished upon him was the typical vocabulary of insult, that is to say, he was called everything which obviously he was not. He was a "savage, a barbarian, a maniac. He was ignoble and monstrous. He did not know how to draw; he painted with a drunken broom." Absurd language to use against a man who, though he painted at white heat, with feverish rapidity, painted with the profoundest respect for Poussin and Raphael, the idols whom, in their ignorance, they imagined he was brutally mocking. Had they objected that his effects were too elaborately premeditated, his designs too coolly rationalized, that he could not deliver himself from tradition, there would have been some justice in their accusations. They did not know it, but instead of a barbarian, they were attacking the most scholarly, the most cultured painter of the nineteenth century.

Delacroix looked down on painters who were painters and nothing more—day laborers of the stripe of Courbet and Manet who worked as methodically as plasterers, and once a job was finished, put it out of their minds and promptly began another. He was a patrician and an aesthete, but naturally so; the rest were talented boors. His tastes in art and letters were sound and catholic; his habits fastidious; his judgments liberal. He read widely—the classical writers and his contemporaries—and

Delacroix: SELF-PORTRAIT.

Louvre, Paris

was emulous of Byron whose poems he read as they appeared. He admired Goethe, Mozart and Beethoven, but could not stand Berlioz; he was one of the first to appreciate Balzac, and to reject the flatulent shrieking of Hugo; he was as generous in his praise of Rembrandt, Rubens and Holbein, as of the Italians; proclaimed the genius of Goya and Daumier; battled for the Englishmen; and defended the rights of all artists whether he liked them or not. A brilliant figure, reserved and incapable of vulgarity, he was the most distinguished conversationalist in Paris, spending his evenings in the company of countesses, elegantly tailored in English clothes—the consummate product of French culture. Delicate of health and extremely nervous, he was forced to conserve his strength, employing, he said, a third of his time getting himself in condition to paint. But in bulk his work compares favorably with the most prolific artists. He composed with astonishing fluency in oil, watercolor, etching and lithography; his feverish intellectual curiosity is recorded in thousands of studies: translations of Rubens, Michael Angelo, Veronese, Rembrandt, Goya, Rowlandson, Velasquez, Daumier; experiments in color to test the practical value of complementaries which he had scientifically charted on a revolving disc. In subject-matter he acknowledged no limit. He gathered ideas from Ariosto, Dante, Scott, Shakespeare, Byron and Goethe; from mythology, the Crusades, the Revolution and contemporary events; he painted portraits, battle pieces, animals, genre, easel pictures and murals, and he painted religious themes. In addition to this, he wrote letters which have passed into literature, and criticism of great charm and not less penetration.

A spectacular figure indeed! And the pictures are as spectacular as the author! But they are, I am pained to say, for all their sincerity, the intelligent planning and brainwork that went into the making of them, disappointing engines. Once, I daresay, when the themes were fresher, and the hollow forms could be filled with swinging emotions supplied by the titles, they were furiously exciting, but today, with Byronism an extinct malady and Greece of less significance than Persian oil fields, they stand out, in their corporeal flimsiness, as magnificent gestures. The solid matter of great painting is not in them. Possibly, as MacColl suggests, after Rubens and Rembrandt it is hard to be fair to smaller men, but it is not hard to discover what is the matter with Delacroix. He has told us himself—unintentionally however: "The most real things in the world are the illusions I create with paint." In other words he could not or did not concern himself with realities, with first-hand experiences providing the substance of art; and like Poussin, fed upon the ideas of others, striving by will-power and intellection to translate into paint emotions other artists had created from direct contacts with life.

His approach to art, subtle, guided by remarkable understanding, cutting like a blade to the kernel of greatness, was a little too academic to allow his imagination to range independently. In beginning a picture, it was not what he had observed, or loved and hated and mastered in France that released his energies, but Rubens, Shakespeare and Byron, and when the hectic labor was over, it was not a new thing he had brought forth, but a complex hybrid. Delacroix was tarred by the brush of French precedent. He too must sweat and suffer and suppress his individuality for the traditional glory of France. He fought like a man to dislodge official oppressors, but at the same time coveted recognition from the society whose ribbons and honors were not worth the having. Six times he applied for a seat in the Academy, and finally, after he had been snubbed and vilified for twenty years, was admitted. What a fall! And this wise and sensitive man, the profound student of Michael Angelo and Rubens, was held in thrall by the marmoreal dullness and immobility of Poussin! It was the academic grandeur of Poussin, the heroic position which he occupied in French painting, that hypnotized Delacroix. He too must be a hero, a lofty, inaccessible soul, a god of painting. Unable naturally to rise to the heights, he resorted to stimulants. He was always inspiring himself. Every morning, before beginning to paint, he made a sketch from Poussin to induce the heroic mood; while working on his *Dante and Vergil* he had the *Comedy* read to him in Italian, painting like one possessed; instead of breakfast, he swallowed a dose of Rubens; he would go all day without eating to goad himself into a nervous frenzy; he doped his brain with literature to escape offensive realities and to lose himself in artificial exaltation. These are not the courses of the healthy mind but the symptoms of morbidity. Delacroix derived small satisfaction from living; ambition intoxicated him, and the incubus of greatness exacerbated his nervousness and drove him into orgies of unnatural toil. Critically, his mind was an unerring instrument; when he began to paint he tortured his faculties into a state of neurosis. He had the Frenchman's love of the exotic and traveled to Morocco for local color. Critically, he was on the side of true classicism; in practice, he was always knocking at the doors of the Academy.

I have no fault to find with his subject-matter. Any subject is legitimate so long as it represents a natural, unforced or special preference on the part of the artist. Nor am I disturbed by his literary qualities, the term literary being a fashionable club to whack painters bold enough to depict characters plausibly occupied, and in the throes of emotions consistent with the situation. Delacroix's subjects were those uppermost in the minds of the Romantics; he came by them honestly; they were congenial to his temperament and a compliment to his scholarship. It was his efforts to fill them with forms and emotions he had never experienced that tumbled him to grief. The nominal subject of a picture—the title in the catalogue—is one thing; the actual subject another thing entirely. Giotto's saints, Rembrandt's Christ, the classical rapes of Rubens, were unquestionably inspired by predilections for biblical and mythological subjects, but the saints are Italian barbers, the Christ a Portuguese Jew, and the raped women the wives of Rubens. These figures carry a meaning because they refer directly to realities, because they are created from forms which the artists have loved and mastered, from attitudes observed and studied, from emotions actually experienced. So it is with all enduring art.

Delacroix unhappily preferred illusions to realities. He had great will power, great courage, but a weak appetite for the gross earthy fare from which art draws its vitality. He was a product of the study and the salon: commerce with the world turned his stomach. He was a poor observer with a specious but very limited knowledge of the human figure. He dealt in ideas and abstractions. He shunned nature, worked only occasionally from life, and admitted that he could not get interested in the model, nor, he might have added, in any object or living thing. Thus his knowledge was inadequate to his ambitions, and when one has recovered from the effects of his incredible facility, one finds in his huge canvases only convulsive attitudes and colossal sketches. By the aid of brilliant color he partly conceals his uncertain draughtsmanship; but the drawing is ragged, and the segments composing his pictures are broken by gaps and fissures. He obtains vividness by his sketchy technique, but the agonized faces, the swirling naked figures, the faked, ramping chargers, the theatrical Medea, the symbol of French Liberty taken bodily from Rubens, are too unsubstantial, too obviously put together by dextrous invention to convey the dramatic truth which Delacroix imagined he brushed into them because he understood so well how Rubens had done it. The great Fleming lurks in all his figures, but it is only the ghost of Rubens. With his universal sympathies, his robust and lusty humanity, and his superabundant knowledge, Rubens expands, as naturally as one breathes, into massive forms. Delacroix endeavors to illustrate Shakespeare and Byron by figures and movements based upon Rubens: the forms, needless to say, are of giant size, and he struggles with the help of stimulants, to expand his meagre experiences, to blow himself up into the stature of a giant. The effort is heroic, the achievement shocking. He is agitated, not dramatic; nervous rather than powerful. He achieves the gesture of greatness—but the substance is wanting.

Why then is Delacroix so highly reverenced by modern France? Mainly, I believe, because he is an influence, a force, a symbol. He comes closer than any one else to France's notion of the romantic aristocrat of art—he towers among the boors like a Renaissance lord. He is a symbol of the heroic, lending a Napoleonic touch to painting. When the Davidian plague lay upon art, he came forward in a blaze of color, and by the force of his courage, his daring attempts to create a new tradition in the face of virulent opposition, changed the base of procedure from the academic morgue to the healthy athleticism of Rubens. But why, it may well be asked, was it necessary to bring Rubens on the scene? It would not have been necessary, had Delacroix been of the stature of Rubens—and modern painting would be another story. To appraise the benefits of the Flemish transfusion, one has but to compare the murals of Delacroix, especially those in the Church of St. Sulpice—the nearest thing to monumental decoration that has come out of France—with the machines of the academic crowd, to compare the independent art of the nineteenth century with the official art, past or present. For there is something of Delacroix in all his successors. Watteau, Chardin and Corot were worthy men, but tame and placid; violence, belligerent recklessness, incessant hostility were needed to turn art into new channels and these Delacroix possessed in fullest measure. He rooted out the still-life growth which was choking French painting to death, introducing action, turbulence, and color. Above all color. "Grey," he said, "is the enemy of all painting." He was a great colorist, not soft and gaudy like the Impressionists to whom he handed the English palette, but strong and brilliant, using a full orchestra of tones and making them all sing together. In the vividness and animation of his color we almost forget his stretched and lurching forms which, flung into the world without the bone and muscle supplied by observation and experience, fall exhausted from his brush. He did not destroy the Academy—that were an impossible task—but he stands in relation to modern painting as France once stood in relation to the whole world, and as the commanding figure stands in one of his most thrilling canvases: the *Spirit of Liberty Leading the People*.

CHAPTER

XVII

DAUMIER

IN PARIS, a city of monuments, there is no monument to Daumier. The French, it seems, would prefer to forget the greatest of their painters. When he was alive, they sent him to jail, and let him die totally blind and without a sou; since his death, in 1879, they have written little that would indicate even an historical concern in his work and his fate. But it is no wonder the French do not love him. He has neither charm nor culture, none of the things they prize in art; he painted only a few nudes, and those the opposite of the chic and the seductive; and he fell upon the cult of prettiness and the catchpenny wares of the Academics with the branding-iron of caricature. There is no one remotely like him; he is so utterly different from the rest that it is hard to believe that he is a Frenchman.

Save for a few portraits of his friends, mostly artists, and his pictures of the poor and miserable to whom he was bound by his experiences as a boy in the streets of Paris and by his feelings of pity, regret, loneliness and oppression which bind together all human souls, his art is that of an active revolutionary. He used it to assassinate second-rate kings and impious politicians; to expose the imbecilities of the mean, hardened and pretentious bourgeoisie for whom he had no compassion but, instead, a healthy hatred that is not without a smile despite its pitiless irony; and he used it with gigantic incision to create the most impenitent gallery of hypocrites ever called into existence by the onslaught of genius on the sordid stuff of mankind. To imitate this man without sharing his convictions, to undertake to learn from him without the knowledge born of such convictions, is to try to make bricks without straw. It has not been tried very often, and those foolhardy enough to hazard it, fancying they could bend his mighty line without being able to wield the substance enclosed within it, have broken their backs like the drones who ventured to draw the bow of Ulysses. On the present generation he has exercised little influence—the present generation has not caught up with him.

Daumier was born in 1808, in Marseilles, and was brought to Paris in his first years. His father, a glazier and a mediocre poet yearning for literary honors, succeeded at nothing, and the family was desperately poor. From his seventh year the boy Honoré, already busy with his pencil, seems to have taken life in his own hands, choosing the career of an artist. Of formal education he had practically none. He lived in the streets and the Louvre, the best possible schools for the radical Frenchman. He studied, entirely in his own way, the masters of the High Renaissance, Rembrandt and the sculptures of Michael Angelo, worked from nature and the nude, and was always modelling in clay or wax. For a while he was an usher at one of the courts of law, and for a shorter time a bookseller's drudge, jobs paying him so little that he decided it were better to starve as an artist than as a menial. Before he was twenty he had mastered lithography, and at twenty-one published in this medium a series of compositions which were, beyond all peradventure, the most original and the most powerful drawings ever done in France.

Daumier had a memory of unaccountable tenacity, or perhaps not so unaccountable, if we think of his extraordinary capacity to observe and study the human animal. He was essentially and exclusively a figure artist, and being a man of genius, his interest in people was so sustained and piercing that he discovered, in the active anatomy of his subjects, salient characteristics, movements, and variations of structure which escape the ordinary eye. This property may have been a gift from God, but it was regulated by a strong will, steadiness in living, fundamental human decency, and common sense, qualities for which artists are not precisely famous. It was not so much what people said as how they looked when they said it, not so much what they did as the shapes they got themselves into and the faces they put on, that fascinated his curiosity. And once he observed things—a windbag of the law defending a guilty minx, or an old woman with a ragged child tugging at her skirts—he never forgot them. He dug into the inmost secrets of their dirty or battered souls, noted the lines and planes of blubbering faces, noted huge violent mouths puffing out casuistries, heaving chests, bowed backs, the ponderous stride of towmen—Paris painted in action, Paris as he saw it, and not off duty posing for artists. His knowledge of the human figure, though furthered, of course, by the Old Masters, was largely gathered from direct observation of those around him, from people performing naturally their daily tasks. He rarely made studies for their own sake; had no need to hire models—the working population of Paris was his model; and with his superhuman memory, watched his victims in action, returned to his garret, his head filled with them, modelled them in clay, and then lithographed them for the press.

His first published work attracted the attention of the editor of a radical sheet called *La Caricature*, and he was invited to join the staff of that unsavory organ. He accepted at once, was allowed gorgeous freedom, and being very young and terribly in earnest—he was only twenty-one—turned his heavy artillery into the ranks of the Orleanist politicians. In a short time he won unenviable notoriety, the respectable artists regarding him as a vicious gamin, the catspaw of rabble-rousers; and the political cowards shaking in their boots at the sight of his masterpieces of slaughter. The bombardment went on, and after three years, on taking a particularly hot shot at Louis-Philippe, he was clapped in prison. But life behind the bars was not so bad to one of Daumier's upbringing; he bore it with good humor, worked at his art, and after his release, resumed his post, unchastened. When his paper crashed, he was called to another, as humorist and social satirist, and till his death continued to earn his bread by cartooning.

It is often said that Daumier did not really have political con-

Daumier: LITHOGRAPH FROM *La Caricature.*

victions, that, being an artist, he could not possibly have cared for the filthy affairs of government arrogated by hard, insensitive men to their own selfish purposes. This opinion does not make sense. Dilettante artists are harmless, never get locked up. Daumier was not so detached from humanity that he could devote his life to the decorous rehashing of past styles, not so timid and ignorant of practical matters that he could remain in a studio aimlessly fretting with subjectivities, or wheedling stereotyped forms into tasteful abstractions. True, he was no fanatic, no wild-eyed anarchist seeking the dubious honors of martyrdom. He did what he thought was right, dealt a powerful blow, and took the consequences without whining; he had the self-control, the formidable calm of a man sure of his fire. No other artist of equal ability ever gave the best of his life to caricature and social criticism, but that is one of art's misfortunes. The deliberation with which he prepared his caricatures—the work and effort and knowledge he bestowed on them—was the direct result of invincible beliefs. Do you suppose that Daumier toiled like a galley-slave merely to afford a few snobbishly endowed connoisseurs a sumptuous drawing-room thrill called the aesthetic emotion? The aesthetic emotion was twaddle to a man of his character. Or that the murderous effectiveness of his lithographs, their tragic emphasis and appalling vigor, is due to some mysterious quality attributed to lines and masses when abstracted from the subjects in which they generate life? Or that his drawings are any less works of art because they show up abominable judges, hateful women and a cringing middle class empty of all honor?

It is also maintained that the world is the poorer by many masterpieces because Daumier was compelled to divert his powers as a painter into the trivial field of satire. This is conjecture, Daumier himself giving credence to the notion. He was overworked and was paid less for his daily labor than a vendor of chestnuts; he got tired of journalism, especially of its demands on his humor, for he was not very funny—working at night so that he might have a little time by day to paint, and hoping, in later years, that each plate would be the last. But no relief came, and he stuck by his stones till death. Whether he would have produced more masterpieces in paint, had he been of independent means, cannot be decided. Let us be grateful for the few that we have, without disparaging the lithographs. He made thousands of lithographs, and some naturally are not so good as others; and the best are inferior to the best oils in the sense that the scope of a fine drawing is more limited than the scope of a fine painting done by the same hand. But the best—and they run into the hundreds—rank far above the most ambitious canvases of the rest of the Frenchmen. He knew their value, and when he was old and tired, continued to serve his journal with little slackening of his powers and with a fortitude which should be a shining light to malcontents and defeated aesthetes. But he felt all along that he could do greater things with his brush, and now and again, he did. Let us bear in mind, however, that his years of hard labor in lithography were good for him, were indeed the making of him, and that he would never have been the great painter he was, had he not educated himself by constant activity in black and white, perfecting his draughtsmanship in the immitigable routine of professionalism. Most cartoonists, needless to say, never learn anything, in fact, grow steadily worse. Daumier pursued the art of caricature as seriously as Michael Angelo pursued the art of sculpture, and with a similarity of attack which led the percipient Balzac first to point out the affinity between the two men.

He lived in an old house on the Quai d'Anjou in the most ancient quarter of Paris with his wife Marie, a seamstress whose father, like his own, was also a glazier. In 1848, about the time of his marriage, he took up oils, painting with mastery on his first trials; but his canvases, while they brought him the admiration of the best artists of Paris, were rejected by the public as crude and incompetent. At the instigation of Courbet, he painted *La République* as a competitive decoration for the Hôtel de Ville to commemorate the Second Republic. The picture, far from winning the prize, was not even praised. He was commissioned by the Director of Fine Arts to paint a religious piece for a provincial church, but failed again with one of his greatest works, *The Good Samaritan*, to satisfy the arbiters. These were his only attempts at official recognition. He bore his defeats with stoical courage and went back to his lithographs, sometimes working on eight stones simultaneously in order to be free to resume his oils. The strain was great and he was never free. The streets of Paris, his early home and his school of art, never ceased to fascinate him: he observed collectors peering into the stalls on the quai, café philosophers, booths of jugglers and acrobats, vagrant musicians, blackgowned lawyers hurrying in and out of the Palais de Justice. At the end of the day he would sit for hours at his windows above the Seine, watching the boats, the fishermen, the laundresses, mothers scrubbing their children—the habits of people as poor as himself. "We have our art to comfort us," he would say to his friends, "but what have these wretched folk?"

Daumier's friends were all celebrities—Delacroix, Courbet, Baudelaire, Corot, Gautier, Barye and Daubigny—but he did not seek them. They came to him in the spirit of comradeship and admiration, came to his humble quarters above the river, sat on the floor by his stove, smoked and drank beer together. He talked little, this square stocky cartoonist with a head like Huxley's; he was a poor talker—the dialogue under his satires was written by his editors—but they all knew who was the great man among them. In 1860 his paper let him go, and for three years he had scarcely enough to eat. The other journals turned him down, declaring his vogue was gone; he could not get fifty francs for a watercolor; his eyes began to fail, and but for his friends he would have starved. In 1863, his paper recalled him and once more he was a professional humorist. Twelve more years of toil. He retired to a little cottage at Valmondois, and ten years later, on his sixty-fifth birthday, nearly blind and facing eviction because he could not pay his rent, received a letter from Corot.

"Old Friend:

"I have a little house at Valmondois which I could not, for the life of me, think what to do with. Suddenly I thought to give it to you, and liking the idea, I have had your ownership legally confirmed. I had no idea of doing you a good turn. The whole scheme was carried out to annoy the landlord.

"Ever yours,

"Corot."

In reply, Daumier said, "You're the only man from whom I can take such a present and not feel humiliated." He sent Corot a painting of some lawyers.

In his last years, through the political influence of friends, he was offered the ribbon of the Legion of Honor, but refused it quietly. When Courbet, the showman, heard of the matter he went to Daumier and said, "Great man! Like me you have rejected the dirty decoration—but one should do such things with show and noise."

"I did what I thought was right," Daumier answered. "It's not the public's business."

In 1878 a large exhibition of his oils and watercolors presented by a committee of which Victor Hugo was chairman did not pay the expenses of the gallery. The following year, he died, blind, paralyzed, and alone, and was buried by the State. At his funeral Forain remarked, "Oh, Daumier, he was different from all of us! He was magnanimous!" Immediately after his death there was some agitation for a public monument but nothing came of it.

Daumier brought his great work to its conclusion before the mania for technical speculation had alienated art from humanity. He told his story completely, definitely and with astounding clarity before the difficulties and imperfections of Cézanne's method had been converted into a philosophy. In his art there is not the slightest evidence of any cult of special meanings or transcendental theories—it is the art of a thoroughly healthy mind. Irrelevant fancies such as "organization for its own sake," with its train of rationalizations, were as foreign to him as they were to Rembrandt. He is classic in the true sense of the term, setting up no technical barriers between himself and his world, never mistaking means for an end, never allowing the implements of presentation to obscure the underlying intention. Not that he was careless of processes—no man ever worked more strenuously to master his technique: he entered emotionally into French life and developed the meanings of his own land and kind. He could not conceive of art as a thing removed from experience, as pretty combinations of cubes and cones; yet an analysis of his painting from a purely structural point of view shows that his organizations in plane and line are superior, as such, to the whole of that great mass of Modernist work done with the sole purpose of proving how interesting an abstraction can really be made. His art is living testimony to the profound importance of subject-matter, and to the great benefits derived by one attaching himself to well-grounded interests and convictions, and adhering to the character of his early impressions.

His subject-matter, gathered from the commonest aspects of French life, is so elemental that it has been called trivial. It is anything but trivial. He painted what he knew and understood, the men and women with whom he had toiled and suffered, the thieves and hypocrites preying on society, and he painted with a depth of feeling surpassing any other Frenchman. His religious conceptions and his illustrations of Cervantes and Molière are not less French and not less his own creations than his pictures of bourgeois gossips. And his deep feeling of which so much has been said—and rightly said—was not the exclusive effect of a single impression, but the accompaniment of his whole expressive program, and his whole life. Never did he attempt to transfer to stone or canvas some fugitive emotion aroused by a single scene or circumstance; in no instance are his figures mere transcriptions of particularities in the manner of Velasquez and Manet—they are massive structures containing a richness of humanity and poetry transcending anything possible in the hit-or-miss reportorial style.

It is one of the caprices of fate, or I should say, one of the cases of divine justice, that Daumier, born into a civilization famous above all else for its culture, should, by repudiating that culture and everything it represents, have attained his unique position as a classic artist. Think of the others! How they coveted the grandeur of the ancients and a niche among the immortal gods! How they ranted and argued, borrowed and imitated, rummaged the past for the secrets of the grand style! How subtle and exquisite they were, how ingenious and refined! How heroic! How they loaded their canvases with Roman cerements and established the Academy to protect their decaying aristocracy; how they went romantic and sought for Style in Rubens and in picturesque legends! How they strove for greatness by appropriating the subject-matter of antiquity, and how, the other day, they imagined they had found the classic formula in the negation of subject-matter—in what was called "the harmonics of abstract composition." Standing between the two extremes is Daumier who, without the trappings of classicism, without heroic achings of any sort, trained his vision on the commonest things, and discovered therein new evaluations, new and epic forms.

His supremacy is not so much a matter of feeling as a matter of purpose and superior knowledge. He had the vehement preferences and passionate interests which keep a man's attention continually centered on his fellows, the instinct of the artist to gather a meaning from every action and to read the changes of form and structure implicit in action—not the detached interest of the scientist in the accumulation of facts. He painted ordinary things—men and women he had observed and studied—and his cartoons of kings and fine people are only more dramatic versions of his next-door neighbors or the outcasts of the streets. He put his knowledge to a humane purpose and this knowledge, as I have already mentioned, was not the hoarding of accurate data, but an integrated experience of life—of poverty, sorrow, rascality, politics, religion, manners and art manifestations—presented in its relation to personal judgments of value. Thus he makes a washerwoman a creature of epic proportions, as sublime as one of Michael Angelo's prophets; his clowns and gamins are as noble as the saints of Raphael, and much more vigorous and living; his ministers of state colossal in their grotesque indecency and subversion of justice. With Daumier it was not a question of taking life lightly, of painting all things with facility and charm, but of painting a few subjects with monumental power.

His knowledge, technically applied, was not a surgeon's equipment; it was simply common knowledge intensified by sustained observation. He knew the whole gamut of muscular actions as they impinge upon the vision; knew from his lifelong habits of observation, as well as from his training in sculpture, the infinite number of planes composing the body, and of this number the few absolutely indispensable to the simplest renderings of condensed bulk and solidity. His use of caricature to which objection has been made by sticklers for antique purity is not a whit different from the enlargements of Michael Angelo, Rubens or El Greco. Like the Old Masters, he picked out essentials and played upon them, exaggerated them to his own end which, in his journalism was ironical, but which in his paintings was to emphasize emotions of tragedy and heart-wringing pathos as inherently spiritual as the religious states evoked by the Italians. The ordinary cartoonist disproportionately exaggerates obvious features to produce a humorous or fantastic likeness, and so doing, disregards the structural connection between all the features; Daumier, in magnifying a nose or mouth, considered the effect of this alteration on the rest of the head, readjusting his planes and welding them into an indivisible block. The result is a new physiology of appalling dimensions. He builds his figures sculpturally, modelling in planes of tone, but the planes are not the fragmentary projections of the Cubists—they are all brushed together into a compact whole and enclosed by heavy contours lest the bulging flesh sag of its own weight.

The Havemeyer Collection recently acquired by the Metropolitan Museum brings permanently to the public some of the choicest examples of Daumier's art, both in oil and watercolor. The *Third Class Railway Carriage*, in this collection, one of the many versions of the subject and one of the best, contains most of the great qualities distinguishing him from his countrymen. It is an unfinished painting rather dark in tone, the color running from the subtlest mixtures of deep reds and greens into a rich monochrome, and among the tricky pastels of Degas and the flower-beds of Monet not likely to engage your attention. For despite the directness of statement, it has a mysterious appeal not at once apparent. It represents three seats in a compartment: in the front two women, one suckling a baby, the other hooded and old, with hands clasped over a basket and by her side a boy asleep with his hands stuffed in his pockets; in the background rows of figures, some facing us, some in profile, several in back view. Here for the first time in French painting the figures are real—not decorated pilferings from the old art, not flat impressions—forms standing out in space with incisive bulk and the force of things experienced intensely and habitually pondered over, filled with pity, with the weight of magnanimity, with the strength and substance poured into them by a great soul; here in hands reduced to outlines, in coarse peasant faces, in bodies as solid as the clay from which they were fashioned and postures of Egyptian simplicity, we have the story of the dreariness of one aspect of French life—and we have more, the whole story of suffering humanity.

Daumier's art does not charm or excite us with new aspects of nature: it offers us new aspects of humanity. It embodies ideas and suggestions of fresh creative tendencies in the growth and expansion of modern painting, leaves us with the feeling that the way is open to new ideals and larger possibilities of expression. To prophesy is rash, but I venture to say that in the new orientation of art which I am confident we shall see, once the technical speculators have recovered their wits, it will be Daumier who will guide the errant band into the path that leads to salvation.

H. Daumier

Daumier: THIRD CLASS RAILWAY CARRIAGE.

Gordon Edwards Collection, Ottawa, Canada

(Courtesy of the Museum of Modern Art, New York)

CHAPTER

XVIII

IMPRESSIONISM

IN ART, conventions die hard; styles live beyond the day of their usefulness; traditions flourish from generation to generation; and the authority of the Old Masters continues to be a source of discipline and a source of evil to painters working in the unfriendly climate of modern society. In considering art as a progressive interplay of tendencies, some salutary, some inconsequential, all corresponding more or less faithfully to the civilizations which they adorn or criticize, I have shown the various contributions of Western Europe, in national movements and individual eminence alike, and how all the tendencies converge into French painting, divide, and run through the nineteenth century in two currents, the Academic and Impressionist. Of the Academic, thank heaven! we have no more to say; the Impressionist, as a local invention, remains to be analysed. But before proceeding to this analysis, let us review briefly antecedent developments which have been dwelt upon at some length in other chapters.

The term Impressionist, broadly speaking, means precisely what it says: an eyeful of nature; an instantaneous vision of the world, or of that very small pocket of the world which may be grasped instantaneously; a glimpse of externals; a sensational record of appearances. We may gather at once that it is opposed to classic art, that it places the simple act of vision above imagination, sight above knowledge, fidelity to natural appearances above a conception of humanity and a criticism of life. From the remotest beginnings of painting, as far back as one cares to go, artists have been occupied with the facts of life, with faces, figures, scenes and events—things accessible to the eye—but never, when men of brains and beliefs, have they treated these facts as isolated fragments to be mechanically recorded in the manner of the camera. When painting was really an important art, as well understood and as widely circulated, let us say, as the art of fiction during the last century; when it was a common language embodying collective beliefs and enlisting the powers of great minds, there were no Impressionists. But gradually, for reasons I have already given, painting declined, and, in the words of MacColl, "the absence of a religion, of an architecture, of a court or a caste of patrons, of a common language, audience and intention, left individual inspiration to its own fires, languors and eccentricities." I do not wish to imply that Western civilization is going to the devil, that because painting has languished, the spirit of art is dead, or, with religion a-mouldering in the grave, there is nothing in modern life worth painting. My point is that the office once held by painting has been usurped by other arts which have adapted themselves to new conditions. Whether it will regain that office is not for me to say, but certain it is that it will never again become a considerable factor in the lives of men as long as it continues to illustrate abstruse psychological theories and to sacrifice the larger centers of human interest to technical exercises.

I do not advocate a return to classical art. The world would not be improved if all the artists presumed to paint like the Old Masters: surely it was not made better by the institutes of the French Academy, and the recent propaganda for El Greco has not redeemed the situation. But I insist that if painters are once more to serve any useful purpose in society, they must know what the world is about, must have some sort of conception of contemporary life—of the value of our manifold inventions and the direction of our gigantic enterprises; they must express their conceptions intelligibly, and give up the habit of squinting at details and of chopping objects into planes to make clever posters dignified by the name of Cubism.

The classical tradition, though sapped by Impressionism, crumbled slowly. The first signs of Impressionism occur in Venetian art when the tastes of the courtesan city were running to material riches and scintillant gewgaws. The aged Titian, after a long life devoted to the painting of faces and stuffs, observed, as he approached the grave, that light falling upon objects breaks up the surfaces into patches of tone, and that, by painting broadly with hints of color in the shadows, the vivid effects of nature may be coaxed into pigment. He was probably aided in his discoveries by his failing eyesight—you may have noticed that painters in order "to see things broadly," peer at them with half-closed eyes—but however that may be, he was the first artist to deal practically with the analysis of natural light. What he found out is now known to every novice, but in his day it was a radical departure marking the beginning of the exploration of the phenomena of light.

Titian's methods were studied in Madrid by Velasquez, the most marvellous eye in painting. Velasquez, both by practice and influence, did more than any other one man to knock the props from under the classical structure. In his art the old method of modelling an object firm and round by a uniform blending of shadows, of making it as solid as it was known to be, was replaced by the illusion of its appearance in a given circumstance and under natural lighting—and at times the illusion is pretty thin and flat. He observed that local colors—the material colors of things, a white dress, for example, or red hair—are distractingly modified by reflections and shadows, and that shadows are not black, as they had been conventionally treated, but filled with color. Here was a difficulty. Painting by eye, he could not effect an harmonious image of nature by reproducing broken surfaces; nor did he know enough about the composition of light to abolish local colors as was ultimately attempted by the modern Impressionists. He got round the difficulty by a process of elimination: by avoiding positive colors, by throwing out disturbing lights and shadows, and by translating the natural scale into an equivalent scheme of silvery greys. But his grey tones are identical in value—in the amount of light and dark they contain—

with the corresponding tones of the model, and the result is a simplified version of nature enveloped in grey atmosphere.

In Holland the Dutch Calvinists, proscribing religious subjects, demanded and got in art little bits of painted matter to remind them of their farms, clinics and taverns, and their glum visages which they regarded as very holy. As a consequence, their artists, Hals, Vermeer, de Hoogh and hundreds of others, expert craftsmen with keen eyes and nimble fingers, developed to perfection the technique of the imitated tone; that is, they painted objects as the eye actually sees them in the clear light of day. But the Dutch, like Velasquez and Goya, were indoor painters, everything, including sea-pieces and landscapes, being done in a studio lighting. The investigation of outside illumination began with the French chef, Claude Lorrain, and was carried forward by Watteau, Corot and the Englishmen, Constable, Bonington and Turner. It was Constable, you will remember, who shocked the British connoisseurs by his discovery that grass is green, and not the dead olive-brown used by painters for centuries. It is hard to believe that such an elementary fact should have been looked upon as a daring innovation in landscape, but, as I have said, conventions in art, when sealed by the masters, are accepted by succeeding generations as final truths. And it was Constable, exhibiting in the *Salon of 1824*, who taught the French how to capture the exciting effects of natural light by dividing colors into streaks of tone placed side by side. The contributions of Turner to the science of light and color we shall examine in due course.

Thus it becomes apparent that the direction of Western painting was towards the problems of light and atmosphere, a tendency in itself legitimate enough had not the higher functions of art been ignored. But in their enthusiasm for a subject the potentialities of which seemed to be limitless, painters abandoned themselves so single-mindedly to subordinate issues that their aim, in the end, amounted to the complete suppression of the imagination—to the frenzied pursuit of novel processes, the recording of ephemeral data, the glitter of surfaces and the mechanical operations of the eye. About 1850, when the fight between the Classics and Romantics was still waging, and to express an opinion on painting was to take sides with Ingres against Delacroix, or the other way round, two men appeared who bridged the gap between the old tone painters and the new and gave the immediate impulse to the technical revolt known as modern Impressionism. These two, Courbet and Manet, in their point of view differed little from Velasquez: both were accomplished workmen; both victims of their own cleverness; both deficient in imagination.

Courbet, the older, was a pachydermatous fellow, a peasant without manners or modesty, and a defiant showman with a strong body and a great pair of lungs. He respected Delacroix but despised his romantic subject-matter, and despised with the same blatant hostility the mincing prettiness and artificial elegance of the Ingres school. His notion of painting was to seize Nature by the throat, as the yokels of Ornans took their women, and to bend her to the will of his vigorous brush. He was given to talking about art and his talk was usually the silly bragging of an over-confident vulgarian; he used, or allowed to be used in his behalf—he would do anything for publicity—for the first time in painting the word *Realism*, by which he meant "things as they are." When asked to paint a religious picture, he roared with laughter. "Show me an angel," he cried, "and I will paint one!" "Painting," he said, "is an art of sight. I will give you real nature with all her crudities and violences." Sometimes, when he was showing off—proving to his enemies what a prodigiously clever fellow M. Courbet really was—he did exactly that, copying the sportive nudity of over-blown women with photographic accuracy and thrusting the hussies, painted indoors, into a faked bower of smudgy vegetation.

What Courbet intended to say was that religious imagery, to the modern Frenchman, was a dead issue and allegory a farce: the painter, to be anything but an academic nuisance, must draw upon the contemporary world for his materials—there is no other source. This doctrine, as expounded quietly by Daumier, was only the best of good sense. Courbet was genuinely desirous of restoring to painting the grandeur and vitality of the old art which, he swore, had been lost because artists, slaves to precedent, had persisted in painting second-hand subjects. He was right, of course. But unfortunately for him his manual competence exceeded his ability to think. It was one thing to repudiate religion and history; quite another to work out a new conception of humanity. He had animal spirits, strong physical desires, and a sensual relish for living, but not much else—and he was not half so radical as he supposed himself to be. In decrying imitation—whether classic or romantic—he should have gone the whole way and invented a new technique for his realism; instead, he compromised, taking the method of Velasquez and Hals for the recording of his sensual impressions.

Yet Courbet's paintings, compared to those of Poussin, Ingres and Puvis de Chavannes, are extraordinarily masculine—even powerful. The man was alive, and if he could not think, at least he could see. The gifts which he brought to art are not of the highest but they are genuine. His arrogance and energy disposed him to paint occasionally very large canvases which today, now that his realism is neither an insult nor a novelty, have something of the flatness of old magazine illustrations. Like Velasquez, he could only paint what the eye could embrace and isolate from its surroundings, and his attempts at the grand style produced nothing better than figures bunched together, or strung out in rows with no reasonable connection. He is more at ease in small nudes, portraits and landscape. If you enjoy nudes—nakedness that has no other meaning than frank, healthy flesh,—a sturdy dish for the lustful eye, large females relieved of superfluous creases and the disagreeable blemishes common to all mortals, yet so close to nature that you are not conscious of the meddling hand of the composer, nakedness that is just a plain fact and not a misshapen apology for a new creed or an idealization—you will like Monsieur Courbet.

And my experience tells me that a good many people do like him. There is in the Metropolitan a Courbet nude that is one of the centers of attraction in a museum not overcrowded with fine paintings. It is a second-rate thing—one of his feats of skill—and so faithful to the model as to be slightly repugnant in the same sense that a large nude photograph is not particularly edifying. And to add to the unpleasantness, the model, unmistakably a domestic animal painted in a studio lighting and painted literally in every fold and hollow down to the flickering ripples of flesh characteristic of women who take no exercise, is placed in a sylvan retreat, like a nymph from the bath, the idea being that a touch of nature lends poetic charm to what otherwise would be only an exhibition of nakedness. The picture unfailingly draws a crowd not only because it is a nude but because of its striking verisimilitude. "How lifelike!" people exclaim. "How natural!" Which, needless to repeat, it is.

Manet added taste to Courbet's realism. He was a Parisian of the old school, well-bred, well-dressed, loyal to his friends and to his brush, a man of the world and a man of principle. He looked upon painting as a routine job in essentials like any other occupation, and punctually every day at the same hour, put aside his gear, changed his clothes, and hurried out to the same table in the same café to chat with his friends and appraise the girls. Not that he was a Bohemian idler—he took his work very seriously—but with him painting began and ended in his studio and its sole connection with the outside world was its connection with the men from whom he had developed his own virtuosity. His views were superficial; he had no interest in what people thought or in what they did; one thing was as good as another, and from the congeries of particles composing the world, he selected a fragment—a dwarfish nude, a bouquet, or a soldier—posed it and made a cunning pattern out of its surfaces. He was interested in tones and values, not in any light which tones and values might shed on the riddle of living. Had he not been a superlative workman, had he not materially advanced the Impressionist technique, he would have been only another Frenchman with a flair for painting.

After studying in various European galleries, Manet found himself in Hals, Velasquez and Goya, and in the brutal realism of Courbet. It may seem evasive to criticize one painter in terms of another, but in this case there is no alternative, inasmuch as Manet's contribution to art is a bold manipulation of a technical process originating in Spain and in Holland. At first even his subjects were similar to those of Goya, but soon he ceased to bother about what he should paint, and concentrated on problems of illumination. Gradually he worked out a formula for the rendering of the visible world which, summarily, was as follows:

He abolished sculptural modelling, arguing that it falsified natural appearances. One's visual impressions are flat, therefore one should paint in flat tones.

Influenced by the Japanese, he substituted the silhouette for the rounded forms of Italian art.

He lighted his models from the front in order to give a more direct approach to nature.

He used shadows as sparingly as possible—they complicated the problem.

He built up his objects in tones, that is, in juxtaposed touches of light and shade, as Velasquez had done before him; only he did not fuse the touches, but enlarged them into mosaic patterns, leaving the eye of the spectator to blend them together.

As time went on, turning to outdoor illumination, he used purer colors, brighter tones, and a more pronounced division of tones thus coming within a step of the granulated art of the Impressionists.

And what, we may well inquire, is the use of this formula? Simply this: to present sharp impressions of nature; to reveal the face of things as they flash suddenly into the field of vision. Manet's paintings have the quality of unexpectedness—the arresting freshness and strangeness of things seen for the first time. Suppose, taking your ease in a café, there should suddenly stand before you a stranger, a woman whose face, figure or costume, whose general appearance immediately captivates you, but who vanishes before you have had time to consider the causes of her appeal. The effect is a vivid impression. So it is with Manet's art. He gives you brilliant silhouettes, vividly apprehended surfaces, radiant patterns. Like the interesting stranger in the café, his figures and forms are abstractions. They tell you nothing of themselves; they are fragments of matter separated from the context of humanity. To *know* an object, to give meaning to the materials composing it, implies a knowledge of its relation to its environment. To convey this knowledge by painting only what flashes upon the retina in a single instance is an impossibility, however cleverly patterned the planes of light and shade may be. Manet was aware of this. Unlike Courbet, he made no exalted claims for his art; but simply asked to be allowed to paint what he saw, and within the terms of his own definition no man ever painted better. In old things, which to the ordinary person with his slovenly habits of observation are devoid of interest, he discovered exciting arrangements of tones, painting them with the greatest dexterity and with a clear caressing elegance that left its mark upon Whistler and upon most modern students; and the ordinary person, beholding the result, is astonished and delighted by new aspects of nature.

But the French were not delighted. They regarded his realism as hideous; and his unexpected aspects of nature provoked a tumult of protest. Two pictures ruined his reputation for life; one a representation of two nude grisettes lunching in the open with a couple of dressed gentlemen—a modernization of the Giorgione idea; the other, the infamous *Olympia*, a snapshot of a nude demirep with her negro maid and her black cat, and her flesh a pale bluish-white instead of the tawny epidermis of Titian's courtesan. The French, of course, approved of nudes and harlots, but for the sake of their culture demanded something less ingenuous—a classical goddess or charming nymph, not an undisguised piece of merchandise. For his honesty, Manet, one of the most estimable of men, paid the penalty of persecution.

In 1874, nine years after the *Olympia* scandal, a group of painters rejected by the official Salons organized a joint stock company and exhibited their works independently in Paris. The group included such familiar names as Monet, Sisley, Pissarro, Renoir, Cézanne, Degas and Berthe Morisot; and its first exhibition was received by the public with jeers and laughter, by the critics with customary Parisian insolence. Taking his cue from one of Monet's pictures called *Sunrise, an Impression*, a smart critic to a comic sheet lumped all the exhibitors together under the name, Impressionists. The word caught on, passing from a token of ridicule to an honorable title now employed to describe modern technicians seeking to record the momentary sensations of light and color. The term had been used before by Turner, and it was from Turner that Monet, while in London to evade the draft, had learned the principles of broken color. The debt to the Englishman was generously acknowledged by the French Impressionists in a letter written to the Director of the Grosvenor Gallery in 1885. The letter, which I quote from Clive Bell's *Landmarks in Nineteenth Century Painting*, states the general aims of the new school.

"A group of French painters, bound together by the same aesthetic tendencies, fighting for ten years against conventions and routine practice to bring into art the scrupulously exact observation of nature, applying themselves passionately to the realistic rendering of form and movement, as well as the fugitive phenomena of light, cannot forget that it has been preceded in this undertaking by a great master of the English school, the illustrious Turner."

In connection with this letter, it is worth noting that in one of the rooms of the Metropolitan Museum where each engraving is accompanied by an explanatory comment, some ill-informed and anonymous member of the staff has attached to a print from *Liber Studiorum* the opinion that "Turner was the last of the dead school of English landscape painters; that he contributed nothing to painting; and that his work contains no ideas for the growth and expansion of landscape art."

The Impressionists, though only technically radical, were responsible for a revolutionary era in art. They announced "the final purity of painting," laying great stress on the "innocence of the eye," the eye that registers nature impartially like the lens of a camera, and is not hampered by the action of a critical and inquiring mind. They invented a code for the transcription of natural statistics, a scientific recipe arrived at by observation but corroborated later in the laboratories of Chevreul, Helmholtz, Rood and Henry. The principles of coloration established by Leonardo da Vinci and applied in moderation by the Dutch and Spanish and by Turner, they examined, tested, and developed to the last degree, making a chromatic formula the end and aim of art, and perfecting a method which, being scientific and mechanical, was proof against all error.

The world, they reasoned, is enveloped in atmosphere in which all things are immersed like a fish in a bowl of water. We can no more paint an object itself than we can paint the fish, or a veiled woman; we can only paint the light and air surrounding it, the patches of bright and darker colors revealing its shape and its position in atmospheric space. The appearance of an object is never constant: it varies with the time of day, the color of the light thrown upon it, the distance from the eye, and the reflections from other objects. The expression, "the thing in itself," "the essence of a thing," is without meaning: an object is a different thing every time we look at it, and the best we can do is to forget its aspect under other conditions, and to paint it as our eye tells us it exists at a given instant. An object is a visual sensation produced by the vibrations of light, and we must find a way to fix these sensations in pigment.

They remembered that Turner, on seeing a black cow standing against the setting sun, had remarked, "She is not black—she is purple"; they were familiar with Manet's broken tones and Delacroix's experiments with complementaries; they had heard that the chemist Chevreul, called in by the Gobelins to analyze certain black wools which, when woven into tapestries, had proved to be brown, had covered up the adjacent colors, and the brown tones had magically turned into black again; they studied their predecessors but none, except Turner in his snow scenes and in his last canvases where he sacrificed relief and modelling to the intensity of color, had approximated the brilliant effects they hoped to win from nature. So to nature they went, probing light relations as they had never been probed before, and sacrificing relief, design, and everything else to their single-minded realism.

They met with many difficulties. They found the out-of-doors to be a maze of complications—pure colors, tones, cross-reflections, blurred contours; they found what we all know today, that the atmosphere is a screen through which the white light of the sun is transmitted purely or decomposed. They rediscovered Leonardo's law that shadow is not absence of light, but less intense illumination from a different source, and that shadows, reflecting colors from many sources, are seldom black. They discovered that natural colors—local colors—are only relative, that shadows are not simply modifications of the general color of an object but planes of an entirely different hue. In other words a red coat is actually a coat of many colors. How to paint these phenomena? Velasquez and Manet had considered local colors as light or dark spots of various intensities, but that was a studio compromise. The Impressionists demanded the primary effects of nature. So they dragged their canvases into the sunlight and went to work. Again they encountered difficulties.

They soon confirmed Turner's dictum that "no color is vivid enough to express the pitch of light of pure white sunshine." "But," Turner had added, "if I must indeed be lower in the key, there is no reason why I should be false in the note. Here is sunshine which glows even when subdued; it has not cool shade, but *fiery* shade." The Impressionists did not wish to lower the key; they sought the blazing splendor of pure sunlight, selecting for study the most pronounced aspects of nature—scenes flooded on one side by the orange rays of the setting sun and lit from above by the blue light of the zenith; trees and grass at high noon; flowers, and snow—anything exhibiting strong contrasts of light and shade, of color and tone. Having learned that the values of natural light, when literally copied in pigment, lose their original life and brilliancy, they began to enliven their canvases by injecting large amounts of complementary tints into the shadows. (A complementary is a color's foil, the color which, in combination with its opposite produces a neutral tint. The primary colors are red, blue and yellow, and the complementary of one is obtained by mixing the two others. Thus the complementary of red is green; of blue, orange; of yellow, violet. This, as Helmholtz first demonstrated, is true only of pigments, the complementaries of light rays being altogether different.) It had long been recognized—the Orientals had proved it—that the maximum of intensity is obtained by juxtaposing a color with its complementary, that is, by underscoring a spot of yellow with a streak of violet, but in Western art the law had been practically inoperative. The Impressionists worked it to the limit, but even this did not satisfy them: pigment was no match for light.

The next step was the invention of the spectrum palette. Since, they argued, the atmosphere is a screen decomposing light into the three primaries and their composites; and since we cannot obtain the brilliancy of light by mixing our pigments, we will use pure colors. Accordingly, they indicated not only shadows but also local colors by facets of pure pigment varying in tint and hue, which, when recomposed by the eye at a distance, produced the vibrant animation of nature itself. For example, in painting grass, they did not use a prepared green, but stippled the canvas with innumerable touches of blue and yellow pigment, leaving the blending process to the spectator. The purpose of this, let me say again, was to compel the painter's colors, which are mud and oil, to serve as light, which is clean and pure. But these clean, refreshing views of nature were greeted with hysterical abuse, the public—and the critics—asserting that Monet and his crew were barbarians, quacks, and incompetents, and their pictures ludicrously at odds with "the world as it really is." If they had condemned Impressionism on the ground that it was too scientific and logical, too close to Nature, their protests would not have been without sense. They were shocked by the violation of local colors. The Impressionists painted faces with orange lights and blue shadows; and to match the intensity of the sun's rays, painted landscapes in a high key, loading their canvases with tones of blue, orange and violet, at the expense of the local colors, to ensure the shimmering effects of nature enlivened by sunshine.

But despite its ignominious beginnings, Impressionism gained momentum, won the sympathies of men of talent, and flourished for forty years without producing anything more vital than a large stock of very real and convincing representations of sunlight. It was essentially uncreative, limiting art to statistics of nature gathered by the eye in the short space of fifteen minutes. It was in line with the psychology of the period the tendency of which was to assign to each organ a specific and exclusive function, the opposite of the more recent theory that every action is the cooperative reflex of all the organs working as a unit. The Impressionist eye, of course, was not so innocent as Monet and William James believed, its vision being conditioned by the attitude of the mind and by all previous sensations and experiences; but the Impressionist school, by reason of its self-imposed limitations, came closer to the immediate effects of nature—the direct transfer of visual sensations—than any other group of painters. The proof of this lies in the paintings themselves, their similarity, their imaginative poverty, their lack of any further appeal after the eye has recovered from the first blast of sunlight. They painted the same haystacks and water-lilies day after day, ten times a day, not because they had any new experiences to express but solely to prove that the color of an object varies with the declination of the sun. The personal deviations are merely preferences in method, one man favoring granulations shaped like commas, another dots and dashes, a third discs, a fourth lozenges—and so on and so forth.

Impressionism spells the victory of technique over the creative spirit. Seduced by a playful mechanics, its practitioners forgot all about art as an expressive medium, painting nature exactly as seen, and dissolving the substance of things into floating veils of atmospheric iridescence. It is an art without design, if such can be called art, since design is not a formula but the fruit of controlled or directed thinking—nature modified by the mind, the imposition of the will on the elements of experience. It reveals, instead of new meanings, and new kinships in the details of the world, new aspects of nature, resembling the incandescent lamp of the theatre which, by slides of different colors, suddenly changes the appearance of the stage. It achieves a certain unity of effect, but this again is only a natural condition; the use of atmosphere as a circumambient medium to hold fragments together as fog seems to give coherence to unrelated things. Like the camera, it reduces nature to an apprehensible scale and discloses a number of interesting facts overlooked by the dull eye of the layman, but the reduction, call it whatever pretty name you wish, is only a piece of nature. Impressionism is nature observed through a peephole.

My excuse for treating this movement at length is twofold: first, to prepare us for its successor, Post-Impressionism, or Modernism; second, to show how painting in intervals barren of creative thought, runs to technical subtleties. But the movement was not wholly negative. It carried on the healthy realism of Courbet and Manet, disposing of academic subject-matter, and by making nature enjoyable, drew attention to the artistic material in the nooks and corners of the everyday world. It explored fully and scientifically the relation of light-values to color, removed quantities of ugly mud from the palette, and taught painters not to be afraid of gay and lively tones. Without its experiments Cézanne and Renoir would not have been possible, and without its sharp contrasts of lights and colors Thomas Benton could never have developed his powerful mural art.

The intricate technique of the Impressionists was reduced to an exact science by a small group of painters generally called Neo-Impressionists, or Divisionists and Pointillists from their method of dividing tones into circular dots. The Neo-Impressionist flurry would deserve no mention but for the efforts of one man, Georges Seurat who, in the present century, has risen to a high position among modern artists. Seurat died in his thirty-second year, leaving only a few pictures, but these, I think, expressing all that he had to say. Gifted with intellect and imagination, as well as patience and good eyes; recognizing the shallowness of the Impressionists, but at the same time approving of their science, he set out to restore to painting classic dignity, forethought, and architectural order. To an extent his purpose was rewarded. He chose, as subjects, things he knew and understood—landscapes he had loved and pondered, circuses, dancers, groups of bathers by the riverside—idealizing his forms, stripping off useless details, emphasizing geometrical structure, but preserving specifically French characteristics of figure and costume. But he tied his hands with the most infernally complicated technique ever contrived by an artist of intelligence.

Seurat painted by rule: he had laws for the emotional properties of curved and straight lines; laws for the manufacture of gay, sad and calm harmonies; and laws, taken from Helmholtz, for the translation of color into light. He applied his pigments in minute points, detached granules of color or tone, which, like the juxtaposed touches of the Impressionists, were fused by the eye into optical mixtures. With patience beyond the endurance of anyone but a madman, or genius, he covered large canvases with thousands and thousands of circular specks, each premeditated and set down with exact knowledge of its action on contiguous specks. An absurd procedure worthy of a mediaeval mystic torturing his soul for the glory of God! One might as well build a temple out of beads of glass, or compose a novel of a thousand chapters, all the chapters containing exactly the same number of sentences, and the sentences containing the same number of words. The effect of this frigidly calculated method was to destroy the emotional powers of his forms. In spite of all that may be said in his behalf, his sense of style, his classical adjustments, his flawlessly articulated designs, his hieratic gravity, and his plastic relationships, Seurat's art is labored to death. His pictures have the motionless perfection of stereoscopical views. His molecular forms, though dead, are wrapped in veils of tone

Cézanne: PORTRAIT OF M. GEFFROY.

Collection Pellerin, Paris

which hold them together, and like a sterilizing gauze, protect them from decay.

It is not altogether just to include Renoir among the Impressionists, but in his simple-minded acceptance of nature, his concern with the sensuous aspects of the world, and his manner of painting, he may, without libellous insinuations, be called a product of this school. Renoir should be the most popular of painters, for his point of view is that of the average healthy man. There is nothing in his art to upset the animal complacency of the average person who wants in painting no more than a sensual experience—nothing that is not immediately apparent and thoroughly enjoyable. The attempts to add intellect to his luscious instincts and to classify him with the great masters have originated with admirers loath to admit that so extraordinarily talented an artist should have been so singularly lacking in ideas. Renoir had no ideas and no need of them: it was sufficient that he loved trees and sunlight, flowers and fruits, bourgeois pastimes, children, and above all, the nude female. He was not squeamish in his choice of models: "I am not hard to please," he once said. "I can get on very well with the first dirty scamp who comes along provided her skin doesn't repel the light." A happy man, he communicated his happiness to his art, having no other aim than to express by means of light and color his innocent pagan joy in the physical world.

Renoir began as a china painter and the trademark of the potter remained with him: the tendency towards surface ornamentation and to treat pictures as patterns of pretty color. He studied Courbet and Delacroix, exhibited with Monet, Pissarro and other specialists in sunlight, and in his last period, after an Italian tour, endeavored, by increasing the amplitude of his forms and heating their color, to rival the decorative opulence of the Venetians. As a painter in the narrower sense he has had few superiors: the texture of his forms is woven of hundreds of separate brush-strokes combining to produce a dominant tone, and the light seems to radiate not only from an external source but from within the web of glowing color. In his use of natural light and color he is frankly Impressionist but with a signal difference. While following the values of natural light, he avoided the flatness of literal rendering by manipulating the illumination to his own ends, focussing the strongest lights on the crests of his forms; that is, he placed light where it was needed to accentuate mass, and not where it would naturally fall. Hence the rotundity of his forms as distinguished from the flat surfaces of Monet. Technically, his major interests were in color and tone, and a decorative line. His pictures, composed on a basis of highly saturated tones and naturalistic values are patterns similar to those of Watteau—obviously more sculptural, but modelled in relief, not in the full round.

Renoir's sentiment is commonplace; his color, especially in his earlier work, disagreeably sweet and vulgar—a peasant girl's dream of beauty; the huge nudes of his last years look as if they had bathed in warm strawberry juice; but when he strikes the happy medium, he brings into modern painting the delicious, bracing sensuality of the natural man.

CHAPTER

XIX

CÉZANNE

"It has come about that a public naturally hostile, but well primed by critics and dealers, has conspired to the apotheosis of a great artist, who remains nevertheless a difficult master even for those who love him best." —*Maurice Denis.*

SINCE his death twenty-five years ago, Cézanne, the most despised artist of his time, has become the most famous painter of the nineteenth century. But he remains hardly less a problem than he was to his friends in Paris, to his family, and to his townsmen of Aix who, had he not been the only son of a rich banker, would have treated him as the village idiot. His friends did not know what to do with him: the painter of whom Renoir said that he could not place two colors side by side without producing remarkable effects was neurasthenically touchy—so terribly sensitive that he was nicknamed "the man without any skin"; he was obtuse and childish in matters calling for the exercise of ordinary judgment, and pietistically shrinking in his relations with his fellows. The public did not know what to do with him, nor the critics; so they howled him down and drove him back to the South. And it would seem that the men of today who have adopted him as the one modern master are at a loss to know what to do with him, if we may judge by the curious uses they have made of his art.

No better proof of the total estrangement of the modern artist from the public is needed than the hostility which greeted Cézanne at every turn in his career. The public would grant him no rights and no merits which the lowest member of society was bound to respect. Of all the Impressionists, he was the arch offender. The rest were wrong-headed and ridiculous but, after all, clever painters who knew their trade. He was a "sublime ignoramus"; "a Zulu"; "a butcher whose procedure recalled the designs that school-children make by squeezing the heads of flies between the folds of a sheet of paper." The press-cuttings compiled by Vollard, his biographer, to illustrate the contemporary estimate of Cézanne rival the list of calumnies edited by William Archer from the published opinions of the British critics on the first performances of Ibsen's plays. But in contradistinction from Ibsen, Cézanne was as innocent as a lamb. He had no message of regeneration, no medicine for the ills of mankind. Instead of wishing to pull down the pillars of society, he leaned heavily upon them, trusting with peasant faith in conventional authority.

He was a painter pure and simple, and his most ardent defenders have been at pains to remind us that his work is not tainted by moral ideas or social criticisms, that it is free from literature, anecdote, historical allusions, and everything else disturbing to a purely plastic conception of art. Out of joint with the world—"I am so feeble in life," he confessed more than once—he retired to the vegetable kingdom where, one would say, a man should be safe from the strictures of critics. But it happened that his conception of nature was particularly repellent, and in addition to constitutional irritations, he was condemned, year after year, to the critical lash which, falling on his tender skin, must have been hard indeed. Without his love for painting he would have been crushed—a weak-kneed skulker with an inheritance. So great was this love, so obdurate his purpose, that he could forget the floggings and approach nature with patience and humility. We shall come to a closer understanding of the man if we approach him in the same spirit.

Cézanne was born in Aix-en-Provence in 1839. His father was of Italian stock, the family coming originally from Cesena; his mother, of Creole ancestry, was a servant in the Cézanne household, and according to Tristan Klingsor, "it was not until 1844 that she was married to the painter's father." The happiest period of his life, in fact the only period of real happiness, was his early youth in Provence where, in company with Zola, another Italian, he wandered about the country filled with the hopes and dreams of a great career. The two Southerners were inseparable: they went to school together, learned some Latin and a little music, and boasted of their talents. The shrewd Zola was ambitious of letters, and Cézanne, his future decided by a box of colors which his father had bought from a peddler, talked of Rubens and Veronese. He was not a dull boy, but he was surely not a prodigy. He took the second prize in drawing at the Aix Museum, overcame parental objections to his bent, and in his twenty-second year, following Zola's example, went up to Paris. Here his troubles began. He was awkward, shy, and ill-bred, with an unpleasant dialect and many inhibitions. And as is so often the case with the excessively shy, he endeavored to disguise his fears by sudden eruptions of temper in which he cursed official juries and Salon favorites with foul-mouthed impudence; and to publish his contempt for the conventional art of Paris, affected a Bohemian swagger that did not become his rustic innocence. Naturally he was a problem to the few who slowly learned to believe in him; for he was not very personable, was by turns, overbearing and pitiably self-effacing, and his remarks on his brethren, though unexpectedly sagacious, were not of the sort to promote good-will among artists constrained by necessity to work together.

Failing to pass the examinations for entrance to the *École des Beaux Arts*, Cézanne attended irregularly one of the more liberal academies, and copied in the Louvre. For ten years he did not seem to get anywhere—he was attempting inventions for which he had no aptitude whatever. But there was merit in his abortive labors. He was never banal, and he had the instinct of the born colorist; but his painful gropings did not commend themselves to the juries, and he went ahead at a snail's pace, unrecognized and harassed by his inability to match the work of cleverer men over whom he felt in his secretive lonely soul the superiority of genius. Paris depressed him and to recover his faith he returned each year to Provence to paint alone on his father's magnificent estate. In 1866 he sent two canvases to—of all things!—the Salon de Bouguereau, and when the pictures were promptly rejected, naïvely appealed to the hanging committee to reconsider its decision. It would be difficult to imagine anything more embarrassing to the epicene Salon exhibits than those raw early Cézannes, but the author of them, while he had only contempt for "that gang," as he called his foes, believed that he was entitled to public notice and said so with brusque resentment. He was moved to outlandish glee, regarding it as a personal vindication, when Zola, now a pushing journalist, gave the show a drubbing in the press. But the official Salons never ceased to haunt him, and again and again he tried the doors, only to find them locked against him. Once, in later life, through pressure brought by a friend, he was admitted by the back door, but his enemies retaliated by hanging his canvas on the top line where it could not be seen.

During the Franco-Prussian war he was a deserter, dividing his time between open-air painting and the studio. It was better so—he would have made poor cannon-fodder. About this time he married a plain and rather stupid woman from Aix who seems, nevertheless, to have been an excellent wife to him. She had no notion of what he was driving at—but who did? She was docile and unquestioning, perfectly satisfied to remain at home while he was away in Paris, or on a sketching tour with Pissarro and Monticelli. It is a little surprising that he should have undergone the ordeal of matrimony, and more that he should have begotten a son. Women frightened him out of his wits and as a consequence he suffered from a repressed eroticism; and he was so nervous that he could scarcely endure the touch of his own child. "Listen," he said to Vollard, "I'm only a painter. Parisian wit gives me a pain. Painting nudes on the banks of the Arc [a river near Aix] is all I could ask for. Only, you understand, all women are cats and damned calculating. They might get their hooks into me. Life's frightful, isn't it?"

Encouraged by Renoir—one of the first to appreciate him—and Pissarro, he exhibited with the Impressionists in 1874 and again in 1877. How he was received, and how the derision hurt him, I have already told. Having no need to sell his pictures and convinced by his own suspicions that he did not belong anywhere, not even among those befriending him, he began to spend more and more time in the South. Fortunately he was spared what would have been for him the greatest tragedy of all—the pains of making money. On the death of his father, in 1886, he became a rich man, but made no change in his abstemious mode of living. In 1895, Vollard, now an art-dealer, taking advantage of the publicity attending the refusal of the Government to accept the Impressionist pieces—there were several Cézannes in the lot—in a bequest for the Luxembourg, hastily assembled about twenty-five canvases in a small gallery and announced an exhibition of Cézanne's work. The reaction of the public may be seen from the following:

"Another day I heard screams through the door. A young woman was struggling to break away from a man who held her with a grip of steel before a picture of *Bathers*. I caught this bit of dialogue: 'How *could* you upset me like this? And I once took a prize in drawing, too!' Then the voice of the man: 'That will teach you to be more respectful to me from now on!' Apparently the husband was compelling his wife to look at the Cézannes by way of punishment."

Soon afterwards, Cézanne retired permanently to his estate in Provence. He was probably the loneliest of modern painters. His friendship with Zola had long ago been discontinued; occasionally an artist came down from Paris to visit him, but the presence of painters better equipped to get along only exasperated his humility; and his townsmen shunned him. He envied men who could face the hard competitive struggles of life with courage and resolution. He was, as he said, only a painter: profound as regards art, in other departments of thought, naïve and lacking in intellectual independence. At times a curious melancholy attacked him, a black hopelessness not unlike the despondency that used to eat into Dr. Johnson, and he would fall back on the church of Rome. But at bottom he was an egoist very much aware of his own ability. The gradual dissolution of his friendship with Zola alternately angered and saddened him. There was no open quarrel but the fine companionship of the early years had ended in silence. Zola, of course, was a parvenu whose interest in art had proved to be no more than a youthful enthusiasm; and in the flood of his great popularity, he forgot the struggles of the painter. Inclined to judge art by fashionable successes, he could not bring himself to display the Cézannes in his possession—pictures which had not cost him a single franc. Cézanne, on the other hand, detesting all popular idols, believed that Zola had been ruined by success, that his old friend had maligned him in *L'Oeuvre*; and in his isolation was morbidly unsympathetic with Zola's heroic stand in the Dreyfus case.

In his last years he carried his canvases into the fields as religiously as his neighbors went about their business of sowing and reaping. Only his harvest was far more uncertain. His difficulties in "realizing his sensations," as he put it, increased with time, and his nervousness became almost pathological. He would get up at all hours of the night and poke his bald head—he was as homely as the busts of Socrates—out of the window to gauge the prospects for the grey weather which he deemed most friendly to his sensations. He grew more savage and exacting, destroying canvases, throwing them out of his studio into the trees, abandoning them in the fields, and giving them to his son to cut into puzzles, or to the people of Aix when they could not refuse the favors of a man of property. "I am one," he lamented, "who has a piece of gold, and can't make use of it." At the beginning of the century, a few connoisseurs discovered the gold, and when Vollard arrived in Provence with intentions of buying on speculation all the Cézannes he could get hold of, the peasantry, hearing that a fool from Paris was actually handing out money for old linen, produced from barns and outhouses a considerable number of still-lifes and landscapes, demanding as much as 150 francs for the windfalls! The old Master of Aix was overcome with joy. At last he was making a little stir in the world! But recognition came too late. In 1906 he died from a fever contracted while painting in a downpour of rain.

The gentlemen of the press showed no more charity for the corpse than they had shown for the living painter. Even Whistler who, as a rule, could detect originality from afar and turn it quickly to his own profit, was for once with the majority. His remark, recorded by Vollard, on Cézanne's portrait of his sister which, as Vollard observes and as everybody today immediately grasps, resembles an El Greco, summarized the general opinion of the press. "If," said Whistler in all seriousness, "a six-year-old child had drawn that on his slate, his mother, if she were a good mother, would have whipped him."

Influenced by Delacroix, for whom he always had the highest admiration, Cézanne, at the opening of his career, spent long hours in the Louvre studying the Old Masters. In his first paintings he emulated Courbet and Daumier, and in subject-matter, Manet, choosing such themes as a nude Olympia crouching on a bed before a bearded pasha who might be Zola, and mixed parties of nude women and dressed gentlemen regaling themselves on the grassy banks of a river. These grotesque conceptions, so far as they relate to his mature canvases, are failures. The ability to visualize situations which could not be observed from nature, or to compose subject-pictures from models, was denied him. But they are the failures of genius misapplied, revealing beneath their scenic absurdities an inchoate power and a spiritual purpose totally foreign to the sensuality of Courbet and the reportorial patterns of Manet. After ten years of discouragement, he was persuaded by Pissarro that the proper way to paint was in broken tones. He became an Impressionist and a good one, his first trials being sometimes mistaken for the work of Pissarro, the most skilful of all painters of natural light. A colorist from the outset, the brilliant palette of the tone-painters delighted him, but only temporarily. Disheartened by the shallowness and want of purpose in Impressionism, he returned once more to the Louvre, made notes and small copies of the masters, and slowly began to evolve a style of painting which was later on to turn the world of art upside down. His ideal was classic art, the three-dimensional design originating with Masaccio but eventually lost, he believed, because of the painter's interest in extraneous issues—in surfaces, textures, and values.

Cézanne's ambition, in his own words, was "to make out of Impressionism something as solid and durable as the paintings of the museums"—meaning the Renaissance masterpieces—and he addressed himself to the problem with the patience of a religious martyr. To put it in another way, his aim was to achieve the monumental in a modern language of glowing, vibrating tones. It sounds very simple, but technically his method was minute, analytical and exceedingly complicated. He would reveal and compose forms in their material and rhythmical aspects by the juxtaposition of colors. The Impressionists, you will recall, translated nature into snatches of pure colors, or tones, placed side by side, but in so doing, destroyed not only the local colors but the structure of objects. Their pictures were flat—emotionally and spatially. Cézanne wanted to retain the natural color of an object and to harmonize it with the various influences of light and shade tending to destroy it; to work out, in each instance, a scale of tones expressing the mass and character of the form.

Accordingly he submitted objects to a series of color-divisions, and by introducing spectrum tints running from yellow to violet into the divisions as they receded from light to dark, did, in a material sense, succeed in uniting form and color. This color-form procedure called for rigid attention to the planes of objects: to gain solidity and deep space in a scheme where darks vibrated and were as colorful as lights, he was instigated to a profound study of the geometrical formation of cubic structure. From his experiments and his occasional sage utterances arose all this talk about planes, cubes and cones, plastic form and functional color, the last signifying color inseparably united with form, color which seems to be a secretion from the constituent planes rather than a thin garment draped over a form modelled in black and white.

But this, I fear, is not very enlightening. Let us state the problem more specifically. Cézanne loved to paint fruit because it afforded him obedient models and he was a slow worker. Before him on a table lies a red apple. From his tactile experience of feeling and handling fruit he knows that the apple, in general shape, is a sphere, but as he examines it in the lighting of his studio, his eye informs him that the contour is broken into planes of various intensities of color and tone. These divisions escape the casual glance of the layman, but to the trained eye are not only evident but confusingly numerous. The old painters, disregarding accidental reflections and shadows, would have taken a red pigment and modelled a spherical object by uniform gradations of one color, that is, by mixing neutral tones with the red to produce the shadows—a perfectly good method but not Cézanne's. His aim is to preserve the solidity of the apple, but at the same time to conciliate the rounded mass with the lights and shadows breaking up the form into planes. Thus he sees before him a sphere the local color of which is red, but the surface divisions, absorbing or reflecting light from different sources —blue from the table cover, green from the trees outside the window, yellow from the walls of the room—he observes are not uniformly red but orange, blue-green or violet. He does not intend to copy the apple. He will keep the dominant color and the character of the fruit, but will heighten the emotional appeal of the form by a scheme of rich and concordant tones. The difficulty is to find the exact tint for each plane. Believing that "form is at its plenitude when color is most intense"—an erroneous notion, for Daumier achieves greater solidity in black-and-white—he begins by painting the first plane, the one nearest the eye, in the brightest tone—red containing a strong injection of yellow. Then, with infinite caution, applying paint in unscrubbed touches, he proceeds from one division to another, the scale of tones gradually diminishing in intensity. But he has begun in so high a key that when he arrives at the last planes—necessarily the darkest since they are in shadow—he must paint them in deep blues or rich violets. He must harmonize the planes one with the other and establish their exact position in space; and he must preserve throughout a balance of red so as not to ruin the local color—all to create a new and more exciting apple.

This tortuous process of *modulating* as he named it, nearly killed the man. Difficult with a single fruit in which he needed to consider only the effect of one plane on another, how much more difficult with a collection of things in which he had also to consider the effect of one object on another! Or with the human figure and all its complexities! Or figures in landscape! No wonder he threw his canvases out of the window and moaned that he was only a primitive blundering in an untraveled road!

It was but rarely that Cézanne mastered his instrument, and his failures may be attributed to his mental, not his manual awkwardness, and to his limited intelligence. Not by training, temperament or experience was he capable of complete knowledge of the things he attempted to present in all their fullness. His art, in words used by Delacroix to describe another painter "is the complete expression of an incomplete mind." A large part of his groping labors went into technical processes. An Impressionist, or at least half an Impressionist, he endeavored to "realize his sensation," as he put it, by knowledge acquired on the spot in a single instance. The contour which, whether it exists in nature or not must exist in art since the extension of a form is limited and the boundary must be indicated by one device or another, escaped him. He painted almost entirely in patches, and his color divisions, too small and fragmentary to function as distinct parts of design, exhibit the planes of objects instead of their mass. His method led him, in spite of himself, into distortions. Let me explain.

Naturally it requires more art to unify many things than a few, and Cézanne, feeling his way round the apple, adding patch to patch, was up against the problem of crowding many segments into a solid whole. On reaching the last planes, he discovered that while he had constructed a solid all the parts of which were in just relationship, he had violated the natural shape of the apple. This was better than a flat pattern but it galled him, nevertheless. To prevent the last segments from spreading out into space and to counteract the unshapeliness of the whole, he resorted to indefinite boundaries—broken outlines more or less detached from the enclosed planes. In composing a number of objects, the distortion of one compelled him to change the actual position in space of all the others, to knock tables out of plumb and to hold objects stationary on inclined planes where, by the laws of motion, they would roll out of the picture. He distorted things because he could not help himself, deliberately, if you will, but with anguish in his heart. It was the only way in which he could bring his forms into agreement—the only way in which he could utilize his little piece of gold. The distortions are less conspicuous in his still-lifes: he knew more about vegetables than about mankind; and simple, geometrical shapes are more amenable to harmonious alterations than the figure. But his "expressive deformities," as they have been called, are expressive in spite of and not because of their deformities.

It is, of course, the prerogative of the artist to take liberties with nature, but in the greatest painting, departures from the norm do not strike us as distortions but as harmonious enlargements and accentuations, as new and more forceful conceptions of nature. In Cézanne, more often than not, the violations give the effect of objects painfully squeezed out of shape, an effect he strove to remedy by using heavy outlines at the juncture of his forms. That the distortions were the unavoidable consequences of his limitations and not effects consciously striven for as his followers would seem to believe, is confirmed by his own confessions of failure—and by his work. They are less numerous in his still-lifes than in his landscapes, and less numerous in his landscapes than in his figures. Where his temperament allowed him to master the structure of forms, there is little distortion. In one of his heads—his own, I need hardly say—the *Self-Portrait* of the Pellerin Collection, holding fast to the color and character of the individual cranium, he arrives at the nobility of the "museum pictures." Here the color truly functions; the planes coalesce into a solid form; and he produces a new style of monumental painting. But the public, considering neither his intentions nor his occasional masterpieces, amused itself by calling him vile names.

Cézanne is a man building a house. He has studied and admired Greek temples and Renaissance palaces but has no desire to live in either. He will make a dwelling place for the modern man. His general notions of design are excellent but he is a slow and uncertain builder. To aid him he has sincerity and heroic patience. The house begins to take form but the construction does not suit him and he remodels it continually. The intersections are clumsily managed; the joints overlap; the disposition of the space leads him astray and he resets the partitions; the walls are forced out of line and the foundation must be extended. At length he puts on the roof and the work is finished, or as finished as possible, for he cannot conceal the evidences of his labor. Those who see it laugh uproariously and call it a barn. But it is a solid structure built to last and he prefers it to the stage-settings thrown together in the traditional French manner. It is his home, his only protection against the unfeeling world, and in it he lives alone, devoting his life to mending the contours and fortifying the architecture against the assaults of time.

The house has endured. After the old hermit builder was dead and buried, an enterprising collector bought it at a bargain, turned it into a museum, and made people pay for the privilege of looking at it. Then it became fashionable. Young Frenchmen began forthwith to imitate its crudities and imperfections; and Americans, copying the latest French models, entered into the mass-production of Cézannesque shacks built in the lopsided style of Parisian Modernism.

Cézanne was on the road which leads to greatness. His goal was reality, to make things real and true by loading them with his own perceptions and first-hand experiences, to create a full, rich, three-dimensioned world in the mass and depth of which we might receive experiences comparable in force to those of practical life. He sought an architectural support for his visual planes, an art as durable as the museum masterpieces. But he learned to his everlasting torment that the museum masterpieces were the fruit of a much greater knowledge than he could ever acquire; a knowledge of mankind, of the habits of people, the character of events and the significance of action; a knowledge attained by manifold interests which drive certain men to explore and command the anatomy of the body and the anatomy of landscape, to relate structure to movement, to understand inside and out, in any circumstance or lighting, the visual objects through which the artist expresses his synthesis of civilization. He attempted to gain such knowledge by regarding human models as pieces of still-life, by isolated studies as concentrated as they were mortifying. His *Portrait of M. Geffroy* required ninety sittings; that of Vollard one hundred and fifteen, after which he remarked, "The front of the shirt is not bad."

He was inordinately timid, pathetically bound to a narrow routine. He had an erotic passion for the nude, and his lifelong desire was to pose a nude woman out-of-doors. He never did; nor did he paint more than two or three in his studio. He was afraid. Thus, owing to meagre knowledge, his figures are no more than crude sketches, his women being distinguishable from his men only by their enlarged hindquarters. Withdrawing to vegetables and landscape, he transferred his secret passions to inanimate forms—apples, pears and farmland. If, in his pictures of men and women, he leaves his forms in a state of paralysis, with inert crusts for heads, and thick clubs for arms and legs, in his paintings of still-life he is a master. His fruit and vegetable compositions are truly dramatic; they have the weight, the nobility, the style of immortal forms. No other painter ever brought to a red apple a conviction so heated, a sympathy so genuinely spiritual, an observation so protracted. No other painter of equal ability ever reserved for still-life his strongest impulses to the creation of new and living things. In his painting of still-life, his "little sensation" is realized.

By sensation he meant his perception of forms: their effect upon him, the poetry they aroused within him, their size, structure, and solidity, their relation to all his memories and experiences. Cézanne restored to painting the preëminence of knowledge—the *knowing* of things—the most essential quality to all creative effort. That is one of his chief claims to distinction. He is the solitary glory of Post-Impressionism, or Modernism.

Cézanne: SELF-PORTRAIT.

Collection Pellerin, Paris

Picasso: ABSTRACTION.
Collection Paul Guillaume, Paris

CHAPTER

XX

MODERNISM

THE world has paid a heavy penalty for Cézanne's genius. The peasants of Aix had hardly sealed the grave of the unloved and misunderstood Master when there appeared in Paris the first of a succession of movements which, under the collective name of Modernism, have mocked the complacency of the orthodox for a quarter of a century. Practically all these movements, or more precisely, cults, have originated, directly or indirectly, from the difficulties and imperfections of the Provençal solitary. In 1906, the year of Cézanne's death, Matisse, Friesz, Braque, Van Dongen, Dufy and Vlaminck, advocating lyrical deformations of nature and the crude rhythms of savages, founded the first Modernist schism in art. They were called, in the spirit of derision, *Fauves*, or wild beasts.

In 1909, Picasso performed his first experiments with congested fractions of geometrical forms, and in the same year, his rival Braque exhibited the first abstract picture. Matisse, with a sneer for his former comrade in crime, tagged the abstract notations with a word of contempt—*Cubism*—and another school was born. Two Americans resident in Paris, Russell and Wright, developing the color-form procedure of Cézanne into an art purporting to combine the properties of architecture and symphonic music, celebrated their day of glory under the banner of Synchromism. Then came Futurism, Orphism, Expressionism, Vorticism, Purism, and a dozen others equally sonorous and Latin. The rivalry was absurdly acrimonious; the distinctions between the sects immaterial. And finally, as a fitting climax to all this school-founding and sciolism, a group of cynical renegades with nothing better to do, contrived, by a campaign of ingenious parody, to burlesque Modernism to death. This flurry which Maurice Raynal wittily described as "sticking a moustache on the smile of Mona Lisa", was called Dada-ism.

During the winter of 1913, the new, or Modernist art, was officially introduced to the American public. The exhibition was adroitly advertised, and a unique furore arose. One picture, a typical specimen of French Cubism provocatively labelled *Nude Descending a Staircase*, sped the issue from aesthetic circles into the field of popular ridicule, and for a moment the new, or immigrant art, loomed on our eastern coastline as a national menace, a Bolshevik spectre threatening our sacred insularity. Most of us remember those vociferous and ill-mannered times: the orgies of indignation, the bravado of nondescript painters intoxicated with publicity, the protests of dealers and antiquarians, and the piteous bleat of academic retainers trembling for the security of their little jobs. But to some of us it seemed that a new era was beginning. The spirit of art was alive again, and under the stress of French ideas an exhilarating burst of vitality began to sparkle in our musty showrooms. Galleries dedicated to the children of Cézanne were subsidized; French libraries interpreting the Modernist gospel of St. Luke were imported; an exclusively American exhibition, the pictures of which were certified by five experts, added authority to the surging scandal; eccentric magazines containing ferocious manifestoes and infantile illustrations sprang up overnight; and Greenwich Village emerged as the American Bohemia of the new order.

It was easy in those days to be hopeful, to prophesy, if not a renaissance, at least an efflorescence of native genius such as had never before occurred in the Western Hemisphere. But since that memorable uprising of 1913 something has happened. The sensational issues are dead and buried; the lust for battle has dwindled into an ignoble truce with the Academy; the creative stream has run dry; and Modernists, at home and abroad, are wearily sifting and resifting its barren deposits. Let us look into the matter.

First, let us keep in mind the source of the new and militant cults. With the single exception of Futurism, every one of them came out of Paris where art, like professionalized vice, flourishes parasitically in a segregated quarter; where painting is a proliferation of styles and techniques; where any clever schemer with a new bag of tricks may get a following among the café-philosophers. There was some charlatanism in the movements but not a great deal: the majority of painters were sincere men consumed with the desire to be original at any price. Had they been impostors they could never have grown hysterical and blood-thirsty over such childish things. At this point I must correct the common impression that the Modernists had never learned to draw, that is, to draw according to the precepts of the Academy, and that they resorted to subterfuges and preposterous distortions to conceal organic deficiencies in draughtsmanship. Some were prize-winners at the art schools; others respectable teachers; almost all of them had passed through what was known as the "sound training of the best French tradition." It was because of this meaningless training that they repudiated the Academy. They were sick of Impressionism, sick of salon frivolity—of naturalism in all its forms. Painting was either a spiritual force, or it was nothing. They found their redeemer in Cézanne, directly or through his missionaries Van Gogh and Gauguin, and the new movement was on.

Van Gogh is one of the tragic figures of modern art. His fanatic enthusiasms, his ungovernable debauches of the spirit and the flesh alike, and his abnormal sensitivity drove him to violent insanity and in the end to suicide. Seven times he tried to save himself—by religion, love, and art—and in each trial his excesses, often repulsive and always pathetic, would have destroyed a man of lesser faith. It would be difficult to name an artist whose life exhibits a more complete and impassioned surrender to the torments of the spirit. Others—Leonardo da Vinci, Rembrandt and Cézanne—have yielded as intensely to the creative impulse and have produced a far more profound and influential art; but for the parallel of this mad Dutchman in religious ecstasy and self-sacrifice we must turn back to the audacious convictions of

St. Francis. His faith in humanity was simply incredible. Alone among Modernists he believed in the indivisible union of art and religion, and in his fierce internal conflicts sought to reconcile his visions with the hard realities of life, and to find in painting a universal language for the regeneration of mankind. We may say that he was only a lunatic reaching for the unattainable, but let us not forget that he was, despite his obvious and deplorable limitations, extraordinarily open-minded, generous and consistent; that he had the courage to face the world honestly; and that his ideas, when put into practice, brought forth canvases of alarming vitality and convincing spiritual truth.

Van Gogh studied Delacroix, Millet, Monticelli, and Japanese prints; his twisted serpentine brush-strokes were derived from Impressionism; but it was from Cézanne that he learned to press nature into the service of his own agitated feelings. While he was essentially a religious painter, he did not make the mistake of trying to paint ecclesiastical subjects. His convictions were not of that sort, and with the best of critical sense he pointed out the falseness of Gauguin's absurd *Crucifixion*. He desired, like Rembrandt, to approach the common things of life with complete spiritual freedom. But his intellectual powers were short-lived and he was incapable of self-discipline. His contacts with nature, indeed with such ordinary things as a postman, a cluster of sunflowers, or a row of cypresses, threw him into a state of frenzy amounting almost to hallucinations. To convey the dramatic force of those terrible contacts he used a symbolical language of his own invention—smiting colors, accentuated contours, forms flattened into violent silhouettes, distorted forms writhing in pain, the pain of his own soul. If his conception of nature and humanity is that of a disordered mind, it is, nevertheless, the most vivid and trenchant conception in Modernist painting. But his art, I fear, is more singular than enduring. It is too remote from normal experiences to influence the world and too dependent upon the excitement of curious sensations to be useful to students. So far, it has proved to be most useful to the dealers. During his lifetime Van Gogh sold four pictures, one for 400 francs, the highest price. Recently one of his canvases went for the record-breaking sum of $85,000.

Gauguin brought the exotic element into Modernist painting. He was an odd compound of the artist and charlatan, of the gypsy and the Parisian *épateur*. Beneath his cruel cynicism lay a vein of brackish sentimentality which, congealing into a savage loathing of humanity, made him sinister and detestable wherever he wandered. A successful stock-broker, he renounced business for painting, took French leave of his wife and children, sailed to Martinique and later to Tahiti where he married a negress. Though he made a grand show of his hatred of "the disease of civilization," his reversion to primitive nakedness was only half-genuine. He was always grumbling for money, always thinking of the effect of his calculated savagery on the effete society of Paris. Returning to Paris for an exhibition of his painting and failing to take the town by storm, he sailed off to the South Seas again and died in the Marquesas in circumstances of unspeakable wretchedness. It is significant that his last painting was a snow scene of the country he had forsaken but could not forget.

He was a man of diversified talents—boxer, fencer, sailor, painter, sculptor, and poet. But it was his sensational subject-matter that won him notoriety. Cunningly he adapted the surface characteristics of Cézanne's art—the planes and distortions—to tropical settings and figures where they seemed to be peculiarly appropriate. The planes expanded into areas of brilliant color, the distortions appeared to be the natural shapes of negroid figures. Thus his pictures, resembling the flat textile patterns of primitive craftsmen, were received as the genuine expression of the barbaric soul, and not the sophisticated borrowings of a malcontent. Cézanne, however, was not taken in. "Gauguin," he said, "has only turned out fantastic figures. He has stolen my little sensation and carted it round in every tramp steamer." Gauguin's exotic magnetism has about run its course. He attracts only the lazy-minded who are tired of life and turn to art for soothing relief, or defeated painters who wander to strange places because there is nothing at home worth painting.

Matisse, the old chief of the Wild Beasts, entered Modernism through the influences of Cézanne and Van Gogh. To these influences he added his own phenomenal sense of color and his gleanings from the study of negro sculpture and the Asiatic decorators. His aim was a decorative style comparable to that of the orientals, clean flat design in which he carried the means of expression to the irreducible minimum, throwing aside the representational baggage which he believed had stifled the creative impulse in European art. His early pictures, at first glance, seem to be only spontaneous sketches; actually, they are built on the premises of logic. For example, he would destroy the proportions of any one of his forms, say the human figure, for the sake of the linear balance of the whole picture, distorting the contour of the hip or limbs into an enormous curve to offset the opposing curve of another form. This process, while unquestionably producing a balanced ensemble, was not without its ridiculous aspects, and eventually he abandoned it for a more seemly approximation of natural contours.

Everything that Matisse touches bears the imprint of ease and joy, the enthusiasm which springs from health and conviction, the direct contact with the living model and the greatest fluency in expressing that contact. By transferring the ingredients of genre-painting to the field of decoration, he has created an original style of art, a style in which the relations of the parts are determined by the artist's sense of free rhythm as distinguished from the geometrical symmetry of conventional arabesques. He converts the charm of fruits, flowers and buoyant nudes into silhouettes which, adhering to the everyday character of the model, suggest the liveliness and simplicity of ancient book illuminations. Design of this sort is not the result of the analysis and organization of planes, as in the case of Cézanne, but of the ready shifting of the proportions of silhouettes—of rendering nature in terms of flat pattern. The bulge of a woman's back or hips is expanded or shortened to meet the exigencies of a given space; the natural aspect of a scene—landscape or interior—is not materially altered but skilfully distributed in the interest of a balanced whole. By this method the spontaneity of direct experience is preserved. There is no grim transformation of nature to serve an ideal purpose, no depth of imagination, nothing dramatic—only the joyous responses to nature arranged with exquisite taste. In brief, *le monde visible* of Gautier presented in decorative style.

Matisse's reputation has suffered from his own errors in scale and from the exaggerated claims of his admirers. Having only a faint imagination, he is most impressive in small canvases, but fancying himself a mural designer, he magnifies his still-life patterns and his leaping nudes into large things which dissipate his charm and expose the poverty of his invention as well as the fragility of his bodiless forms. Like Whistler he deals in minor harmonies and subtle arrangements where taste and tact take the place of creative vigor and knowledge. With him Modernism begins to turn back from the strength and substance of Cézanne into the old French tradition of boudoir hangings. He is essentially a light talent, an ornamentalist whose designs are more applicable to silks, cretonnes and ceramics than to pictorial space. His nimble figures are closer to the sprightly nudes of *La Vie Parisienne* than his infatuated followers have ever suspected.

The most famous of the Modernists is that astonishing Spaniard, Picasso, the mainspring, if not the actual founder, of Cubism. Picasso's prominence, however, rests upon his influence, not upon his artistic achievements. If, at any step in his career, he has painted a picture that is more than an experiment, more than an exercise in technical ingenuity, I do not know where he has hidden it. For cleverness alone art has reared no workman more prodigious, but his inventiveness, I submit, would have been more useful in the field of mechanics. By his early contrivances in blue and rose, by his Cubism, his sculpturesque nudes, and his late super-realistic horrors, he has demonstrated that a picture may be perfectly composed, in the narrow or mechanical sense, and yet contain no meaning, and contain no emotional stimulus beyond the temporary shock of surprise or deprecation. He has proved that one cannot create an art by subjecting facts to the tyranny of processes; that true composition is not an extrinsic equation evolved from the styles of others but the final form, the personal tone and order assumed by materials experienced at first-hand. He has attempted to make art out of other art—an academic business; his work is a series of abstractions from the art of his rivals and predecessors. His eclectic searchings are endless: he has imitated Steinlen, Toulouse-Lautrec, negro sculpture, Cézanne, Van Gogh, Gauguin, the archaic Greeks, El Greco, Ingres and Corot. His paintings are detached studio inventions, laboratory performances destitute of human relationships and all relationships save those pertaining to the sources he has plundered. Picasso is generally credited with having a mighty intellect. I find no evidence to support this opinion. Mighty intellects do not exhaust themselves playing with trifles.

There is nothing mysterious in a cube or a cone; nor is there anything mysterious in Cubism if taken for what it is—an experiment in structure. All artists, the classic especially, have considered the geometrical formation of objects—that is part of their equipment—and in the studies of Uccello and Dürer, we may discover analyses of structure antedating by centuries the Modernist examples. But Cubism, as a distinct school of painting, owes its origin to Cézanne whose forms were composed of colored planes, one defined against the other. Picasso, in his first phase, enlarged upon the planes and changed the contrasting colors into simple areas of light and dark. This process, carried further, abstracted an object into its nearest geometrical equivalent; that is, a human head, though still recognizable as a head, was reduced to an assemblage of geometrical fractions. In his second phase, Picasso split the head into sections and then arbitrarily shuffled the sections together again so as to bring into a single focus aspects observed from several points of view. Or, as his satellites glibly put it, "moving round an object, he seized several successive appearances which, when fused into a single image, reconstituted it in time." The head is now only an eye, a nose and an ear scattered among a splintered wreckage. In its last phase Cubism paradoxically went flat. The three visible planes of the cube, by

Orozco: PROMETHEUS. (Detail.)
Pomona College, Claremont, California
(Courtesy of the Delphic Studios, New York)

a gradual process of extension, were projected beyond the limits of vision—to the frame of the canvas—ceasing to function as indications of solidity and becoming automatically three flat tones. The head, needless to say, disappeared. Representation was annihilated. Art at last was pure, perfect, abstract, absolute—and intolerable.

There is nothing unreasonable in Cubism, and there would have been nothing sensational in it had painters kept their experiments in their studios instead of offering them to the world as the loftiest manifestations of the human soul in a state of ecstasy. The contagion spread for several reasons. It was the strongest possible reaction against the stupidities of Impressionism, the diametrical opposite of imitation; it attacked conventional painting in the most combative terms, and its radicalism, being nonrepresentational, was a tonic to young minds surfeited with the Academy; it was a legitimate effort to increase the reality of objects by emphasizing structure and excluding sentimental attachments. But here the good in the movement ends. It was a transitional measure; like Pragmatism, a method and not a philosophy. To argue that it was an independent growth, an art complete in itself, is frankly absurd; and Picasso's defense of his cubes on this ground is obvious rationalization.

Cubism erroneously presupposes that design is an end and not a means, and that all human attributes are irrelevant. It limits the meaning of art to the perception of the abstract relations of the various parts, and shrouds simple processes in an element of mystery by using such awful terminology as "plastic dynamism," "the integration of the plastic consciousness," "the quality of the form is the incommensurable sum of the affinities perceived between the visible manifestations and the tendency of the mind." It postulates the idea that geometrical parts of design—a cube or a triangle—can be identified with specific factors in our psychic life—an idea that has no foundation in experience. Cubism is the apotheosis of structure. It strips objects of all the features and characteristics with which the emotional life is inseparably connected, leaving only the denuded concepts of the physicist and mathematician.

All art, to be sure, implies a certain amount of selection—one cannot include everything—but normally the purpose of selection is to set down one's experiences in forms objectively valuable. Such is its biological function—a means to an end. Why then should the Cubists carry the process to its second stage, to abstract the primary selection until nothing remains but dry bones? The answer is that they have no experiences worth communicating, or in plainer speech, nothing to say. Without a teleological basis, art, if sufficiently pursued, leads to insanity. When the means, let us say, of sexual gratification are withdrawn from actual experience, the victim wanders in a world of fantasies and ineffectual visions; when art is removed from experience and intelligible meaning, the deluded painter begins to read arbitrary and subjective values into his work, denies objective achievement, and in the end suffers a complete drying-up of creative energy.

The last of the shockers was Futurism, a cult manufactured in Italy and launched into Paris amid the beating of drums and the dodging of vegetables. On its practical side it borrowed from Cubism the idea of trying to illustrate simultaneous aspects of movement; theoretically it was a derivative of Croce's *Expressionism.* It had propaganda to offer and was bent on driving it home in the most sensational modern style. The argument of its manifesto was as follows. "The language of the old art is dead. We have a new and more exciting idiom, a set of personal symbols composed of anything and everything. We will translate into graphic form live states of the soul; we will jerk your sensibilities into the most acute responses. Without shocking emblems of brilliant color and free line we will make you feel art against your will." The argument captivated beginners and defeated professionals: to break with the past, to abolish tradition, to step out like a child into a world of freedom, to invest life with fresh symbols, to feel and to express—thus to create art. Everything was art so long as it was inspired by true feeling.

The influence of Futurism has been of a cryptic nature. As a school it is extinct, having been absorbed by *Expressionism*, a movement which has played havoc among all the arts. Like the other sects, *Expressionism* has flaunted a far-fetched aesthetic, but at bottom it professes a fairly simple creed: "Our contacts with nature—the facts of the visible world—for creative purposes are more important than any amount of learning or traditional knowledge. Given a genuine insight into the world of everyday experience, it is possible for the artist to dispense with all old forms and to create directly, trusting to the pull of such impulses as follow his sensations. Working thus, new forms are inevitable. The burden of dead learning which stultifies academic production is overthrown by an earnest and truthful expression of experience." Again we have "the purity of direct sensation"—the happy notion that "true feeling makes true art"—the Expressionist slogan which has become the painter's panacea and his silencing answer to the inquiring laymen. This notion lends authority to that brand of self-satisfaction which parades as genius; it allows for every imaginable kind of stupidity, and lack of knowledge; and raises the scratches of freaks and incompetents into the ranks of the masters. Hence its popularity. But, like many of the ideas of faith-healers, it holds a grain of truth. It states positively that the artist must have a natural and not a forced interest in his subjects, and rules out of court all virtuosity and academic precedent.

Expressionist theory ignores the fact that individuality develops through convention and the heritage of accumulated knowledge, and that unless we pass our lives totally isolated from a social milieu—which would result in savage ignorance—we are obliged to see, feel, and act on the basis of established conduct. Our mental habits, on the whole, are conventional, and we are permitted to see and construct only through and by the corpus of these conventions. What is called originality is but a slight addition to the mass of accepted and habitual opinions composing the ego. Hear Havelock Ellis on this point: "The self that he thus expresses is a bundle of inherited tendencies that came the man himself can never entirely know whence."

Such, in brief, are the principal divisions of the Modernist revolt. In retrospect, the movement does not seem to be so revolutionary after all, and now that the excitement has subsided, we may wonder what it was that caused so much controversy. It appears that the good in the movement is no different from the good in the schools of the past, a fact witnessed by virtually all Modernist painters who have never missed an opportunity to link their work with the most ancient traditions and to establish their affinity with the Old Masters. The controversy arose from the pretentious claims of the artists and their backers and from the sensational methods of exploitation.

The Modernists were men of the strongest anti-social propensities. They took pride in their aloofness and gloried in their refusal to traffic in bourgeois sentiments and vulgar emotions. "To hell with the public!" they cried. "There is no such thing as popular art! The public has always demanded trash and we will leave that to the academicians!" But these aristocrats of art, these aesthetic thoroughbreds, were not wholly above commerce with the rabble: they employed the most extraordinary tactics in order to persuade, cajole, and bully the public into buying their pictures. In such an atmosphere art turns inward, feeds upon itself, takes refuge in abstractions. It was only natural that men living in a little world of metaphysical disputations should have produced an art divorced from its human context; it was to be expected that the defence of this art should be the hopeless effort to separate social, moral and sentimental activities from what was snobbishly labelled "pure aesthetics." This critical attitude, propped up by the tenets of an unstable psychology, sprang from two bases, the scientific and the emotional, but the machinery involved was identical.

It consisted in restricting the significant factors in the production and appreciation of art to those whose understanding rested upon special training or unusual experience. Thus technique, essentially a matter for painters and a few specialists, became the whole of art, a field completely isolated from vulgar understanding. Into this exclusive field the thoroughbreds dragged the values belonging to the profoundest art and annexed them to minor technical issues. Furthermore, by describing technical problems in the terms of physiological mechanics and psychology, painters made the simplest processes enormously impressive. The "purification of painting" was the fine name given to this dehumanizing tendency, and to be looked upon as in the know, one was forced to subscribe to the high-sounding chatter about abstraction, empathy, significant form, dynamic relationships, and so forth.

The purification of painting! An enchanting fallacy indeed! "Pure beauty," as Winckelmann said long ago, "is like pure water —it has no taste." Yet this tasteless art multiplied by leaps and bounds. The various purity cults founded on the technique of line and color organization raised mediocrity to a glorious eminence and provided the initiate with the regalia for personal distinction. Poor old Cézanne's little sensation was father to a thousand perversions. To be "highly sensitive" in the esoteric fashion was the supreme honor, and any painter ingenious enough to erect a precious mythology round a few lines, or daubs of color, was assured of enviable notoriety. A tangle of lines, a swirl of tones, and he had produced a subjective cryptogram entitled *Psychic Portrait, Symphony in Blue-Green*, or *Centripetal Force.* Every little technical operation, every shade and detail, was magnified to epochal proportions. He was willing to die to make a table cloth pictorially interesting, willing to sacrifice his life to a pattern of spots and curves, the sole value of which lay in its "abstract beauty"—a theme for the humorist. He was so self-contained that he esteemed man as less valuable than a bowl of fruit or a congestion of cubes. The growth of humanity did not concern him—he was painting the growth of abstractions or the soul of pots and pans. Eventually he talked more about himself and his strange soul-states than about his art, and consulted the Freudian doctors to ascertain the full import of the psychic orgasms aroused within him by a piece of still-life.

Increasing in purity, painting shrank proportionately in human values until, at last, it appealed to a few souls divinely endowed with the "aesthetic emotion." This emotion by means of which one responds purely to art, that is, to its abstract harmonics, has been regarded with suspicion by eminent investigators unable to separate it from other emotions and unable to admit that man, being what he is, a gross bundle of appetites, memories and experiences all bound together into a single receiving system, can react purely to any stimulus. But the suspicion, I believe, is ill-founded. The aesthetic emotion is the unique property of those who love only art and not life; whose receptive apparatus, through disuse, has so shrivelled that it is no longer capable of responding to anything but abstractions. Painters possessing this peculiar emotion are really convinced that they have symbolized the grace of the human body, and the dynamic power and movement of modern machines, by abstract combinations of lines and masses bearing no discoverable relation to the objects in question. They maintain that an abstract art is the reflex of a machine age, and that its technique is the organic expression of the scientific trend of the times, a theory echoed by many writers. It happens, however, that the Modernists, by their own confession, are aggressively hostile to our machine age, and that they live as far from it as possible, preferably in the more romantic quarters of Paris. In the ways of contemporary civilization, they are poorly educated, and their pseudo-scientific technique is an arbitrary method deduced from Cézanne, a Provençal recluse for whom the machine age never existed.

Yet, making allowances for all that is excrescential in Modernism, I find the movement vastly more interesting than its sworn enemy, the official art of France. Even in its slightest activities—the child's play of the customs-house officer Rousseau, the consumptive art of Modigliani and the smartness of Dufy—there are evidences of creative ability—of a personality moulding materials into new and arresting forms instead of faithfully recording the dimensions and visual appearances of nature. On certain departments of the crafts—costume-designing, weaving, print-cloths, pottery and kitchen wares—the influence of Modernism has been gay and beneficial; on the wholesale decoration of interiors its effect has been abominable, largely because the

Cubist designers, ignoring the animal and spiritual needs of man, have imposed an eccentric pictorial formula upon utilitarian objects. What the movement will lead to I do not know. In France the more intelligent men, following the example of Lhote, are gradually returning to representational art; the others, professing to symbolize sub-conscious nightmares by indecipherable diagrams which they call *Super-Realism*, are beyond redemption. Matisse, growing old, turns out pretty sentiments for the American trade; and Picasso, to judge by his prize-winning exhibit at the Carnegie Institute, is a candidate for the Academy. The present condition of French painting is not one to make the heart rejoice. There is more hope in North America.

CONCLUSION:
HOPES AND FEARS FOR AMERICA

HOME again, after our long journey through European traditions, we enter a new environment for art. We are confronted not only with new physical conditions, but with what is more significant, a new mental attitude toward the world of the spirit. America possesses no revered or time-honored art-culture, and our country as a whole, in word and deed, does not seem to regret it. If we do not look ahead, we surely do not look very far into the past for salvation, and the absence of an art tradition does not in the least interfere with our industrial development. America is the land of machines, and our new attitude toward the world—our indifference to cultural precedents and observances—is both the cause and the effect of our mechanized civilization. Our psychology is profoundly conditioned by our changing instruments and our control over them. Our machines wear out and we construct newer and better models; we build and invent, destroy and replace, attaching no value to our handiwork beyond that of function and service. Thus we have come to have no use for things themselves, and no time to polish up memories of things when the moment of their usefulness is over.

This, translated into terms of aesthetics, means that art for its own sake, or beauty's sake, or for the sake of any abstraction whatever, will not thrive in America. It means that the kind of painting exploited by our international dealers is a hot-house product nurtured in little pots of imported soil, and that it will never exert an iota of influence on American life or thought. It means that if we are ever to have an indigenous expression, it will be an art proceeding from strong native impulses, simple ideas, and popular tastes, an art reflecting the color and character of a machine age. We had some years ago in the United States a popular expression of a minor sort in prints and illustrations, the form of which, intimately related to the social scheme, is not to

sando como le hará
a su dinero
para que vay

Rivera: THE BILLIONAIRES.
(Ministry of Education, Mexico City, Mexico)
(Courtesy Weyhe Gallery, New York)

be sneered at; and we have today all the talent and energy requisite to great painting, as well as an environment of immeasurable artistic richness.

But, the idealists object, the machine is strangling the creative impulse. This terrible ogre, by destroying handicrafts, has destroyed the background of the fine arts, leaving the sensitive soul no foundation for a spiritual edifice. Furthermore, the machine is supposed, in some mysterious fashion, to have affected our responses to "formal relationships." Again, the overwhelming material productiveness of the machine has robbed us of all leisure, crushed the soul of man, and turned the Americans into a nation of robots automatically engaged in manufacturing a civilization that has no goal and no purpose.

Civilizations are like trees: they are not conscious of goals and destinies. What pray was the goal of Florence? From Machiavelli we might infer that it was political intrigue and conquest. If there was ever a civilization which, on the face of it, was unfavorable to art, in which leisure was unknown, bloodshed and insurrection the order of the day, and no man's life worth a florin, in which material aggrandizement was the absorbing ambition, it was Florence at the height of her glory. And what was the goal of the Dutch traders during the half-century in which they produced their thousands of artists? As for leisure, what art was ever begotten of leisure? The whole moral of Vasari's *Lives* is that Italy would not allow her artists a moment's rest. Imagine Rubens, Balzac, Shaw, or any man of signal achievement, crying for leisure! Why should painters demand leisure and not architects and engineers? What the artist needs is work and more work, the incessant pressure of active life, exorbitant demands on all his powers driving him onward to higher and harder problems.

Man has always been affected and conditioned by his instruments. We sometimes forget that the leaders of Italian art were masters of tools—goldsmiths, architects, and engineers, as well as painters and sculptors—eager for scientific knowledge and capable of mechanical inventions. The modern painter spends his time worrying about his soul instead of educating himself to a new age. The fact that the instruments of today are more complex and effectual does not mean that the sensibilities of man have grown correspondingly duller; it means that they have been sharpened, and I venture to say that everywhere, but particularly in the industrial centers, man is a more alert and sensitive organism than ever before. He has to be, or he would endanger what is as precious to him as his soul—his life. The formal relationships of his beautiful machines call for the most intelligent appreciation. Why then does he not produce art? The simplest answer is that art is produced for him by a leisured group of Franco-Americans immersed in cultures having no significance in an industrial age—cultures in which the meanings of life and art, like the superstitions of theologies professing ultimate and eternal realities, are hangovers from civilizations where smaller instrumental capacities were united to conceptions of value now obsolete.

If the mechanized United States has produced no plastic art of any richness or vitality, it is because she has borrowed her art from foreign sources, and refused to utilize the most exciting materials that have ever challenged the creative mind. The other arts are not afraid of American realities: there is plenty of vitality in fiction and the theatre, and our architects have created the only original style since the seventeenth century. But our poor painters mope and suffer, complaining that they were born too late! Too late to grasp the immensity of New York; too late to experience the Renaissance banditry and racketeering of Chicago; to explore the cotton belt and the hill-billies of the South; to observe the tractors in the Kansas wheat fields; the cow gentlemen of the Southwest; the Rockies; and the proud breed of Californians—an epic in itself!

It does not follow that the painter has finished with man, that to be thoroughly modern and American he must represent only our instruments of production. Man remains the most interesting feature in the terrestrial landscape. He is still the slave of his instruments, but he is also, on occasion, the master. Today, more than ever before, he is in a state of passionate agitation. He is building portentously. With his complex and powerful engines he is cutting swiftly into the fog of his destiny. But he loves and struggles, conquers, loses, and dies, as he has always done; and in his face and his actions, as well as in the great background of his experiences, there are subjects for pictorial consideration as thrilling and dramatic as those which invited the powers of Leonardo da Vinci. "But how is the painter to begin without a tradition of handicrafts?" ask the Spenglerians and the collectors of precious objects. The question is answered by the current art of Mexico in which the work of the leading painters springs from a corpus of popular cartooning rather than from laborious lace-making, lacquers and weaving. For the Mexicans, in conjunction with the utilitarian arts, have the story-picture, the so-called primitive drawings, the significance of which is largely social. And their healthy mural art, while of the first importance in its plastic qualities, is not less important as a social document. During the past generation, before the appearance of Rivera and Orozco, there was among cultivated Mexicans a European bias toward art, an official tendency to look to France for aesthetic provender. But there was never a rich economic background lending support to galleries and trained salesmen employed to handle the vapid refinements of the European studio; and Mexico happily escaped the iniquities of high-pressure exploitation of art objects, and the servility and imitation of artists involved in this artificial system.

Here in the mechanized United States we have scores of painters who far surpass the Mexicans in surface craftsmanship but who cannot touch them in genuine artistry. As a matter of fact, the close relationship between painting and handicraft has been grossly overestimated. The essentials of the craft of painting are simple and readily acquired. A child of ten or twelve may easily possess all the craft necessary to be a great artist. If you doubt this, visit an art school and watch the children draw. The painter's problem is to organize color and mass the meanings of which are determined by his experiences and his concepts of value. The tricks of doing are as nothing. Whoever can paint a house or a chair, can learn, so far as the manipulation of pigment is concerned, to paint a picture. Every year hundreds of thousands of pictures are turned out which, as pieces of craftsmanship, leave nothing to be desired. Once in a while art breeds a man like Hals or Sargent whose manual dexterity is something to marvel at; but this form of cleverness, though prized by dealers, has little to do with the spiritual meaning of art. One of the greatest obstacles to the growth of art in the United States is the pressure brought to bear on painters by dealers who insist that a canvas shall be surfaced like a gem—a hand-rubbed affair of glittering textures. I know many painters, by nature indisposed toward the work they are paid to do, who forget to be artists in the miserable business of polishing little nothings to the last degree so as to convince the connoisseur that he is getting his money's worth. But there are signs of a better day, of new conditions affording the artist an escape from the service of the ivory tower.

The architect is coming to his senses. After years of dressing up his buildings in borrowed ornament, he seems finally to have recognized the necessity of original planning—of new designs and decorations commensurate with the magnificent work of the engineers. He is discarding bridal cake ornament; his structures shoot upward with unbroken lines; his surfaces grow cleaner. He has even gone so far as to call in the artist. The suspicion is spreading that designs produced by living artists might be more appropriate for modern buildings than anything stolen from the relics of Europe. Which means that the art of painting may enjoy a revival of function; that it may cease to be a plaything of the rich and stand upon its own feet; that it may find, in the big designs and the swift execution demanded by the modern architect, the proper stimulus to monumental decoration.

Wall painting on a grand scale—a sweeping social commentary taxing the organizing ability of the artist to the utmost—has received its first modern impetus in the murals of two powerful and energetic Mexicans, Rivera and Orozco. These two men have

Benton: THE MINER.

(New School for Social Research, New York)

penetrated to the depths of Mexican life with its curious mixture of contradictions—the savage and the civilized, the sanguinary and the pastoral, the religious and the revolutionary. Their work is free from the stench of the studio and the niggling polish extolled by professional art lovers. The spiritual fervor and the profound understanding of the tragic struggles and sufferings of man, which are the special characteristics of Orozco's genius, have been lost to mural art since the early Italians. Rivera displays brutal force, satire that burns, vast knowledge of the ferments and clashes of his people, and a prodigious command over pictorial space. The achievement of two Mexicans—as a whole, and in terms of meaning and function, in terms of structure and plasticity, in organizing power and draughtsmanship, in human significance and social criticism—puts to shame the combined efforts of the modern Europeans.

Luckily, the fame of the Mexicans has crossed the northern border of their country. They do not deal in small wares; they have no pictures to sell; they ask for walls to write on. Rivera, the revolutionist, has been commissioned to decorate the San Francisco Stock Exchange; Orozco, having finished a monumental job for Pomona College, has been employed, with Thomas Benton, to paint the walls of *The New School for Social Research*, in New York. Benton, in his historical murals, but especially in his latest work in *The New School for Social Research*, is the first American to attempt an inclusive picture of his time. He has none of Orozco's loftiness of spirit; he is hard and matter-of-fact, with a nervous and disturbing—one might almost say annoying, style. But his ability to express the American character and scene, his energy, and his individual style, when added to the great work already accomplished by the Mexicans, should go far toward the development of a new and emancipated tradition of art in North America.

There are other painters who have looked beyond their studio walls into the fascinating American environment, whose pictures point out the road which our artists must travel in order to deliver themselves from European masquerade and create something of their own. There is the example of the late George Bellows, the most popular of modern Americans. Bellows, exhilarated by the riotous and gaudy, the loud and belligerent aspects of native subject-matter, proved that it is possible for a man to paint without addressing himself to the fads and philosophies of the Continent. Among contemporary etchers, John Sloan has no rivals worthy of notice; his caustic renderings of New York life are the most distinguished specimens of the etcher's art that have appeared since the death of Meryon. Boardman Robinson, for years our most artistic cartoonist, has completed, for a department store, a set of decorations which needs only a more incisive study of actualities to rank with the best of modern mural paintings. And Charles Burchfield, less vigorous than heretofore, possibly because of the pressure of dealers, depicts the shabbiness of the small town with unsparing realism. Among the artists deriving from European schools are Preston Dickinson, John Marin, and William Yarrow. Dickinson is a painter of exceptional capacities who, with larger interests, might easily become a figure of considerable importance. Marin, a product of French Impressionism, is a nature poet whose fragile watercolors express the magical play of light and color on broken waters and unsubstantial hills. Yarrow, after a long period of sequestration in the Renaissance atmosphere of Florence, has returned to America, where he belongs, and is now designing, for one of our universities, a series of murals on popular sports. I conclude with Georgia O'Keeffe who, besides being the foremost woman-painter of the world, is an artist of genuine originality. Her forms are as thin as paper or leaf-metal, but she wisely confines her talents to flowers and leaves which demand delicacy of execution and clean color rather than structural draughtsmanship.

Among the younger painters there is plenty of talent worth mentioning, but more important than talent is the growing desire to throw off the European yoke, to rebel against the little groups of merchants and esoteric idealists who control the fashions and markets in American art, and who maintain little stables of thoroughbred artists just as the sporting millionaires deal in thoroughbred horses. These little groups, comprising collectors, connoisseurs whose fathers got rich in pork, oil, or iron, lady art students, and students of philosophy mired in aesthetics, feed on transplanted European cultures—or American imitations of the same—support museums, cliques and various uplifting societies, but they have only the mildest of contacts with the swift and brutal realism of American energy. The consciousness of slavery among the younger men has bred unrest and dissatisfaction with foreign cults, and this unrest, together with the immense possibilities in architectural decoration, augurs well for a revival of painting in America. For it is in North America, or Russia, or perhaps in a combination of the two, that we must plant our hopes for the significant expression of the new age. Certainly we have profited little by the culture of Western Europe.

END

outclassed [illegible]. These little groups, comprising collectors, connoisseurs, whose [illegible] got rich in [illegible], or from lady-art students and students of philosophy [illegible] in academies, [illegible] on [illegible] — at [illegible] imitation of the same — [illegible] and various uplifting societies but [illegible] the [illegible] of contact with the [illegible] and [illegible] of [illegible]. The consciousness of slavery among [illegible] men has [illegible] and [illegible] than what foreign [illegible], together with the [illegible] possibilities of architectural decoration, augurs well for a revival of painting in America. For it is in North America, or Russia, or [illegible] of a combination of the two, that we must plant our hopes for the [illegible] expression of the coming age. Certainly we have [illegible] [illegible] of Western Europe.

END

BIBLIOGRAPHY AND ACKNOWLEDGMENTS

PART of the chapter on Blake was first published in *The New Republic*; the account of Ryder is revised from an article in *The American Mercury*; some of the material on the modern Frenchmen is taken from essays published in two magazines now deceased, *The Dial* and *The Freeman*.

The bibliography of art is unfathomable. For an exhaustive list relating to every school and period the reader is referred to Reinach's *Apollo*, the best manual of art in existence. The following brief selection is intended for those who have only a moderate appetite for the barbarous terminology of aesthetics.

For general use: Tolstoy, *What Is Art?* (absurd in some of its conclusions but one of the most profound inquiries into the meaning of art ever written); Faure, *History of Art* (rhapsodic appreciation but inspiring in small doses); Taine, *Lectures on Art, Philosophy of Art* (a behavioristic view on a large scale by a master of past environments); Ruskin, *Modern Painters* (eloquence, exaltation, and spiritual valuations); Ogden, Richards and Wood, *The Foundations of Aesthetics* (a devastating attack on absolute systems of beauty). See also the *Ars Una* series of one-volume histories of various national arts.

Burckhardt, *Cicerone, The Civilization of the Renaissance in Italy*; Berenson, four small and instructive volumes on the Italian Renaissance; Symonds, *Short History of the Italian Renaissance*; Ruskin, *Giotto*; Vasari, *Lives of the Painters*; Cellini, *Autobiography*; Wölfflin, *Art of the Italian Renaissance*; Symonds, *Michael Angelo*; Rolland, *Michael Angelo*; Richter, *Literary Works of Leonardo da Vinci*; Siren, *Leonardo da Vinci*; Gronau, *Titian*; Ricketts, *Titian*.

Rooses, *Art in Flanders, Rubens*; Fromentin, *Masters of Past Time*; Bertram, *Life of Rubens*; Bode, *Rembrandt* (a monumental work); Van Loon, *R. v. R.* (an absorbing account of the life and times of Rembrandt).

Meier-Graefe, *A Spanish Journey* (El Greco and Velasquez

compared); Rothenstein, *Goya*; Beruete y Moret, *Goya*; Stevenson, *Velasquez*; Cossío, *El Greco*; see also Langdon-Davies, *The Spanish Woman*, Harpers Magazine, November, 1929.

Armstrong, *Art in Great Britain and Ireland, Turner*; MacColl, *Nineteenth Century Art* (a brilliant analysis of British and French schools); Meier-Graefe, *Modern Art* (a masterly work on the English and modern French painters); Leslie, *Life of Constable*; Damon, *William Blake*; Dobson, *Hogarth* (a perfect biography).

Delacroix, *Journal*; Hourticq, *Art in France*; Klossowski, *Daumier*; Fry, *Vision and Design, Transformations.* (Miscellaneous essays on art by one of the best of living critics. Fry is an ardent champion of Modernist art which he defends with the highest intelligence.) Bell, *Art, Since Cézanne* (art for art's sake applied to the Modernists). Gleizes and Metzinger, *Cubism* (a sample of the esoteric side of Modernist theory).

Index

A NOTE ABOUT THE AUTHOR

THOMAS CRAVEN'S major interest has always been the criticism and history of art. He has contributed outstanding articles on the subject to *The American Mercury, The Dial, The Nation, The New Republic,* and other periodicals. His essay *Have Painters Minds?* which appeared in *The American Mercury* for March, 1927, stirred up more controversy than any other article on art ever published in this country. MR. CRAVEN's writings have been commended by such noted critics as Roger Fry in England, Elie Faure in France and Lewis Mumford, one of the most authoritative writers on art in America.

He was born in Kansas in 1889, and received all his formal education there. He has since lived in various parts of the country—Alabama, Missouri, California, New Mexico, Porto Rico and New York. He arrived in New York in 1912, determined to become a poet, and at once sold two poems to the *American Magazine.* During the next eight years he placed not a single manuscript.

MR. CRAVEN also confesses that he has proved a failure at the following occupations: newspaper reporting in Denver, school-teaching in California, night-clerking for the Santa Fe Railroad in Las Vegas, sailing before the mast into the West Indies and teaching English in Porto Rico.

from THE INNER SANCTUM *of*
SIMON *and* SCHUSTER
Publishers · 386 Fourth Avenue · *New York*

DESIGNED BY ROBERT S. JOSEPHY
PRINTED AND BOUND BY J. J. LITTLE AND IVES COMPANY
NEW YORK